THE MARKETISATION OF FRAMEWORK AGREEMENTS IN THE UK

This book examines the increasing marketisation of framework agreements in UK public procurement and proposes reform to refocus the purpose of this vital purchasing tool and renew the emphasis on public service delivery.

Through detailed empirical research, the book examines how contracting authorities set up and use framework agreements in practice, the behaviours of centralised procurement authorities and the private sector, and how these have been addressed or not under the Public Contracts Regulations 2015 implementing EU Directives. This reveals the scale of marketisation, the effect of legal rules on framework agreement efficacy, and the need for regulatory and other reform. Going further, post-Brexit, this book also examines the relatively limited impact of the new UK Procurement Act 2023 in addressing these issues and identifies a pressing need for further regulatory, institutional, and industry reform.

The book provides the reader with a detailed understanding and analysis of the rules and policies on framework agreements as developed and applied under EU law and UK law, including the UK's post-Brexit efforts at reform, and the resulting legal uncertainty. It also provides insight into the less explored attitudes, behaviours and practices. This includes everything from centralised purchasing authorities competing against each other to provide framework agreements across the public sector to private sector organisations seeking to run framework agreements for profit.

The book will be of interest to practitioners keen to understand and mitigate legal and commercial risks in setting up and using framework agreements. It will also guide policy-makers on the key priorities for targeted reform. Civil society organisations will gain insight into the ongoing challenges of ensuring transparency and accountability. The book will also be of comparative interest in the EU given the UK's experience as a Member State and internationally for countries looking to reform their approach to regulating framework agreements.

The Marketisation of Framework Agreements in the UK

Practice, Regulation and Reform

Steven Brunning
and
Luke RA Butler

•HART•
OXFORD • LONDON • NEW YORK • NEW DELHI • SYDNEY

HART PUBLISHING

Bloomsbury Publishing Plc

Kemp House, Chawley Park, Cumnor Hill, Oxford, OX2 9PH, UK

1385 Broadway, New York, NY 10018, USA

Bloomsbury Publishing Ireland Limited, 29 Earlsfort Terrace, Dublin 2, D02 AY28, Ireland

HART PUBLISHING, the Hart/Stag logo, BLOOMSBURY and the Diana logo are trademarks of Bloomsbury Publishing Plc

First published in Great Britain 2025

A catalogue record for this book is available from the British Library.

A catalogue record for this book is available from the Library of Congress.

Library of Congress Control Number: 2025945740

ISBN: HB: 978-1-50998-562-3
ePDF: 978-1-50998-560-9
ePub: 978-1-50998-561-6

Typeset by Compuscript Ltd, Shannon

For product safety related questions contact productsafety@bloomsbury.com

ACKNOWLEDGEMENTS

Steven would like to thank everyone who participated in the empirical research and his employers who supported him throughout his PhD. Special thanks go to Steven's brilliant co-author and PhD supervisor, Luke Butler, to Sue Arrowsmith who started him on his PhD journey and provided expert guidance and his other PhD supervisors Ping Wang and Peter Trepte for their great insights. Steven would also like to thank his wife, Áine, for humouring his daily musings on frameworks during every dog walk, his children Shay and Malachy for their understanding, his parents, Ann and Peter for absolutely everything and sisters Theresa and Siobhan and other close family and friends for providing a bedrock of support.

Luke would like to thank Steven for capturing the zeitgeist of UK framework practice and bringing his extensive expertise to bear. However, this book would not have been possible without his family. Luke would like to thank his wife, Holly, for the years of enduring love and support, especially on those miserable sacrificial Sundays where work has too often taken over. He would also like to thank the best mum in the world – Gale, sister – Carly, brother-in-law – Adam, nieces – Elsie and Ever, and dad – Buster. In particular, the book is dedicated to his greatest achievements, Béatrice and Tobias.

More generally, the authors express thanks to Roberta Bassi, Verity Stuart, and Linda Goss for their professionalism, dedication and patience in commissioning and/or managing the project. Similar thanks are extended to Claire Banyard for attentively reviewing the manuscript. The authors are also indebted to Vicky Taylor who, in her personal capacity (outside the day job as senior operational lead on the Executive Programme in Public Procurement Law & Policy), volunteered expert and assiduous assistance in sense-checking the manuscript.

Tables 1 and 2 in chapter 2 reflect the position as at 2022 and the data is based on estimates as of 2022–23.

CONTENTS

PART I

The Marketisation of Frameworks in the UK

1

Introduction

1. Frameworks in the United Kingdom

Public procurement involves a contracting authority from the public sector buying goods, services or works to deliver public services. It will identify a need (eg, ICT hardware) to be met. If it cannot be met 'in-house', it will enter into a contract with a private sector supplier. It does so by inviting suppliers to a competition to submit tenders based on a defined specification and pre-defined criteria (although sometimes a contract may be awarded without competition). Tenderers will be assessed based on their ability to perform and their tenders evaluated based on price and/or quality. A losing supplier may bring a legal challenge in respect of this process and obtain a remedy, if successful.

The tendering and management of public contracts is subject to regulation through legislation and policies. Regulation may support the achievement of various objectives which may, in turn, realise lower prices and/or better-quality goods and services or other form of value. Until Britain's exit from the European Union ('Brexit'), procurement was legally regulated largely by Regulations implementing EU Directives,[1] the public sector-wide regulations being The Public Contracts Regulations 2015 ('PCR 2015').[2] These were retained pending reform by which the UK replaced its EU-derived model with a new Procurement Act 2023 ('PA 2023') which came into force on 24 February 2025, supplemented by the Procurement Regulations 2024 ('PR 2024').[3]

The importance of procurement and its regulation has grown. Outsourcing of governmental functions (including procurement) and service provision to the private sector have necessarily increased the role of contracts as a vehicle for their discharge and, with it, regulated processes for their award. Whereas historically, contracting authorities would be expected to procure requirements themselves, they increasingly enter into contracts with the private sector to procure on their behalf. Similarly, whereas they would have performed certain public services 'in-house', many are now contracted

[1] Directive 2014/24 on public procurement and repealing Directive 2004/18 [2014] OJ L94/65; Directive 2014/25 on procurement by entities operating in the water, energy, transport and postal services sectors and repealing Directive 2004/17 [2014] OJ L94/243; Directive 2014/23 on the award of concession contracts [2014] OJ L94/1; Directive 2009/81 on the coordination of procedures for the award of certain works contracts, supply contracts and service contracts by contracting authorities or entities in the fields of defence and security, and amending Directives 2004/17 and 2004/18 [2009] OJ L217/76.

[2] SI 2015/102. The other implementing Regulations comprise The Utilities Contracts Regulations 2016 SI 2016/274; The Concession Contracts Regulations 2016 SI 2016/273; and The Defence and Security Public Contracts Regulations 2011 SI 2011/1848.

[3] SI 2024/692.

out. Moreover, for certain requirements, it may no longer be the case that a contracting authority procures these from the private sector but, rather, from or through another public sector provider within a 'quasi-' or 'internal' market. This is in addition to routine procurement of requirements from the private sector. More generally, the professional and public consciousness around procurement has increased. Once regarded as a 'back office' function, procurement is now highly professionalised attracting well-trained civil servants, matched by an expert industry selling to the public sector; both buyers and suppliers have increasingly good awareness of regulation. Procurement is also a matter of major public interest, the media often reporting on the latest failure, which is heightened given significant challenges to public spending.

In 2023/24, gross spending on public sector procurement in the UK was £407 billion.[4] In 2024, HM Treasury included procurement as one of five areas expected to create further efficiency savings.[5] Further, the Cabinet Office, the Ministerial Department responsible for promoting governmental efficiency, including setting much of the UK's procurement policy, has observed that, whilst it is not possible to accurately model the impact of procurement reform on competition, increased competition could deliver annual benefits of between £4 billion and £7.7 billion based on cost reductions of 2–3.8 per cent.[6]

The 'framework agreement' or 'framework' is a prominent procurement tool sometimes referred to as an 'umbrella contract' in other contexts. To briefly explain its function, there may be instances in which a general need is identified but it is not known when a specific requirement may arise, the precise quantities, and/or price. Therefore, a 'framework' is established setting terms for future contracts to be entered. To borrow a definition under EU law, the basic concept is:

> an agreement between one or more contracting authorities and one or more economic operators, the purpose of which is to establish the terms governing contracts to be awarded during a given period, in particular with regard to price and, where appropriate, the quantity envisaged.[7]

Frameworks involve two stages. As conceived under EU law (other systems may differ), in stage one a contracting authority conducts a competitive procedure to appoint to the framework one or more suppliers that best meet the selection and award criteria. This also establishes the key terms and procedures under which 'call-off' contracts may be made. The parties may or may not give undertakings to request or supply requirements; typically, there will be no guarantee of future orders. In a conventional framework model, once the framework is established, the framework is closed, often for several years, and cannot be reopened to new suppliers. In stage two, as and when the need arises, a contracting authority calls off a contract. Depending on the framework terms, this may be done following a further 'mini-competition', enabling suppliers to submit updated tenders, or a 'direct award' to a supplier without further competition based on

[4] L Booth, 'Procurement statistics: a short guide', Research Briefing, Number 9317, House of Commons Library, 30 August 2024, 3.

[5] HM Treasury, *Seizing the Opportunity: Delivering Efficiency for the Public* (March 2024) 9–11.

[6] Cabinet Office, Impact Assessment, Procurement Reform Bill IA No: CO2024, 21/04/2022, 30.

[7] Article 33(1) Directive 2014/24/EU.

the application of the terms established in the framework. Frameworks may be 'single-supplier', ie awarded to a single supplier, sometimes in the form of a strategic partnership for more complex requirements, or 'multi-supplier' and which often concern commoditised items (although sometimes complex requirements).

Where contracting authorities do not have the capacity to set up a framework, a larger or more specialist contracting authority may do so and allow others to use it. Such 'centralised purchasing authorities' ('CPAs'), as termed under section 1(4) PA 2023, may aggregate demand for common requirements across contracting authorities and set up and operate frameworks for their use. A framework can reduce the administrative burden and transaction costs given that contracting authorities do not have to conduct a new procurement each time a requirement arises. Rather, they can simply call off contracts from suppliers who should, in theory, have already demonstrated their offers following a competitive award process when establishing the framework. Further, they can benefit from economies of scale through demand aggregation which may lead to reduced prices, as well as security of supply.

Since at least the 1990s, successive UK Governments have attempted to make better use of frameworks to deliver efficiency savings and their use has since grown exponentially. According to a 2023 National Audit Office ('NAO') report, the UK Government procured 72 per cent of its large contracts through frameworks in 2021–22.[8] Further, the Crown Commercial Service ('CCS'), an executive agency and trading fund of the Cabinet Office and the UK's largest CPA, has agreed that 'there is a pronounced trend', in terms of value, towards increasing use of frameworks as distinct from other procurement options.[9]

Various factors may explain their ubiquity. One is, perhaps, an ideological trend in recent decades towards greater promotion of neoliberal values in the public sector. For instance, since the 1980s, the UK's focus on 'new public management' ('NPM') has concerned making the public sector more 'business-like'; this includes introducing greater competition into the public sector, incorporating private sector styles of management, disaggregating centralised bureaucracies into agencies, outsourcing, and separating the roles of purchasers and providers of services. In turn, this has been summarised as comprising three main strands: (1) market-type mechanisms ie increasing use of markets and competition in the provision of public services; (2) managerialism and organisational restructuring; and (3) customer orientation.[10]

Further, frameworks have been viewed as a means of introducing competition in procurement and driving efficiency. CPAs who set up frameworks are attuned to the purported rationalities of the 'market'; CPAs encourage framework use not only because their frameworks can aggregate demand leading to reduced prices but because they can charge fees to access and use their frameworks which may generate profits beyond

[8] NAO, *Competition in public procurement: lessons learned*, Cabinet Office, Session 2022–23, 19 July 2023,10.

[9] House of Commons, Committee of Public Accounts, 'Competition in public procurement', Sixth Report of Session 2023–24, 13 December 2023, HC 385, 13.

[10] JM Alonso, J Clifton and D Díaz-Fuentes, 'Did New Public Management Matter? An Empirical Analysis of The Outsourcing and Decentralization Effects on Public Sector Size' (University of Munich Personal RePEc Archive, December 2011) 5.

covering their operating costs. Many other examples can be identified of behaviours which might constitute 'marketisation'.

Another factor is less ideological and more a reality of prevailing economic conditions. Global recessions have necessitated 'efficiency savings'. Yet another factor is the practical utility of a framework for the reasons indicated.

Ultimately, as reflected in the extent of their use, frameworks can be an effective purchasing mechanism when established with a well-defined scope, accurate estimated overall value, identifiable user contracting authorities, select suppliers, clear and transparent processes for awarding call-offs, and monitoring. However, frameworks have not been beyond criticism. As discussed below, the experience of the US and certain European countries suggests that frameworks have been overused in abandonment of traditional, open competitive procedures that may more efficiently obtain best value. For instance, questions arise as to whether frameworks actually provide meaningful competition by whatever measurement. They are closed off to anyone but those admitted for the framework duration. There may be little chance of securing work when many suppliers are admitted. Direct call-offs may be made to certain suppliers in circumstances in which there was no robust upfront competition to be appointed to the framework. If frameworks are poorly established by CPAs, user contracting authorities may have to do more work at the call-off stage in verifying the terms of their use or of supplier offers that were not properly assessed at the point of framework award. There is no necessary guarantee that offers in call-offs represent the best price or quality available on the market given that the framework is closed. Also, certain types of complex requirement may be unsuitable for procurement through frameworks. These issues and many more call into question whether it would have been more suitable to run a different type of procurement process, quite apart from whether framework outcomes justify their use.

2. Framework Marketisation

The intuition of this book is not simply that frameworks have become too popular or overused where other purchasing tools might be more suitable. Rather, there has been a paradigm shift in the regulated framework model which is increasingly being instrumentalised to serve market interests as much as (if not more than) public service needs.

For context, as early as 2008, it was observed that frameworks were being overused. It was argued that, in an efficient system, when choosing a procurement method, an official would typically be assumed to weigh costs and benefits to achieve best value. These would include the administrative costs of conducting the procurement, any legal constraints on choice, the likely participants in and outcome of the competition, and potential delay in the event of challenge. However, it was suggested that that choice of method had been distorted because officials had become 'enticed by administrative efficiencies' leading to overuse of frameworks.[11] Two explanations were given.

[11] C R Yukins, 'Are IDIQS Inefficient? Sharing Lessons with European Framework Contracting' (2008) 37(3) *PCLJ* 545.

The first was that frameworks had simply become 'expedient' tools used 'not to make procurement more efficient, but rather to bypass the procedural steps required by law'. It was suggested that frameworks make it 'quite easy to avoid competition and transparency', because, although generally awarded in full and open competition, call-offs are not typically subject to normal competition or transparency requirements.[12] As a result, once frameworks are in place, contracting authorities and suppliers 'pass into a much darker, uncompetitive world, where normal public procurement principles often do not apply', where call-offs can be made 'with far less process, and often with little risk of accountability', such that the 'gain in *administrative* efficiency may come at the cost of a deep loss in procurement value'.[13] In respect of the EU Directives, it was observed that frameworks have been used not because of their efficiency but to 'provide a ready means of avoiding the burdens and inefficiencies *of the procurement directives themselves*'.[14]

Thus, frameworks had grown, at least in part, due to purchasers' strategic response to '*regulatory* pressures and opportunities, not necessarily economic forces'.[15] Similarly, in countries such as the US, it had been observed that framework contracting 'blossomed in response to an increasingly stringent regime of procurement rules'.[16] Because normal procedural steps should, in principle, reflect policymakers' considered judgements as to an optimal balance of process and efficiency, 'a shortcut around those steps suggests a suboptimal choice'.[17] Thus, this view appeared to be predicated to some extent on a correlation between increasingly strict regulation and frameworks as a means of avoiding the full regulatory rigours of conventional competitive procedures.

The second reason given for overuse was that CPAs incentivised framework use because they typically receive fees for each purchase. It was observed in the US, for example, that CPAs were criticised for being 'entrepreneurial to a fault' and that, in both the US and Europe, such authorities 'driven by self-interest have encouraged the growth of frameworks arguably beyond an efficient level'.[18] This appeared to discern a correlation between commercially oriented behaviours and increasing use of frameworks. Notably, that research did not expressly refer to such fees as merely constituting part of the 'administrative costs of conducting the procurement'. Ultimately, procurement regulation (as historically conceived) is about regulating processes for award, not how procurement is organised and executed such as through operational financing of purchasing models, eg 'fees'. Thus, the above would suggest that market-oriented practices (eg, fee charging) not caught by procurement regulation but impacting on a key procurement tool may constitute another reason for overuse.

This book accords with the foresight of that earlier thinking but considers that UK practice has gone beyond excessive framework use for the above reasons towards behaviours that call into question its very defining characteristics, standing out from at least some other European countries. The palpable sense (reinforced by an empirical qualitative study) is that the issues go beyond a tendency to bypass procedural steps set out

[12] ibid 546.
[13] ibid 546–47.
[14] ibid 554 (emphasis in the original and footnote in quotation omitted).
[15] ibid (emphasis in the original).
[16] ibid 548.
[17] ibid 567.
[18] ibid.

under the law or incentivisation of use by CPAs in return for fees. Market-led behaviours that were scarcely mentioned in earlier decades seem to have become so prevalent that they exert an equal, if not greater, influence than 'regulatory pressures' or genuine 'economic forces', leading to improper use. There has been a regressive shift in the way that the regulated framework model is understood and operated. It is not only that regulatory controls exert limited pressure now, but that highly marketised framework models have developed largely unchecked. These even appear to have shaped the new legal definition of a framework in the UK, including rules that encourage rather than facilitate framework use based on accepted (but not necessarily best) market practice, subject to few appropriate regulatory constraints.

To further explain, the above 2008 research had recognised the historical provenance of frameworks as a more 'advanced form' or evolution of the earlier 'supplier list' provided in national and international regulated procurement systems.[19] Supplier lists did not involve extensive upfront competitions for the identification of suppliers and orders but, rather, established standing lists of suppliers for future procurements still to be undertaken. Frameworks were considered more developed forms of these, enabling a procurement process not only to identify pre-approved suppliers but also ensure pre-negotiated availability of requirements which supplier lists lacked. However, many large frameworks today bear a closer resemblance to supplier lists than to traditional understandings of a framework. As indicated, the idea is to hold a competitive award process to establish the basis of an agreement, to such extent that contracts could merely be called off from it or only supplemented by a 'mini' competition (a proper competition having already been undertaken to establish the framework). Instead, today, many frameworks may involve only a notional competition to appoint hundreds or thousands of suppliers; a skeletal framework may establish only basic terms for future awards, the details of which are fleshed out at the call-off stage. Frameworks can admit an unlimited number of suppliers subject to limited checks at the framework award stage. Further, at the call-off stage, procedures may deviate from the established terms with much left to purchaser discretion; and there may be a propensity to make direct call-offs instead of running mini-competitions, bearing in mind that the framework itself may not have been awarded pursuant to a rigorous competition. When the frameworks end, the next iteration is developed on the same or bigger scale. Thus, it is less a case of focused frameworks and more Frankenstein frameworks, the product of successive iterations, with the needs of many different contracting authorities and suppliers stitched together and lacking the proper control by their creators and users.

To give concrete examples, an apparent contrast is noted between the general definition of a 'framework agreement' under EU Directives provided above and the new highly generic definition of a 'framework' under the PA 2023. Section 45(2) simply defines a framework as:

> a contract between a contracting authority and one or more suppliers that provides for the future award of contracts by a contracting authority to the supplier or suppliers.

[19] ibid 556.

In this much simplified definition, there is no longer a reference to a framework's fundamental purpose, namely upfront establishment of key terms governing future awards. Indeed, the above would be an apt description of the generic pan-public sector frameworks in operation in the UK. Thus, it is no longer a case of frameworks being overused to avoid regulatory constraints. Procurement law *itself* is now being designed to facilitate the very marketised framework models that were created despite regulatory controls.

Reinforcing this sense, the earlier research seemed to suggest that the full general requirements of the EU Directives otherwise exerted a strong regulatory pressure, which must have necessarily been the case if frameworks were considered a means of avoiding them. This, in turn, seemed to be predicated on an understanding that frameworks were subject to less regulation than conventional procurement procedures involving a single award. By contrast, it is submitted that whilst EU rules on frameworks certainly provided more flexibility than running a full open competitive procedure, particularly in respect of the call-off stage, in actuality, there are not extensive differences between the rules to which frameworks are subject and those requiring a full open competitive procedure. It is still necessary to apply one of the conventional competitive procedures in awarding the framework. Further, call-offs remain subject to regulatory controls, some of which are actually more stringent than rules on simple openly competitive procurement. In addition, general legal procurement principles continue to apply with the same force to *all* forms of competitive procurement, whether a fully open competitive procedure or framework. Indeed, under earlier EU Directives, frameworks were even subject to an anti-avoidance rule that did not apply to procurement generally. On this view, it is not the case that frameworks have provided a major incentive for avoidance due to their being subject to far fewer rules. In theory, the regulatory pressure applied to frameworks is not much less substantial than in respect of fully open competitive procurement. Therefore, even where similar regulatory controls are applied to frameworks as to conventional procurement, that regulatory pressure is exerting increasingly little force. Worse, frameworks may actually be set up in direct contravention, or complete disregard, of certain fundamental rules that would apply to *all* procurement.

That being so, something more than avoiding regulatory pressure explains the exponential increase in framework use. To give another example, legally, only a public 'contracting authority' as defined by procurement law can set up and operate a framework. This has not prevented private sector organisations which clearly do not meet such a definition attempting to do so. This is not simply avoidance of certain rules or exploitation of grey areas by legally and market savvy contractors but, rather, wilful disregard of basic procurement law.

As a further example, that earlier research suggested that introducing rules that subject frameworks to review and remedies would remove a 'false incentive' for using them, namely, to 'dodge review'.[20] This was said to be a means of restoring balance so that frameworks would only be used because they 'truly provide the best value in procurement' rather than as a 'sly shelter from transparency, accountability or competition'.[21]

[20] ibid 568.
[21] ibid.

Around that time in 2008/9, the EU did introduce revised review and remedies rules.[22] Again, this suggested that regulatory pressure through such enforcement rules could be brought to bear on frameworks to prevent their overuse. However, the authors' experience has been that frameworks have been deliberately designed to practically eliminate the risk of legal challenge even where, by doing so, it creates a theoretical risk of challenge that may be high. An instance would be the admission of hundreds or thousands of suppliers to mitigate any risk of challenge from suppliers for not being admitted to the framework (when it might have been thought that admitting so many would increase the probability of that risk for other reasons) or the readmission of excluded suppliers (particularly, large market players). Perhaps ironically, therefore, frameworks may be created in contravention of the law to avoid being subject to legal challenge for other contraventions. This has created a perception that some frameworks are simply impervious to challenge. This must be considered in light of the fact that there have been few direct legal challenges to the ways in which frameworks are set up and operated in the UK.

Of course, this is not to give the impression that frameworks are the regulatory 'Wild West'. Contracting authorities may try to act compliantly, consult legal advisers, and are aware of legal risks. However, the point remains that something more than seeking to avoid the full force of procurement rules now explains the increasing proliferation of frameworks. The authors attribute this, at least in part, not only to the general lack of effectiveness in the operation of regulation but also to an endemic marketisation. Various market forces have been applied to the practice of frameworks, such that they have become 'too big to fail', the law acting not as a major constraint but as a mere risk to be acknowledged or even ignored. No one doubts that commercial considerations (eg concern to ensure value for money for the taxpayer) should inevitably be at the forefront when setting up and using frameworks, with regulation acting only as an enabler or limitation. Regulation should not be an inhibiter of good commercial practice. That said, there is a sense that regulation is largely subordinated to market-led determinations.

As will be discussed, many marketised behaviours that directly impact on frameworks have emerged which, in theory, would not even be caught by conventional procurement regulation. As indicated, procurement regulation primarily governs the processes for awarding contracts and, moreover, the rules are addressed to the public not the private sector. It does not generally address market behaviours which, if anything, are largely a matter of competition law. Using fee arrangements as an example, fees do not directly pertain to the award of contracts such as to naturally fall within the purview of procurement law but rather reflect commercial or market-based measures which are not addressed by it. This is so, even though the imposition of fees could conceivably affect access of suppliers to a procurement market, for example. Therefore, it is not only the case that the regulatory pressure of *procurement* regulation is now much less; some of the market-led behaviours would not be subject to procurement regulation in any event. Added to which, other forms of regulation (eg competition law) may not directly

[22] Directive 2007/66/EC of the European Parliament and of the Council of 11 December 2007 amending Council Directives 89/665/EEC and 92/13/EEC with regard to improving the effectiveness of review procedures concerning the award of public contracts OJ L 335/31.

address such practices. Therefore, another reason for the current position is the lack of other effective regulatory constraints on practices which are not directly concerned with the award of public contracts but clearly play a prominent role in procurement.

To fast-forward to 2025, as CPAs continue to expand their 'market share', HM Treasury has questioned the record 'surplus' profits being generated through fees. It has intervened to propose schemes to repay fees to contracting authorities in order to reinvest them back into public services.[23] This redistribution of wealth (of sorts) is an indirect acknowledgement of the way in which a framework market has developed and the need to refocus on the public service mission.

It is also possible to identify various ways in which contracting authorities have become more business-like in their use of frameworks. Examples include 'framework shopping' among overlapping frameworks and frequent reference to CPAs 'competing' against each other in a notional 'market' for the provision of what are, effectively, buying services on behalf of other contracting authorities.

Even more significant is the increasing involvement of the private sector beyond simply providing goods or services, or even consultancy services to contracting authority framework providers. Contracting authorities are awarding contracts to private sector providers to set up and manage frameworks on their behalf. If this were to be passed off as conventional 'outsourcing' in which the private sector merely acts as an 'agent' led by its public sector principal, some of these arrangements effectively create new types of framework, calling into question who is the real framework provider. Further, outsourcing is, of course, a decision driven by the public sector. In a further development, private sector firms have sought to persuade contracting authorities to host frameworks run by them. Going further still, there are instances in which private sector organisations are using (rather than simply managing) public sector frameworks and benefitting from prices charged to the public sector. Suppliers are also marketing their ability to secure direct call-offs from frameworks and leading customer contracting authorities to frameworks on which they are suppliers. The private sector is inevitably not subject to the same standards of probity and ethics as the public sector accountable to taxpayers.

However procurement is viewed, whether as the exercise of public power to deliver a service in the public interest or as a 'commercial function' to deliver the same, or a combination of both, and whatever the understandable reasons and incentives (perverse or otherwise) that explain the current position, it is strongly arguable that the balance is shifting too far away from the focus on public service and too far towards market-led considerations. A framework is no longer viewed as one of several available purchasing tools for a discrete purpose but rather the axiomatic choice, a default 'commercial vehicle' (as it is sometimes described) with high volumes of public spend being driven through them to meet both public service needs and profit motives. A recalibration is necessary to reassert the characteristics that define it as well as to provide the regulatory controls that discipline it. Importantly, this is on the assumption that frameworks continue to offer a very useful, functional purchasing tool with more advantages than disadvantages. After all, it is possible to use frameworks to develop and deploy good

[23] NAO, *Efficiency in government procurement of common goods and services*, CCS, Session 2024–25 HC 116, 42.

practices. There are examples of frameworks that are legally compliant and well run and ensure optimal outcomes leading to better public service delivery. But this is not the case for all frameworks. Sights must remain firmly fixed on the public service mission, it being necessary to curb some of the excesses of marketisation.

Therefore, *The Marketisation of Framework Agreements in the UK: Regulation, Practice and Reform* provides the first ever legal-empirical analysis of how regulation on frameworks has been applied 'end-to-end'. It reveals the extent to which market forces have been brought to bear on the framework model and the role which regulation has played – or not – in ensuring its efficacy. This fully up-to-date text will also examine post-Brexit efforts at reform in anticipation of future practice. In doing so, it seeks to establish a discourse on how to better regulate frameworks not only in the UK but internationally.

3. Aims and Objectives in Context

Originally, the working hypothesis was that problems in practice may be due largely to a failure of legislation. The issues were, therefore, very much viewed from a legal perspective. The starting point was that whilst frameworks are regulated, questionable commercial behaviours are arising, and which must necessarily be the result of a disconnect between the law and practice eg rules not covering a particular issue or being uncertain and creating grey areas ripe for exploitation etc. On this basis, it was considered that problems with the law were largely causative of the commercial behaviours emerging. There has been limited rigorous empirical evidence to substantiate this hypothesis and which merited further investigation.

However, the findings of an empirical research PhD project conducted by one of the authors called this hypothesis into question.[24] The issues arising in respect of regulation have, indeed, to some extent created conditions conducive to certain behaviours or failed to address them. But, perhaps even more fundamentally, many of the trends appear to be attributable to factors which have less to do with the effectiveness of regulation and more with the way in which various market forces have been brought to bear on how frameworks are set up and operated.

This was an important finding because it cannot therefore be assumed that better *procurement* regulation will necessarily solve many of the issues. As indicated, certain behaviours or practices are not targeted by procurement regulation at all. It follows that procurement regulation and other regulatory regimes will need to be reformed in conjunction. Further, regulation of whatever kind cannot be the sole solution given that some of the problems have arisen in ignorance or disregard of the law and may continue whatever regulation is introduced. Thus, other reforms are needed, not least a change in culture. Regulation can help play a part in nudging behaviours but is not a substitute for institutional and industry reform.

[24] S Brunning, 'The Commercialisation of Multi-Supplier Frameworks in The UK Public Sector: The Divergence between Law and Practice' (Thesis submitted to the University of Nottingham for the degree of Doctor of Philosophy 2024).

3.1. Aims, Objectives and Key Arguments

The principal aims of this book are as follows:

- to raise public awareness of complex public sector purchasing arrangements;
- to explore how frameworks are regulated and regulatory policy decisions made;
- to provide empirical evidence of the factors influencing framework use and (non-)compliance with regulation in practice;
- to encourage reform in ways that are evidence led; and
- to provide the basis for future sector-specific and comparative research which could inform the reform of other regulated procurement systems

The objectives are:

- to identify evidence of marketisation and other factors affecting the efficacy of frameworks and their regulation;
- to analyse current legislation and policy underpinning the regulation of frameworks;
- to examine the apparent disconnect between the 'black-letter' law and commercial practice in respect of the use of frameworks;
- to critique the latest reform efforts, in particular, under the PA 2023; and
- to explore certain areas of potential reform.

The central arguments are as follows.

First, empirical qualitative research supports a trend towards increasing 'marketisation'.

Second, there is a disconnect or discord between the current black-letter law and its operation in practice. Fundamentally, frameworks are emerging which do not bear the core characteristics of a regulated framework. Further, there are grey areas of the law that do not appear to be the result of intended flexibility or constructive ambiguity and which have created legal uncertainty ripe for exploitation, in particular, to serve market interests. This legal uncertainty has not only led to poor procurement practice which is not legally compliant but also contributed to conditions conducive to the marketisation of frameworks.

Third, the current position is not exclusively or even largely attributable to issues arising under EU law. The UK has not taken sufficient domestic initiative to address many of the issues raised. This has been confirmed by a failure to take more decisive action post-Brexit under the PA 2023.

Fourth, certain of the issues arising are not attributable to procurement regulation on frameworks at all but, rather, market behaviours in respect of the set-up and administration of frameworks, particularly, through centralised purchasing. Some of these issues raise competition law and other considerations which have not been directly addressed by procurement regulation.

Finally, it is necessary to introduce further regulation and other reforms. The law seems to continue to perpetuate a myth that frameworks are a seemingly innocuous purchasing 'tool' in need only of largely facilitative rules subject to minimal constraints.

Practice indicates that these are not just tools but entire business models sustaining a significant market and that current regulation is insufficient to address them. However, regulation alone is not a complete solution. Institutional and industry reform is also required.

3.2. Wider Contribution to Debate on Procurement and its Regulation

To date, there has been much useful research on frameworks, including analysis of the fundamental concept,[25] the law and economics of frameworks,[26] the relationship between frameworks and competition law,[27] as well as frameworks in the context of centralised purchasing, which includes country and comparative studies.[28]

This book fills an important gap by seeking, for the first time, to undertake a more focused, legal-empirical analysis, exemplified by: a focus on one jurisdiction, framework contracting from set-up to call-off, and on a sectoral basis. This provides an opportunity to explore in more detail the factors informing framework choice, use and regulatory compliance, the efficacy of regulation, and wider market-related elements that bear on framework contracting. In doing so, it seeks to better understand how regulation operates holistically in the framework eco-system. The empirical component focuses on the ICT sector but the findings are likely to be generalisable across other sectors in need of similar research such as construction, defence, healthcare, education, etc. Further, the book considers the choice between frameworks and other commercial purchasing tools, such as dynamic purchasing systems, indicating the possible susceptibility of other such tools to marketisation and which also require further study.

This book is also timely, as the PA 2023 has just entered into force. The PA 2023 represents the UK's vision of what a reformed regulated procurement system should look like decoupled from the EU regulatory model (albeit both being products of political compromise). Whilst the empirical research was based on application of the PCR 2015 which remained in force until 24 February 2025 (and is of relevance to any legacy frameworks still operating), the authors also provide updated analysis of the corresponding rules in the PA 2023. The analysis of past practice in light of the new rules is significant because, with limited exceptions, the provisions on frameworks have not been substantially reformed to address many of the issues raised in this book. Further, there has been increased activity in respect of frameworks within the last few years, with

[25] S Filipon, *Framework Agreements, Supplier Lists, and Other Public Procurement Tools: Purchasing Uncertain or Indefinite Requirements* (Hart Publishing, 2023).

[26] GL Albano and C Nicholas, *The Law and Economics of Frameworks: Designing Flexible Solutions for Public Procurement* (Cambridge University Press, 2016).

[27] D Kristensen Balshoj, *Public Procurement and Framework Agreements: The application of competition law to contracting authorities in a procurement context* (Djøf, 2018).

[28] C Risvig Hamer and M Comba (eds), *Centralising Public Procurement: The Approach of EU Member States* (Edward Elgar, 2021) and C Risvig Hamer, K-M Halonen and M Socha (eds), *Public Procurement: Centralisation and new trends* (Djøf, 2024).

a 2022 High Court case shedding light on blatant abuse.[29] Frameworks, particularly in the context of centralised purchasing, are also attracting increasing attention from audit institutions such as the NAO and the media. In June 2024, the authors were cited in two consecutive articles in the *Financial Times* highlighting major problems with transparency and profiteering in the UK framework market.[30]

The book will provide essential insights for policymakers considering further implementation and reform of the PA 2023 and other initiatives relevant to frameworks. The book is also directed at contracting authorities, as an authoritative guide to understanding what is required to ensure legal compliance and key areas of risk. It should also be of interest to institutions with auditing functions in the UK such as the Parliamentary Public Accounts Committee ('PAC') and the NAO, as well as civil society organisations.

The UK is also an interesting 'case study' from a comparative perspective because, of course, it was formerly an EU Member State which largely 'copied out' EU Directives. Therefore, many of the legal and practical issues arising will be relevant to EU Member States. Importantly, the EU has begun an evaluation of the functioning of the Directives with a review to reform.[31] As the EU is the most developed form of international instrument on procurement, discussion of UK regulation that was formerly based on that model could also inform debate on reform of other international agreements eg the UNCITRAL Model Law[32] or World Trade Organisation Government Procurement Agreement ('WTO GPA'),[33] neither of which are examined in detail in this book.

4. Structure

This book is composed of four Parts, of which this Introduction is Part I. Part II titled 'The Marketisation and Regulation of Frameworks' comprises three chapters. Chapter two briefly explains the basic components of a framework, the relevant actors involved, and its operationalisation, in particular, through centralised purchasing. It introduces the concept of 'marketisation' and identifies select examples from the empirical research explored in Part III. Chapter three examines the objectives underpinning EU procurement legislation which is important for understanding how framework rules must be interpreted and applied. By contrast, Chapter four considers the UK's domestic approach to the regulation of frameworks, including its policy position taken on the Directives and its decision-making on the options open to it as regards implementation in domestic law. It also considers the limited extent to which the UK has introduced further domestic policy initiatives. Combined, these chapters explain the extent to

[29] *Consultant Connect Ltd v NHS Bath and North East Somerset, Swindon and Wiltshire Integrated Care Board & Ors* [2022] EWHC 2037 (TCC).

[30] G Plimmer, 'Process for UK government contracts erodes "transparency", warn experts' *Financial Times* (London, 3 June 2024) and G Plimmer, 'Private providers winning big fees on UK public sector contracts, experts warn' *Financial Times* (London, 7 June 2024).

[31] Information is available at single-market-economy.ec.europa.eu/news/commission-launches-call-evidence-and-public-consultation-evaluation-public-procurement-directives-2024-12-13_en.

[32] UNCITRAL Model Law on Public Procurement 2011.

[33] World Trade Organisation, Agreement on Government Procurement 2012 and related WTO legal texts 2012.

which frameworks have been regulated at the supranational and domestic levels and the limitations of initiative in this area to date.

In light of that context, Part III titled 'Practice in the UK' comprises five chapters and includes an extensive legal-empirical study of the application of the PCR 2015 originally carried out by one of the authors as part of a PhD but expanded and substantially revised to consider the potential impact of the PA 2023. Part III has been arranged according to different themes which largely correspond to the sequential phases of the set-up and management of a framework. Chapter five examines certain decisional factors that often inform the choice to use a framework. Chapter six explores the key preparatory decisions made when establishing a framework, namely, preliminary market engagement, choice of procedure for award and formulating a call for competition, identifying users, estimating and disclosure of framework value, setting the duration of a framework and call-offs, and use of lots. Chapter seven examines the process for identifying suppliers to be admitted to a framework, namely, limiting the number, use and application of selection criteria, formulation and use of award criteria and weightings, establishing call-off procedures for direct awards and mini-competitions, and establishing pricing terms. Chapter eight examines how frameworks are used by contracting authorities, including use of direct call-offs, running mini-competitions, finalising call-off terms, evaluating price, use of a 'framework within a framework', and contract modifications. Chapter nine examines issues in respect of review and remedies in challenging a framework. Each chapter is divided into separate sub-topics with each setting out the legal position under the PCR 2015 followed by a summary and analysis of the empirical data collected, and concluding with a consideration of the PA 2023 and its likely practical impact.

Part IV simply titled 'Reform' comprises a single Chapter ten which draws the threads of analysis together and establishes the case for further reform. It focuses primarily on reform through regulation but also highlights the need for a much clearer understanding of the characteristics and economics of the UK framework market to inform regulatory policy, as well as the need for institutional and industry reform. This chapter does not set out a comprehensive and prescriptive set of reforms as this would necessitate a book in its own right. Rather, it should provoke further discourse on areas in need of focus in the short, medium and longer term.

5. Research Methods and Methodology

This book includes desk-based doctrinal analysis of legal and policy materials and qualitative empirical research. As indicated, the empirical component derives from PhD research undertaken by one of the authors between January 2021 and June 2022.[34] The focus was qualitative rather than quantitative, its aim being to systematically identify key thinking around, and features of, procurement practice and how the rules on frameworks were applied in the context of multi-supplier frameworks. It investigated what (if any) discrepancies exist between the black-letter law and its application in practice and

[34] The research received ethical approval. Information on the research methods used can be found in Brunning (n 24) 11–19.

the perceived positive and negative aspects of current regulation. This included consideration of what strategies were being adopted to resolve any issues arising. Its principal focus was to investigate how rules were being interpreted and whether there was a need for further guidance or reform.

5.1. Research Questions

The key research areas and questions in the empirical phase were organised as follows.

The supply and proliferation of multi-supplier frameworks:

(a) Given the lack of centralised controls over the supply of frameworks in the UK, how are multi-supplier frameworks made available to contracting authorities?
(b) What commercial practices have developed as a result?
(c) Why do contracting authorities decide to set up or use multi-supplier frameworks instead of using other procurement routes?
(d) What types of requirements are they considered most useful for?

Setting up a new multi-supplier framework:

(a) What issues do contracting authorities encounter when applying the PCR 2015 to the set-up of a new multi-supplier framework?
(b) How have these been addressed in practice?

Using an existing multi-supplier framework:

(a) What issues do contracting authorities encounter when applying the PCR 2015 to the use of an existing multi-supplier framework?
(b) How have these been addressed in practice?

Legal challenges and remedies:

(a) What are the perceived legal risks and remedies in relation to the award of multi-supplier frameworks and/or call-offs?
(b) What strategies are used to deal with these risks?

As evidenced by the questions, the empirical research was not explicitly designed to validate concerns about marketisation. Rather, the focus was very much on critiquing the efficacy of the technical legal rules in practice, and explains why much of Part III is 'legalistic' in its systematic analysis of the rules. However, starkly, interviewees consistently raised and, in some cases, prioritised relaying their concerns about emerging behaviours within the market. Interviewees attributed some of the market-related issues to uncertainty in the legal rules, questioned the relevance and effect of legal rules on certain behaviours, and even put forward arguments for using reformed legal rules to address some of the market-related issues. Therefore, regulation seems to feature heavily in this discourse even though, as the book shows, marketised behaviours have emerged sometimes in ignorance or disregard of legal rules. It is because the marketisation theme became so prominent against the backdrop of a largely technical legal analysis that marketisation became a central feature of the book, alongside a more general technical legal analysis.

5.2. Research Methods and Methodology

A combined doctrinal in context[35] and socio-legal approach[36] was adopted. The choice to use qualitative empirical research was informed by the need to explore opinions, behaviours and processes, providing explanations that are not possible from analysing statistics alone.[37] By providing an understanding of the context in which rules are applied, qualitative research can produce evidence of the effects of law in practice, which can, in turn, contribute to evidence based policy-making.

Correspondingly, it was considered that the research should not be restricted by pre-formulated targeted questions using a 'tick-box' survey. This would produce data based on a pre-conceived set of assumptions about the most significant issues. Instead, it was decided to use semi-structured interviews to allow respondents to prioritise the areas of focus.[38] It was this approach that elicited concerns about the market-related aspects of frameworks despite the initial focus on questioning how rules were applied in practice. Where responses led to follow-up questions and entered sensitive topics (eg, around exposure to risk of breaches of legal requirements in specific cases etc), indirect questions were asked on the basis of hypotheticals and generalising scenarios in accordance with good practice.[39]

Interviewees included contracting authorities, CPAs, legal advisers and suppliers. The research design was mindful to acknowledge a conceivable overlap between categories of respondents because some contracting authorities may be involved in both the set-up and use of frameworks. The fact that an entity may act in more than one capacity did not produce any significant findings but is an important reminder that a buyer in one market may be a service provider or seller in another, and which may have various implications. When presenting the empirical evidence in Part III, the following abbreviations are used to identify interviewee(s): central purchasing bodies ('CPBs'), contracting authorities ('CAs') and legal advisers ('LAs'). It is recalled that section 1(4) PA 2023 now uses the term 'centralised procurement authorities' ('CPAs') whereas under EU law, including the PCR 2015, the term 'central purchasing bodies' ('CPBs') was used. As will be discussed, CPB and CPA may generally be used interchangeably, although it should be noted that the definition of a CPA under the PA 2023 introduces new elements which will be discussed. The Appendix sets out anonymised, generic descriptions of the role of each interviewee.

The validity of the empirical research findings must be acknowledged but so must their limitations. The research was not intended to produce extensive quantitative data sets taking account of variables such as characteristics of the individual questioned (although seniority and experience were catalogued). It was more important to capture experiential, cultural and behavioural factors that informed views and which was better

[35] This conceptualises law in the context in which it develops, exists and operates. See, generally, F Cownie, *Legal Academics – Cultures and Identities* (Hart Publishing, 2004).

[36] The socio-legal research focus is 'to understand law as it is embedded in the larger society'. See, generally, M Feeley, 'Three Voices of Socio-Legal Studies' (2001) 35 *ILR* 175.

[37] R Barbour, *Introducing Qualitative Research*, 2nd edn (SAGE, 2014) 13.

[38] ibid 18.

[39] H J Rubin and I S Rubin, *Qualitative Interviewing: The Art of Hearing Data* (SAGE, 2004) 28.

served by a qualitative research method. Further, as with much empirical legal research in the field of procurement regulation, the findings are typically treated as 'anecdotal'. The data cannot be treated as being statistically representative of the sector or any other, given that they relate to the experiences of a selection of willing participants. It also should be acknowledged that whilst the authors have sought to be as objective as possible, both are lawyers, providing legal advice or consultancy in the field.[40] This experience has enhanced the quality of the research but the authors have also been mindful not to over- or under- state the significance of legal considerations in practice or, indeed, their own experiences.

The limitations of the sample size must also be acknowledged. In respect of the identification of contracting authorities and suppliers, the Government has not maintained a single, central repository of frameworks and their supply base. There are publicly available lists of framework representatives of suppliers but these are not comprehensive. By contrast, law firms publicise their expertise and were easier to identify, which partly explains their proportional representation in the sample and is also justifiable given the main focus of this book on regulation. In the absence of a systematic data capture of the various frameworks, participants were recruited following: desktop internet searches, online professional network providers, and any publicly available lists of contact details for representatives of suppliers, down-selected to be most representative of the sector. Participants included: representatives of CPAs, representatives of contracting authorities from central government, health authorities, educational institutions and other contracting authorities, representatives of suppliers, and external legal advisers (as distinct from in-house contracting authority lawyers who were otherwise recorded as falling within the category of contracting authority). Given the sheer volume and proliferation of frameworks in the UK and the number of contracting authorities and suppliers who use them, it was not feasible to interview the entire user population. Instead, it was decided to take a representative sample to gather an understanding of all relevant perspectives. This also informed the decision to focus on a particular sector.

Only approximately 10 per cent of CPA, contracting authority and supplier representatives contacted responded, with 20 per cent in the case of external legal advisers. Notwithstanding, the sample yielded 57 interviews (12 CPAs, 18 contracting authorities, seven suppliers, and 20 legal advisers) of approximately two-hour duration per respondent and, thus, a fairly reliable data set, evidenced by saturation of responses on certain key issues. It is suggested that the sample size is justifiable given that, as will be explained in more detail, the empirical research only focused on one sector, namely the ICT sector. This is a more detailed data set than other interview-based studies undertaken within the academic discipline of public procurement law and many official studies undertaken by UK's audit institutions. Further research would be necessary to determine if trends are replicated in other sectors but which seems highly likely given that there are no sector-specific rules on frameworks which radically differ from each other. Of course, there may be different market characteristics and behaviours typical in

[40] It is confirmed that there is no conflict of interest between the authors acting in any capacity outside research.

a particular sector which may impact on framework practice and which requires further research.

It should also be acknowledged that, unsurprisingly, legal advisers engaged most on specific issues of the interpretation of legal rules. That said, there is perhaps a tendency to suggest that lawyers only offer legal expertise in the procurement space. Many procurement lawyers are also procurement experts, providing practical solutions tailored to particular markets. Interviews with lawyers were illuminating because they were as, if not even more inclined, to speak more widely about the effects of marketisation, not just the rules. Equally, it may be said that it is difficult to claim true procurement expertise without some basic understanding of legal regulation given that it is the main form of governance of procurement practice. Therefore, perspectives on the rules given by non-lawyers were equally instructive.

As indicated, the empirical phase was conducted before the PA 2023 came into force. Responses therefore mainly concerned the regulatory regime under EU law as implemented in the PCR 2015. However, importantly, various interviewees referred to the incoming PA 2023 reforms. Therefore, it is reasonable to assume that many legal advisers (and, indeed, practitioners) will have been aware of these reforms when giving their responses and which informed their thinking. Thus, many of the findings in relation to practice under the PCR 2015 are just as relevant to the application of the PA 2023.

Finally, as a matter of style, it should be noted that where a term is defined in brackets for the first time in a chapter, the defined term will be used throughout the book eg Public Contracts Regulations 2015 ('PCR 2015') and Procurement Act 2023 ('PA 2023'); the full definition is not generally repeated. The same is the case for certain entities eg centralised procurement authorities ('CPAs') and organisations eg National Audit Office ('NAO'). Further, the book generally uses the term 'framework' rather than 'framework agreement' throughout, except where the EU law definition of 'framework agreement' is discussed. This is simply for expediency and accuracy to reflect that 'framework' is now the term used under the PA 2023. It should be noted, however, that the title of the book retains the term 'framework agreement'. This is deliberate, reflecting the authors' view of the conceptual importance of agreeing from the outset a firm basis governing terms for future purchases.

6. Scope

Regarding subject-matter, this book focuses on multi-supplier frameworks. Single-supplier frameworks are slightly different in the issues they raise, such as to merit a separate frame of analysis and research. For instance, they have features similar to standard binary contracts that establish strategic partnering arrangements and do not involve a closed market of suppliers, thereby creating a different dynamic and where marketisation is not as readily apparent. Further, interviewees were particularly keen to comment on multi-supplier frameworks given the size, scale and extent of their use in practice. Notwithstanding, the book refers to single-supplier frameworks where mentioned by interviewees as this may be useful for future research.

It is also important to acknowledge the selective sectoral focus of the empirical research. Generally, the book focuses on regulation in the public sector, not other sectors or types of contract such as utilities or defence and security, to ensure a focus on the main rules applicable across the UK. It also acknowledges that sector- or contract-specific features of frameworks will necessitate further research. However, occasional reference will be made to rules on frameworks in other context for comparison. Within the public sector, the empirical research focuses on the ICT sector. As it was expected that the sample size for interview would be relatively small, it was best to concentrate on maximising findings by concentrating on a particular sector to ensure that these were at least substantially representative within that sector. In retrospect, this was a suitable choice because the research revealed that many of the issues have been experienced in other areas and certain market behaviours unique to, or characteristic of, the ICT sector reinforced the findings on marketisation by offering sector-specific examples.

After desktop searches of various sectors, it was decided to focus on ICT sector for several reasons. Firstly, as discussed in chapter three, the EU had this sector in mind as one area of importance when conceiving rules on frameworks. Second, the UK Government clearly considers ICT to be important in transforming public service delivery. According to a 2025 NAO report, at least £14 billion is spent annually on digital procurement.[41] Third, frameworks are used for the purchase of a wide range of ICT goods and services. This avoids the risk of any conclusion that problems experienced in the ICT sector are largely attributable to the types of goods and services procured. ICT sector frameworks involve a diverse range of products and services from highly commoditised low-value peripherals through to complex and integrated software solutions. Further, within this sector, there is a wide range of frameworks set up by central government[42] and regional purchasing consortia.

Regarding disciplinary focus, this book is mainly concerned with the legal and policy aspects of frameworks. In particular, it focuses on 'regulatory policy', which is often understood as how a Government achieves its objectives through the use of regulations, laws and other instruments to deliver better economic and social outcomes and thus enhance the life of citizens and business.[43] Further research in economics and other fields will be necessary to inform thinking on regulation going forward. More specifically, the main focus is on public sector procurement regulation under the PCR 2015 rather than on other sector-specific sets of regulations (eg, defence, utilities and concessions). This is on the basis that the PCR 2015 is the general model from which other regulations have been adapted, although, technically, as will be discussed, frameworks were regulated under EU law in the context of utilities before the public sector. It should be added that the principal focus is on procurement above the contract value thresholds for which the majority of rules under the PCR 2015. It does not consider below-threshold

[41] NAO, *Government's approach to technology suppliers: addressing the challenges*, Department for Science, Innovation & Technology, and Cabinet Office, Session 2024–25, 16 January 2025 HC 543, 5.

[42] A list of 'technology' frameworks set up by CCS can be accessed at www.crowncommercial.gov.uk/agreements/pillar/technology.

[43] This is the standard definition used by the Organisation for Economic Co-operation and Development. Information on its work on regulatory policy can be found at www.oecd.org/gov/regulatory-policy/#:~:text=%E2%80%8C%E2%80%8CRegulatory%20policy%20is%20about,life%20of%20citizens%20and%20business.

frameworks in any detail. Further, the focus is not on the whole of the UK but rather the applicable rules in England, Wales and Northern Ireland given that the PCR 2015 apply common rules across these countries. Scotland implemented the EU Directives in separate regulations,[44] although did not introduce significantly different provisions on frameworks. Notwithstanding, the empirical research component involved interviews from representatives in England, Wales, Northern Ireland and Scotland.

It should be added that whilst the book makes very occasional reference to practice in other countries, particularly EU Member States, it is not intended to have a comparative law focus. Indeed, the UK could learn lessons from other jurisdictions and which ought to be the subject of further study.

As indicated, the book focuses on the PCR 2015 and PA 2023. Post-Brexit, the UK has introduced supplementary Regulations on discrete aspects eg The Health Care Services (Provider Selection Regime) Regulations 2023[45] for the procurement of healthcare services in England. These are occasionally referenced as a point of comparison against the PA 2023 but are not examined in detail.

Finally, it is important to emphasise that this book is not to intended to denigrate stakeholders or to pronounce on the legality of particular frameworks or organisational behaviours but rather to open a constructive dialogue. The authors are acutely aware that contracting authorities have had to find ways to make savings under significant pressure. Suppliers can hardly be blamed for taking advantage of opportunities within the market if there is a demand, or for creating it. Additionally, central government will have been alert to many of the issues but will have needed to exercise certain choices or trade-offs and see whether markets may correct themselves before deciding on further regulatory interventions. However, in trying times, it is easy to see how the values of public service provision can be compromised by cost-cutting and profit-making. Conflicts of interest and misaligned incentives are bound to arise as stakeholders negotiate this challenging public-private interface. The book should be treated in a spirit of candid reflection on how frameworks and their regulation have developed, how they currently operate, and how they can be improved.

This book does not constitute legal advice. It is as accurate as possible at the time of submission in May 2025.

[44] The Public Contracts (Scotland) Regulations 2015, SI 2015/446, reg 34.
[45] SI 2023/1348.

PART II

The Marketisation and Regulation of Frameworks

2

Frameworks and their Marketisation in the UK

1. Introduction

A framework is often described as a 'tool' by which a contracting authority uses a procedure to establish through competition a basis for sourcing future requirements from suppliers appointed to the framework. For many reasons, frameworks have become ubiquitous in the UK.

An important factor is an ideological shift in recent decades in how public service delivery is viewed, characterised, in particular, by the promotion of neoliberal values. Theorists have described certain forms as 'New Public Management' ('NPM') or, framed in regulation terms, 'new public contracting'.[1] This is typified by increasing use of markets and competition, managerialism, organisational restructuring, and customer orientation.[2] Outsourcing and competitive tendering have been described as forms of 'marketisation' because they rely on the award of contracts to the private sector. They are seen as ways to secure value for money, among other things, as well as open up markets to international trade, and frameworks are seen as 'commercial' tools to achieve efficiency. In turn, procurement laws and policies are viewed instrumentally as ways to facilitate that marketisation. Another factor is prevailing economic conditions. The global financial crash and austerity measures have, as a matter of economic necessity, forced the public sector to make 'efficiency savings'. Yet another factor is the practical utility of frameworks because they avoid the need to re-run full procedures for each individual requirement and are an increasingly quick route to market.

It is recalled from chapter one that it is argued that there has not simply been overuse of frameworks to avoid legal rules otherwise applicable to full and openly competitive awards or because their use is incentivised by CPAs. Rather, there has been a fundamental shift in the regulated framework model in which procurement laws and policies generally exert limited pressure on framework use. Further, market-related factors increasingly compromise the basic characteristics of a typical framework, exemplified

[1] P Vincent-Jones, *The New Public Contracting: Regulation, Responsiveness, Relationality* (Oxford University Press, 2006).

[2] JM Alonso, J Clifton and D Díaz-Fuentes, 'Did New Public Management Matter? An Empirical Analysis of The Outsourcing and Decentralization Effects on Public Sector Size' (University of Munich Personal RePEc Archive, December 2011) 5.

by generic pan-public sector frameworks which do not involve a substantial upfront competition to appoint select suppliers and establish clear terms for call-offs.

This chapter introduces the framework agreement concept within a regulated procurement system. First, it considers its advantages and disadvantages, by extension, how these align with the objectives of the system overall, and the implications for regulation (Section 2). This provides the basis for understanding the role that regulation may play or not in ensuring the efficacy of frameworks and addressing marketisation (Section 3). Second, it introduces the notion of a UK 'framework market', comprising the public sector entities involved, suppliers and sectoral use, the operationalisation of frameworks through centralised purchasing (Section 3), and the increasing role of the private sector (Section 4). Third, it explains 'marketisation' as a theoretical frame of reference to explain factors and behaviours influencing frameworks in practice and even, increasingly, regulation (Section 5). It will also highlight various examples of marketised behaviour. The chapter then concludes (Section 6).

2. Framework Agreements

2.1. 'Framework Agreement'

As discussed in chapter five, the legal definition of a framework agreement in Article 33(1) Directive 2014/24/EU (as transposed in regulation 33(1) PCR 2015) involves an agreement between one or more contracting authorities and suppliers, the purpose being to establish the terms governing contracts to be awarded during a given period.

Frameworks involve two stages in a typical 'closed' model.[3] In stage one, a contracting authority establishes a framework for sourcing future requirements. It conducts a procedure to select suppliers to be admitted to it. This procedure would typically be either an 'open' procedure which is a single tender stage process inviting all suppliers or a 'restricted' procedure, whereby only those meeting qualitative selection criteria (economic and financial standing, technical and professional ability, etc) are invited to tender. In theory, the competition to be admitted will result in the establishment of clear terms governing future call-offs (ie, the agreed 'framework'). This would include setting call-off procedures, namely, whether awards will be made according to the terms set by the framework, eg a so-called 'direct award' or 'direct call-off' or require a further 'mini-competition', or a combination. It would also include price (or indicative prices) and other conditions. Only suppliers admitted can supply under the framework for its duration, such that it cannot be reopened to admit new suppliers. In stage two, a call-off procedure is undertaken to award contracts as needs arise based on the framework terms. This procedure will generally be quicker than a full competitive procedure because certain preliminary due diligence checks and much of the contractual agreement should have been completed at stage one.

[3] For a discussion of different framework models, see GL Albano and C Nicholas, *The Law and Economics of Frameworks: Designing Flexible Solutions for Public Procurement* (Cambridge University Press, 2016) 16–20.

There are two forms, namely, a 'single-supplier' framework (ie only one supplier is appointed) or 'multi-supplier' framework. As the Cabinet Office's Government Commercial Function ('GCF') has observed, there are around 8,000 construction frameworks in the UK, many being single-supplier frameworks.[4] This is likely due in part to the fact that these can be a means of setting up strategic partnering arrangements necessary to deliver bespoke construction services by a trusted supplier, as opposed to repeat delivery of commoditised items from many suppliers. These often involve the establishment of legally binding obligations to purchase and supply between the parties, not dissimilar to a conventional public contract. However, by far the most common type is a multi-supplier framework that imposes no legally binding obligations, except under a call-off.

A contracting authority can create a framework that can be used by other contracting authorities. For example, a group of contracting authorities in the National Health Service ('NHS') or local authorities may collaborate to create their own frameworks and may open them up for use by others. However, the most common multi-supplier framework is one set up by a contracting authority which aggregates demand and offers 'centralised procurement', namely, as a centralised procurement authority or 'CPA'. In this scenario, a CPA awards a framework to many suppliers and the CPA and suppliers become parties to the framework, usually by the CPA entering into separate agreements with each supplier. The framework might be made available for use by a range of other eligible contracting authorities who may be required to enter into an access agreement with the CPA setting out the terms of use, apportionment of legal responsibilities and liabilities, and reporting requirements as regards use.

As discussed in chapter five, the main alternative to frameworks is what Article 34 Directive 2014/24/EU calls a 'Dynamic Purchasing System' ('DPS'). Unlike a framework, a DPS is a completely electronic process. The first stage involves a process for identifying pre-qualifying suppliers eligible to supply future requirements; this is not a procedure to award an opportunity to supply according to established terms, as with a framework. It is only at the second stage that a full procedure is conducted to invite suppliers admitted to the DPS to submit tenders. Further, a DPS is open for suppliers to join at any stage whereas a framework is closed. In addition, the scope of a DPS is confined to commonly used purchases whereas a framework is not.

As also discussed in chapter five, the EU law definition of a framework agreement is broad and uncertain. A broad definition alone is not necessarily problematic in principle, especially under an EU system designed only to coordinate rules commonly applicable across Member States (as discussed in chapter three). Such a definition may thus recognise that different countries may develop different framework models. However, when combined with a lack of clear regulatory constraints on whatever framework model is applied and how it is operationalised, this has enabled different types of framework to arise which may involve significant variances in practice, from tightly defined strategic partnering arrangements to loosely defined arrangements with thousands of suppliers. As will be discussed, the PA 2023 introduces an even looser definition and accompanying provision.

[4] House of Commons, Committee of Public Accounts, *Competition in public procurement*, Sixth Report of Session 2023–24, 13 December 2023, HC 385, 13.

2.2. Advantages and Disadvantages

As discussed in detail in chapter five, many different factors may inform the choice to use a framework. There are certain perceived advantages and disadvantages, even if their effects in practice are not always possible to empirically substantiate. A consideration of these is important from not only a user but also a regulatory perspective. Regulation needs to ensure that it can facilitate the benefits and/or limit the drawbacks of frameworks and enable contracting authorities to effectively weigh these up. For example, frameworks may achieve certain short-term efficiencies but may also limit competition. This raises the question of how to regulate to balance these considerations depending on the underlying objectives of the procurement system.

It has been identified that the most relevant motivations for using frameworks comprise enhancing administrative efficiency; avoiding unnecessary use of urgent procurement methods; improving performance in simple, low-value and urgent procurement; ensuring security of supply; enhancing small- and medium-sized enterprise ('SME') participation; and fostering competition through aggregation. These can reduce transaction costs and achieve economies of scale.[5] Albano and Nicholas have indicated that the rise in framework use has coincided with an increase in average contract size, likely to reflect the potential for economies of scale and the amortisation of administrative costs over a larger aggregate value.[6] Frameworks might avoid or limit warehousing, inventory control and distribution costs where orders are placed as needs arise.[7] As regards security of supply, frameworks create a closed, finite 'micro-market', making it easier to buy from capable and credible suppliers and manage the procurement; although, as will be discussed, this is not necessarily the case for generic multi-supplier frameworks involving many suppliers.

However, as the NAO has observed, inappropriate framework use may also have disadvantages. There may be inflated prices where a supplier enters the framework and sets a rate but that price will not reflect the outside market rate over time. Further, frameworks may limit competition either because there may be an insufficient number of suppliers admitted necessary to conduct effective mini-competitions or, conversely, too many to make an effective choice, including, in the latter case, the possibility of their receiving little or no work. Another disadvantage may be less competition where it is possible to directly award to suppliers without reopening competition.[8] Also, if large frameworks take time and cost to set up and administer, it may simply be preferable to run a normal procedure.

Techniques for operationalising frameworks may also have distinct advantages and disadvantages, in particular centralised purchasing.[9] For smaller contracting authorities that do not have the resource to set up frameworks, CPAs can do so and on a much larger scale to achieve greater efficiencies given access to a wider supply market.

[5] Albano and Nicholas (n 3) 5–9.
[6] ibid 24.
[7] ibid.
[8] NAO, *Lessons learned: competition in public procurement*, Cabinet Office, Session 2022–23 19 July 2023, HC 1664, 25.
[9] For a useful discussion in this regard, see Albano and Nicholas (n 3) ch 11.

However, as discussed in chapter five, a perceived drawback is that the provider may not necessarily be clear as to the precise needs of user contracting authorities when setting up the framework and user contracting authorities may be unclear on the precise terms on which the framework is intended to be used.

However, as indicated in chapter five, contracting authorities do not necessarily make calculated economic and operational decisions about frameworks based on a cost-benefit analysis of their relative advantages and disadvantages. As with any procurement choice, decisions may equally be based on convenience or familiarity or sector customs. Similarly, CPAs may set up and operationalise frameworks for the financial incentives as much as for providing an effective and efficient means of procurement.

The UK does not explicitly legally require contracting authorities to make cost-benefit or other comparisons between frameworks and other options. As will be discussed, some policies mandate a 'frameworks first' approach which nudges towards their use. This is not to say that individual contracting authorities may not undertake careful assessments of the options.

2.3. Frameworks and the Objectives of the Regulated Procurement System

As discussed in more detail in chapter three, it is important to understand not just the advantages and disadvantages of frameworks but also their role within the scheme of objectives of a procurement system overall.[10] This will influence how frameworks themselves are regulated and their provisions interpreted and applied and how they ought to be regulated when considering reform.

To explain, it was discussed above that frameworks are perceived to deliver efficiency in public spend. However, a procurement system may be designed to achieve any number of objectives, in certain instances subordinating efficiency or, more broadly, value for money, to other objectives. This matters because it means that laws and policies on frameworks and their set-up may need to take those other objectives into account. For example, in a country experiencing extensive corruption, the importance of preventing corruption as an objective may impact its approach to regulating frameworks. Examples might include: mandating use of frameworks over other procedures; prioritising use of open frameworks rather than closed frameworks; restricting discretion to set certain award criteria and use direct call-off procedures; mandating use of central government CPAs to minimise local corruption; or preventing private capital participation in CPAs. Such restrictions on choice could undermine value for money or efficiency in the short term but may reduce corruption.

The above scenario is not necessarily one of an economically developing country. As discussed in chapter three, a real-life example which led to litigation in the EU is the *ASMEL*[11] case in which Italy introduced legislation limiting private sector participation

[10] For a useful introduction to this debate, see SL Schooner, 'Desiderata: Objectives for a System of Government Contract Law' (2002) 2 *PPLR* 103.

[11] Case C-3/19 *ASMEL v ANAC* ECLI:EU:C:2020:423.

in a contracting authority which operated frameworks, in part, to address the influence of the mafia in local government procurement. In that case, a question arose as to whether such rules may be contrary to EU law given EU objectives in preventing restrictions on the freedom to provide services.

In other systems with lower corruption risks, the emphasis may instead be on securing value for money, in particular, maximising efficiency. Thus, in a decentralised system (ie one prioritising choice and flexibility for contracting authorities), that system may nevertheless encourage the use of centralised CPA-established frameworks in order to secure efficiencies through aggregated demand but stop short of mandating their use. If procurement rules are broadly drawn to facilitate flexibility in the set-up and operation of frameworks, this may also allow different models of framework contracting to develop, including extensive involvement of the private sector which can offer ways of managing frameworks. If that procurement system does not have particularly clear overall objectives for the procurement system and specific objectives for use of frameworks, and provides a largely deregulated or light-touch regulatory environment, it is possible to see how behaviours may also develop in ways that could also undermine value for money, including efficiency. Examples might include the set-up of many overlapping frameworks involving thousands of suppliers. These may be set up by highly professionalised CPAs which then charge suppliers for their services (which could deter access by small suppliers) or even compete against each other to attract users. This may also invite extensive private sector profit led organisations. All of this may call into question the actual objectives of frameworks and, indeed, the regulated procurement system overall.

If a discussion about objectives seems abstract, it can be put into a specific context. As discussed in chapter four, historically, the UK did not adopt dedicated procurement legislation pursuing a clear set of domestic objectives. Rather, it largely copied out EU Directives into UK Regulations and, by extension, EU objectives. UK procurement policy has referred to the need to ensure 'value for money' (and suggested that giving effect to EU Directives is consistent with this objective) but this is not exactly the same as the EU Directives' objectives of preventing discrimination and removing market access barriers to create an internal market. As a result, the UK has been somewhat ambivalent as to the objectives of UK procurement regulation given that it seeks to pursue value for money whilst the bulk of its procurement legislation does not explicitly pursue this objective. As will be shown, this may impact on the approach to regulating frameworks.

As will be discussed in chapter three, matters have been further complicated because the EU itself has not been clear to what extent it may pursue other distinct objectives such as 'competition' beyond the traditional objectives identified above. Relevant to the analysis in this book, it has been argued there is a competition objective and that its effect is such that the EU Directives' rules on frameworks must be interpreted and applied in a way that takes account of their effects on competition. This has created uncertainty as to what kinds of constraints apply to contracting authorities in applying the rules on frameworks, given such an objective. The EU's own ambivalence in this regard is also reflected in its decision to introduce a generic rule to ensure that frameworks are not used improperly or in ways that prevent, restrict or distort competition, the scope and application of which has been unclear.

The above must also be considered in light of the fact that, by definition, the Directives are 'directory', coordinating procedural rules for the award of contracts across EU Member States but leaving space for them to introduce further legislation and policies in pursuit of domestic objectives, provided these are compatible with EU law. However, as indicated, the UK has not taken any domestic initiative in this regard.

These conceptual issues are relevant to the UK's experience and this book for several reasons. First, as the UK has copied out the EU Directives, the above uncertainty that pervades EU law on the objectives of procurement regulation is necessarily replicated under UK law. As EU rules have only been couched in fairly general terms and have not categorically addressed concerns about the effects of frameworks and their operationalisation on competition, it is possible that EU law and policy has contributed to some of the problems now experienced in the UK. However, as chapters three and four will discuss, caution should be exercised not to overstate the EU's responsibility. It is arguable that the UK has failed to take sufficient initiative domestically to address these behaviours.

Second, this is now a live concern because, following Brexit, the UK has chosen to design a procurement system and regulation that gives effect to the UK's own internal domestic objectives. Of course, it remains a domestic objective to open up its procurement market to international trade in accordance with international agreements, but it is no longer a significant objective of UK procurement regulation to assist in creating an EU internal market. This raises fundamental questions, such as: will there be much clearer objectives regarding the pursuit of value for money, including efficiency, or even maximising competition? What effect, if any, could such objectives have on the design and operation of rules on frameworks? Further, what role, if any, will a reformed competition law (or, indeed, other regimes such as state aid/subsidies) play in addressing the anti-competitive effects of frameworks and their use? However, as will be discussed in chapter four, the UK has not, in fact, articulated a clear set of objectives for its new system, including the role of frameworks in this regard, except a set of generic statutory objectives (in section 12) to have regard to, for example, value for money and maximising public benefit etc. It is by no means clear how the rules on frameworks must be applied in light of these objectives. Most importantly, the PA 2023 includes new rules on frameworks but these do not fundamentally address many issues raised in this book and the competition law aspects have not featured much at all in the debate on reform.

In short, therefore, there is a need to think critically about the objectives of a procurement system, how regulation is used to achieve them, and how this relates to frameworks but which has so far been demonstrably absent in UK discourse.

3. The UK Framework Market

It would be possible to provide an overview of frameworks in the UK without referring to it as a framework 'market'. However, it is appropriate to do so for several reasons.

Procurement itself is often referred to as constituting a 'market'. Contracting authorities wish to buy goods, works and services and suppliers wish to sell to them. Transactions are effectuated through the award and conclusion of contracts. However, barriers to procurement opportunities may be erected through laws, policies and practices which can lead to favouritism. From the perspective of international trade, domestic preferences in the award of contracts risk discrimination that shuts out foreign suppliers. This necessitates initiatives, including regulation, to open up national procurement markets to cross-border trade. This is often referred to as trade 'liberalisation' as distinguished from 'marketisation', as discussed below.

As will be discussed, official publications regularly refer to a 'framework market' and to CPAs as having a 'market share' of certain categories of good or service. It is said that when frameworks are set up, they create 'mini-markets' for admitted suppliers. The proliferation of frameworks has also led to contracting authorities 'framework shopping'. Indeed, the very fact that the language of the 'market' was referenced so often by interviewees, is, itself, an indicator of marketisation.

As will also be discussed in chapter three, it has been a point of debate under EU law the extent to which a CPA provides services on a 'market' such as to be subject to competition law.

As will be discussed below and in Part III, there are numerous examples of behaviours which are clearly market oriented.

The following is not intended to provide a comprehensive picture of the UK framework market. In fact, it is not possible to do so because it is not actually known how many frameworks exist. As discussed in chapter ten, going forward, there is a need for more systematic mapping and analysis of the framework market in order to better understand the implications for regulation. Moreover, this book is careful not to single out particular organisations for criticism and therefore avoids too much detail or analysis of specific frameworks.

3.1. Public Sector Entities

Contracting authorities may set up frameworks solely for their own use. Alternatively, they may join together with other contracting authorities in a consortium to set these up for their use instead of using a CPA. Framework arrangements may exist at regional level for pooling the purchasing requirements of local authorities procuring commonly used goods and services such as school meals, energy and stationery.[12] Sectoral frameworks are also set up for other types of contracting authority, such as universities. In addition, central government departments have set up frameworks, the most prominent example being CCS which acts as a CPA for the whole public sector.[13]

The NAO has identified the most significant framework providers by value of contracts awarded under them as well as the number of frameworks provided by each provider:

[12] NAO, *Efficiency in government procurement of common goods and services*, Cabinet Office, Session 2024–25 HC 116, 18.

[13] Information is available at www.crowncommercial.gov.uk/.

Table 1 Key Framework Providers in the UK

Framework provider	**Value of contracts awarded using its frameworks (2022–23) (£bn)**	**Number of frameworks**
Crown Commercial Service	16.8	175
Ministry of Justice	1.2	25
Department of Health & Social Care	0.7	19
National Highways	0.7	43
Department for Education	0.7	42
Ministry of Defence	0.6	97
Yorkshire Purchasing Organisation	0.5	179
Eastern Shires Purchasing Organisation	0.5	139
Torus62 Ltd	0.4	12
NHS Shared Business Services	0.4	52
Fusion 21 Ltd	0.3	24
Hampshire County Council	0.3	94
Lincolnshire County Council	0.3	34
NHS England	0.3	93
Communities & Housing Investment Consortium (CHIC)	0.3	20
NHS London Procurement Partnership	0.3	23
Homes England	0.3	29
NHS Supply Chain	0.3	118
Scottish Government	0.2	59
Portsmouth Water Ltd	0.2	1
Total	**25.3**	**1,278**

Source: NAO, *Efficiency in government procurement of common goods and services*, Figure 3 Providers of frameworks to the UK public sector, based on NAO analysis of information from Tussell (a third-party data provider).

Several standout features are readily apparent from this basic table. Most importantly, framework providers may set up many more than one framework. CCS alone operates 175. This will require extensive resource and pose difficulties for ensuring effective oversight, as discussed in chapter five.

Further, CCS is by far the largest provider, being twice as large as the next 19 biggest combined.[14] This evidences the extent to which there is a significant degree of centralisation of procurement of common goods and services despite the tendency to suggest that procurement in the UK is largely decentralised. As will be discussed below, this raises a number of issues that merit further investigation. One is that CCS, an executive

[14] NAO (n 12) 18.

agency of the Cabinet Office, the department responsible for setting much of the UK's procurement policy and guidance, is also the largest framework provider. This prompts questions about the extent to which policy may be shaped by its own experience, quite apart from any potential for conflict in these roles. This degree of centralisation is further corroborated by the prevalence of central government departments, which is, perhaps, unsurprising given their spend relative to local authorities as well as the constellation of regional purchasing organisations which operate over large combined geographical areas. Naturally, this degree of centralisation also raises the question of the extent to which there is any concentration of demand-side market power by these actors when providing their framework services and what are the implications for smaller locally based suppliers seeking to access contract opportunities for increasingly large volume aggregated requirements. However, it may be noted that some of the major local government framework providers are not major combined authorities in large city regions, eg Hampshire County Council and Lincolnshire County Council.

As evidenced, there are also sector-specific framework providers, notably, in the health and social care and housing sectors. NHS Supply Chain and others are increasingly used to procure clinical and non-clinical needs; in some instances, NHS policies mandate use of 'approved framework agreements' to procure requirements for agency staff[15] and ICT.[16]

It is also important to acknowledge the devolved context. Wales, Northern Ireland and Scotland have established many frameworks, with each government (or its respective executive agency) acting as a CPA. For instance, according to the Scottish Government, in 2022/23, total spend through collaborative frameworks was over £1.3 billion, achieving over £135 million (10 per cent) in savings.[17]

3.2. Suppliers

As it is not known how many frameworks exist, it cannot be known how many suppliers there are. Concerted efforts have been made by contracting authorities, in particular, CPAs, to increase the number of suppliers admitted to frameworks. There is an early incentive to attract suppliers given that once awarded, frameworks cannot be reopened to admit new suppliers (although, as discussed in chapter four, the PA 2023 has introduced open frameworks for the first time).

According to a NAO report, CCS has 'brought more suppliers to the market for public contracts'; there are now over 9,500 suppliers on CCS frameworks.[18] Suppliers reporting spend through a CCS framework have grown from 2,039 in 2017–18 to 3,926 in 2022–23. In 2022–23, the average revenue generated by each such supplier was £6 million, and no single supplier had more than 7 per cent of the £25 billion spent by

[15] Information is available at www.england.nhs.uk/reducing-expenditure-on-nhs-agency-staff-rules-and-price-caps/agency-rules-list-of-approved-framework-agreements-for-all-staff/.

[16] Information is available at www.england.nhs.uk/nhs-commercial/central-commercial-function-ccf/procurement-framework-strategy-recommendations/.

[17] Scottish Government, *Annual Procurement Report 2022–2023*, 39.

[18] NAO (n 12) 28.

the public sector.[19] The NAO has used metrics adopted by competition authorities to assess whether buyers have a large choice of potential suppliers. For instance, frameworks may be divided into lots to increase the chances of suppliers (particularly SMEs) winning a share of contracts. The NAO analysed 308 lots within 107 frameworks with spend above £100,000 in 2022–23. It found CCS frameworks involving 24 or more lots where contracts were awarded to a single supplier even though others were available, suggesting that a number of frameworks have a few suppliers winning most of the work and creating highly concentrated markets.[20] In response, the Cabinet Office stated that reported figures would need to take account of a variety of factors, including: overall market conditions at stage one of the framework; the commercial strategy of the framework provider; and plans to use mini-competitions at stage two; however, the NAO's view was that this illustration provides a useful starting point to encourage CCS to make more use of its data to understand competition and refine its strategy to enhance value for money.[21] This suggests that there is a need for more in-depth analysis of the extent of, and reasons for, any concentration within the framework market.

The GCF maintains a list of the Government's so-called 'strategic suppliers', which generate significant revenue from CCS frameworks, as indicated below.

Table 2 Strategic Suppliers on UK Frameworks

Supplier	**Recorded spend from CCS frameworks in 2022–23 (£bn)**
EDF Energy Ltd	1.62
Alexander Mann Solutions Ltd	1.33
Corporate Travel Management (North) Ltd	0.64
Totalenergies Gas & Power Ltd	0.60
Mitie FM Ltd	0.57
Capgemini UK plc	0.44
Calder Conferences Ltd	0.44
NHS Professionals Ltd	0.41
Vivo Defence Services Ltd	0.36
Deloitte LLP	0.32
PA Consulting Services Ltd	0.30
Softcat plc	0.26
Boxxe Ltd	0.25
Amazon Web Services EMEA Sarl	0.24
BT Group plc	0.24
GBT Travel Services UK Ltd	0.23

(continued)

[19] ibid.
[20] ibid 37.
[21] ibid.

Table 2 *(Continued)*

Supplier	Recorded spend from CCS frameworks in 2022–23 (£bn)
Fujitsu Services Ltd	0.23
Vodafone Ltd	0.23
OMD Group Ltd	0.23
Atos IT Services UK Ltd	0.22

Source: Based on NAO Figure 8 Top suppliers by amount of spend recorded through the Crown Commercial Service's (CCS's) frameworks, 2022–23, according to information provided by the Crown Commercial Service.[22]

Separate data published by Tussell indicates that, in FY22–23, 37 per cent of the combined contract value of contracts won was won through frameworks, up from 12 per cent in FY18/19.[23] Tussell has also published the top frameworks by value of contracts awarded by sector in FY22/23:

Table 3 Contract Value on Frameworks Awarded to Strategic Suppliers

Sector	Framework	Value of contracts awarded to strategic suppliers
Outsourcing & FM	Prison Operator Services	£890m
Technology	Technology Services	£801m
Construction Engineering	Delivery Integration Partnership	£460m
Consulting	Management Consultancy Framework	£153m
Telecoms	Network Services	£277m
Aerospace & Defence	Technology Services	£55m

Source: Tussell, UK Strategic Suppliers Report 2023.

As discussed in Part III, EU and UK laws and policies have neither placed particular constraints on the number of suppliers admitted to frameworks nor developed specific initiatives to increase market access on frameworks, as distinct from typical measures often taken in relation to procurement generally (eg, rules on division into lots).

3.3. Prominence of Certain Sector-specific Frameworks

As discussed in chapter five, there is no UK-wide list of frameworks although, as the NAO has observed, third-party market data providers have identified anything from 8,000

[22] NAO (n 12) Figure 8 Top suppliers by amount of spend recorded through the Crown Commercial Service's (CCS's) frameworks, 2022–23, 30.

[23] Information is available at www.tussell.com/insights/uk-government-strategic-suppliers. Access to the 2022–23 report is by request only (report on file retained by the authors).

to more than 21,000.[24] The NAO has suggested that this fragmentation prevents the government from acting as a single buyer across numerous categories of common goods and services, resulting in duplication of effort and increasing bidding costs.[25]

Nevertheless, there are certain sectors where it is known that frameworks play a particularly prominent role, eg construction, healthcare and ICT. As indicated in chapter one, the empirical research for this book focused on the ICT sector. According to a 2025 NAO report, at least £14 billion is spent annually on digital procurement in the UK, comprising hardware and software.[26] In 2022–23, £9 billion was spent through CCS frameworks with its technology category having the most spend above corporate and estates.[27]

It is recalled that, in certain sectors (eg NHS), central or local government policies have mandated use of frameworks for various types of requirement. The same is true of the ICT sector. For context, the UK has sought to transition towards better digital public services which necessitate complex IT systems to manage increasing amounts of data through closer collaboration between the public and private sectors.[28] However, the pressure to drive efficiencies and limit spending is challenging given the pace of technological development and the technical expertise required when procuring ICT solutions. Contracting authorities need to develop sophisticated and agile purchasing techniques to ensure they procure fit-for-purpose and up-to-date ICT solutions that offer the best value for money. Frameworks provide one such option. In 2017, the GCF issued guidance stating that 'services should be procured from a government framework where possible and appropriate, with consideration being given to the terms and conditions of frameworks and their appropriateness in a disaggregated model'.[29] Similarly, the former Conservative Government's Technology Code of Practice advocated 'a commercial approach that supports the disaggregation of contracts' and reminds central government departments of CCS's 'technology' category of frameworks when developing purchasing strategies.[30] A prime example in this sector is the G-Cloud framework which, at the time of writing, is in its 14th iteration.[31]

In 2022, the Government published its first Digital, Data and Technology Playbook.[32] This provides guidance on sourcing and contracting for digital, data and technology projects and requires all central government departments and arms-length bodies to follow the guidance on a 'comply or explain' basis. It states that 'we should look first to available frameworks to see whether the need we are procuring for is already met

[24] NAO (n 12) 21.

[25] ibid 7.

[26] NAO, *Government's approach to technology suppliers: addressing the challenges*, Department for Science, Innovation & Technology and Cabinet Office, Session 2024–25, 16 January 2025 HC 543, 5.

[27] NAO (n 12) Figure 7 Categories of spend managed by the Crown Commercial Service (CCS), 2022–23, 29.

[28] See generally, HM Government, 'Industrial Strategy: building a Britain fit for the future', 27 November 2017.

[29] GCF, 'Government Shared Learning – Exiting Major IT Contracts: Guidance for Departments', November 2017, 6.

[30] Information on the Code of Practice is available at www.gov.uk/government/publications/technology-code-of-practice/technology-code-of-practice.

[31] Information is available at www.crowncommercial.gov.uk/agreements/RM1557.13.

[32] HM Government, 'The Digital, Data and Technology Playbook, government guidance on sourcing and contracting for digital, data and technology projects and programmes', June 2023.

by existing contracts and contracting mechanisms' whilst highlighting that, despite certain benefits, 'using frameworks inappropriately can have negative consequences for contracting authorities, markets and suppliers and can unintentionally inflate prices'.[33]

A 2025 NAO report has highlighted some of the challenges of procuring digital solutions and how this may lead to increased framework use. This includes, among other things, the technological complexity, 'unknown unknown' risks, and a lack of personnel, digital and commercial skills necessary to effectively procure digital solutions which 'can increase reliance on generic commercial frameworks which are not well suited to complex requirements'.[34] It also identified the pressure to award contracts within limited timescales before developing a proper understanding of what are complex requirements. It gave an example of a CCS framework used to procure a voucher scheme within a tight timescale where the requirement was still being developed at the time of procurement. It was described as 'a standard government contract with pre-assessed suppliers' and was the only option to procure within timescales that would also minimise the risk of legal challenge and high costs. However, it was noted that it could only procure from the limited pool of framework suppliers and according to its standard terms which included a cost-plus pricing model that did not provide the required performance incentives.[35]

As discussed in chapter five, it is questionable whether multi-supplier frameworks are a suitable tool for purchasing complex requirements. Further, as discussed in chapter seven, a fundamental issue concerns how and when pricing mechanisms are established for a framework. Whilst there is a risk that pricing mechanisms may only be set out in very broad terms at the framework award stage (or not at all), leaving too much to the discretion of user contracting authorities at the call-off stage, the above example also highlights the issue of user contracting authorities potentially having little choice but to accept pricing models under which they will bear much of the cost risk at the call-off stage. It is also interesting that it was observed that a framework was used to minimise the risk of legal challenge. As discussed in chapter nine, generic cross-public sector frameworks may be designed in such a way as to significantly reduce the risk of challenge, sometimes ironically in violation of the procurement rules and at the expense of the efficacy of the framework itself.

3.4. Levels of Competition on Frameworks

It is difficult to empirically verify the extent to which known frameworks provide for competition. 'Competition' and how it is identified and measured might include any number of aspects, including: how, where and how often frameworks are advertised; the number and type of suppliers that submit tenders to be appointed to the framework and the number admitted (or re-admitted having been excluded); the extent to which lotting structures are included to facilitate market access; the form that competitions may take (eg, on price or price and quality); the extent to which frameworks provide for and are reopened to mini-competitions as against direct call-offs; the number and type of lots

[33] ibid 66.
[34] NAO (n 26) 38.
[35] ibid 41 citing Figure 11 Case example: awarding contracts too quickly.

awarded to single or multiple suppliers and the value of each lot; and the number and value of awards made relative to the number of suppliers admitted to the framework. Of course, there may also be other ways of identifying the extent to which frameworks provide for competition. An example is the maximum duration set for a closed framework which will necessarily set a limitation on competition. In 'open frameworks' under the PA 2023, this would include the extent to which frameworks are reopened to competition and the effects of reopening given that initially admitted suppliers will need to compete against new entrants.

There appears to be limited data and economic or other research on competition in UK frameworks. The NAO has observed that the Government does not assess whether, or to what extent, the number of suppliers on a framework affects competition.[36] Similarly, the PAC has found that there was a lack of clear understanding of levels of competition within the framework market.[37] There is also the difficulty of measuring competition. As the NAO has observed, 'it is difficult to assess competition through a single measure as, for example, the number of bidders does not fully correlate to effectiveness of competition'.[38]

One issue concerns uncertainty around a contracting authority's control over the extent to which it permits competition. For example, the PAC has noted that the GCF has not seen any evidence of favouritism in contract awards and is trying to find the 'sweet spot' between having too many bidders, in which case all but one of them will have wasted bid costs thereby eventually inflating the cost to the public purse, and too few, which it said was also the wrong answer.[39] The GCF has stated that rather than extending frameworks, bringing the framework back to market and getting competition is the right thing to do.[40] However, it is not clear what analysis has been done to determine what the likely 'sweet spot' would be or the levels of competition across successive reiterations of frameworks.

The NAO has also found that the number of suppliers on frameworks can vary significantly. As of October 2022, it found that 48 per cent of frameworks had over 20 suppliers with 11 per cent only one or two.[41] Of course, the number of suppliers on a framework is not necessarily a good indicator of the extent to which it provides for competition. As will be discussed in Part III, a multi-supplier framework may admit hundreds or thousands of suppliers but if there is no robust competitive process to appoint them or most do not receive any work, it is questionable the extent to which it can be said to be 'competitive'.

It is also questionable whether contracting authorities have developed effective mechanisms to improve competition. For instance, the PAC has asked CCS what mechanisms are in place to look at a sector and identify where the market is 'thin' in terms of competition, where there were too few bidders, or perhaps where suppliers were not as good as needed. CCS said that it had experienced staff who could assess the markets

[36] NAO (n 8) 10.
[37] House of Commons Committee of Public Accounts, *Competition in public procurement* (n 4).
[38] NAO (n 8) 29.
[39] ibid 13.
[40] ibid.
[41] ibid 28.

and was working to bring more suppliers onto frameworks such as the G-Cloud framework. It commented that 99 per cent of business done through G-Cloud is below £5 million but that it was not the only vehicle for opening the market to small businesses, and that during the COVID-19 pandemic it put in place a low-value procurement platform for any contract below £140,000. When asked how government ensures that there really is competition, CCS noted that it was not mandatory for government buyers to engage with suppliers on CCS frameworks and that for procurement of less than £140,000 government buyers can directly award without reference to CCS frameworks. More generally, it said that the Cabinet Office was focusing on sectors where it sees an excessive concentration in terms of the focus on certain suppliers to the exclusion of others (particularly, smaller suppliers).[42] The PAC did not appear to be satisfied by the responses given, concluding that poor quality and incomplete data has meant that the Government is unable to evaluate competitive trends and understand how effectively markets are open to SMEs and others outside government's strategic suppliers, noting that the Cabinet Office expects the PA 2023 to help address the data issues.[43]

As indicated, there appear to be very few reliable statistics on the numbers and contract values of call-offs awarded by mini-competition or direct award. Further, even if there were reliable statistics indicating a trend in favour of using mini-competitions, this would not necessarily constitute clear evidence that frameworks are competitive. Whilst a mini-competition may indicate a 'refresh' of competition, it could equally be the result of a failure in the framework award process to effectively establish the original terms through an initial competition; this is quite apart from the fact that a mini-competition also introduces inefficiency because a further process has to be conducted. Similarly, it cannot necessarily be concluded from a prevalence of direct call-offs that there is a lack of competition. This might be the case if the process for framework award did not involve a robust competition to appoint suppliers such that there has not been sufficient competitive tension at both stages but if there was a robust competition at the framework award stage, direct call-offs may simply be the efficient result of a well-established framework.

That said, as discussed in Part III, interviewees indicated a high prevalence of, or preference for, direct call-offs as a quick route to market and which suppliers even marketed as such to their customer user contracting authorities; the sense was that this undermined competition. Again, CCS lacks data on the number of direct call-offs made because there are gaps in data provided by user contracting authorities and that the Cabinet Office agrees that it needs more structured data and effective processes to track procurement through the commercial lifecycle to monitor savings effectively. It was considered that this data gap will be plugged by new transparency provisions under the PA 2023 that will allow government to see where those are 'and to close them down'.[44]

Finally, perhaps most importantly for the purposes of this book, it is also difficult to discern the extent to which *regulation* may affect competition.

[42] House of Commons Committee of Public Accounts (n 4) 12.
[43] ibid 5.
[44] ibid13.

4. Centralised Purchasing

As indicated, public sector entities may cooperate to realise the advantages of aggregated demand. This may include going beyond joint cooperation to centralised purchasing through the creation of, or recourse to, a CPA. This book does not examine in detail the legal and practical operation of centralised purchasing in the UK.[45] However, given the fundamental role it plays in the operationalisation of frameworks, it is important to explain its regulation.[46]

As discussed in chapter three, according to Article 2(16) Directive 2014/24/EU, a 'central purchasing body' is a contracting authority providing 'centralised purchasing activities' and, possibly, 'ancillary purchasing activities', as defined. Such bodies can act as wholesalers (ie buying, stocking and reselling supplies to other contracting authorities) or intermediaries (ie acting on behalf of other contracting authorities by setting up frameworks and other tools for use by others). Article 37 provides that this includes the possibility for contracting authorities to use a framework concluded by a 'central purchasing body' offering centralised purchasing activities.

Over the past two decades, the prominence of CPAs has grown with many providing a full range of frameworks and DPS. Again, many factors may explain this development. One is a wider push from central government to centralise procurement. In the UK, procurement is largely decentralised in that contracting authorities make their own decisions about their procurement options. Supporters of the decentralised approach view this as placing the procurement function closer to the needs of an individual buyer. However, as the NAO has observed, a decentralised approach risks losing the savings and benefits that a centralised approach offers through standardisation of terms, aggregation of demand and economies of scale.[47] In the UK, much procurement policy is driven centrally. It is a central government department (the Cabinet Office) which promulgates most of the procurement policies. Some of these apply to central government departments but with a recommendation that they also be emulated within local government and some have broader application across all contracting authorities. Further, it is a central government CPA (namely, CCS) which is the largest framework provider.

In 2007, in its *Transforming Government Procurement*[48] document, HM Treasury highlighted that acting collectively rather than through separate departmental action can be an important driver of value for money. It also noted that the former Office of Government Commerce ('OGC') (effectively a precursor to CCS) would have strong derived powers to require departments to take up centrally negotiated deals for certain goods and services to use the Government's collective buying power to get better value for money on a whole-life costing basis or agree any alternative 'only where justified'.[49] It would also require departments to collaborate in their dealings with key suppliers

[45] For a brief introduction, see A Manzini, L Butler and M Trybus, 'Central purchasing bodies in the United Kingdom' in C Risvig Hamer and M Comba (eds), *Centralising Public Procurement: The Approach of EU Member States* (Edward Elgar, 2021).

[46] For a useful discussion of frameworks designed for aggregation, see Albano and Nicholas (n 3) ch 11.

[47] ibid 16.

[48] HM Treasury, 'Transforming Government Procurement', January 2007.

[49] ibid 19.

and markets.[50] It has been observed that this led to more widespread use of such CPAs, the OGC being among the first to develop CPAs via OGCbuying.solutions, an executive agency of HM Treasury also responsible for developing procurement capability across the public sector.[51] Thus, CPAs might have initially been seen in the UK both as a means of aggregating requirements but also developing procurement capability and promoting collaboration. As discussed in chapter five, the increasing trend is towards competition rather than collaboration between CPAs and their specialist procurement capability as something to market as an advantage to user contracting authorities with lesser capability.

It is beyond the scope of this book to examine the policy question of the extent to which procurement in the UK should be more centralised or decentralised but this will necessarily affect debate on future framework models and their regulation. As discussed in chapter four, it has been raised whether the UK should legally mandate the use of certain CPAs but which has been rejected.

Attempts have been made to identify the most well-known CPAs but there is no comprehensive list.[52] Within local government, there exist a number of regional local authority CPAs. As indicated above, Yorkshire Purchasing Organisation (which is local government owned and sponsored) appears to be the largest by value of contracts awarded using its frameworks (£0.5 billion) and number of frameworks operated (179) in 2022–23.[53] According to the NAO, its customers are public sector and private sector organisations for services which include framework provision, direct sales and assisted procurement. Its total spend managed in 2022–23 was £1.2 billion and its funding model is a levy on frameworks and profit from direct sales with a typical range of 0.4 per cent–2 per cent.[54] As discussed above, within central government, the largest CPA by far is CCS.

As early as 2008, UK academic commentary observed that procuring common requirements through CPA led frameworks can have advantages but CPAs may not always meet purchasers' needs, may lead to changes in the market which limit supplier availability in the future, and may increase the risks of procurement processes being challenged under either the procurement rules or competition law eg for abuse of a dominant position.[55] It was further identified that there are two implications of CPAs that merit particular focus. The first is the effect they might have on market structures, without necessarily having legal consequences. The second is the extent to which they may create or increase the risk of a legal challenge to their activities, particularly, in relation to competition law.[56] As discussed in chapter five, whilst there is some evidence of collaboration, a significant amount of *de facto* competition also occurs between CPAs as they seek to encourage contracting authorities and suppliers to use or join their

[50] ibid 18.

[51] J Chard, G Duhs and J Houlden, 'Body beautiful or vile bodies? Central purchasing in the UK' (2008) 2 *PPLR* NA26.

[52] NAO, 'A review of collaborative procurement across the public sector: List of professional buying organisations', May 2010.

[53] NAO (n 12) Figure 3 Providers of frameworks to the UK public sector, 19.

[54] ibid, Figure 4 Comparison of different centralised procurement authorities (CPAs) 20.

[55] Chard, Duhs and Houlden (n 51) NA 26–34.

[56] ibid 28.

frameworks. The legal aspect of a CPA's operation, particularly as regards their effects on competition, is considered in more detail in chapters three and five. Various NAO and other reports have also observed since as early as 2010 that many CPAs operating frameworks for similar goods and services incurred unnecessary administration costs by duplicating procurement activity and a wide range of prices were being paid for the same commodities, even within the existing collaborative arrangements.[57]

As indicated, the largest CPA is CCS. CCS was established in 2014 as a trading fund and executive agency of the Cabinet Office. It is a key part of the GCF, a network procuring or supporting procurement for the Government. Originally, CCS was tasked to buy common goods and services for departments directly, but this approach changed in 2016. CCS states its responsibilities as including: managing the procurement of common goods and services (although there is no definition of such[58]) in order that public sector organisations achieve value by buying as a single customer; increasing taxpayer savings by centralising buying requirements and bringing together smaller projects; and leading on procurement policy on behalf of the UK Government.[59] CCS has proposed to update its purpose as follows: 'to help the UK public sector to better extract value from its commercial and procurement activity'.[60] This might suggest a reorientation and more proactive focus on how value for money is actually achieved rather than largely assuming this to be the case through use of CCS purchasing mechanisms. CCS develops government-wide category management strategies for common goods and services to help organise the types of purchases that may be made.

CCS has a financial objective set by the Cabinet Office (with HM Treasury agreement) to deliver a 5 per cent return on capital employed.[61] The majority of CCS's income is from the levy suppliers pay as a proportion of the value of business they win through CCS's frameworks.[62] Other framework providers use a similar model. The typical levy range charged is 0 per cent–2 per cent.[63] It has been reported that some CCS frameworks also impose other charges; for example, one of CCS's technology frameworks charges a 1 per cent levy and a 10 per cent management fee, and another framework for recruitment had a combined charge of 4 per cent.[64] CCS's average levy is 0.7 per cent, double the rate it requires to achieve its financial objective.[65]

According to the NAO, in 2022–23, CCS had 238 frameworks and 19,606 customers.[66] CCS has estimated that the market it serves is worth around £125 billion, approximately 32 per cent of estimated spending on procurement of goods and services in 2022–23,[67] of which £25 billion goes through CCS's frameworks.[68] Eight central government departments accounted for almost 50 per cent of the spend through CCS

[57] NAO and Audit Commission, *A review of collaborative procurement across the public sector*, May 2010, 6.
[58] ibid,14.
[59] Information is available at www.gov.uk/government/organisations/crown-commercial-service/about.
[60] CCS, *Annual Report and Accounts 2023/24*, 24 July 2024, 11.
[61] NAO (n 12) 25.
[62] ibid 8.
[63] ibid 20, Figure 4 Comparison of different centralised procurement authorities (CPAs).
[64] ibid, fn 4.
[65] ibid 11.
[66] ibid 27.
[67] ibid 14.
[68] ibid 6.

frameworks in 2022–23, which included the Cabinet Office (£0.7 billion).[69] Thus, even the department to which CCS is attached is a major user of its frameworks. CCS has more than doubled the annual value (in real terms) of the transactions through its agreements from £12 billion in 2017–18.[70] CCS's annual report for 2022–23 showed that it supported customers with procurements worth a total annual contract value of over £2.3 billion but it also stated that there are still areas such as the NHS and local communities and housing where CCS believes greater usage of its frameworks can help secure better value for money.[71]

In terms of actual outcomes for the public sector, CCS reported 'commercial benefits' of £3.6 billion in its 2022–23 annual report and accounts, comprising 10.37 per cent of the gross spend managed.[72]

Going forward, CCS's target 'market share' has remained relatively unchanged at around 21 per cent, with aims to achieve a 50 per cent market share in the next four years.[73]

Several general observations can be made based on existing reports. First, according to the NAO, CCS was seen as the 'default organisation' for certain categories of common requirements and contracting authorities were broadly satisfied with CCS's performance, although a number alluded to inconsistencies in the quality of 'customer service'.[74] As discussed in chapter five, interviews have raised concerns about support offered in CPA-led frameworks.

Second, it is clear that CCS is increasingly market oriented. Its corporate performance measures have focused on growth in spend through frameworks. CCS's metrics also measure commercial benefits and customer satisfaction, but no other measures (eg, speed or quality of framework), and it has been observed that CCS's business plan for 2024–25 includes actions to amend its metrics and deprioritise spend growth.[75] Further, its levy model is not simply intended to cover CPA operating costs but to exceed its financial objective and effectively make a profit. The use of fee charging mechanisms by CPAs is discussed in more detail in chapter five. Moreover, since 2014, CCS has collected customer feedback using a Net Promoter Score as the only proxy measure for its customer satisfaction; the measure does not include supplier feedback or evaluate specific CCS frameworks but rather uses consumer experience style questions such as 'would you recommend CCS to a friend?'. CCS has stated that it is moving away from using this as its sole measure due to its limitations.[76] CCS also told the NAO that it saw growth in spend as a means to enable better value for money for procurement because it meant more transactions were being undertaken using the terms, specifications and maximum price it sets through the framework and because greater spend through its arrangements gives it more influence with suppliers. However, as the NAO observed,

[69] ibid 31, Figure 9 The Crown Commercial Service's (CCS's) biggest customers, 2022–23, 31.
[70] ibid 26.
[71] ibid.
[72] ibid 34.
[73] ibid.
[74] ibid 8.
[75] ibid 45.
[76] ibid 32.

'growth on its own does not lead to an efficient central purchasing system, and there is a risk that incentivising growth means it is prioritised over maximising value'.[77]

Third, an important NAO finding was that CCS's calculation of commercial benefits is not well understood by its customers and is not aligned with departments' own savings calculations. In economic terms, whilst HM Treasury defines efficiency as being able to spend less to achieve the same or greater outputs, or to achieve higher outputs whilst spending the same amounts, CCS's approach is not a measure of the value of the framework or the genuine reduction in cost from using the framework.[78] It was noted that CCS does not currently collect data from public sector organisations on the prices of goods and services included in contracts awarded but relies on data from suppliers. CCS then uses its category specialists and third parties to identify reliable market comparators but is not always able to obtain reliable market prices, meaning this picture is incomplete.[79] The NAO has also observed that public sector organisations use different systems which do not always allow for data to be easily shared with CPAs.[80] More generally, the NAO considered that there is no relationship between the levy and commercial benefit generated by frameworks.[81] CCS also does not benchmark itself or its frameworks against other CPAs.[82]

Finally, of particular relevance to this book, the NAO has reported that CCS frameworks were seen as compliant with legislation.[83] As discussed in Part III, however, based on the empirical evidence, it is certainly questionable whether all CPA led frameworks are always legally compliant.

5. Private Sector Organisations

As discussed in chapter five, private sector organisations feature increasingly prominently in the framework landscape beyond simply providing the goods and services for end users.

First, the NAO has noted the emergence of frameworks hosted by small contracting authorities and operated by private sector organisations.[84] In these instances, a contracting authority is a 'flag of convenience', notionally identified as setting up the framework but which is run by the private sector. As discussed in more detail in Part III, under Directive 2014/24/EU only contracting authorities can enter into frameworks and only contracting authorities can operate as CPAs. A private sector supplier is highly unlikely to satisfy the definition of a contracting authority, therefore raising various issues in respect of legal responsibility and accountability.

Second, as discussed in chapters five and eight, a practice has emerged by which contracting authorities expressly award contracts to private sector organisations to set

[77] ibid 8.
[78] ibid 32.
[79] ibid 9.
[80] ibid 10.
[81] ibid 42.
[82] ibid 45.
[83] ibid 27.
[84] ibid 8 and 40.

up and operate framework-type arrangements which are more typically single-supplier frameworks than multi-supplier. The private sector entity acts as a 'neutral vendor' or 'managed service provider' awarded a contract to source a wide range of requirements for a varied contracting authority base (often the entire UK public sector and sometimes also the third sector eg charities). Again, as the NAO has observed, such speculative frameworks have been established without direct reference to contracting authorities and offer 'direct awards' with suppliers potentially earning fees from buyers and suppliers.[85]

Third, as discussed in chapter three, private sector organisations may provide procurement consultancy services to contracting authorities without these necessarily having been subject to a procurement procedure in accordance with the PCR 2015.

The above is quite apart from any use of frameworks by private sector organisations to secure prices obtained by public sector contracting authorities.

6. The Marketisation of Procurement and the Role of Regulation

It is recalled from chapter one that there has arguably been a shift in the regulated framework model, in part because of its 'marketisation'. Before identifying various indicators in this regard, it should be considered whether 'marketisation' is a useful explanatory frame of reference. It is submitted that this concept, as developed through the multidisciplinary social sciences (and law) literature, seems to adequately capture what is occurring.

6.1. Marketisation

Literature across a range of disciplines (economics, sociology, political science and public administration, regulation studies and law) has sought to rationalise the increasing extent to which public service provision is subject to market considerations howsoever defined. Terms such as 'privatisation', 'liberalisation', 'marketisation', 'commercialisation', 'corporatisation', 'commoditisation' and 'commodification' are used, often interchangeably or indiscriminately. As will be discussed, there is a tendency to root marketisation in neoliberalism in the form of NPM and similar thinking.[86] It is not uncommon for academic studies referencing the phenomenon to then focus on privatisation, outsourcing or the introduction of competition through procurement. Health and welfare markets are identified as 'case studies' for exploring marketisation which is, perhaps, unsurprising given that welfare maximisation is a key feature of economic theories and where inalienable rights of the person and profit making may be perceived

[85] ibid 21.

[86] S J Dutta, S Knafo and I Lovering, 'What is neoliberal about new public management?' in C Scherrer, A Garcia and J Wullweber (eds), *Handbook on Critical Political Economy and Public Policy* (Edward Elgar, 2023).

to conflict. A literature review has revealed how research tends to identify the negative rather than positive effects of introducing market thinking, eg in terms of the impact on public sector values, reduced quality of services etc, although it does also acknowledge the purported benefits, eg increased efficiency.[87]

There is no accepted theoretical conception of 'marketisation'. Indeed, research surveying its use has found much variation such that it runs the risk of losing its analytical force and becoming a 'buzzword'.[88] However, as will be discussed, it has been used in literature on procurement and, if nothing else, provides a useful shorthand to capture the range of market-related behaviours and influences which appear to have impacted on framework contracting.

A useful starting point is to distinguish marketisation from other concepts. Hermann and Verhoest state:

> The terms liberalisation, privatisation and marketisation are often used to describe the profound transformation of public services in the last two decades, from the abolishment of public sector monopolies to the sale of public assets and the introduction of new, performance-based funding schemes, and sometimes even the introduction of New Public Management (NPM) techniques. The wide use of these terms has the potential to obscure some causes and effects of the restructuring of public services.[89]

'Privatisation' in its narrowest meaning refers to the sale of public assets to private providers. By contrast, in their view, 'liberalisation' means the abolition of public sector monopolies and the creation of public service markets with at least two providers competing for customers. Liberalisation thus aims at establishing perfectly competitive market structures, with many providers which have no market dominance and where oligopolistic markets ought to be avoided. On their conception, a special form of liberalisation is regular competitive tendering. Here, providers compete for contracts rather than customers, giving them an exclusive but temporary right to provide a public service. As customers cannot choose between different services, providers compete *for* the market rather than *in* the market.[90]

By contrast, Hermann and Verhoest characterise 'marketisation' as any changes that amount to the introduction of 'market elements' in public service provision; its purpose is not to have different providers compete for customers or contracts but, rather, the introduction of market elements is part of an internal reorganisation of service production and delivery, which supposedly should grant the service providers greater autonomy. In this regard, they identify the UK healthcare sector as an example which has transitioned from integrated healthcare service provision to 'quasi-' or 'internal' markets.[91] To explain, in the UK, a so-called 'purchaser-provider' split was

[87] A Mankell and J Hvenmark, 'Variations on a theme: exploring understandings of the marketisation concept in civil society research' (2020) 30(3) *Int. J. Sociol.* 443, 454.

[88] ibid 461 and which examined a sample of 210 peer-reviewed articles in civil society studies published between 1993 and 2017.

[89] C Hermann and K Verhoest, 'The Process of Liberalisation, Privatisation and Marketisation' in C Hermann and J Flecker (eds), *Privitization of Public Services: Impacts for Employment, Working Conditions, and Service Quality in Europe* (Routledge, 2021) 7.

[90] ibid 7–8.

[91] For a discussion of the accountability implications of encouraging NHS bodies to act as 'market players', see ACL Davies, 'This Time, it's for Real: The Health and Social Care Act 2012' (2013) 76(3) *MLR* 564–88.

introduced between the organisation funding services and the organisation delivering them. Formerly, hospital doctors largely decided which services would be provided. This was replaced by a system in which commissioning bodies were set up to act on behalf of patients to buy services according to need. Health authorities and general practices became 'purchasers' and were given budgets to buy healthcare services. These were to be purchased from acute hospitals, social care organisations and others who became 'providers' of those services set up as NHS 'trusts', separate organisations with their own management. Funding was changed from full-cost coverage to performance-based reimbursement in which individual hospitals can make profits or losses as if operating on liberalised markets. As Hermann and Verhoest observe, 'marketisation has been fuelled by the spread of NPM strategies' in which there has been a shift from hierarchical control to markets, leaner organisational structures, use of public-private partnerships and contracting out, and that whilst advocates of NPM promise greater efficiency and better service quality, governments introduce NPM reforms in order to cut costs, as a result of which service providers feel the same pressures as if they were competing for market shares.[92] Similarly, regulation literature has identified marketisation as a variant of NPM that has been particularly prevalent in Britain, defined as the attempt by the state to harness economic incentives in the organisation of public services through new forms of purchaser choice and provider competition; this includes the use of 'economic contracts' as instruments of regulation.[93] Therefore, on this conception, central to marketisation is the idea of *internal* reorganisation within the public sector of ways in which public services are delivered.[94]

Outside the specific context of quasi- or internal markets, marketisation has been described as the process by which market forces are imposed in public services, which have traditionally been planned, delivered and financed by government, and comprises: (1) the commodification of services and infrastructure; (2) the commodification of labour such as the reorganisation of work and jobs to maximise productivity and assist transfer to another employer; (3) restructuring the state for competition and market mechanisms; (4) restructuring democratic accountability and user involvement; and (5) embedding business interests and promoting liberalisation internationally.[95]

As discussed in Part III, some interviewees referred to the 'commercialisation' of frameworks, observing CPAs 'seeking to make it much more commercially attractive for contracting authorities to use a framework'.[96] There have been attempts within local government to define 'commercialisation' as: 'the principles, practices, and spirit of commerce applied to the public sector in order to deliver greater environmental, social and financial value'.[97] This has a grounding in theory which has suggested that it

[92] ibid 9.

[93] Jones (n 1) 46-48.

[94] For a discussion of the development of 'triangular' public service relationships involving the state, intermediate public service provider, and the citizen, see M Freedland, 'The Marketisation of Public Services' in C Crouch, K Eder and D Tambini (eds), *Citizenship, Markets, and the State* (Oxford University Press, 2001).

[95] D Whitfield, 'A Typology of Privatisation and Marketisation', European Services Strategy Unit, Research Report No.1, November 2006.

[96] LA3.

[97] This definition has previously been provided by Local Government Association on its 'commercialisation' webpages. The latest information on its commercialisation initiatives is available at www.local.gov.uk/free-commercialisation-support-available-lga.

can be characterised as modelling the public sector on private firms and organisation of services into business units operating with business values.[98] Thus, at first glance, commercialisation captures some of the behaviours explored in this book. However, 'commercialisation' is insufficient as a descriptor because behaviours go beyond public sector entities becoming more 'business-like' in how they procure public services; as indicated, more fundamentally, private sector organisations may also be assuming the role of contracting authorities and using frameworks themselves for their own commercial advantage.

Relating the above to frameworks specifically, it may be difficult to argue that the framework market is a 'quasi-market' per se and this book is cautious not to draw overly simplistic or superficial comparisons with other market structures. Ultimately, user contracting authorities that provide public services procure from the private sector. They are not generally buying from a public sector entity service provider (eg CPAs tend to act as their agents not wholesalers). Therefore, there is no clear purchaser-provider split. However, similar to conventional quasi-markets, contracting authorities are increasingly relying on other public sector entities to undertake the buying for them (sometimes under payment of a fee) and those public sector entities are notionally competing against each other to provide those services. As discussed in chapter three, EU case law has indicated that when CPAs offer their services to contracting authorities, they are not acting as economic operators or undertakings within a market (rather, they are acting as contracting authorities on behalf of others), and that a market of centralised procurement activities does not exist. Whatever the economic or legal classification of such activities, it is difficult to refute that they are in the business of buying for others and some sort of economic model is sustaining it. Of course, many frameworks are also used to procure *in* quasi markets eg where contracting authorities purchase within the NHS internal market.

The idea of the marketisation of the public sector has been identified as reflective of a wider marketisation of society that has even extended to non-profit civil society organisations eg charities:

> market structures, logics, identities and activities are spreading throughout society with a trend towards more business-like appearances and behaviours due to an increased presence of, for example, competitive tendering, contract management, commercial activities and managerial practices typical for the corporate world.[99]

Research has identified the extent to which marketisation may be driven by external forces (eg pressure to adopt certain practices in light of changes to market structures outside the organisation) and internal (eg funding pressure that means that an organisation may seek new partnerships with others in a particular sector, increased marketing to attract business, sales of surplus goods and services etc); although, of course, external influences can also affect internal changes.[100]

Again, applying this to the framework context, as Part III will evidence, internally, contracting authorities are becoming increasingly influenced by certain pressures when

[98] Whitfield (n 95).
[99] Mankell and Hvenmark (n 87) 443.
[100] ibid 457–61.

making choices about framework use and set-up. This includes factors such as the timing of other frameworks coming on to the market, the need to market frameworks to attract users and suppliers given competition from others, and the perceived need to partner with private sector organisations. This has also been influenced by other 'external' factors such as economic conditions favouring aggregation of public spend as well as a central government push to use frameworks.

6.2. Marketisation in the Context of Procurement

Political science and public administration literature has considered the extent to which the organisation and delivery of the procurement function has changed to 'sustain and expand the rationalities of marketisation of the public sector', in particular, by changing the role of civil servants.[101]

First, consistent with the literature outlined above, it has observed that marketisation is occurring in both the public sector and society more generally, thus:

> [W]e use the term marketisation in an inclusive way in relation to this development. Marketisation consequently refers to both specific processes and practices within the public administration that are part of the creation and installation of markets as systems of resource allocation, as well as more general tendencies in society where market rationality is expanding into more or less all areas of human activity.[102]

It has further observed that:

> [A]cademic interest in public procurement has mainly been, and continues to be, dominated by research questions concerning judicial interpretations, economic efficiency and specialised issues pertaining to public procurement of various goods or practices such as construction, IT services or management [...] In this sense, aspects of public procurement are well researched. However, there are a number of important questions that are seldom explored [...] In particular, this concerns what we might label *the politics of public procurement*, or in other words, issues of how practices of making markets, tendering and contracting out affect governing, control and the bureaucratic organisation.[103]

That research has referred to the concept of 'public procurement *as* marketisation' ie 'public procurement is understood as an instrument of governing associated with the rationalities of marketisation'.[104] This captures the sense in which there is an ongoing re-conceptualisation of the role for public administration and civil servants as public functions are increasingly transferred to private actors, creating and enhancing competition, and focusing on 'narrow economic efficiency'.[105] For instance, empirical research of local government procurement stakeholders in Sweden found that three marketisation themes emerged. The first concerned organisational set-up ie procurement functions

[101] A Öjehag-Pettersson and M Granberg, 'Public Procurement as Marketisation: Impacts on Civil Servants and Public Administration in Sweden' (2019) 23(3–4) *Scand. J. Public Adm.* 43.
[102] ibid 43–44.
[103] ibid 44 (emphasis in the original).
[104] ibid 44–45.
[105] ibid 46.

were becoming increasingly centralised including increasing need for specialisation of expertise that involved administrative costs. The second concerned increasing use of 'market language and thinking' not typical of civil servants and the perceived need for public sector entities to distinguish themselves as assets for external actors when it came to doing 'good business'.[106] In this regard it stated that:

> [...] [T]hey strive to be an organisation that can beat all other public organisations in terms of being the most desirable business partner for private companies with products and services being procured. The mindset is that they are in competition with other local governments and public organisations and must be, and remain, the most attractive public procurement organisation in order to succeed in procuring what they are aiming to procure.[107]

The third was increasing use of external consultants instead of, or supplementing, in-house procurement capability due to lack of resource (in particular, use of lawyers) and changing roles of civil servants.[108] It was indicated that it was sometimes difficult to communicate the expectations of a civil servant to someone in the private sector eg not simply being a good salesperson but that civil servants must also be transparent and accountable to taxpayers.[109]

Again, the above is likely to resonate with procurement practitioners. As discussed below, market-type language is pervasive in the framework contracting space with emphasis on contracting authorities being described as 'customers' of CPAs instead of collaborators in the delivery of public services, CPAs competing against each other for business, including marketing to attract suppliers and private sector partners, and balancing this with the fact that contracting authorities will remain legally responsible, ie accountable.

6.3. Marketisation and Procurement Regulation

Kunzlik has explored the relationship between neoliberal ideology and EU procurement law.[110] As discussed in chapter three, this is, in part, a response to academic arguments for the further neoliberalisation of EU procurement law based on the view that 'competition' (the efficiency concept of competition) and 'value for money' are dominant norms for that system. Putting that debate to one side momentarily, Kunzlik's conception of 'marketisation' essentially appears to be as follows. His starting point is to explain neoliberalism as being based on three core beliefs: (1) the state is a threat to economic freedom, such that state regulation of the market should be constrained; (2) the free market provides superior efficiency on the basis of producing an optimum allocation of resources and alignment of factors of production; and (3) the market can act as both a constraint upon state action and as a guarantor of neoliberal freedom and efficiency,

[106] On UK Government use of 'service provider' and 'customer', see G Mautner, *Language and the Market Society: Critical Reflections on Discourse and Dominance* (Routledge, 2010) ch 4.

[107] ibid 52. See relatedly, J W Campbell, 'Marketization and Public Service Motivation: Cross-Country Evidence of a Deleterious Effect' (2023) 52(1) *Public Pers. Manag.* 91.

[108] Öjehag-Pettersson and Granberg (n 101) 53.

[109] ibid 54.

[110] P Kunzlik, 'Neoliberalism and the European Public Procurement Regime' (2013) 15 *CYELS* 283.

given a supporting legal framework which imposes constraints on governmental discretion to limit its imposition of excessive or inefficient regulation. On the basis of the latter, international regimes on free trade are central to neoliberalism, being superior laws that constrain governments' ability to interfere in the market and capital flows.[111] Further, he indicates that neoliberalism asserts the importance of three particular normative values: efficiency, competition and profit-maximisation,[112] and offers policies that reflect these, namely: (i) a *laissez-faire* approach and the role of the state in maintaining market institutions; (ii) expansion of the market to create new fields for profit-making and capital accumulation; and (iii) preference for market-based policy instruments rather than regulation or other command and control instruments.[113] Concerning expansion of the market, he states that:

> This expansive impulse is reflected in a number of specific policies, including: the creation of de-regulatory international trade regimes to expand the market geographically by assuring international free trade and international capital flows; the 'commodification' of things previously not thought properly subject to property rights and therefore excluded from the scope of the market; and the 'marketisation' of activities that were previously considered to have an especially public character and which were therefore traditionally undertaken by the state itself rather than by private enterprise for private profit. 'Marketisation' involves subjecting the provision of public services or functions to market forces by having them delivered by private firms in pursuit of profit and subject, whenever possible, to competition. It has been implemented by several means: privatisation (where erstwhile state activities such as state-owned utilities, railways, airports and the air traffic control services are transferred to the private sector to be operated for private profit), the outsourcing of state activities (where, although responsibility for a given function is retained by the public sector, its delivery or an aspect of its delivery is contracted out to private firms) and by engaging in public-private partnerships […].[114]

Rendering the link between marketisation, procurement and its regulation explicit, he continues:

> The marketisation of public sector activity not only reflects neoliberalism's belief that the private sector is inevitably more efficient than the public sector but also its political agenda to 'roll back the state' and expand the market to open up new opportunities for global business interests and for capital accumulation, hence the argument that neoliberalism's 'primary aim has been to open up new fields for capital accumulation in domains hitherto regarded off-limits to the calculus of profitability' […].[115]
>
> Since marketisation by means of outsourcing and public-private partnerships (including PFI contracting) depends upon the award of public contracts, it has enhanced the importance of public procurement and its regulation. Neoliberals favour it on ideological grounds and it is rhetorically said to be justified by assertions of the superior 'efficiency' of the private sector, including its flexibility and capacity for innovation.[116]

[111] ibid 292–97.
[112] ibid 297–300.
[113] ibid 301–303.
[114] ibid 302 (footnotes omitted).
[115] ibid 304.
[116] ibid 305.

> Marketisation has [...] also intensified the ideological importance of the regulation of public procurement. This is because, by expanding the range of government activities whose delivery depends upon the award of contracts, the use of outsourcing and public-private partnerships also expands the zone of activity in which the discretion of public bodies may be controlled by public procurement law [...] We shall see that the fact that public procurement is regulated by an EU regulatory regime subjects the exercise of dominium to rule of law constraints. The fact that, as a result of outsourcing and public-private partnerships, more government activities are now delivered under public contracts than before enhances the importance of these constraints, a welcome development from the neoliberal perspective.[117]

Kunzlik acknowledges that the regulation of procurement is also welcome from a neoliberal viewpoint because procurement raises three particular challenges to neoliberal values. The first is that the state is a buyer and, thus, market participant but is not motivated by the profit-maximisation rationality and may be motivated by non-market goals that may produce inefficient outcomes. The second is that, when purchasing, public bodies do not compete with each other. The third is that the fact the state is not geographically bounded means that 'non-economic policies' it may pursue to give preferential treatment to domestic firms may impede market access for foreign firms and restrict capital flows.[118] The neoliberal response to these 'problems' would be to: (1) require public purchasers to behave like profit maximisers by requiring them to base their purchasing decisions on the same sort of economic factors that would feature in a private firm's calculations eg pursuit of value for money; (2) emphasise the need for maximum competition as regards public contracts in order to achieve efficiency and value for money; and (3) impose international trade rules that constrain government discretion.[119] From this perspective, international procurement regulation should go beyond simply removing cross-border barriers to trade and require public authorities to conduct themselves in ways that will maximise competition for public contracts in order for the market to achieve a degree of 'efficiency' approximating to that in private markets.[120]

It is beyond the scope of this book to explore in detail the objectives of procurement regulation. However, as already indicated above, in order to properly grapple with the issue of how best to regulate frameworks, it is necessary to determine the objectives of procurement regulation. As discussed, if there is a particular emphasis within the system on maximising competition and efficiency, this could condition approaches to the way in which rules on frameworks are formulated and interpreted, in particular, in ways that may place questionable constraints on contracting authority discretion. Kunzlik's insight is thought provoking because, on his conception of marketisation, behaviours such as outsourcing as a prime example of marketisation, in turn, depend on awarding public contracts, the province of procurement regulation. As a result, marketisation has enhanced the ideological importance of procurement and its regulation. From a neoliberal perspective, this acts as a welcome constraint on governmental discretion. However, taken to its extreme, as will be discussed in chapter three, some appear to

[117] ibid 310.
[118] ibid 310–11.
[119] ibid 311.
[120] ibid.

consider that those constraints reflect certain broad competition or efficiency objectives for EU procurement law; in other words that EU procurement law should be interpreted in a 'pro-competitive' or 'pro-market' way. This includes the rules on frameworks even though this could potentially act as a significant constraint on discretion. As will be discussed, this poses a challenge where EU rules have conferred broad discretion to act, knowing that this conferment may limit competition, but which is tolerated to facilitate flexibility in setting framework terms. As will be explained, it is certainly questionable whether EU procurement law does have such broad competition objectives.

More generally, it is interesting that Kunzlik appeared to characterise certain challenges that procurement presents to neoliberal values as reflecting a basic distinction between procurement as not significantly involving market elements (except the state acting as a buyer from the market) and the private sector where the market is prevalent. It is recalled that, on this conception, the state is not motivated by profit and public bodies do not compete with each other. Of course, he appeared to have only been speaking about procurement in general terms, not 'commercial' purchasing tools (as they are often described) which blur the lines between public sector and private sector provision. Thus, as discussed, in the context of CPAs operating frameworks, there is an extent to which, whilst a user contracting authority is a buyer and, thus, market participant not motivated by profit, another aspect of the state on which it relies (to which it effectively outsources its buying function), namely, a CPA, is, at least to some extent. Further, notionally at least, it could be said that elements of the state are competing against each other in the provision of procurement-related services. As will be discussed in chapter three, there is a sense that procurement regulation has not been able to clearly work out how it addresses the fact that some public sector procurement practices are not necessarily a challenge to neoliberal values but, rather, the very embodiment of them.

Other research has suggested in more general terms that the EU Directives have contributed to marketisation, particularly, through the introduction of competitive tendering; however, importantly, it also suggests that there was a longstanding trend towards marketisation in the UK before any influence of EU law and policy, an issue discussed in chapter four. That research provides an important qualification that EU regulation is not solely responsible for emergent trends, responsibility also falling to the UK. To explain, the political science and public administration literature has questioned whether the EU is, in part, responsible for the increasing extent to which national health and social service governance regimes are converging towards a 'neo-liberal model', that is, being 'marketised'.[121] The gist is that increased efficiency is supposed to translate into welfare gains, with the market providing the most suitable tools to address socio-economic challenges, and that public welfare services, particularly in 'Anglo Saxon' countries (including the UK), are becoming increasingly organised via the market with 'market instruments' applied to pursue social goals and an increased role for 'commercial providers'.[122] In this vein, it has identified NPM reforms, including competitive

[121] O Busck, 'Marketisation of the public sector leads to socially and environmentally irresponsible contracting: the case of Denmark' (2007) 13(4) *Transfer* 611–30 and S Bock Segaard, N Brookes and J Benedikt Pahl, 'What Shapes National Responses to EU Public Procurement Policy? The Case of Health and Social Services in Norway, Germany and England' (2020) 24(1) *Scand. J. Public Adm.* 25.

[122] Bock Segaard, Brookes and Benedikt Pahl (n 121) 25.

tendering procedures in which profit-making and non-profit-making organisations compete against each other, as contributing to this trend. The EU procurement Directives are said to play an important role in specifying the conditions for contracting out health and social services although it has been acknowledged that it is unclear what role EU legislation plays 'when it comes to the processes of marketisation of health and social services'.[123] Research has identified a possible bias in EU legislation towards policies which create markets, rather than those which correct markets, which could reinforce the trend towards marketisation.[124] That said, research has found that the position is more nuanced than a straightforward implementation of the Directives to achieve 'pro-market' objectives, national responses being highly dependent on a range of factors. In respect of England, one study observed that there had been a shift since the 1980s from social services funded and delivered by local authorities to a dominant for-profit sector, characterised as a 'pro-market' approach to the delivery of social and health services.[125] It further observed that in more recent years, the Government was committed to a strategy of reforming procurement processes to stimulate economic growth and that its response to the 2014 procurement Directives was to incorporate this into a narrative of being strong on the economic with new rules supporting priorities of deficit reduction, being promoted as making procurement faster and less costly and enabling better outcomes for government and industry.[126]

Thus, it has been observed that the UK Government has, for a long time, evidenced a strong commitment to neoliberal values, which clearly underpinned the agenda for the wider transformation of public services and the welfare state. Further, 'the narrative about the directives situated them as part of an unquestioned, pro-market approach' and which also tended to the liberal model, 'placing flexibility above all else', with all stakeholders supporting market principles, including non-profit consultees.[127]

In light of the above, the important takeaway from such research is that whatever the claimed impact of EU Directives on the creation or control of markets, the reality is that the UK has, for many years, adopted a 'pro-market' approach to the provision of public services and aligned the implementation of the Directives with that approach. In other words, it is not the case that the Directives have necessarily driven many of the pro-market behaviours that might be seen in UK procurement.

The above insights are relevant to the themes of this book because, as will be discussed in chapters three and four, it cannot be said that the EU Directives push some overt 'pro-competitive' or 'pro-market' approach that has contributed significantly to the marketisation of frameworks. Indeed, such a conception of EU objectives could even lead to interpretations that would place potentially significant constraints on the use of frameworks and the application of rules on frameworks in order to safeguard competition. As will be discussed, there has been little evidence in the UK that frameworks and the rules on frameworks are being considered in light of their potential effects on competition, whether negative or positive. Therefore, at most, the general

[123] ibid 26.
[124] ibid.
[125] ibid 33–34.
[126] ibid.
[127] ibid.

directory rules on frameworks under the Directives may have created certain conditions conducive to enabling marketised framework models to develop through their general uncertainty or lack of focus on specific behaviours. It is not the case that some dogmatic pro-competition objective of EU regulation is responsible. Rather, the UK has itself emphasised the role of procurement in market creation. As will be discussed, the UK has also not taken the initiative domestically to address behaviours that have led to framework marketisation.

7. Indicators of Framework Marketisation

Part III will identify many possible indicators of framework marketisation but it is useful to give some examples for context.

Fundamentally, it is submitted that one major indicator is the proliferation of increasingly generic pan-public sector frameworks that seem somewhat removed from the conventional regulated framework model conceived under EU law. As discussed in chapters three and five, the definition of a framework agreement under Directive 2014/24/EU was broad in its scope, permitting various models to develop. Nevertheless, it indicated a clear purpose on using an upfront competition to establish key terms and one or a limited number of select suppliers as the basis for governing future call-offs. However, a broad definition combined with very general provision on framework procedures and centralised purchasing have created conditions whereby a highly marketised model has emerged. It is often characterised by a dominant entity setting up and operating it, sometimes with significant private sector support, designed for many user contracting authorities and hundreds or thousands of suppliers, and providing very flexible call-off procedures. The framework may be broadly established but leaves much of the substantive procurement to be done later.

Regarding the decision of whether to use a framework, as discussed in chapter five, a 'framework first' mentality has emerged. Even though the use of certain frameworks or CPAs is not legally mandated above other options, central government policies effectively steer contracting authorities towards them. Concern has been expressed about the fact that the same department that has encouraged their use through policies and guidance is the same department that has created the largest CPA. At its worst, there is a risk of it leveraging its conflicted position to gain a market advantage over other CPAs. Further, from a user contracting authority perspective, the proliferation of overlapping frameworks means that contracting authorities may have to invest considerable resource 'framework shopping' and even preparing business cases to justify framework choices. As discussed in chapter five, internal organisational decisions made within contracting authorities may be influenced by the external market environment. An example is the desire by some contracting authorities to find the quickest means of setting up frameworks not only to improve their own efficiency but because of pressure from the market where competing frameworks are regularly set up and made available for use in successive iterations.

Relatedly, concerning the nature of the framework market, as identified in chapter five, there is an increasing blurring of the 'buyer-supplier' or 'buyer-provider' divide.

On the buyer side, CPAs are effectively offering their services as procurers on behalf of purchasing contracting authorities and providing ancillary purchasing activities in support. This raises the question of the extent to which CPAs themselves are engaged on a market for the provision of such services. More generally, CPAs are considered to be competing against each other and developing marketing and business-winning strategies to attract contracting authority 'customers' (as well as suppliers). On the supplier side, the private sector is not simply selling goods or services. They may effectively operate frameworks through host contracting authorities or run frameworks for them. This is in addition to any other procurement consultancy services provided. In extreme cases, private sector organisations are even using frameworks set up by the public sector, taking advantage of public sector obtained prices, and there may even be some trading in framework models for use. It is difficult to identify more characteristic forms of marketisation than effectively outsourced procurement functions (to CPAs) being further outsourced (to the private sector).

Concerning market behaviours, any number can be identified that go as far as raising competition law issues. There are a range of different arrangements between contracting authorities working in close collaboration to establish frameworks in specific sectors that could conceivably create buyer dominance. As discussed in chapter five, central government departments have entered into memoranda of understanding with suppliers to set prices that are used in frameworks. Further, as discussed in chapter six, framework providers are using preliminary market engagement not only to scope requirements but also to attract user contracting authorities and suppliers, using external consultancies in support. Some may even be taking their marketing strategy a step further by providing additional marketing support to suppliers to market their services to user contracting authorities in return for additional fees. As indicated, CPAs are also offering a range of ancillary purchasing activities alongside private sector providers but it is not necessarily clear to what extent these have been subject to any proper process for award or general accountability. There also appears to be considerable market power exercised by suppliers. As discussed in chapter five, original suppliers may enter into preferential arrangements with resellers who then tender on frameworks; original suppliers may dictate prices, thereby potentially rendering any mini-competition between resellers on price redundant. Further, as discussed in chapters six and seven, some suppliers direct their customer contracting authorities to certain frameworks and advise them on their use and even market their ability to secure direct awards.

Considering the influence of marketisation on the specific operation of the framework model, again, any number of examples can be identified. As discussed in chapter six, the advertisement process, which should be used to alert the market and show transparency, has essentially been reduced to a formality, given that suppliers will be alerted to framework opportunities in other ways (aided by proactive marketing of frameworks). CPAs have also broadly defined the scope of frameworks in terms of product or service categories and allowed products to be added by suppliers providing they fall within the overall scope. Frameworks set up in such a generic way may not be attuned to the specific requirements of user contracting authorities. By not providing accurate information about the specific services required, the estimated value of purchases and scope and regularity of use, bidders might not be able to submit the best tenders. Regarding the establishment of the framework award and call-off processes, as discussed in chapter five, CPAs have introduced various features in the award and call-off stages that are specifically designed to render them as attractive as possible to user contracting authorities and suppliers. The fact that a CPA can be remote from its user contracting authorities may move the purchasing tool away from a collaborative one centred on a public service mission towards a more transactional 'arms length' arrangement. Further, supplier interests may even be put before user contracting authority interests and which is a difficult balance for CPAs to strike There is also considerable scope to make direct call-offs subject to few controls or transparency, as marketed by suppliers.

Regarding monitoring and oversight, as discussed in chapter five, the set-up of generic and flexible frameworks by CPAs can mean that frameworks can be too unwieldy to effectively manage. A 'hands off' or reactive approach to problems encountered may be directly contrasted with one of the claimed benefits of private sector managed frameworks, namely, experience of offering better 'customer service' support.

As discussed in chapter nine, and a sign of the times, frameworks are being created and operated in ways that significantly limit the risk of challenge in practice even where the risks may, in theory, be high. As frameworks become too big to fail, the triumph of the market over regulatory pressure becomes even starker. As will be shown, ironically, frameworks may be set up in certain ways to avoid legal challenge which may themselves be unlawful and which undermine the efficacy of the framework.

Finally, perhaps the most concerning indicator of marketisation is the extent to which it has influenced regulatory reform. As will be discussed, not only have successive Governments failed to acknowledge or address the issues, there is also evidence that their approach to regulatory reform tolerates, if not implicitly endorses, marketised behaviours. As will be discussed in chapter five, the PA 2023 definition of a 'framework' (rather than framework 'agreement') is even broader than under EU law in omitting any reference to the core purpose of a framework; instead, it simply defines a framework as a contract providing for the future award of contracts. This legal definition mirrors in practice the multi-supplier pan-sector framework. Moreover, there is explicit provision on fees for the first time but which expressly authorises rather than regulates them.

In the interest of balance, it should be acknowledged that not all of the indicators of marketisation should necessarily be viewed as negative. Ultimately, contracting authorities need to allocate scarce resources and achieve efficiency and quick, familiar procurement routes can be seen as a solution. Further, some CPAs are collaborative and do achieve clear savings and other benefits. Moreover, some framework providers (including from the private sector) offer good customer service.

However, this book suggests that the balance has tilted too far towards market imperatives above the public service mission and few would likely disagree with this candid assessment.

8. Conclusions

This chapter has explained the significance of frameworks as a purchasing tool and the existence of a framework market in the UK. Whilst individual contracting authorities may establish frameworks, there is increasing recourse to CPAs.

As indicated, there has been a process of extensive 'marketisation' of frameworks, characterised by various facets. Fundamentally, there has been a shift in the regulated framework model as conventionally understood. It has been reimagined from a tool focusing on an upfront competition to establish a firm basis governing future derivative call-offs to a commercial vehicle facilitating a notional competition to establish a basis for future awards to be determined. In the case of multi-supplier frameworks, the broadly regulated framework model has been exploited to allow unclear estimations of value, many unspecified user contracting authorities, hundreds or thousands of suppliers, generic terms, and considerable flexibility in the design and application of call-off procedures. Many other indicators of marketisation have been identified and will be corroborated in Part III.

This raises the question of the extent to which regulation has enabled or failed to address issues that have contributed to this trend, acknowledging, of course, that the role of regulation should not be overstated. Ultimately, procurement regulation may contribute to the conditions conducive to certain behaviours but it will be one of several factors. In the same way, regulatory reform may, through introducing certain controls, prohibit or nudge certain behaviours but other reforms will also be necessary especially where behaviours are culturally entrenched. chapters three and four explore the development of EU and UK regulation on frameworks, which will provide further context for Part III concerning how regulation on frameworks has been applied in practice.

3

Regulation of Frameworks in the EU

1. Introduction

Chapter two identified a trend towards framework marketisation, raising questions about the role of regulation in enabling or failing to prevent certain behaviours as well as the extent of any other legal uncertainty on the efficacy of frameworks in practice.

Before exploring the law in practice in Part III, the development of regulation on frameworks must be explained, starting with EU law. First, it is important to understand the objectives of EU regulation to determine how the rules must be interpreted and whether those objectives contribute to marketisation. Second, it is necessary to explain the origins of the regulated framework concept and its supporting rules. Third, understanding EU regulation is important because it was the foundation for UK regulation discussed in chapter four.

This chapter begins with a brief discussion of the objectives of EU regulation, distinguishing between accepted objectives of preventing discrimination and removing market access barriers, and contested objectives, namely, some distinct 'competition' competition objective (Section 2). It then traces the development of EU regulation on frameworks (Sections 3 and 4) up to the present (Section 5). Given the importance of centralised purchasing in operationalising frameworks, this aspect is also discussed (Section 6). Further, whilst this book focuses primarily on procurement regulation, it briefly discusses the relevance of competition law, because the EU has been ambivalent in addressing the effects of frameworks on competition and competition law issues were raised in interviews (Section 7). The chapter then offers concluding observations (Section 8).

2. Objectives of EU Procurement Regulation

The fundamental principles and rules are set out in the Treaty on European Union ('TEU')[1] and the Treaty on the Functioning of the European Union ('TFEU').[2] Relevant to this book, the TFEU covers, among other things, aspects of trade, an objective of the EU being the creation of an internal market.[3] This includes so-called primary

[1] Treaty on European Union (Consolidated Version 2016) OJ C 202, 7.6.2016.
[2] Treaty on the Functioning of the European Union (Consolidated Version 2016) OJ C 202, 7.6.2016.
[3] Article 26 TFEU.

Treaty provisions guaranteeing free movement of goods[4] and services,[5] and freedom of establishment,[6] including a prohibition on discrimination on grounds of nationality.[7] Such freedoms are designed to prevent Member States imposing measures of equivalent effect to quantitative restrictions on trade in ways that restrict the free flow of goods[8] or the ability to provide services across borders. As will be discussed, the ways in which Member States control the award of public contracts has created a risk to free movement, which has been addressed through the coordination of national rules.

These Treaty provisions were originally considered to impose only negative obligations but the European Court of Justice, now Court of Justice of the EU ('CJEU'), interpreted them as also imposing positive obligations, from which various broad 'principles' were derived, including ensuring transparency, equal treatment and proportionality.[9]

The EU has chosen to regulate procurement mainly through Directives adopted on the basis of Articles 53, 62 and 114 TFEU. Article 26 provides that the EU shall adopt measures with the aim of establishing or ensuring the functioning of the internal market and Article 114 TFEU provides for the adoption of measures for the approximation of provisions laid down by law, regulation or administrative action which have as their object the establishment and functioning of the internal market. To this end, Article 288 TFEU provides that the EU institutions must adopt regulations, directives, decisions, or recommendations. A directive is binding as to the result to be achieved but leaves the choice of form and methods to Member States. Directives are, therefore, essentially 'directory', setting coordinating rules which, whilst binding, are necessarily general (albeit increasingly prescriptive). As discussed in chapter four, the UK has tended to 'copy out' the minimum required by the Directives.[10]

It is recalled from chapter two that it is important to understand the underlying objectives of the procurement system, including its regulation, when considering frameworks. This may seem abstract, given the focus of this book on the practicalities of applying the law, but is essential.

There is a risk (to be avoided at the outset) of misattributing much responsibility for framework marketisation to a failure of EU regulation on the erroneous assumption that its rules promote some generic 'pro-market' or 'pro-competitive' objectives. Whilst, as chapter two explains, the Directives are necessarily a means of effecting marketisation because they facilitate the award of contracts, their objectives are limited to setting general rules preventing discrimination and removing market access barriers. There is no express 'competition' objective requiring the Directives to be interpreted to constrain contracting authority discretion because of their potential effect on competition. Similarly, it would be incorrect to suggest that the Directives pursue value for money and have failed to

[4] Article 34 TFEU.

[5] Article 56 TFEU.

[6] Article 53 TFEU.

[7] Article 18 TFEU.

[8] For an introduction to procurement under the TFEU, see S Arrowsmith, *The Law of Public and Utilities Procurement: Regulation in the EU and UK*, 3rd edn, Vol I (Sweet & Maxwell, 2014) ch 4.

[9] See eg Case C-324/98 *Telaustria Verlags GmbH & anor v Telekom Austria AG* ECLI:EU:C:2000:669, [2000] ECR I-10745.

[10] For a detailed introduction to UK implementation, see Arrowsmith (n 8) ch 3.

do so in the context of frameworks, being a characteristic objective of national systems. It is, of course, still possible that EU Directives have contributed to creating conditions conducive to marketisation where certain objectives are unclear and have resulted in legal uncertainty or the Directives have not addressed issues within the EU's competence.

2.1. Non-discrimination and Removal of Market Access, not Competition, Efficiency and Value for Money

Arrowsmith has argued that EU procurement regulation focuses on non-discrimination and removal of market access barriers as objectives, not value for money.[11] The EU's main concern is economic integration through trade and the main interest of Member States is securing the benefits of comparative advantage through opening markets to trade. The EU therefore subjects national systems to coordinated regulatory controls which prevent national laws or practices that may discriminate against, or erect other barriers to, foreign suppliers. In turn, such controls enable equal conditions for market access to procurement opportunities across the EU. Requiring advertising and competitive award processes are ways of ensuring the transparency necessary to realise such conditions.

However, more recently, it has been argued that there is a 'competition' objective or principle,[12] that is broader than requiring competitive tendering as a means of verifying observance of the prohibition on non-discrimination and ensuring equal conditions of access. Such wider 'competition concerns' for procurement rules have been identified as including preventing contracting authorities and suppliers from engaging in anti-competitive behaviour.[13] In *Sintesi*, Advocate General ('AG') Stix Hackl suggested that there is a 'principle of free competition or principle of competition in relation to the directives' which is one of the 'fundamental principles of Community law on the award of public contracts'.[14] Academic commentary has placed further reliance on this Opinion to suggest that there is a longstanding competition principle 'embedded' in the Directives, a particularisation of a more general principle of competition in EU law.[15] This entails that procurement rules have to be interpreted and applied in a 'pro-competitive way' so that they do not hinder, limit or distort competition.[16]

On this conception, contracting authority discretion is constrained, sometimes significantly, by a requirement to ensure that procurement rules do not have an anti-competitive effect in their application, even where such rules confer discretion. The conception adopted in *Sintesi* goes as far as identifying contracting authorities as 'undertakings' which can be dominant on a market,[17] seemingly importing the application of competition law in the context of procurement.

[11] S Arrowsmith, 'The Purpose of the EU Procurement Directives: Ends, Means and the Implications for National Regulatory Space for Commercial and Horizontal Procurement Policies' (2012) 14 *CYELS* 1.

[12] See generally, A Sanchez-Graells, *Public Procurement and the EU Competition Rules*, 2nd edn (Hart Publishing, 2015).

[13] ibid 195.

[14] Case C-247/02 *Sintesi* ECLI:EU:C:2004:593, [2004] ECR I-9215, paras 29, 33.

[15] Sanchez-Graells (n 12) 203–205.

[16] ibid 205.

[17] *Sintesi* (n 14) para 35.

Of course, procurement practice changes and procurement law and its objectives may evolve. That said, the EU institutions and Directives have never given a definitive indication that the traditional objectives have changed such that a new conception of regulation is built around addressing the effects of procurement (and procurement regulation) on 'competition'. Whilst creative arguments have been made to advocate such, there appears to be no compelling evidence to confirm it. It is beyond this book to engage this fundamental debate. However, it is necessary to briefly consider it given the impact of its uncertainty on the regulation of frameworks.

Suffice to state, interpretations of the Directives and the reasoning of EU courts are questionable.[18] To give one illustration that takes the wording of the earliest Directives alone and from which much reasoning predicated upon it unravels, AG Stix Hackl cites Recital 20 Directive 92/50/EEC,[19] Recital 14 Directive 93/36/EEC[20] and Recital 10 Directive 93/37/EEC[21] to support the view that 'the development of effective competition in the field of public contracts is expressly stated as an objective in the preamble to each of them'.[22] Sanchez-Graells states that:

> the very broad terms of these recitals are a clear indication of the existence of a *general* competition objective in the public procurement directives, which should not be narrowed down or interpreted only as implying an 'operational' requirement of promotion of access to the public procurement procedure.[23]

In actuality, those references were to unnumbered preambular statements, not legal provisions, and hardly constitute a concrete basis on which to divine a 'fundamental' principle. AG Stix Hackl was also incorrect in citing Recital 20 Directive 92/50 which makes no reference to the development of effective competition but instead to eliminating practices that restrict competition in general; AG Stix Hackl does not explain how the two are synonymous. AG Stix Hackl also cites cases involving Directive 71/305/EEC[24] in which reference to 'ensure development of effective competition in the field' is first found. However, this is a selective reading of the preamble; the full citation is: 'Whereas to ensure development of effective competition in the field of public contracts it is necessary that contract notices drawn up by the authorities of Member States awarding contracts be advertised throughout the Community'.[25] Thus, construed in context, Community-wide advertisement is the focus and a means of ensuring the development of competition; it does not support a 'general' competition objective. Perhaps indicatively, AG Stix Hackl's formulation was not expressly adopted by the court.

[18] Arrowsmith (n 8) 3–16 going as far as to suggest that AG Stix Hackl's reasoning is, in parts, based on wrong assumptions, in particular, that transparency supports competition instead of the other way round.

[19] Council Directive 92/50/EEC of 18 June 1992 relating to the coordination of procedures for the award of public service contracts OJ L 209/1.

[20] Council Directive 93/36/EEC of 14 June 1993 coordinating procedures for the award of public supply contracts OJ L 199/1.

[21] Council Directive 93/37/EEC of 14 June 1993 concerning the coordination of procedures for the award of public works contracts OJ L 199/54.

[22] *Sintesi* (n 14) para 31.

[23] Sanchez-Graells (n 12) 196, fn 4 (emphasis in the original).

[24] Council Directive 71/305/EEC of 26 July 1971 concerning the coordination of procedures for the award of public works contracts OJ L 185/5.

[25] ibid, preambular statement 9.

As indicated, this example is by no means exhaustive of possible critique of that Opinion nor various other cases. To give another example, more recently, in *Archus*, the CJEU has stated that the equal treatment principle has the aim of 'promoting the development of healthy and effective competition' which 'lies at the very heart of the EU rules on public procurement procedures'. Whilst various cases are cited in support, it is nowhere clear the legal basis for any such vague notions.[26] This is relevant to the UK because in the post-Brexit English Court of Appeal judgment in *Optima* (a case involving a framework) Coulson LJ stated that 'the EU, and now the UK, have detailed rules relating to public procurement' and which 'are designed to ensure healthy and effective competition', citing *Archus*.[27] This could be interpreted as referring to healthy and effective competition as a means of ensuring value for money. As discussed in chapter four, section 12 PA 2023 includes a new statutory objective to the effect that, for covered procurement, a contracting authority must have regard to the importance of delivering value for money. However, section 12 makes no express reference to competition. This simple textual analysis calls into question the view that a broad competition objective has been declared 'with pristine clarity'.[28] Indeed, it has even been argued that there has been a 'consolidation' of this competition principle in Article 18(1) Directive 2014/24/EU, discussed below. However, even those citing Article 18(1) to this effect have acknowledged that this is far from clear.[29] To put this in the context of frameworks specifically, most recently, research on the relationship between frameworks and competition law has argued that there is no such competition principle.[30]

It may be added that Article 67(1) provides that contracting authorities must base awards on the most economically advantageous tender ('MEAT'). Article 67(4) further provides that award criteria must not have the effect of conferring an unrestricted freedom of choice and 'shall ensure the possibility of effective competition'. Recital 90 also states that:

> Contracts should be awarded on the basis of objective criteria that ensure compliance with the principles of transparency, non-discrimination and equal treatment, with a view to ensuring an objective comparison of the relative value of the tenders in order to determine, in conditions of effective competition, which tender is the most economically advantageous tender.

Therefore, conditions of effective competition are intended to be the product of criteria that reflect traditional EU objectives.

It is recalled from chapter two Kunzlik's observation that arguments have been advanced to further 'neoliberalise' the EU procurement regime and, thus, curtail contracting authority discretion even further than it is at present.[31] An example is the attempt to argue (as above) for the application of 'competition' (the 'efficiency' concept

[26] Case C-131/16, *Archus and Gama* [2017] ECLI:EU:C:2017:358, para 25. This cites Case C-496/99 P, *CAS Succhi di Frutta* ECLI:EU:C:2004:236, [2004] ECR I-3801 at para 110 which refers to the same concepts but does not cite any authority.

[27] *Optima Health v Secretary of State for Work and Pensions* [2025] EWCA Civ 127, para 59.

[28] Sanchez-Graells (n 12) 195 and 198–99.

[29] ibid 195–96 and 207–214.

[30] D Kristensen Balshoj, *Public Procurement and Framework Agreements: The application of competition law to contracting authorities in a procurement context* (Djøf, 2018) ch 4.

[31] P Kunzlik, 'Neoliberalism and the European Public Procurement Regime' (2013) 15 *CYELS* 283.

of competition) and the pursuit of 'value for money' as dominating norms for the system. Kunzlik argues that those norms are not legally justified because the concept of 'competition' to which EU procurement regulation refers is not the neoliberal 'efficiency' concept, but a concept based upon economic freedom concerned with 'competitive equality' and the structure of competition in public markets.[32] Further, concurring with Arrowsmith, he states that the legal bases of EU procurement legislation do not permit it to mandate the pursuit of 'value for money' as a requirement of EU law, although its pursuit is the central goal of domestic procurement regulation.[33]

Returning to the themes introduced in chapter two, whilst it is thus possible to superficially claim that the Directives are the embodiment of marketisation, it does not necessarily follow that they dogmatically promote competition and efficiency objectives, therefore providing neither the basis for encouraging market-oriented behaviours nor general constraints on how procurement rules (including those on frameworks) must be applied. Again, as Kunzlik has argued, the Directives may have a neoliberal foundation but this does not necessarily mean that such rules support the view that the EU regime has as its objective, or imposes any specific duty of, efficiency linked, in some way, to some notion of objectives relating to the pursuit of competition.[34] It should be acknowledged that Kunzlik did not expressly consider such a debate in the context of frameworks specifically; however, he briefly refers to the EU's proposals for modernisation of the Directives (discussed below) which include an increased emphasis on centralised purchasing. He states that such proposals might assist in achieving value for money by coordinating public sector demand, thereby allowing the exercise of greater 'buying power'; however, importantly, such references neither imply an obligation to pursue any specific version of 'value for money' nor mandate the imposition of an overriding duty to pursue 'efficiency'.[35]

EU case law has also sought to explain the role of efficiency considerations in relation to the pursuit of the traditional objectives of EU procurement regulation. Thus, in *Spezzino*, AG Wahl stated that:

> [T]he degree of advertising must be sufficient to enable the public contract to be opened up to some degree of competition, and for the impartiality of procurement procedures to be reviewed: even though a call for tenders may not be necessary, the contracting authority should, nonetheless, ensure that there is some form of call for competition which is adequate to the circumstances.[36]
>
> Opening up award procedures to other potential tenderers may provide contracting authorities with more offers (and thus with more choice in terms of both quality and price), and should encourage operators which are interested in the award to be more economical and efficient.[37]

Alternatively put, advertising enables some degree of competition, with competitive procedures providing transparency to ensure that decision-making is impartial; doing so may ultimately lead to more offers, incentivising suppliers to be more efficient.

[32] ibid 283.
[33] ibid.
[34] ibid 346.
[35] ibid.
[36] Opinion of AG Wahl in Case C-113/13 *Spezzino* ECLI:EU:C:2014:29, para 49 (footnotes omitted).
[37] ibid para 57.

Therefore, it is possible to relate efficiency to the pursuit of traditional objectives, as opposed to there being some general duty or constraint under EU law to act efficiently.

However, even if there is no distinct 'competition' objective or principle, certain procurement rules expressly refer to competition-related concerns, to which this chapter now turns.

2.2. Effects of EU Procurement Rules on Competition and Competition Law Considerations

The Directives have included various references to 'competition' and 'efficiency' of relevance to frameworks. Recital 2 Directive 2014/24/EU refers to procurement as 'one of the market-based instruments to be used to achieve smart, sustainable and inclusive growth while ensuring the most efficient use of public funds' and 'for that purpose' the Directives 'should be revised and modernised in order to increase the efficiency of public spending'. The reference to efficiency of public spend has been identified as problematic in the context of centralised purchasing.

As Comba has observed:

> [T]he potential conflict between new EU Directives and already existing Member States' legal institutions was not only related to the legal structure but even to the scope of centralised procurement, which was created by Member States mainly to get more efficient purchases through economies of scale and professionalisation, while the legal basis for EU procurement Directive is not – and cannot be – concerned with efficiency in public spending, but rather with fostering competition and eliminating discrimination against economic operators on the basis of nationality.[38]

As discussed below in the context of centralised purchasing, Comba states that there is a 'contradiction' or 'misconception' in the rules. His argument appears to be that Member States have introduced aggregated purchasing techniques (eg, frameworks) in pursuit of domestic objectives of efficiency (which is not an EU objective) and the EU also introduced rules to facilitate aggregated purchasing. The apparent contradiction is that such techniques may achieve efficiency, but may also have anti-competitive effects (eg, in limiting access for SMEs and others) contrary to a purported EU objective of fostering competition and eliminating discrimination. As indicated, it can be questioned what is meant by 'foster competition', this not being an express objective of the Directives (unless perhaps meant in the sense of providing equal conditions of market access) but, nevertheless, the gist of his criticism seems to be valid. This is that the EU has introduced aggregated purchasing rules to achieve efficiency (even though this is not an EU objective) but these can also potentially undermine EU objectives. As discussed below, the EU has tried to address this issue by including procurement rules to the effect that they must not be applied in ways that restrict or distort competition, although such rules are stated at a level of generality, are not entirely unequivocal, and perhaps reflect the EU's ambivalence about how to reconcile this apparent contradiction. This

[38] M Comba, 'CPBs in the European legal space: an unresolved misconception' in C Risvig Hamer and M Comba (eds), *Centralising Public Procurement: The Approach of EU Member States* (Edward Elgar, 2021) 22.

uncertainty poses obvious problems in respect of the application of rules on frameworks and their operationalisation through CPAs, namely, to what extent they must be applied in consideration of the effects on competition.

There are other problematic references to 'competition' in the Directives. As will be discussed, Article 18 is titled 'principles of procurement'. In this regard, Article 18(1) refers to equal treatment, non-discrimination, transparency and proportionality but there is no explicit reference to competition. Yet, in the sub-paragraph of Article 18(1), it is provided that 'the design of the procurement shall not be made with the intention of excluding it from the scope of this Directive or of artificially narrowing competition' and that '[c]ompetition shall be considered to be artificially narrowed where the design of the procurement is made with the intention of unduly favouring or disadvantaging certain economic operators'. Article 18 has been cited in the debate on the extent to which EU procurement rules, including on frameworks, must be interpreted specifically to consider the implications of their application on competition generally and their anti-competitive effects, in particular.

Going further, as will also be discussed, recent EU case law has raised the question of whether contracting authorities, in particular, CPAs operating frameworks, are subject to EU competition law. This has, in turn, led to revisitation of the debate discussed above regarding whether the objectives of the Directives include 'competition'.

The upshot is that, given these various references, it remains unclear to what extent procurement rules, including those on frameworks, must be interpreted and applied in consideration of their effects on competition.

3. Development of EU Regulation on Frameworks

Directives on procurement were developed as early as the 1970s.[39] However, these did not include any provisions specific to frameworks. In any event, the UK did not fully implement the Directives until the early 1990s. In 1985, a European Commission White Paper set out a vision to improve procurement regulation and complete the single market by 1992.[40] Following this, a new set of amending directives for the public sector[41] was introduced. Of these, only Directive 93/38/EEC[42] which applied to utilities

[39] Commission Directive 70/32/EEC of 17 December 1969 on provision of goods to the State, to local authorities and other official bodies OJ L 13; Council Directive 71/304/EEC of 26 July 1971 concerning the abolition of restrictions on freedom to provide services in respect of public works contracts and on the award of public works contracts to contractors acting through agencies or branches OJ L 185/1; Council Directive 71/305/EEC of 26 July 1971 concerning the coordination of procedures for the award of public works contracts OJ L 185/5; Council Directive 77/62/EEC of 21 December 1976 coordinating procedures for the award of public supply contracts OJ L 13/1; Council Directive 89/440/EEC of 18 July 1989 amending Directive 71/305/EEC concerning coordination of procedures for the award of public works contracts [1989] OJ L210/1.

[40] White Paper from the Commission to the Council 'Completing the Internal Market' COM(85) 310 Final June 1985.

[41] Council Directive 93/36/EEC of 14 June 1993 coordinating procedures for the award of public supply contracts OJ L 199/1; Council Directive 93/37/EEC of 14 June 1993 concerning the coordination of procedures for the award of public works contracts [1993] OJ L199/54; Council Directive 92/50/EEC of 18 June 1992 relating to the coordination of procedures for the award of public service contracts OJ L 209/1; Council Directive 93/38/EEC of 14 June 1993 coordinating the procurement procedures of entities operating in the water, energy, transport and telecommunications sectors OJ L 199/84.

[42] See definition of 'framework agreement' in Article 5.

procurement included explicit high-level rules on frameworks (in Article 5). Therefore, it was not clear whether frameworks were permissible in the public sector.

In 1996, the Commission published a Green Paper[43] to initiate a debate on procurement policy issues but, again, did not mention public sector frameworks. By contrast, Arrowsmith considered that:

> Possibilities for regulated purchasers to make use of flexible purchasing techniques such as frameworks and mandatory qualification lists are essential if these purchasers are to obtain the best possible value for money. Further, these techniques can be provided for under the directives without any significant damage to the Community's policy of preventing discrimination in public procurement.[44]

As discussed below, the EU subsequently introduced rules on frameworks based on what appeared to be a dual concern. First, it was not clear whether frameworks were being awarded in violation of EU law, such that there was an EU interest in at least providing clarification to ensure compliance with EU objectives. Second, frameworks were recognised as efficient purchasing techniques, such that these rules could also facilitate Member States' objectives provided these were compatible with EU law, with Member States given discretion as to whether to enable contracting authorities to use them. Arguably, therefore, there was a degree of restraint in the purpose and formulation of such provisions, ie to clarify what was permitted under EU law in broad terms and to recognise Member State use of such techniques. The EU did not from the outset develop rules on different types of framework model, or rules on centralised purchasing to increase the 'efficiency' of public spend or maximise competition.

Arrowsmith considered different potential framework transactions under the directives in force in the 1990s, demonstrating that despite the ambiguity, most single- and multi-supplier framework-type arrangements could be set up using the Directives' award procedures but that a regulated contract may come into being at different points of the contracting process depending on the type.[45] Framework-type arrangements were being used widely in a number of European countries, including the UK.[46] Even the EU institutions had frequent recourse to them in the public sector.[47]

December 1997 was a turning point as the Commission announced its decision to refer the UK to the CJEU for improper use of 'framework arrangements' for procuring architectural, engineering and other construction-related services.[48] The Commission acknowledged that the Utilities Directive explicitly provided for use of frameworks but

[43] Commission, *Public Procurement in the European Union: Exploring the Way Forward*, Brussels, 27.11.1996 COM(96)583 final.

[44] S Arrowsmith, 'Framework purchasing and qualification lists under the European procurement Directives: Part 2' (1999) 4 *PPLR* 161, 186; S Arrowsmith 'Framework purchasing and qualification lists under the European procurement Directives: Part 1' (1999) 3 *PPLR* 115.

[45] Arrowsmith 'Framework purchasing and qualification lists under the European procurement Directives: Part 1' (n 44) 129.

[46] See generally, GL Albano and C Nicholas, *The Law and Economics of Frameworks: Designing Flexible Solutions for Public Procurement* (Cambridge University Press, 2016) ch 5.

[47] P Trepte, *Public Procurement in the EU: A Practitioner's Guide*, 2nd edn (Oxford University Press, 2007) 210. See also Case T-19/95 *Adia Interim SA v Commission of the European Communities* ECLI:EU:T:1996:59, [1996] ECR II-321.

[48] European Commission, Public procurement infringement proceedings against the United Kingdom, Austria, Germany and Portugal IP/97/1178 Brussels, 19 December 1997.

stated that they were not authorised under the public procurement Directives, albeit without giving any specific reasons.

Bovis has suggested that the Commission may have based its action on a distinction between two types of framework, namely, those comprising substantive terms that can be lifted verbatim into a call-off and incomplete frameworks that leave terms to be concluded in the call-off, the latter then being prohibited.[49] He alluded to *Commission v Greece*[50] in support, where AG Lenz noted on the facts that '[a]ll the principal contractual elements, in particular the exclusive purchasing obligation and the price calculation, are already laid down in the framework agreement, with the result that the individual supply contracts do little more than specify the quantity to be supplied'.[51] He took the view that 'a framework of this kind must be treated as a supply contract within the meaning of the directive',[52] observing that if this did not meet the definition of a supply contract subject to the Directive:

> the framework agreement would then quite certainly have to be classified as a measure having equivalent effect to a quantitative restriction on imports within the meaning of Article 30 of the EC Treaty in so far as it prevents tenderers from other Member States from supplying specific customers in Greece.[53]

However, this case did not decisively address the status of a multi-supplier framework as a public contract.[54]

Regarding official statements, the Commission was concerned about circumstances in which 'a tender notice is published in the EC Official Journal indicating a general category of services to be provided rather than giving details of a specific contract' and when 'once a list of approved suppliers has been established by this procedure, entities may choose suppliers from the list without going through a new competitive procedure for each individual contract'.[55] Otherwise, such agreements or arrangements would effectively constitute a list of approved suppliers who could be awarded future work without any proper process being applied. However, again, the Commission was less clear as to the formal status of such arrangements, appearing to treat an arrangement in which key terms had been established with little to specify at a later stage as a public supply contract (rather than a framework *per se*), whereas arrangements that left matters to determination at a later stage were simply prohibited.

Arrowsmith has noted that if this case concerned a multi-supplier framework, it provided 'implicit support for the use of such frameworks, at least in the case where the choice of supplier for each order is set by the terms of the offers made at the time the framework is placed'.[56] Anecdotal evidence and the experience of the Northern Ireland case suggested that, in the UK, legal violations were occurring both because the terms

[49] C Bovis, *Research Handbook on EU Public Procurement Law* (Edward Elgar, 2016) 127.
[50] Case C-79/94 *Commission of the European Communities v Hellenic Republic* ECLI:EU:C:1995:120, [1995] ECR I-1071.
[51] Opinion of AG Lenz, para 25.
[52] ibid.
[53] ibid.
[54] Arrowsmith, 'Framework purchasing and qualification lists under the European procurement Directives: Part 1' (n 44) 140.
[55] IP/97/1178 (n 48).
[56] Arrowsmith, 'Framework purchasing and qualification lists under the European procurement Directives: Part 1' (n 44) 140.

of supply were insufficiently complete when the framework was established and because orders were being placed by impermissible methods, for example, by rotating awards between suppliers, in disregard of the Directives' requirement to select using the pre-stated contract award criteria relating to the nature of the offer.[57]

In a subsequent press release, the Commission appeared to row back from its harder lined position that framework arrangements were prohibited in the public sector by stating 'if the terms of a framework agreement are sufficiently specific as to detail the key elements of any individual contracts to be awarded subsequently, and if these are set out in binding form, when those individual contracts are awarded, it is not necessary to follow the detailed procedural requirements of the Directives'.[58] However, questions remained unanswered such as what 'key elements' of a call-off needed to be specified at the outset and what processes could be used to award call-offs.

In 1998, the Commission issued a Communication highlighting the need to simplify the legal framework.[59] It cited 'framework contracts' as one of the more flexible forms of procurement that it was planning to introduce 'in response to the criticism sometimes levelled at the system that procedures are excessively rigid and formalistic'.[60] The Commission explicitly recognised the importance of 'framework purchasing' observing that 'on markets, which are constantly changing, such as the markets for information technology products and services, it is not economically justifiable for public purchasers to be tied to fixed prices and conditions', that public sector purchasers 'increasingly feel the need to manage their procurement on a long-term basis', and that this type of contract should offer the necessary flexibility.[61] It noted many responses to its Green Paper questioning the compatibility of such flexibility with the directives then in force and planned legislative amendments 'to permit more extensive use of flexible contracts allowing product developments and price changes to be taken into account'.[62]

Whilst acknowledging the risk that long-term contracts may be problematic 'in that they could cause positions to become entrenched and certain firms to be shut out', it advocated that 'precise rules be laid down for the use of these procedures' and indicated that 'objective and transparent information should be published on framework contracts'.[63] It referred to the possibility of setting up lists of potential contractors which 'should either be valid only for a limited period or be kept permanently open to new firms'.[64] At this point, therefore, the Commission was entertaining different permutations of 'framework purchasing'. It appears that the main concerns expressed related to the effect of excessively long frameworks on competition; there was little indication of any specific concern about anti-competitive practices or effects (eg concentration of market power by suppliers or contracting authorities).

[57] S Arrowsmith, 'The Past and Future Evolution of EC Procurement Law: From Framework to Common Code?' (2006) 35(3) *PCLJ* 337, 362.

[58] European Commission, Public Procurement: Commission refers United Kingdom to Court' IP/00/813 13 July 2000.

[59] European Commission Communication Public Procurement in the European Union (COM(98)143) 11 March 1998.

[60] ibid 6.

[61] ibid.

[62] ibid 8.

[63] ibid.

[64] ibid.

In May 2000, the Commission published proposals for a new legislative package,[65] resulting in a new Directive 2004/18/EC,[66] which introduced explicit regulation of public sector frameworks.

In the Commission's Explanatory Memorandum to the Proposal,[67] it reiterated the above concerns about the need to be able to respond to market developments and avoid repetition of procedures each time in the case of repeat purchases.[68] It also drew a distinction between frameworks and purchaser order contracts. Frameworks were not considered public contracts within the meaning of the Directives on the basis that 'they do not lay down specific terms and thus cannot give rise to performance as a contract does' whereas 'contracts with several economic operators (such as widely used purchaser order contracts)' for future supply were.[69]

The Commission decided to exempt the award of contracts under a framework from the obligation to follow the normal procedures in the Directive subject to the following dual condition: (a) the framework itself was to be awarded in accordance with the normal procedures in the directive; and (b) the contracts based on a framework were to be awarded 'in accordance with provisions aimed at ensuring compliance with the principle of equality of treatment when choosing the tenderer' with the 'choice being made after the reopening of competition between the economic operators party to the framework'.[70]

The Commission also noted that frameworks enable a contracting authority's purchases to be aligned with the constant development of the market by inviting suppliers to submit tenders with 'scope to adjust the initial tender in line with market developments, such as technical obsolescence or significant price changes'.[71] It considered that the new provisions would not foreclose the market to competition or new entrants as a contracting authority would be free to tender a new contract. However, it was stated that the proposal also contained a 'clause concerning anti-competitive abuses (notably the risk of cartels)' and 'to ensure effective competition limits the duration of framework agreements to three years in principle'.[72] Therefore, at this stage, there appeared to be a concern about supply-side anti-competitive agreements (as opposed to demand-side anti-competitive practices). Further, the proposal appeared to indicate that a pre-determination or policy trade-off was made that, whilst no limit on framework duration would undermine competition, 'effective competition' would be ensured by limiting it to three years; in other words, a tolerable limitation on competition was permitted.

[65] Proposal for a Directive of the European Parliament and of the Council on the coordination of procedures for the award of public supply contracts, public service contracts and public works contracts final, COM(2000) 275 final – 2000/0115(COD), C 29 E/11.

[66] Directive 2004/18/EC of the European Parliament and of the Council of 31 March 2004 on the coordination of procedures for the award of public works contracts, public supply contracts and public service contracts OJ L 134 /137.

[67] Explanatory Memorandum to COM(2000)275 – Coordination of procedures for the award of public supply contracts, public service contracts and public works contracts, 10-05-2000.

[68] ibid 4.1.

[69] ibid.

[70] ibid 4.3.

[71] ibid 4.4.

[72] ibid 4.6.

Whilst noting the benefits of long-term purchasing and flexibility that might be generated by frameworks, the Commission gave no clear reasons for distinguishing between the conclusion of the framework and subsequent purchases and why some aspects would be subject to the Directive and others either to EU Treaty principles such as equal treatment or not at all. A tension can also be identified between the Commission's notion that a framework would enable purchases to be aligned with market and technological advances whilst limiting participation in the framework to the appointed suppliers during a fixed term.

The original draft proposal for what became Article 32 Directive 2004/18/EC catered only for multi-supplier frameworks with a maximum term of three years (or up to five years in exceptional circumstances) during which mini-competitions would be run to award call-offs. The proposal was subjected to an iterative review led by a Working Party within the Council. The UK delegation initially found no need to introduce specific legislation on frameworks as it considered that the old Directives already permitted these. It felt the 'proposed procedure' in draft Article 32 to be too 'rigid'.[73] This appears to be an early indication of the UK's attitude to flexible use of frameworks.

In December 2000, an Opinion from the Committee of the Regions complained about (a) the lack of flexibility in the new draft provisions on frameworks (eg the need to reopen the competition every time a framework was used, a requirement for at least three framework suppliers, and limiting the framework duration); and (b) the lack of clarity as to what falls within the definition of a 'framework agreement'.[74] It noted the Commission's distinction between 'framework contracts' and 'framework agreements', the former covered by the Directive's definition of a 'public contract' and the latter not 'since they do not include all the necessary elements for them to be used as the basis for a delivery'.[75] It identified the Commission's Explanatory Statement that gave the example of a contract with an order form as an example of a 'framework contract'.[76] It highlighted the regular use in some Member States of non-binding agreements that use 'order forms' such as customer choice model contracts (involving a contracting authority contracting with several suppliers and the individual citizen later choosing the supplier) and the uncertainty about whether these would fall within the new definition.[77]

Amendments to the original draft Article 32 were tabled and rejected. For example, it was proposed that 'intellectual services' be excluded due to the framework being considered 'totally unsuitable' for such services.[78] It was also proposed that public works contracts be excluded as frameworks were considered to concern 'small, recurrent

[73] Council of the European Union Brussels, 1 August 2000 2000/0115 (COD) 2000/0117 (COD). It is not clear in what respect the UK delegation considered the Article 32 provisions 'rigid'.

[74] Opinion of the Committee of the Regions on the 'Proposal for a Directive of the European Parliament and of the Council on the coordination of procedures for the award of public supply contracts, public service contracts and public works contracts' and the 'Proposal for a Directive of the European Parliament and of the Council coordinating the procurement procedures of entities operating in the water, energy and transport sectors' (2001/C 144/08) OJ 144 16/05/2001 P. 0023–0029, 2.3.

[75] ibid 2.3.2.

[76] ibid 2.3.3.

[77] ibid 2.3.5.

[78] Amendment 16, European Parliament Committee on Legal Affairs and the Internal Market, 2000/0115 20 March 2001, Draft Report.

transactions'.[79] Other amendments tabled included use of the negotiated procedure without competition for the award of call-offs, the limitation of 'framework contracts' to a term of one or two years[80] and the introduction of rules for the set-up of 'qualification systems' similar to those in the Utilities Directive,[81] demonstrating how qualification systems were conceptually different from what was envisaged in the framework model.[82]

On 25 March 2003, the Commission issued a Communication[83] to the European Parliament stating the Council's common position that draft Article 32 had been revised, altering the maximum framework duration to four years and including the possibility of concluding a framework with a single supplier, and it was a matter for each Member State to decide whether to authorise or limit framework use.

4. Frameworks under Directive 2004/18/EC

4.1. General Rules on Frameworks

Recital 16 Directive 2004/18/EC stated that to take account of the 'different circumstances obtaining in Member States', they should be allowed to choose whether contracting authorities may use frameworks. Correspondingly, Article 32(1) provided that 'Member States may provide that contracting authorities may conclude frameworks'. Given that there was discretion on whether to even make frameworks available it is unsurprising that there was discretion to decide on the frameworks models to be developed. The UK Government opted to enable free use of frameworks and implemented the supporting provisions in the Public Contracts Regulations 2006 ('PCR 2006')[84] regulation 19, subject only to some slight differences in language used to align with UK legislative drafting style.

Article 1(5) Directive 2004/18/EC defined a 'framework agreement' as an:

> agreement between one or more contracting authorities and one or more economic operators, the purpose of which is to establish the terms governing contracts to be awarded during a given period, in particular with regard to price and, where appropriate, the quantity envisaged.

As Arrowsmith observed:

> It is important to emphasise that the concept of a framework agreement as envisaged under the 2004 Public Sector Directive refers to an arrangement that involves the substantial part of the competition being completed 'up front' when one or more economic operators are chosen for the framework, with all the terms of the arrangement – including the price – being

[79] Amendment 130 by Joachim Wuermeling European Parliament Committee on Legal Affairs and the Internal Market 13 July 2001 Draft Report PE 298.409.

[80] Amendment 27 Opinion of the Committee on Industry, External Trade, Research and Energy 29 June 2001 COM(2000) 275.

[81] Amendments 151, 68 and 78 European Parliament Consolidated Legislative January 2002 2000/0115(COD) – PE1.

[82] Qualification systems permit utilities to limit participation in contract award procedures to candidates that are registered to a 'qualification system' operated in accordance with Directive 93/38/EEC.

[83] Communication from the Commission to the European Parliament, 25.03.2003 SEC(2003) 366 final.

[84] SI 2006/5.

> established at that point as far as possible. It is envisaged that the ordering stage will involve merely placing orders based on the tenders submitted in that earlier stage or, at most, supplementing that earlier competition in minor ways (for example, by seeking details of how those on the framework will carry out the specific project).[85]

As explained in chapter four, the UK adopted this definition although broadened it slightly to include not only agreements but also 'other arrangements' (regulation 2(1)).

This definition encompasses both single- and multi-supplier frameworks. Article 32(4) Directive 2004/18/EC / regulation 19(6) provided that for multi-supplier frameworks, there should be a minimum of at least three suppliers. Article 32(2) / regulation 19(10) provided that the maximum framework term could be four years 'save in exceptional cases duly justified, in particular by the subject of the framework'.

Directive 2004/18/EC set explicit procedural rules on frameworks with an estimated financial value exceeding prescribed thresholds (in Article 9(9)). Article 32(2) provided that the main substantive provisions applicable to the award of public contracts for goods, services or works were made equally applicable to the award of frameworks. Regulation 19(2) clarified that either the open, restricted, negotiated or competitive dialogue procedures could be used. For awarding call-offs, Article 32(3) and (4) / regulation 19(7)–(8) set out procedural rules to be followed, such rules only to be applied between the original parties to the framework.

Directive 2004/18/EC differentiated regulation of single-supplier and multi-supplier frameworks. For single-supplier frameworks, contracting authorities were to award call-offs 'within the limits of the terms laid down in the framework' and the contracting authority could consult in writing the supplier requesting it to supplement its tender if necessary (Article 32(3) / regulation 19(5)). For multi-supplier frameworks, call-offs could be awarded by: (a) applying the terms laid down in the framework without reopening competition; or (b) where not all the terms were laid down, by reopening the competition between the appointed suppliers based on the same and, if necessary, more precisely formulated terms and other terms referred to in the framework. Contracting authorities were required to consult the suppliers capable of performing the contract and fix a time limit sufficiently long to allow tenders to be submitted. The call-off was to be awarded to the tenderer who submitted the best tender based on the award criteria set out in the framework specifications (Article 32(4) / regulation 19(9)).

Directive 2004/18/EC also provided that 'the parties may under no circumstances make substantial amendments to the terms laid down in that framework' (Article 32(2) / regulation 19(4)).

As discussed in chapter six, there have been EU cases on the Directive 2004/18/EC rules. In *Autorità Garante*,[86] the CJEU had to address whether it allowed a single-supplier framework by which a contracting authority acted on its own behalf and for others not directly parties to the framework. The case concerned the use of a framework by an Italian regional health authority that was not a signatory to it, but the tender specifications included a clause allowing the possibility of extending the framework to several regional authorities identified in that clause. The CJEU considered Article 32(2)

[85] Arrowsmith (n 8) 11-02.

[86] Case C-216/17 *Autorità Garante* [2018] ECLI:EU:C:2018:1034.

which provided that the procedures used for award under a framework can only be applied 'between the contracting authorities and the economic operators originally party to the framework'. The CJEU held that only economic operators are required to be 'original parties', and it was not necessary for a secondary contracting authority to be a signatory for it to be able to award a contract under it. The CJEU also noted the second sub-paragraph of Article 33(2) Directive 2014/24/EU,[87] which provides slightly more clarity by stating that the procedures can only be applied 'between those contracting authorities clearly identified for this purpose in the call for competition or the invitation to confirm interest and those economic operators party to the framework as concluded'.

For completeness, as discussed in chapter five, Directive 2004/18/EC also introduced Article 33 containing rules on dynamic purchasing systems ('DPS'), another purchasing technique implemented in regulation 20 although DPS are not examined in detail in this book.

4.2. Frameworks May Not Be Used Improperly or to Prevent, Restrict or Distort Competition

It is recalled that there is uncertainty about whether there is an EU objective or principle of competition. Various provisions have been cited in support.

One is Article 32(2) which provided that '[c]ontracting authorities may not use framework agreements improperly or in such a way as to prevent, restrict, or distort competition'. Such a provision does not feature elsewhere in Directive 2004/18/EC except regarding recourse to electronic auctions in Article 54(8). No clear indication was provided as to the circumstances that may give rise to the improper or anti-competitive use of frameworks. Equivocation or ambivalence is further suggested by the fact that Directive 2014/24/EU removed this reference from the main provisions on frameworks and reinserted it in Recital 61 whilst also introducing a more general provision in Article 18(1).

To add further uncertainty, CJEU case law indicates that the Article 32(2) general prohibition on improper or anti-competitive use may *itself* be embodied in other more specific framework rules. The fact that other more specific framework rules share the same purpose calls into question the mischief against which a discrete general prohibition is addressed. Indeed, it may be queried on this basis whether the rationale for such a prohibition could simply be related back to the traditional objectives of EU procurement regulation.

To illustrate by reference to EU case law, Article 1(5) provided in the definition of a framework that the purpose is to establish the terms governing contracts to be awarded, in particular, 'where appropriate, the quantity envisaged'. In *Autorità Garante* (discussed in chapter six), the CJEU held that a contracting authority that is not a signatory to the framework cannot refrain from determining the quantity of services that may be required when it concludes call-offs or do so by reference to their usual requirements. The CJEU's reasoning was, in part, that if they do, the principles of transparency and

[87] ibid paras 49–56 referring at para 54 to the Opinion of AG Campos Sánchez-Bordona at para 62.

equal treatment of suppliers with an interest in the conclusion of a framework would be infringed.[88] This was also supported by the fact that:

> [A] requirement that the contracting authority that is an original party to the framework agreement indicate therein the quantity and amount of the services that that agreement will cover is a manifestation of the prohibition on using framework agreements improperly or in such a way as to prevent, restrict or distort competition, as laid down in the fifth subparagraph of Article 32(2) of Directive 2004/18.[89]

The CJEU had already identified that the requirement to state the total quantity is necessary to ensure non-discrimination and equal treatment.[90] On this view, if the definition of a framework (which the CJEU appeared to consider to be strict)[91] is intended to safeguard certain EU objectives, the same could arguably be said of the more general Article 32(2) prohibition without necessary recourse to some distinct competition objective.

Arrowsmith has observed that Article 32(2) arguably states a relatively broad principle that in the context of frameworks, contracting authorities must not act in a manner that prevents the replication in the public sector of conditions of a competitive market. Arrowsmith continues that whilst the better view is that the Directives do not have a broad competition objective at all, regardless of whether this is so, it might be argued that such a principle is applied to the specific area of frameworks.[92] Thus, on her view, a narrower interpretation of Article 32(2) is that it is directed merely at ensuring that contracting authorities do not behave in a manner that gives rise to the kind of behaviour controlled by competition law, including collusive behaviour by suppliers, since in the context of frameworks, the market may be limited to a small number of known suppliers, or agreements that shut off competition in the market for an unreasonable period of time. Arrowsmith gives as an example the packaging of a variety of products and services not generally offered by individual suppliers into a single framework, with an obligation to bid for the whole requirement. Further, it might catch conduct designed to circumvent the general four-year limit on frameworks, or any conduct that has that effect, such as the award of unjustifiably lengthy contracts towards the end of the life of a framework.[93] Similarly, it is possible to conceive of scenarios whereby contracting authorities may create conditions under frameworks which facilitate collusion and which might be caught by Article 32(2).[94]

Earlier, in 1999, Arrowsmith addressed the issue of framework duration which, as explained above, was not at that time explicitly regulated. Arrowsmith considered it possible that controls over framework duration may exist under EC competition law and, regardless, limits might be implied based on a 'principle of competition which, like

[88] Case C-216/17 *Autorità Garante* (n 86) para 64.

[89] ibid para 69. See also Case C-23/20 *Simonsen & Weel* EU ECLI:EU:C:2021:490, para 67.

[90] Case C-216/17 *Autorità Garante* (n 86) paras 60–68.

[91] ibid para 59.

[92] Arrowsmith (n 8) 11–102.

[93] ibid. See also earlier Arrowsmith, 'Framework purchasing and qualification lists under the European procurement Directives: Part 1' (n 44) 142–43.

[94] See generally, P Arden, 'Legal Regulation of Multi-supplier Framework Agreements and the Potential for Bid-rigging: A Perspective from the UK Local Government Construction Sector' (2013) 22 *PPLR* 165.

the principles of transparency and equality, might be seen to underlie all the directives'.[95] Arrowsmith characterised this as a possible 'special rule' based on the fact that public purchasers might not otherwise be constrained by their own commercial interests from making unfavourable deals if it could enable them to favour national suppliers; however, it was qualified that this was not explored in detail and only considered *whether* this existed, not necessarily that it did.[96] Arrowsmith also prevised that a time limit of two to five years would often be reasonable[97] which seemed to be confirmed by the maximum four-year duration rule subsequently introduced. This therefore begs the question of whether, given that Directive 2004/18/EC introduced a four-year maximum, this would constitute an express limit imposed by the Directive, and so there is no need to consider competition law controls when considering the duration of a framework up to the maximum.

The Commission Explanatory Note on framework agreements stated that a longer framework duration could be justified 'in order to ensure effective competition' for the contract in question if its performance required investment with a depreciation period of more than four years.[98] This was on the basis that 'the development of effective competition in the public procurement sector is one of the objectives of the Directives dealing with this area' and refers to *Sintesi* as 'established case law' as well as this objective being 'moreover more or less restated in the fifth subparagraph of Article 32(2)'.[99] Recital 62 similarly provides that such exceptional cases might arise 'where economic operators need to dispose of equipment the amortisation period of which is longer than four years and which must be available at any time over the entire duration of the framework'.

However, the Commission's explanation is questionable. First, as indicated, caution must be exercised in treating *Sintesi* as 'established case law'. Second, it is not clear why such an express rule permitting a justified extension to the maximum must be predicated on an unclear objective of ensuring effective competition. The EU decided to create a rule setting a maximum framework duration and another rule for exceeding it if there is a justification. There is clearly greater emphasis here on allowing discretion, not subjecting it to significant constraints. It is not clear that either rule is predicated on some objective of ensuring effective competition. Rather, it may simply be the result of a trade-off between ensuring that frameworks cannot continue indefinitely, not least because of the risks of discrimination in favour of national suppliers, and allowing contracting authorities the time to make a framework viable or even to extend it, given various operational and other reasons eg in devising and applying call-off procedures. Both rules seem to tolerate a limit on competition. Third, the example given by the Commission seems intuitively odd. A contracting authority would not generally wish to exceed the maximum duration because it wants to 'develop effective competition'. The Commission seems to suggest that a contracting authority may wish to set a longer duration because the contract may require a longer-term investment and the return may

[95] Arrowsmith, 'Framework purchasing and qualification lists under the European procurement Directives: Part 1' (n 44) 142.

[96] ibid.

[97] ibid 143.

[98] European Commission, Explanatory Note – Framework Agreements – Classic Directive, Ref. Ares (2016)810203–16/02/2016, 5.

[99] ibid and fn17.

take longer. Whilst not unequivocal, it is possible to see why setting a longer duration may open up market access for those sorts of contracts. However, in most cases, a contracting authority seeking to set a longer-term framework duration will be doing so for reasons that have little or nothing to do with enabling competition for certain types of contracts. Indeed, it will likely be acutely aware that it will close off competition but that there are other good reasons for exceeding the maximum and which are not a deliberate attempt to prevent, restrict or distort competition. Fourth, this guidance provides further indication of a certain ambivalence about what effect rules on framework duration have on competition. It does not assist for the Commission to then simply state that '[m]oreover, it should be noted that the public procurement directives do not operate in a legal vacuum – both Community and national competition rules apply to them'.[100]

If the above discussion seems somewhat abstract, it may be related specifically to a practical scenario that demonstrates how potentially far reaching such a general prohibition on improper or anti-competitive use could be. Sanchez-Graells has asserted that Article 32(2) was provided 'in very clear terms', that equivalent reference is now contained in Recital 61 Directive 2014/24/EU and that there is a 'principle of competition in article 18(1) of Directive 2014/24/EU'.[101] On this basis, he argues that it is possible to analyse ways in which the use of frameworks can alter or distort competition and, consequently, how rules can be applied in a 'pro-competitive manner that ensures the effectiveness of the principle of competition embedded in the EU public procurement Directives'.[102] In his view, the limitation on the maximum duration of frameworks of four years except in duly justified cases 'must clearly be restricted by competition considerations' under Article 18(1) such that, even where a contracting authority sets a term under four years (ie, within the maximum duration), contracting authorities must set the validity of the agreement to avoid unnecessary restrictions and distortions of competition on a case-by-case analysis; further, the fact that call-offs can extend beyond the four-year limit should be subject to a strict proportionality assessment based on competitive distortions such longer duration could create.[103] It has been argued that the duration should be determined by balancing 'administrative and commercial grounds' against potential restrictiveness of competition in the market concerned and, 'where a clear conflict emerges, competition considerations should trump commercial justifications and impose a limitation on the duration of the framework'.[104] However, he suggests that frameworks of a very short duration eg less than a year 'probably lack interest'.[105]

It is submitted that this analysis is potentially problematic. As a matter of principle, as indicated, it is axiomatic that the rules cited do not state anything in very clear terms. Further, presumably, in providing for the four-year maximum rule and the possibility to justifiably exceed it, the EU has already determined that four years is a tolerable limitation on competition. At most, any such decision might need to comply with recognised EU

[100] ibid 5.
[101] Sanchez-Graells (n 12) 358.
[102] ibid 358.
[103] ibid 358–59.
[104] ibid 359.
[105] ibid.

Treaty principles but certainly no more. The EU appears to have implicitly traded off that whilst any duration up to the maximum will necessarily restrict some aspect of competition, it is outweighed by other factors eg that a contracting authority can choose to award contracts outside the framework, that the framework does provide competition, albeit only for those admitted during its term, that this may be the kind of duration necessary to make a framework viable, etc. Further, if there were some limitation on discretion to set the duration up to the maximum, it is not clear why another explicit rule is provided which permits a justified extension. If the Directives placed unspecified constraints on the application of rules conferring discretion (beyond those already applicable under recognised EU principles), the fundamental utility of a Directive as a legislative instrument would be called into question; Directives would not be able to meaningfully set rules that confer discretion and would not, therefore, be 'directory'. It would also undermine legal certainty for the contracting authority that thinks, as a matter of common sense, that if a rule set by the EU gives them a discretion to do something, they should reasonably expect to be able to do it. It may be added that if closing off a market were such a major problem so as to necessitate a maximum duration, it is not clear why a specific rule has not been introduced to curb long-term public contracts that are not frameworks eg by expressly requiring a periodic review of the effects on competition. The EU has also not thought twice about providing much longer maximum durations for defence and utilities contracts.

As a matter of practice, such an interpretation could mean that contracting authorities could be required to make a prospective assessment of the potential market impact, weigh up various reasons, and, having done so, resolve to a decision that favours 'competition considerations' when setting framework duration. A contracting authority already concerned about the costs of setting up a supposedly efficient purchasing tool might query whether this is a proportionate exercise. This is especially considering that setting the framework duration is unlikely to be the primary means by which a framework is manipulated to prevent, restrict or distort competition howsoever conceived. As discussed in chapter six, the empirical evidence in the UK indicates a general satisfaction of both contracting authorities and suppliers with the four-year maximum.

To give another example of the extent to which choices made in respect of frameworks might be subject to constraints based on consideration of their effects on competition, as discussed in chapter five, 'parallel framework agreements' have become a source of academic debate.[106] Thus, a contracting authority party to one framework may set up another, the scope of which is identical or similar, or a user contracting authority may exercise a choice between similar CPA led frameworks. The Directives have not expressly prevented contracting authorities from using more than one framework. However, it has been argued that this parallelism is likely to limit competition,[107] and even violate the Article 32(2) prohibition.[108] Similarly, Arrowsmith has suggested that, on the basis of the principle of transparency as well as Article 32(2), an obligation is arguably implied to show objective commercial grounds for choosing one particular framework, to ensure that the discretion to choose is not abused for illegitimate reasons, such as favouring national

[106] See generally M Socha, 'Competitive landscape of parallel framework agreements' in C Risvig Hamer, K-M Halonen and M Socha (eds), *Public Procurement: Centralisation and new trends* (Djøf, 2024).

[107] ibid132 and citations therein at fn 5.

[108] ibid 134.

providers.[109] This would appear to impose a more limited justification requirement than some detailed prospective assessment of anti-competitive effects.

The Supreme Court of Finland has held that a CPA-run framework violated Article 32(2) because the framework was 'too large' and created barriers to most suppliers.[110] That framework involved a large number of user contracting authorities, requirements for suppliers to bid across all categories of products with no possibility of division into lots, and various other requirements.[111] However, this appears to be a relatively rare example and it is not inconceivable that such frameworks could be held to be unlawful on the basis of breach of the recognised EU principles in any event.

To put the above discussion in its chronological context, in the subsequent consultation on reform of Directive 2004/18/EC, there was no clear Member State appetite for requiring contracting authorities under EU law to consider the effects of their procurement decisions on competition. Thus, in its 2011 Green Paper on modernisation which led to Directive 2014/24/EU, in a section titled 'fair and effective procurement' (concepts not explained and which also discussed 'efficient competition' under that heading), it was stated that public procurers often buy in markets with anti-competitive market structures, the ICT sector being identified as an example.[112] It was further stated that:

> On such markets, the aim of public procurement rules – namely open and effective competition – may be difficult to achieve by simply applying the procedural rules provided for by the current Directives. Procurement decisions which are taken without regard to market structures, even if they are fully in line with the rules of the Directives, entail the risk of consolidating or even aggravating anti-competitive structures. This is particularly true in cases of high contract values and in sectors where public authorities are the main clients and private demand is not big enough to compensate the impact of the public authorities' purchases on the market.
>
> Intelligent procurement aimed at maximizing competition in such markets would require in the first place that procurers are aware of the structure of the markets in question. Furthermore, they would have to adapt their procurement strategies (design of contracts and procedural choices) accordingly. For instance, contracting authorities should avoid tendering contracts which can only be executed by one or a small number of market player(s), as this would solidify oligopolistic structures and make new market entries almost impossible. In the worst case, the contracting authority would end up with one dominant supplier who could dictate contract terms and prices.
>
> The right shape of contracts obviously depends on the structure of the relevant market. If smaller competitors on the market are able to deliver the service or products in question on a smaller scale, efficient ways to maximise competition may include reducing the volume / duration of contracts. Efficient competition could also be achieved by splitting contracts into lots, possibly accompanied by a maximum number of lots that can be awarded to one bidder. If there are not enough competitors amongst the smaller firms, an alternative way to ensure efficient competition might be to group several purchases into one contract, in order to attract potential competitors from other Member States.[113]

[109] Arrowsmith (n 8) 11–101.

[110] A Sanchez-Graells, 'Public procurement by central purchasing bodies, competition and SMEs: towards a more dynamic model?' in Risvig Hamer and Comba (eds) (n 38) 78 and citations at fn 41 therein.

[111] ibid.

[112] European Commission, Green Paper on the modernisation of EU public procurement policy: Towards a more efficient European Procurement Market, Brussels, 27.1.2011 COM(2011) 15 final, 30.

[113] ibid.

On this basis, the Cabinet Office consultation asked: 'Do you agree that public procurement can have an important impact on market structures and that procurers should, where possible, seek to adjust their procurement strategies in order to combat anti-competitive market structures?' and 'Do you think that European public procurement rules and policy should provide for (optional) instruments to encourage such pro-competitive procurement strategies? If so, which instruments would you suggest?'[114] In the synthesis of replies, this issue was given scant attention. It was stated that '[m]any respondents' essentially agreed with the first question. By contrast, a 'slight majority' were in favour of specific EU level instruments, on condition that such remain optional and do not entail additional administrative burden.[115] Ultimately, the above was rendered moot as nothing to this effect was introduced in Directive 2014/24/EU.

To repeat, this book is not intended to resolve theoretical debates on the objectives of EU procurement law given the focus on the UK's experience. However, it is an important reminder that there has never been a clear regulatory response to the effects of procurement rules and practices on competition and which reflects a more fundamental underlying uncertainty about the purposes of procurement regulation. As will be discussed in chapter four, the UK does not appear to have been much clearer than the EU in its response in this regard. As discussed in chapter ten, the objectives for the regulated procurement system, including rules on frameworks, is an important issue when considering reform.

5. Frameworks under Directive 2014/24/EU

Following implementation of Directive 2004/18/EC, a 2010 Commission report highlighted the need to further reduce the 'complexity, administrative burden and SME-unfriendliness' of the rules.[116] In 2011, a new Green Paper[117] observed that the directives provided a number of tools for the aggregation of demand, including CPAs, and, importantly, that there were other instruments not specifically designed for aggregating demand, but which may be used for this purpose, such as 'framework contracts'.[118] However, it queried whether CPAs and frameworks were working well or should be modified or additional instruments introduced.[119]

As discussed in chapter four, the UK's formal response to the Green Paper[120] advocated for the replacement of the various purchasing systems available with a single, highly flexible tool. Whilst acknowledging that frameworks could be 'extremely useful', it criticised their closed nature 'which can limit competition over the life of the framework, locking out new and potentially innovative suppliers'.[121] It suggested that 'any new

[114] ibid 31.

[115] European Commission, Green Paper on the modernisation of EU public procurement policy: Towards a more efficient European Procurement Market: Synthesis of replies, Ref. Ares(2016)4907186-01/09/2016, 14.

[116] M Monti, 'A new strategy for the Single Market – at the service of Europe's economy and society', Ref. Ares(2016)841541-17/02/2016, 9 May 2010.

[117] European Commission Green Paper (n 112).

[118] ibid 23.

[119] ibid 24.

[120] United Kingdom response to the European Commission Green Paper on the modernisation of EU public procurement policy (COM (2011) 15 final), 25 July 2011.

[121] ibid 10.

tool enables (but does not require) frameworks to be 'open' to new competition/entrants over the life of the framework'.[122] Suffice to state, the Commission did not take this up.

The Directive as adopted is Directive 2014/24/EU as implemented in the PCR 2015. Ultimately, the provisions on frameworks have largely replicated those in Directive 2004/18/EC with only some very minor changes and clarifications, as discussed below and in more detail in Part III.

Again, for completeness, it should be added that Article 34 has continued to include provisions on DPS.

Regarding the legislative scheme of provisions on frameworks, from the outset, Recital 60 states that 'the instrument of framework agreements has been widely used and is considered as an efficient procurement technique throughout Europe' and 'should therefore be maintained largely as it is'. It then identifies various aspects which needed to be clarified in the rules.

As discussed further in chapter five, the definition of a 'framework agreement' in Article 33(1) replicates that in Directive 2004/18/EC. Importantly, however, rather than leaving it to Member States to decide whether contracting authorities may conclude frameworks, Article 33(1) provides that '[c]ontracting authorities may conclude framework agreements, provided that they apply the procedures provided for in this Directive'. In practice, this did not affect the UK which already allowed free use.

Again, Article 33(1) provides that the term of a framework must not exceed four years, save in exceptional cases duly justified by the subject of the framework.

Concerning preliminary or preparatory steps, as discussed in chapter six, when a framework is fully regulated by Directive 2014/24/EU,[123] the framework must be advertised and competitively tendered by publishing a call for competition in the Official Journal of the European Union ('OJEU').[124] Further, prior to commencing a procurement, Article 40 provides that a contracting authority may engage in 'preliminary market consultations' for the purposes of 'preparing the procurement and informing economic operators of their procurement plans and requirements'. Whilst this provision is not specific to frameworks, the empirical research suggests that preliminary market consultations have played a role in framework marketisation.

Concerning the scope of a framework, as also discussed in chapter six, despite not being an explicit requirement in Directive 2014/24/EU or PCR 2015, in *Autorità Garante*[125] and *Simonsen*,[126] the CJEU held that there is an obligation to publicise at the outset the total maximum volume and value of the framework. In *Autorità Garante*, the CJEU referred to the provisions in Directive 2004/18/EC on the methods for calculating the estimated value of frameworks and the requirements for the content of a contract notice and held that 'a framework must, at the outset, determine the maximum volume of supplies or services that may form the subject of subsequent contracts'.[127] In *Simonsen*, the CJEU analysed the relevant provisions of Directive 2014/24/EU[128] and

[122] ibid.
[123] Articles 74–76 set out a 'light-touch' regime allowing Member States to establish national rules for the award of public contracts for certain social, health and other services.
[124] Note the different rules for publishing a call for competition in the UK post-Brexit explained in ch 4.
[125] Case C-216/17 *Autorità Garante* (n 86).
[126] Case C-23/20 *Simonsen & Weel* (n 89).
[127] Case C-216/17 *Autorità Garante* (n 86) para 60.
[128] Part C of Annex V 2014 Directive.

considered the principles of equal treatment and transparency in holding that 'a failure by the contracting authority to indicate, in the contract notice, a maximum value of the supplies under a framework cannot be accepted'.[129] The CJEU clarified that 'the indication of the maximum quantity or the maximum value of the supplies under a framework can appear in either the contract notice or the tender specifications'.[130]

Regarding the choice of procedure to award the framework, the open and restricted procedures (under Articles 27 and 28, respectively) are freely available. The open procedure is a single-stage procedure that involves the publication of a call for competition which invites suppliers to submit a tender. No negotiation is permitted and all tenders submitted must be evaluated. According to Article 67, the framework must be awarded to the MEAT based on the award criteria set out in the contracting authority's invitation to tender. The restricted procedure similarly does not provide for any negotiations, being a two-stage procedure whereby suppliers submit an expression of interest in response to the call for competition following which shortlisted bidders are invited to tender. As with the open procedure, the framework is awarded based on the MEAT criteria. A multi-supplier framework would usually be set up using open or restricted procedures.

As discussed in chapters seven and eight, for multi-supplier frameworks, Article 33(2) provides that contracts based on a framework must be awarded in accordance with prescribed procedures which may be applied only between those contracting authorities clearly identified for this purpose in the call for competition or the invitation to confirm interest and those economic operators party to the framework, as concluded. Article 33(4) provides for call-offs to be awarded following the terms and conditions of the framework without reopening competition, partly without reopening competition and partly reopening competition, or reopening to competition.

Article 33(3) provides that for single-supplier frameworks, contracts based on that agreement must be awarded within the limits of the terms laid down in the framework. For the award of those contracts, contracting authorities may consult the economic operator party to the framework agreement in writing, requesting it to supplement its tender, as necessary.

Article 33(2) further provides that contracts awarded under the framework may under no circumstances entail substantial modifications to the terms laid down. Aspects of modification will be examined in chapter eight.

Other procedural rules are examined in more detail throughout Part III.

6. Regulation of Centralised Purchasing

Several European countries had adopted legislation on centralised purchasing before rules were introduced in Directive 2004/18/EC.[131] However, most Member States have not adopted additional rules relating specifically to framework use in the context of

[129] Case C-23/20 *Simonsen & Weel* (n 89) para 54.
[130] ibid para 71.
[131] M Comba and C Risvig Hamer, 'EU perspective on CPBs' in Risvig Hamer and Comba (eds) (n 38) 9.

centralised purchasing, although practice is becoming more advanced.[132] Research has indicated that centralised purchasing activities may be characterised in different ways in different countries and treated accordingly in national legislation eg as the provision of public services pursuant to the exercise of public power or commercial services subject to private law.[133] Therefore, how different Member States treat procurement as a function may influence how they regulate centralised purchasing, including frameworks. As discussed in chapter four, the UK Government treats procurement as a 'commercial function'; there appears to be no particularly sharp characterisation as 'public' or 'private' that conditions how frameworks and centralised purchasing are treated in regulatory terms.

6.1. Regulation under Directive 2004/18/EC

Rules on centralised purchasing were first introduced in Directive 2004/18/EC. Recital 15 observed that certain centralised purchasing techniques had been developed in Member States, stating that 'in view of the large volumes purchased, those techniques help increase competition and streamline public purchasing'. It was therefore considered necessary to introduce EU law definitions of central purchasing bodies 'dedicated to contracting authorities', as well as 'the conditions under which, in accordance with the principles of non-discrimination and equal treatment, contracting authorities purchasing works, supplies and/or services through a central purchasing body may be deemed to have complied with this Directive'. Recital 16 further stated that in order to take account of the different circumstances in Member States, they should be allowed to choose whether contracting authorities may use frameworks, CPAs or DPS. Article 1(10) defined a central purchasing body by reference to the concept of a 'contracting authority' as defined in Article 1(9). Article 11(1) provided that Member States may stipulate that contracting authorities may purchase works, services or supplies from or through a CPA. Article 11(2) provided that contracting authorities that do so are to be deemed to have complied with the Directive insofar as the CPA has complied with the Directive.

A 2006 evaluation of the implementation of the Directives observed that contracting authorities were using CPAs and frameworks more frequently because of the 'facilitation of compliance' (an unclear statement), they provide better value for money, and CJEU case law and negotiations regarding the new Directives helped clarify their use.[134] However, as a general evaluation of all aspects of the Directive, these findings were not comprehensive or clear as regards the specific use of centralised purchasing and frameworks. It simply observed that suppliers regarded CPAs as less transparent, less fair and more bureaucratic than other procurement bodies and, overall, less efficient but more competitive and frameworks were less transparent, less fair and less competitive but

[132] M Comba and C Risvig Hamer, 'Introduction to Centralising Public Procurement' in Risvig Hamer and Comba (eds) (n 38) 2.

[133] Comba (n 38) 24.

[134] Europe Economics, Evaluation of Public Procurement Directives Markt/2004/10/D Final Report,15 September 2006, Executive Summary, v.

slightly less bureaucratic; overall, frameworks were found to be about as efficient as other procurement.[135]

6.2. Regulation under Directive 2014/24/EU

Directive 2014/24/EU contains various rules and references to CPAs, and which continue to facilitate flexibility as regards their set-up and use.

Recital 59 refers in general terms to the emergence of centralisation and the risks, stating that:

> There is a strong trend emerging across Union public procurement markets towards the aggregation of demand by public purchasers, with a view to obtaining economies of scale, including lower prices and transaction costs, and to improving and professionalising procurement management. This can be achieved by concentrating purchases either by the number of contracting authorities involved or by volume and value over time. However, the aggregation and centralisation of purchases should be carefully monitored in order to avoid excessive concentration of purchasing power and collusion, and to preserve transparency and competition, as well as market access opportunities for SMEs.

In the proposals for the Directive, the Commission considered that the introduction of aggregated purchasing tools such as CPAs would 'would have to strike the right balance between allowing a stronger aggregation of demand in strategic sectors, and not restricting competition in procurement markets (in particular to the detriment of SMEs), eg by dividing contracts into lots'.[136] However, it did not appear to go as far as imposing specific controls in the rules on centralised purchasing or frameworks to address these possible risks. General rules on division into lots were included under Article 46 but no specific provisions on the use of lotting structures in frameworks, for example. Moreover, Recital 59 only refers to the need for concentration of purchasing power and collusion to be 'carefully monitored'; there are no specific rules on monitoring or reporting on CPAs or frameworks and Recital 59 did not indicate who was intended to do the monitoring.

The Recitals also refer to the role of CPAs in respect of frameworks and the need to clearly determine who can use a framework set up by a CPA. Thus, Recital 60 acknowledges that the identity of the users and suppliers as parties must be clear. It is stated that this implies for instance that where a CPA uses an overall register of the contracting authorities or categories thereof (such as the local authorities in a given geographical area), it should do so in a way that allows verification of not only the identity of the contracting authority but also the date from which it acquires the right to use the framework.

More generally, the Recitals include extensive reference to centralised purchasing and provisions to strengthen it, although Recital 71 qualifies that strengthening them should not prevent occasional joint procurement, as defined. This reinforces that, ultimately, it is a national choice as to how procurement is organised.

[135] ibid 87–92.
[136] Green Paper on the modernisation of EU public procurement policy: Towards a more efficient European Procurement Market (n 112) 23.

Recital 69 acknowledges that CPAs have an increasing role in making acquisitions, managing DPS or awarding contracts or frameworks for other contracting authorities, 'with or without remuneration' but makes no further mention of funding models. It observes that in view of the large volumes purchased, such techniques 'may help increase competition' and should help to professionalise public purchasing. On this basis, it states that provision should therefore be made for an EU-wide definition of CPAs dedicated to contracting authorities. In this regard, Article 2(1)(16) provides that 'central purchasing body' means a contracting authority providing centralised purchasing activities and, possibly, ancillary purchasing activities. Article 2(1)(14) provides that 'centralised purchasing activities' means activities conducted on a permanent basis, in one of the following forms: (a) the acquisition of supplies and/or services intended for contracting authorities, or (b) the award of public contracts or the conclusion of frameworks for works, supplies or services intended for contracting authorities. Nothing in that definition expressly precludes a CPA from providing its services to the private sector; however, the extent to which it effectively operates as a commercial entity will likely be relevant to its status as a contracting authority in respect of the application of the EU procurement rules. As will be discussed in chapter five, the above raises the question in practice of whether certain entities that are setting up and operating frameworks always meet the definition of a contracting authority enabling them to act as CPAs, especially where these operate for profit or involve extensive private sector participation (or are, indeed, private sector organisations).

Recital 70 states that contracting authorities should be allowed to award a public service contract for the provision of centralised purchasing activities to a CPA (including ancillary purchasing activities) without applying the Directive's award procedures. Article 2(1)(15) provides that 'ancillary purchasing activities' means provision of support to purchasing activities, in particular: (a) technical infrastructure enabling contracting authorities to award public contracts or conclude framework agreements; (b) advice on the conduct or design of procurement procedures; and (c) preparation and management of procedures on behalf of and for the account of the contracting authority concerned. Article 37(4) makes provision to this effect. Recital 70 continues that public service contracts for the provision of ancillary purchasing activities should, when performed otherwise than by a CPA in connection with its provision of central purchasing activities, be awarded in accordance with this Directive. Further, the Directive should not apply where centralised or ancillary purchasing activities are provided other than through a contract for pecuniary interest which constitutes procurement within the meaning of the Directive. As discussed in chapter five, it is questionable whether ancillary purchasing activities which are not provided by CPAs (eg private sector organisations) are being awarded in accordance with the Directive.

Recital 70 also states that it should be clarified that CPAs operate in two different ways. First, they should be able to act as wholesalers by buying, stocking and reselling. Article 37(1) states that Member States may provide that contracting authorities may acquire supplies and/or services from a CPA offering the acquisition of supplies and/or services intended for contracting authorities (in Article 2(1)(14)(a)). Second, they should be able to act as intermediaries by awarding contracts, operating DPS or concluding frameworks to be used by contracting authorities. Research suggests that a CPA most frequently acts as an intermediary when it concludes frameworks for use by others.[137] Recital 70 also states that such an intermediary role might in some cases be carried out by conducting the relevant award procedures autonomously, without detailed instructions from the contracting authorities concerned; in other cases, by conducting the relevant award procedures under their instructions, on their behalf and for their account. Again, Article 37(1) provides for this possibility (in Article 2(1)(14)(b) and Article 33(2)). The fact that it is possible for a CPA to operate without any requirement to act on instruction is a significant flexibility. This is important because, as discussed in chapter five, issues have arisen in multi-supplier frameworks in which there is no substantial instruction or input from user contracting authorities which may then have implications at the call-off stage.

Article 37(1) further sets out that Member States may provide that certain procurements are to be made by having recourse to CPAs or to one or more specific CPAs. European countries have introduced various models regarding mandatory or voluntary use of CPAs, eg where contracting authorities can freely choose which CPA to use, can only procure without recourse to a CPA if the price is lower than using a CPA (ie, a presumption in favour of use of a CPA), or even where it is mandatory to use certain CPAs.[138] As will be discussed in chapter four, the UK decided not to mandate use of CPAs.

Recital 69 states that rules should be laid down for allocating responsibility for the observance of the Directive's obligations, as between the CPA and user contracting authorities. Where the CPA has sole responsibility for the conduct of the procurement procedures, it should be solely and directly responsible for their legality. Article 37(2) provides that the contracting authority is responsible for fulfilling the obligations under the Directive in respect of parts it conducts itself, such as conducting a reopening of competition under a framework that has been concluded by a CPA or determining which of the suppliers party to the framework will perform against a given task under a framework concluded by a CPA. As will be discussed in chapter five, this does not necessarily provide absolute legal certainty, however, in instances in which both the user contracting authority and CPA have potentially jointly contributed to a breach.

For completeness, it should be added that there is also reference to the role that CPAs may play in the context of electronic procurement. Recital 72 states that electronic means of communication are particularly well suited to supporting centralised purchasing because of the possibility they offer to re-use and automatically process data and to minimise information and transaction costs. Article 37(4) provides that all procedures conducted by a CPA shall be performed using electronic means of communication (in accordance with Article 22).

6.3. CPAs and the Objectives of EU Procurement Regulation

As is the case in respect of frameworks, there is uncertainty about the extent to which the rules on centralised purchasing must be applied in consideration of their effects

[137] Comba and Risvig Hamer (n 131) 13.
[138] Comba (n 38) 27–28.

on competition and whether centralised purchasing, including through frameworks, is subject to EU competition law, given the unclear objectives of EU procurement regulation.

As indicated above, Recital 2 equivocally suggests that a purpose of Directive 2014/24/EU is to ensure the 'efficiency of public spending'. Comba has observed that Member States widely used centralised purchasing to pursue domestic objectives of securing efficiency but that certain practices were at risk of legal challenge before EU courts as being in violation of EU law. Thus, it was necessary to effectively 'legalise' such widely accepted practices as a matter of 'real politik' to avoid further challenges rather than being a deliberate EU policy decision to foster aggregated procurement.[139] He continues that:

> That would explain the apparent contradiction of the 2004 public procurement Directives: their main scope is to promote competition but they foster a new legal scheme for aggregated procurement, even if it can be an obstacle to competition, especially in respect of the participation of SMEs; so much so that they have to warn against its possible anti-competitive effects [...] That seems to be the unresolved misconception underlying the whole discipline of central purchasing bodies: European legislation tries to force them into a model of a pro-competition institution, but they have a different nature and were originally conceived by Member States for another scope – pursuing cost efficiency – which does not necessarily coincide with promoting competition and, rather, can have serious anti-competitive consequences [...].[140]

Thus, Comba's view is that whilst pursuing cost efficiency in procurement is 'a sound legal ground' for national public administrations, it is not so for EU procurement legislation which should be based on the principles of free circulation of goods and services, prohibition of discrimination and the approximation of laws, which promote competition;[141] although, as indicated above, this is traditionally meant in the sense of facilitating equal access to an EU-wide market rather than promoting the outright maximisation of competition. Therefore, by bringing central purchasing as an activity within the Directive's scope (in recognition of Member State use), there is the problem that it can also have anti-competitive effects contrary to the EU's focus on opening up markets to EU-wide competition; centralised purchasing can potentially reduce the number of competitors due to the high requirements needed to participate in award procedures for very large aggregated contracts.[142] This ambivalence and the need to reconcile facilitating central purchasing with EU objectives may, in turn, be reflected in the fact that the EU has not introduced specific rules to address its anti-competitive effects but rather, only, broadly 'warns against' them.[143] This may, in turn, be an instantiation of a more general uncertainty about how to deal with the issue of the extent to which the application of procurement rules and practices may impact negatively on competition, and which is only dealt with in the form of a highly generic and vague provision safeguarding against artificial narrowing of competition in Article 18, rather than specific rules. Similarly, elsewhere, it has been further observed that the Directives do not contain any mandatory rules that would seek to avoid or limit these effects eg rules requiring

[139] ibid 22–23.
[140] ibid 23.
[141] ibid 34.
[142] ibid.
[143] ibid 23.

division of contracts into lots (as observed above) or to award contracts to several suppliers where CPAs are used or specific targeted monitoring of CPA activities.[144] On this basis, it has been argued that these issues should be addressed in the next round of reform of the Directives.[145] As discussed in chapter four, the UK has similarly not taken any domestic initiative to address any such effects.

Comba also goes further, stating that 'a clear example of this unresolved misconception is the problematic relationship between CPAs and competition laws, both from the perspective of CPAs as purchasers, potentially altering the market, and from that of competition among them'.[146] This chapter now turns to consider this matter by reference to EU case law.

6.4. CPAs Offering Services on a Market

As indicated in chapter two, it has been questioned whether CPAs are effectively offering their services on a market and competing against each other in such a way that their operation may contravene not just procurement rules but also EU competition law.

ASMEL[147] provides a useful illustration of how certain Member States have introduced domestic legislation to address the role of CPAs and EU law's response to the issue of CPAs offering their services on a market. Asmel, a limited liability company owned by Italian municipalities and private associations, acted as a CPA for local authorities. It arranged invitations to tender for frameworks and was remunerated for its services payable by the successful tenderer at 1.5 per cent of the contract price. Following complaints, the National Anti-Corruption Authority investigated and made various findings. First, Asmel did not comply with national legislation which required CPAs to constitute public bodies acting through associations of local authorities as Asmel was governed by private law. Second, whilst private entities may be used, they must be in-house bodies operating only within the founding municipalities' territory whereas Asmel did not, nor was it subject to comparable oversight. Third, the local authorities were only indirectly involved in the CPA. Fourth, Asmel could not be classed as a 'body governed by public law' because it operated only indirectly to meet the needs of its member local authorities and therefore did not directly serve the public interest. Asmel challenged this decision.

On a reference for a preliminary ruling, the question for the CJEU was whether Directive 2004/18/EC precluded national legislation limiting organisational models for CPAs by not allowing private participation. The referring national court's position was that a limitation could be contrary to EU principles of free movement of services and 'maximum possible competition' because the provision of such services can be classed as 'commercial activities and which, as such, could be better provided under a system of free competition within the internal market'.[148]

[144] K-M Halonen and E Puhakainen, 'The reflection of economic objectives in centralised procurement rules' in Risvig Hamer, Halonen and Socha (eds) (n 106) 95.
[145] ibid.
[146] ibid.
[147] Case C-3/19 *ASMEL v ANAC* ECLI:EU:C:2020:423.
[148] Opinion of AG Campos Sánchez-Bordona, para 27.

By contrast, the CJEU reasoned that the only restriction in the Directive on the choice of a CPA is for it to meet the definition of a contracting authority, which is defined broadly and in functional terms, and that a wide margin of discretion applies to their organisation.[149] This was consistent with the Directive's 'underlying principles, namely, freedom to provide services and opening up to undistorted competition in all Member States'.[150] This was because, although contracting authorities that use a CPA are not subject to the Directive's procedures, the CPA was, thereby, securing those principles.[151] On this basis, there was nothing precluding tailoring organisational models to their own individual circumstances and stipulating purely public models.[152] It transpired that the legislation was intended to safeguard against mafia infiltration and to provide a means of controlling expenditure.[153] Further, this legislation did not place any private undertaking at an advantage over its competitors.[154] Nor did it give preference to any national tenderer but, rather, protected small local authorities from the risk of a cartel arising consisting of a CPA and a private undertaking that holds capital in that CPA.[155]

The CJEU further stated that, 'in any event', CPAs cannot be regarded as offering services on a market open to competition by private undertakings.[156] It considered that a CPA acts in fact as a contracting authority, to satisfy the needs of a contracting authority, not as an economic operator in its own commercial interests.[157]

Concerning the geographical restriction on the CPA's operation, the national referring court believed that it may give rise to exclusive operating zones for CPAs, undermining free movement and opening up markets to competition. The CJEU reasoned that Member States have a wide margin of discretion in setting limits on the CPA's territorial operation.[158] The restriction ensured that those CPAs act in the public interest of their participating authorities instead of their own commercial interests beyond those territories and was consistent with Article 1(10) that a CPA must be classed as a contracting authority and meet those conditions. It reasoned that Article 1(9) provides that a contracting authority is an entity not having an industrial or commercial character which performs a task in the general interest; it was considered that, as a general rule, such a body does not pursue gainful activity on the market.[159] Therefore, the national legislation imposing the restriction fell within the bounds of the margin of discretion.[160] Consistent with its other determination, the CJEU also considered that this did not place any private undertaking at an advantage over its competitors.[161]

In addition, AG Campos Sánchez-Bordona stated that the fact that a CPA may be classed as an economic operator in its relations with third parties (ie, Asmel's clients

[149] Case C-3/19 *ASMEL* (n 147) paras 54 and 56.
[150] ibid para 57.
[151] ibid para 58.
[152] ibid para 61.
[153] ibid para 62.
[154] ibid para 65.
[155] ibid para 66.
[156] ibid para 63.
[157] ibid para 64.
[158] ibid para 69.
[159] ibid para 70 citing Case C-305/08 *CoNISMa* ECLI:EU:C:2009:807, para 38.
[160] ibid para 70.
[161] ibid para 71.

paid for its services) was not sufficient by itself to determine the application of principles of free movement of services when that concept cannot be separated from that of a contracting authority covering only the State, local authorities, bodies governed by public law or such associations.[162] Further, '[u]nder Directive 2004/18, those central purchasing bodies did not compete in a non-existent *market for central purchasing bodies' services* with private legal persons who provided the same services to public bodies'.[163] The fact that private undertakings or entities may be able to supply the contracting authorities with purely ancillary activities in support of their procurement activities (eg, consultancy services) in return for payment was a separate matter.[164] The AG further observed that the situation may have changed following Directive 2014/24/EU, Article 37(4) of which permits the award of a 'public service contract for the provision of centralised purchasing activities to a central purchasing body'.[165] It was stated that the fact that such an award may be made without applying the Directive's procedures could be due to the fact that the award must be made to CPAs governed by public law (which may include some limited private participation under public oversight); otherwise, if the award could be made to a private legal person, 'it would be hard to see how such a person could be awarded the contract without first having been made subject to the procedures in Directive 2014/24/EU'.[166]

Further, the AG acknowledged (in a footnote) that from the perspective of competition law, the risk that competition will be distorted may be prompted more by the aggregation and centralisation of purchases which, as noted by Recital 59, could give rise to an 'excessive concentration of purchasing power and collusion'.[167] However, he did not consider that the national legislation was in breach of competition law, stating that '[t]he competition which EU law seeks to protect in this field is, fundamentally, competition between economic operators who provide works, goods or services to contracting authorities'. Provided that those authorities (in this case, CPAs) complied with the Directive's procedures when obtaining them, competition between economic operators was preserved.[168] In other words, the requirement for small local authorities to use their own CPAs (through associations or consortia of municipalities) did not mean that the competitive market for the supply of goods, works or services to those public authorities by the economic operators concerned was thereby closed.[169] On the issue of the geographical restriction, the AG added that whilst the scope of the CPA's operation may be confined to the area in which the participating local authorities operated, there was nothing to indicate that works, services or supplies must come from undertakings based in that territory and so there was nothing to suggest the market was closed.[170]

[162] AG Opinion para 70.
[163] Emphasis in the original at para 72.
[164] ibid.
[165] ibid para 73.
[166] ibid para 74.
[167] ibid para 76, fn 39.
[168] ibid para 76.
[169] ibid para 77.
[170] ibid para 94.

Therefore, *Asmel* is instructive because it confirms that Member States have discretion to place restrictions on CPAs in pursuit of domestic objectives. On the facts, this included preventing corruption, controlling expenditure, and ensuring that CPAs act in the public interest not their own commercial interest. Such restrictions could also be imposed to prevent potential anti-competitive effects such as collusion. Further, the CJEU indicates that CPAs must meet the definition of a contracting authority and, in so doing, are acting effectively in the public interest, not offering services on the market for commercial interest in a way that is incompatible with EU procurement law or competition law.

Before this judgment, given the increasingly commercial market-facing activities of CPAs, it might well have been questioned whether a CPA meets the definition of a contracting authority on the basis that, whilst it may meet needs in the general interest, it may also meet other needs that have an industrial or commercial character. It is certainly questionable whether CPAs satisfy the definition of a contracting authority as readily as *ASMEL* suggests. CPAs may charge not only fees to suppliers but also management fees to contracting authorities that go beyond covering operating costs and generate a surplus, may involve extensive private sector participation in delivering services, and may even offer services to the private sector. As will be discussed in chapter four, section 2 PA 2023 has introduced a new definition of 'contracting authority' and s.1 has introduced a new definition of a 'centralised procurement authority' which means a contracting authority in the business of carrying out procurement for or on behalf of, or for the purpose of the supply to, other contracting authorities. As will be discussed, this is unlikely to add much legal certainty on this issue.

Of course, the judgment must also be put in context. It only concerned whether a national restriction placed on a CPA for public interest reasons was compatible with EU law; it was not concerned with a challenge to the CPA's conduct as regards the kinds of framework being set up, the type of services that it might offer, the size of its 'market share', or any arrangements that may have been entered into with suppliers.

As will be discussed in chapter four, the UK did not introduce any explicit controls on CPAs of any similar kind. Whilst this could be criticised on the basis that a lack of regulatory controls may have enable marketised CPA behaviours to develop, *Asmel* shows that adopting further domestic regulatory controls could have potentially resulted in a legal challenge such that refrain might have been prudent. Notwithstanding, going forward, there is the question of whether such controls should be introduced in the UK either in procurement legislation or in the application of competition law, or both.

7. Frameworks and Centralised Purchasing in the Context of Competition Law

As indicated, *Sintesi* and *Asmel* have raised the issue of the extent to which frameworks and centralised purchasing may be subject to competition law. It is beyond the focus of this book to examine competition law and related areas (eg, State aid or subsidies); however, it is important to briefly explain its relevance to the overall regulation of frameworks and their operationalisation, not least because, as will be discussed in Part III, interviewees repeatedly raised competition law implications in practice.

In outline, Article 101 TFEU provides that certain forms of conduct are prohibited as incompatible with the internal market. These are: all agreements between undertakings, decisions by associations of undertakings and concerted practices which may affect trade between Member States, and which have as their object or effect the prevention, restriction or distortion of competition within the internal market. Article 102 TFEU provides that any abuse by one or more undertakings of a dominant position within the internal market or in a substantial part of it shall be prohibited as incompatible with the internal market insofar as it may affect trade between Member States.

In the UK, as early as 2008, the issue was raised of the potential implications of CPA activity according to EU competition law,[171] and which has subsequently been considered in academic research in relation to frameworks.[172]

7.1. Contracting Authorities Operating as 'Undertakings'

It has been queried whether contracting authorities, and, therefore, CPAs can be considered 'undertakings' exercising economic activity and, thus, subject to competition law. In the UK, it has previously been observed that UK regulatory authority decisions and Competition Appeal Tribunal judgments suggested that a 'contracting authority' under procurement law may also constitute an 'undertaking' under competition law.[173] However, none has explicitly considered the status of a CPA in this regard.

The TFEU does not define an 'undertaking'. According to the case law, the definition covers any entity engaged in an economic activity, regardless of its legal status and the way in which it is financed.[174] The characteristic feature of an economic activity is offering goods and services on a given market and which could, at least in principle, be carried out by a private operator in order to make a profit.[175] This raises the question of whether the circumstances in which a public entity purchases (not offers) goods or services from the market constitute an economic activity.

The seminal EU case is *FENIN*,[176] in which SNS provided healthcare through managing the Spanish healthcare system as well as insurance to members of the national health insurance system. SNS comprised various public entities which, in order to provide care services, purchased supplies from FENIN, an association of undertakings selling medical equipment to Spanish hospitals. FENIN's members claimed that those public entities abused their dominant position by taking longer to pay debts owed to them than to other suppliers. The Commission rejected the complaint on the basis that those public entities were not undertakings; they were not carrying out an economic activity when

[171] J Chard, G Duhs and J Houlden, 'Body beautiful or vile bodies? Central purchasing in the UK' (2008) 2 *PPLR* NA26-34.

[172] See generally, Kristensen Balshoj (n 30).

[173] These are referenced in Chard, Duhs and Houlden (n 171) 30, namely, Case CW/00842/06/05, *Complaint from Independent Media Support Limited about BBC Broadcast's provision of television access services to the BBC*, case closure issued May 30, 2007; Case 1006/2/1/01, *Bettercare Group Ltd v Director General of Fair Trading* [2002] CAT 7; and Case CP/1139-01, *Companies House, the Registrar of Companies for England and Wales*, decision dated October 25, 2002.

[174] Case C-41/90 *Höfner and Elser* ECLI:EU:C:1991:161, [1991] ECR I-1979, para 21.

[175] Case C-475/99 *Amublanz Glockkner* ECLI:EU:C:2001:577, [2001] ECR I-8089.

[176] Case C-205/03 *FENIN* ECLI:EU:C:2006:453, [2006] E.C.R. 6295.

they purchased goods on the market and managed the public health service. Further, their purchases could not be dissociated from their subsequent use. Proceedings for annulment of this decision at the General Court were rejected.[177] It stated that 'it is the activity consisting in offering goods and services on a given market that is the characteristic feature of an economic activity [...] not the business of purchasing, as such'.[178] An appeal to the CJEU was also rejected on the basis that there is no need to dissociate the activity of purchasing goods from the subsequent use to establish the nature of that purchasing activity, which must be discerned according to whether the subsequent use of the purchased good amounts to an economic activity.[179]

Thus, it was considered that whether an entity is an undertaking or not depends on the subsequent use of the purchased good or service *not* on its activity in purchasing. This left scope for debate on when a subsequent use will demonstrate an economic activity. The General Court stated that an organisation purchasing goods for an activity of a purely social nature eg managing health funds on a not for profit basis does not act as an undertaking simply because it is a purchaser on a given market.[180] SNS fulfilled a social function, was funded from social security contributions and other state funding, and provided its services free of charge to members on the basis of universal cover.[181] The General Court also found that arguments raised as to whether treatment of patients privately and for a fee would render SNS an undertaking were inadmissible on the procedural point that they were not raised to the Commission before its decision.[182]

This then raises the question of what is the position where goods or services are procured which may be for social and commercial purposes eg where there may be some element of profit-making because fees are paid for the services ultimately provided to service users. In this regard, it was observed in 2008 that in respect of larger CPAs, it may be difficult to determine to what use certain goods or services are put.[183] It was therefore suggested that the use must be closely analysed, particularly because the increased interaction between the public and private sector means that activities that were not previously deemed economic in nature may increasingly acquire such status. It was suggested that CPAs may be deemed to be operating as undertakings in procuring goods on behalf of contracting authorities operating on commercial markets; for example, educational institutions or healthcare providers that provide certain services on a commercial basis and in competition with private bodies.[184]

FENIN is not necessarily definitive because it did not concern a challenge to the way in which a CPA provides its central purchasing activities. It could conceivably be argued that how a CPA is set up to operate and 'compete' against others in providing services could contravene competition law. For instance, it has been argued that when a CPA acts a wholesaler, eg reselling on the market, it will be subject to competition law.[185] Before

[177] Case T-319/99 *FENIN* ECLI:EU:T:2003:50, [2003] ECR II-357.
[178] ibid para 36.
[179] Case C-205/03 *FENIN* (n 176) para 26.
[180] T-319/99 *FENIN* (n 177) para 38.
[181] ibid para 39.
[182] ibid para 34.
[183] Chard, Duhs and Houlden (n 171) 31.
[184] ibid.
[185] Kristensen Balshoj (n 30) 274.

Asmel, academic commentary had suggested that a CPA acting as an intermediary could also conceivably be held to be providing an economic activity. Various arguments have been made in support. First, *FENIN* has been distinguished because it involved an assessment of the subsequent use of services purchased by a public body, whereas a CPA is only acting as a 'middleman' for user contracting authorities that purchase the goods or services; thus, issues such as whether services are free of charge to ultimate service users is irrelevant in determining the CPA's activity and status.[186] Second, it has been suggested that an entity which is dependent on the contracting authority (ie, does not receive remuneration, provides services free of charge) and, thus, does not carry out an economic activity, should be distinguished from one that is independent (ie, does receive remuneration for services rendered instead of being paid a contribution fee and participates in the market), and, thus, does carry out an economic activity. One commentator has emphasised the issue of remuneration and pointed to a Danish survey in which municipalities perceive a large Danish CPA's 'business model as one based on revenue maximization rather than optimization of the value for the municipalities using the agreements'.[187] It has been argued that the market for entering into agreements on behalf of others is a market in itself and where private sector suppliers may also operate for remuneration.[188] Therefore, it might be argued that such an entity is operating as an 'undertaking'.

However, as indicated above, the more recent *Asmel* case has called this into question; the CJEU has intimated that this is not the case but is by no means settled.

7.2. Competition Law Issues in Practice

Whatever the legal status of a contracting authority as an 'undertaking' under competition law, much academic research has identified the potential for CPA practices to raise competition law issues.

Concerning Article 101 TFEU, regarding the supply side, it has been argued that if central purchasing leads to a reduced number of suppliers, this may increase the potential for concerted action between suppliers. It has been suggested that CPAs may facilitate supply-side collusion because a framework may effectively create a closed market, including lotting structures open to only certain types of supplier.[189] Similarly, on the demand side, it has been suggested that, where contracting authorities act together on a coordinated basis through a CPA which has the effect of reducing the number of suppliers in a market, aggrieved suppliers may argue that there has been collusion in concluding agreements with the object or effect of restricting competition.[190] In the UK, arguments in relation to collusion on purchasing were heard (but not decided upon) by the Competition Appeal Tribunal in the former Office of Fair Trade's decision in

[186] ibid 277–78.
[187] ibid 277 and citation at fn 27 therein.
[188] ibid 280.
[189] ibid 355–58 and citations therein. See also, generally, Nicholas and Albano (n 46) ch 9 on addressing risks of collusion in frameworks.
[190] Chard, Duhs and Houlden (n 171) 32.

Cityhook,[191] a case involving, among other things, allegations of a collective boycott by purchasers of underwater cable technology.[192]

Concerning Article 102 TFEU, it has been argued that where a CPA is a dominant purchaser, there is risk of an abuse of a dominant position, particularly in markets where the public sector has an impact on private sector sales. The UK case of *Napp*[193] has been cited as an example in which (publicly procured) sales of morphine in the hospital sector were key to securing retail sales in the community sector which led *Napp* to engage in predatory pricing in the hospital sector (to secure excessive prices in the community sector). It has been suggested that central purchasing encourages such behaviour because it makes it easier for a dominant supplier to target the limited public sector gateways to the private sector market (in contrast to the position in the absence of a CPA where there is a large number of tenders and, therefore, a number of points of entry to the market).[194] It has also been suggested that if contracting authorities are considered undertakings, then, by purchasing goods centrally, the risk of them being found to be collectively dominant is increased. In this regard, it has been observed that potential abuses may be directed towards either suppliers to the dominant contracting authorities or horizontal competitors of contracting authorities, citing *FENIN* as an example.[195] Another example is the UK case of *Bettercare*, in which North & West Belfast Health & Social Services Trust was accused of abusing a dominant position by offering unreasonably low prices and unfair contract terms to Bettercare Plc, another supplier of residential healthcare services.[196] Similarly, it has been observed that potential abuses that have a horizontal effect may arise, for example, out of supply arrangements that unfairly 'lock in' a supplier to supply their key product to the CPA to the disadvantage of others.[197]

Part III identifies other possible examples of practices that may engage competition law considerations, including close collaboration between consortia in certain sectors in the set-up of frameworks; rebate sharing arrangements; memoranda of understanding between central government departments and original suppliers which set certain prices and terms; and allowing private sector organisations to use frameworks, taking advantage of pricing agreed with public sector customers.

Again, the UK has not adopted any specific procurement laws or policies to address the potential anti-competitive effects of the set-up and operation of frameworks through CPAs or investigated framework practices under competition law. This may be considered in the context of an environment in which, as mentioned in chapter four, the Competition and Markets Authority is signalling increased willingness to investigate procurement practices. As discussed in chapter ten, there is a clear need to investigate frameworks from a competition law perspective in the UK.

[191] Case 1071/2/1/06 *Cityhook Limited v Office of Fair Trading* [2007] CAT 18.

[192] Chard, Duhs and Houlden (n 171) 32.

[193] Case 1001/1/01 *Napp Pharmaceutical Holdings Ltd v Director General of Fair Trading* [2002] CAT 5.

[194] Chard, Duhs and Houlden (n 171) 32, also stating that similar considerations were raised in respect of continence products in an OFT Report, *Assessing the impact of public sector procurement on competition*, September 2004, Vol 2, 23.

[195] Chard, Duhs and Houlden (n 171) 32.

[196] ibid.

[197] ibid.

8. Conclusions

Chapter two identified a trend towards framework marketisation. Research suggested that the Directives are not only integral to marketisation because they regulate an instantiation of it (ie, the award of public contracts to the private sector following increased outsourcing) but also push some overt 'pro-competition' ideology. This begged the question to what extent has EU procurement regulation therefore contributed to some of the issues arising? This, in turn, requires a fundamental understanding of its objectives and how the rules on frameworks have developed.

It cannot be said that the Directives do pursue a clear 'pro-competition' ideology that would give licence to contracting authorities to engage in all manner of commercial behaviours to encourage competition or, indeed, place significant constraints on discretion on how framework rules and practices are engaged because of the risks to competition. Instead, somewhat ambivalently, EU law has introduced rules designed to safeguard against the potential for frameworks and procurement rules to be applied in ways that could have anti-competitive effects. However, these vague rules have created uncertainty. There should also be wariness of the potentially far-reaching implications of claims that EU procurement rules must be interpreted in consideration of their effects on competition; an example was given of placing restrictions on the ability to set the duration of a framework up to the maximum. This uncertainty also arises when considering central purchasing, in particular, whether CPAs can be said to be acting as economic entities in providing services on the market.

To be clear, general uncertainty under EU law as regards the objectives of the rules on frameworks and centralised purchasing is unlikely to have been a significant contributory factor in the marketisation of frameworks in the UK. Nevertheless, the fact that the EU has not decisively addressed such issues may have at least contributed in some way. The position might have been different had large-scale CPA framework practices been challenged before EU courts or subject to competition law investigations, for example. It is therefore unsurprising that the UK has not taken its own domestic initiative. Importantly, as will be discussed, the PA 2023 has not directly addressed competition issues through its rules and frameworks have not been the subject of detailed investigation under competition law.

This chapter has also considered the development of the rules on frameworks and which is instructive. First, basic rules were introduced in recognition of the prevalence of frameworks in practice and to address risks to free movement. As indicated by early EU case law, there was an apparent concern to ensure that frameworks focused on establishing the key terms through a competition because of the risks if subsequent purchases were called off with little transparency. The basic rules that were introduced in Directive 2004/18EC were not intended to constitute a comprehensive regulatory code for frameworks. There appeared to be an early emphasis on leaving Member States to address frameworks within the constraints of the basic rules provided and some did take up this opportunity. The same could be said in respect of central purchasing.

Second, frameworks were seen as arrangements for responding to issues such as volatile pricing in ICT markets not for the procurement of mass volume requirements in stable conditions, involving many user contracting authorities and hundreds or thousands of suppliers. Interestingly, the regulatory regime on frameworks was never specifically adapted to reflect how the use of frameworks has changed over time.

Third, any early concerns about the effects of frameworks on competition tended to focus on supply-side risks of collusion rather than demand-side risks of abuse of dominant position by contracting authorities. This concern only became more prevalent as EU policy began to refer to aggregated procurement, including through CPAs, although as indicated, the EU stopped short of introducing substantial rules to address such risks, instead encouraging monitoring.

In the second wave of reform culminating in Directive 2014/24/EU, there appeared to be certain changes of emphasis whilst the rules largely remained the same. Firstly, there was more explicit recognition of the effects of procurement rules on competition in a new Article 18 on principles of procurement, although not expressly identifying a principle of competition. The general prohibition on improper or anti-competitive use of frameworks was relocated to a Recital. Secondly, it was no longer a case of Member States having the choice to enable frameworks but rather free contracting authority choice. Thirdly, there was recognition that large frameworks, in particular, those operated through CPAs, gave rise to various issues. As indicated, CJEU case law concerned who should be permitted to use a framework where they were not originally a party as well as the need to clearly identify scope for use; whilst these issues can arise in single-supplier frameworks, it is clear that the EU was alert to some of the issues arising from multi-user contracting authority frameworks. However, only clarifications were added in the rules. More radical proposals by the UK to introduce a more flexible model, including open frameworks, were not taken up. Finally, CJEU case law began to test the extent to which measures introduced by Member States to regulate centralised purchasing are subject to EU law, including whether CPAs can be said to be offering services on the market which might engage EU competition law. Whilst the CJEU indicated that this is not the case, the issue is by no means resolved.

Ultimately, therefore, the Directives have developed a functional regulatory model for frameworks and their operationalisation through centralised purchasing. However, it must be acknowledged that the rules have given rise to legal uncertainty and contributed to framework marketisation, as explored in Part III.

To link this EU law discussion to UK practice even more explicitly, during interviews, a legal adviser took issue with the 'one-size-fits-all approach adopted by the European Commission for all Member States when setting the procurement rules'. They viewed the rules 'as a failure of the principle of subsidiarity'.[198] According to Article 5(3) TEU, subsidiarity is a principle whereby the EU does not act (except in the areas that fall within its exclusive jurisdiction), unless it is more effective than action taken at the national, regional or local level. They continued that 'they should have limited the legislation to enunciating broad principles instead' with Member States having 'the flex to put in place arrangements that fit in with the national legal and commercial context'. In their view, frameworks are being used in practice as a tool 'to circumvent public procurement discipline, transparency and a proper regulated competition'.[199]

This frustration is perhaps understandable but it is possible to offer a more balanced analysis of the EU's position. Ultimately, the EU needed to introduce rules on frameworks.

[198] For an explanation of this principle see www.europarl.europa.eu/factsheets/en/sheet/7/the-principle-of-subsidiarity.

[199] LA11.

As discussed in chapter four, it was not the case that the UK (which had been identified as in violation of EU law) had introduced its own set of rules. Therefore, it was entirely appropriate for the EU to adopt at least some regulation that has not been developed at the national level. Further, Directives are necessarily 'directory' in their design to coordinate national approaches. Indeed, initially, only general rules on frameworks may have been introduced precisely in order to respect how Member States organise and conduct procurements using which tools (and the same may be said in respect of central purchasing). Nothing precluded Member States from simply 'copying out' the Directives and avoiding 'gold plating' but it is for them to then bear the consequence of this domestic policy choice. As will be discussed in chapter four, the UK chose not to introduce further domestic regulation. Whilst this might have reduced the risk of challenges to the compatibility of additional domestic rules with EU law, not regulating or attempting to mitigate or clarify legal uncertainty domestically that behaviours develop subject to few regulatory controls within an already uncertain legal environment under EU law. Thus, it is difficult to see how the EU can be held largely responsible for much of the legal uncertainty (except that which arises under EU law) and widespread marketisation of frameworks. Indeed, no doubt, had only a set of broad principles been enunciated at the EU level, this would have been subject to even greater criticism and potentially contributed to an even worse position than at present in the UK.

However, EU procurement regulation is not wholly beyond criticism. As discussed in Part III, many provisions are perhaps too generic in their drafting (notwithstanding their directory nature), creating a risk of inconsistent interpretations and which has inevitably affected compliance. The CJEU case law indicates that obvious grey areas have not been conclusively resolved. Further, as indicated, the EU has not categorically addressed the effects of frameworks and CPAs on competition. Whilst Member States may have rejected the use of procurement rules to address competition risks, there was little precluding the Commission from issuing guidance in this area.

4

Regulation of Frameworks in the UK

1. Introduction

Historically, the UK did not develop detailed legislation governing procurement, instead regulating largely through soft law, ie policy and circulars mandated for use but not expressly by statute. The eventual implementation of the EU procurement Directives marked a seemingly irreversible trend towards more hard-law regulation. As the UK adopted a 'copy-out' approach to the Directives, EU law has provided the foundation for much of the UK's regulation. Successive UK Governments have not gone further in developing specific regulation on frameworks, with limited exceptions. Therefore, as indicated, whilst it is arguable that EU regulation has, to some extent, contributed to issues examined in this book, much responsibility necessarily falls on the UK itself.

This chapter begins by explaining the development of UK legislation relevant to procurement before the PA 2023 (Section 2), as well as policy guidance relating to frameworks (Section 3). It briefly acknowledges the extent of albeit limited private sector-led initiatives to address frameworks, an important dimension that should be considered in the context of regulation because it is suggested that industry should play a more responsible role in self-regulating in this area (Section 4). It then introduces the PA 2023 replacing the EU-derived UK Regulations, which came into force on 24 February 2025 and was further implemented in the PR 2024 (Section 5). As discussed in more detail throughout Part III, this new regulatory regime introduced by the outgoing Conservative Government has not fundamentally addressed many of the issues raised in this book, calling into question whether further reform is necessary. At the time of writing, the new Labour Government's future approach to the regulation of frameworks is uncertain. For instance, on 13 February 2025, it published a revised National Procurement Policy Statement ('NPPS') which has acknowledged but not addressed some of the issues arising.[1] Further, a Ministerial statement has referenced the possibility of yet further primary legislation but it is unclear whether this will address frameworks. The chapter then offers concluding observations (Section 6). This considered in parallel with chapter three on EU regulation will provide the context for the analysis in Part III.

[1] Cabinet Office, *National Procurement Policy Statement*, 13 February 2025.

2. UK Procurement Legislation before the Procurement Act 2023

2.1. Approach to Procurement Regulation

Historically, the UK did not adopt dedicated legislation to regulate the award of public contracts. There was not even legislation equivalent to the directory rules found in the EU procurement Directives.[2] Before the full transposition of the EU Directives into UK law, the main statutory requirements were contained in the Local Government Acts. For instance, the Local Government Act 1972 (which remains in force today) provides in section 135 that a local authority (but not other public bodies) must issue 'standing orders' with respect to the making of contracts. These must include provision for securing competition for such contracts and for regulating the manner in which tenders are invited. However, as Arrowsmith has observed, whilst there is a legal duty to comply with this legislation, it has not generated significant enforcement activity by suppliers.[3] Further, the Local Government Act 1988 (also still in force) provides in section 17 for certain restrictions on the extent to which local authorities may take into account non-commercial considerations in procurement.

Rather, much procurement was governed by internal instructions and suggestions for best practice which have been described as 'regulatory rules'.[4] These were initially issued by HM Treasury's Central Unit on Procurement in the 1980s and 1990s, a function passed to the OGC in 1999 and then to the CCS. This combination of more limited hard-law regulation (in contrast to traditions in civil law countries) and soft law reflects 'a conscious policy choice in the modern era based on an appropriate balance between rules and discretion'.[5] Again, as Arrowsmith has observed:

> This 'philosophy' of public procurement views public procurement more as a commercial and professional function than a bureaucratic one, seeking to learn from the private sector while at the same time recognising the distinct character and values of the public sector.[6]

In other words, the UK has sought to avoid a highly bureaucratic system involving prescriptive hard-law rules in favour of flexibility, allowing the exercise of discretion and trusting the professional judgement of procurement officers to balance commercial and public sector considerations.

However, this philosophy has arguably been called into question in the context of frameworks. It has been a case of relying extensively on the private sector to conduct procurement and replicating commercial and market behaviours that compromise the distinct character and values of the public sector. Further, in the absence of overly prescriptive hard-law rules, it might have been expected that there would, as a minimum,

[2] For a general history of the UK's approach to regulating public procurement, see S Arrowsmith, 'The Evolution of Procurement Law in the United Kingdom: A Common Law Perspective on Regulating Contract Award Procedures', 12 April 2024, SSRN. Available at papers.ssrn.com/sol3/papers.cfm?abstract_id=4756144.

[3] ibid 12.

[4] ibid.

[5] ibid 15.

[6] ibid.

be high-quality guidance but this has not materialised despite repeated calls for it. It is difficult to find many convincing arguments to justify or excuse this, even acknowledging the UK's lighter touch approach to regulation in the common law tradition.

It was not until the 1990s that the UK implemented EU Directives into UK law.[7] The UK adopted a 'copy-out' approach which implemented their detailed procedural rules but did not introduce further hard-law rules prescribing statutory objectives or supplemental rules for the procurement system. As will be discussed, 'the domestic objectives, such as commercial value and integrity, were left to the traditional approach'.[8] Nevertheless, the implementation of EU law effectuated a profound change in the UK, creating a 'new public procurement culture' and 'industry'.[9]

Notwithstanding, the UK has not become a particularly litigious procurement culture, unlike some countries which experience hundreds or thousands of cases each year[10] (although, in 2024, procurement disputes were at a record number (79) up 39 per cent from 2023[11]). As discussed in chapter nine, only a limited number of cases have involved frameworks.

2.2. Objectives of UK Procurement Legislation

Given that much of the UK's hard-law regulation has derived from EU Directives, which, it is recalled from chapter three, are predicated on trade objectives, the question arises of what are the UK's own domestic objectives for procurement and its regulation beyond giving effect to EU objectives because of its own interest in securing the benefits of trade. As Arrowsmith has observed, as the UK's system was largely limited to doing the minimum required to give effect to EU legal requirements, its own system 'was far from comprehensive in its objectives and scope, as well as in the detail and content of its obligations and, consequently, the limits placed on discretion',[12] leaving much to be addressed by the traditional 'soft law' approach and affording discretion within the boundaries set by the EU rules.[13]

Often, it is claimed that the objective of UK procurement law and policy, is the pursuit of 'value for money'. For example, the NAO has stated that:

> [p]ublic sector procurement in the UK is subject to a legal framework which is intended to encourage value for money and free and open competition, in line with internationally and nationally agreed obligations and regulations.[14]

However, this should be clarified because there is little indication that procurement in the UK has either of these as its *principal* or main objective.

[7] Public Works Contracts 1991 SI 1991/2680 and Public Supply Contracts Regulations 1991 SI 1991/2679.

[8] Arrowsmith (n 2) 22.

[9] ibid 21.

[10] S Arrowsmith and R Craven, 'Public procurement and access to justice: a legal and empirical study of the UK system' (2016) 25 *PPLR* 227.

[11] Solomonic, 2024 Year in Review, Litigation trends in the English High Court and the Competition Appeal Tribunal 2025, 11.

[12] Arrowsmith (n 2) 2.

[13] ibid 33.

[14] NAO, *Efficiency in government procurement of common goods and services*, CCS, Session 2024–25 HC 116, 5.

First, as indicated, much UK regulation derives from EU law and which does not have value for money as its central objective. Occasionally, it is said that the EU law rule on the 'most economically advantageous tender' and 'best price-quality ratio'[15] reflects value for money considerations. However, the UK's implementation of such rules is simply an example of it aligning its approach with the EU (as confirmed below) rather than adopting any such specific domestic objective. To confirm, as discussed in chapter three, the objective of the Directives is not to secure value for money even if their application can have this effect. For example, rules that prevent discrimination and remove market access barriers may increase the range of suppliers able to make competitive offers that, in turn, may lead to lower prices and/or better quality. However, it is equally possible to conceive of ways in which such rules in pursuit of EU objectives could place constraints on discretion which may undermine value for money.

Second, although the UK has adopted policy guidance which, in relation to public spending, refers to the objective of securing value for money, such policies do not specifically concern processes for awarding public contracts or make characteristically vague statements about the objectives of UK procurement. Thus, Managing Public Money, a HM Treasury-issued document identifying the main principles for dealing with resources in public sector organisations in the UK, states that 'it is important to secure value for money in asset management through sound procurement' and that 'public sector organisations should normally acquire goods and services through fair and open competition, acting on Cabinet Office advice'.[16] It continues that:

> Good procurement practice demands that public sector organisations buy the goods, works and service they need using fair and open procurement processes, guarding against corruption and meeting the standards in MPM. European Union (EU) law and World Trade Organisation (WTO) agreements underpin these principles.[17]

However, the above speaks only in vague terms. It is inaccurate to state that EU law underpins value for money because the application of EU law may curtail discretion in ways that can compromise the achievement of value for money. Moreover, as indicated in chapter three, it is questionable whether even the EU has as its objective 'free and open competition'. It is also possible to identify instances in which free and open competition is most certainly not government policy. For example, in the context of defence procurement a pre-Brexit 'global competition by default' policy (in place whilst the UK was an EU Member State complying with EU procurement Directives) has been replaced with one focusing on long-term strategic partnerships reliant primarily on single source procurement.[18]

Third, the notion that UK procurement and its regulation seeks to achieve value for money is not readily apparent from the legislation regulating *procurement*. This should be distinguished from legislation that does not specifically concern the process of awarding contracts but may impose statutory duties on public authorities when exercising

[15] See Recital 89 and Article 67 Directive 2014/24/EU.

[16] HM Treasury (2018) *Managing Public Money*, 114–119, Annex 4.6.

[17] ibid 114.

[18] HM Government, *Defence and Security Industrial Strategy: A strategic approach to the UK's defence and security industrial sectors*, CP 410 March 2021, 6.

public functions, which include procurement. For instance, section 3 Local Government Act 1999 provides that local authorities and other public bodies have a duty to 'make arrangements to secure continuous improvement in the way in which its functions are exercised, having regard to a combination of economy, efficiency and effectiveness'. This is *not* specific to procurement but covers value for money in all spending decisions and is referred to as the 'best value' regime.[19] Another example is the Public Services (Social Value) Act 2012 which concerns statutory duties applicable to contracting authorities when proposing to procure or making arrangements for procuring. Section 1 provides that if a relevant authority procures services by entering into a public services contract or concluding a framework agreement, it must consider: (a) how what is proposed to be procured might improve the economic, social and environmental well-being of the relevant area, and (b) how, in conducting the procurement process, it might act with a view to securing that improvement.

The upshot is that it is not clear precisely what are the objectives of the UK procurement system and how these are given effect through regulation. As discussed below, the *Transforming Public Procurement* Green Paper which precipitated the PA 2023 identified a range of different objectives but which were not clearly articulated. Further, the PA 2023 includes a statutory requirement in section 12 to have regard to certain 'objectives', including value for money, but their scope, content and effect are not well defined. Moreover, there seems to be some confusion on the distinction between 'objectives' and 'principles' that has not been satisfactorily resolved, with some duties and obligations in section 12 reading more like general legal principles of the kind featured under EU law (eg, equal treatment and transparency) but are not expressed in identical terms (eg, same treatment and sharing of information). Importantly, there has been no clear indication of how these objectives or principles may be given effect and balanced in the event of potential conflict. For instance, as discussed below, guidance on covered procurement objectives states that the PA 2023 does not intend for any of the objectives (citing value for money as an example) to disapply, override or take precedence over the obligation to have regard to the other objectives. Equally, the new NPPS states that value for money is always the overarching priority in procurement. Also, significantly, there has been no committed view as to the role of 'competition', eg whether this should be treated as an aspect of securing value for money or some other objective (eg, maximising public benefit). What is apparent is that there is no distinct principle of 'competition' of the kind which has been argued to exist under EU law, as discussed in chapter three.

Such discussion of objectives can be related to concerns raised in this book for several reasons. As indicated in chapter three, the above means that whatever criticism can be made of UK Regulations in failing to secure value for money, including in the context of frameworks, it cannot be claimed that this is largely attributable to EU Directives as this is not their objective. Similarly, it cannot be said that UK regulation reflects a strong commitment to the pursuit of domestic objectives that are not being upheld when frameworks are being used. Importantly, the lack of a clear policy vision and legal certainty regarding the domestic objectives of the UK procurement system may have implications going forward.

[19] See generally, Ministry of Housing, Communities & Local Government and Department for Levelling Up Housing & Communities, *Statutory guidance, Best value standards and intervention: a statutory guide for best value authorities*, 8 May 2024.

For example, is it clear what are the objectives for the use of frameworks under the post-Brexit procurement system and what are the objectives of the new rules on frameworks under the PA 2023? To what extent must the new rules on frameworks be applied in consideration of the new section 12 statutory objectives under the PA 2023? Will they need to be interpreted and applied in consideration of their effects on competition, even though competition is not an express statutory objective? As indicated in chapter three, recent post-Brexit UK case law has suggested that the 'purpose' of procurement regulation in the UK includes 'promoting the development of healthy and effective competition'.[20] In practical terms, will the interpretation of objectives constrain how rules on frameworks are applied, or, indeed, allow even more flexible use in practice? It is recalled from chapter three that a principle of competition could limit contracting authority discretion when applying framework rules such as on setting the maximum duration of a framework. More generally, to what extent should rules on frameworks (and centralised purchasing) be designed to require consideration of their anti-competitive effects? The PA 2023, for example, does not include an equivalent rule found in Directive 2004/18/EC regarding the prohibition on improper use of frameworks or use such as to prevent, restrict or distort competition. Thus, understanding the objectives of the regulated procurement system is important when thinking about the regulatory regime on frameworks and its reform.

2.3. EU-derived Domestic Procurement Legislation

As discussed in chapter three, it was not until Directive 2004/18/EC (as implemented in the PCR 2006) that the EU introduced specific provisions on frameworks. It follows that the UK had not previously adopted detailed legislation or policy on frameworks.[21] It is recalled that the UK's early practice and position on proposals for the adoption and/or reform of the Directives had been to ensure flexibility as regards their availability and use. Indeed, it has been suggested that 'the UK's concerns to ensure adequate flexibility to implement a commercial approach, where appropriate' had 'substantially influenced developments in the EU legislation from 2004 onwards', citing, in particular, explicit provisions on framework agreements as reflecting the influence of UK practice prior to the 2004 reforms.[22] In transposing the EU procurement Directives into UK law, the UK Government's position was one of 'maximising flexibility in the rules, deregulating where possible, and avoiding gold-plating'.[23] Therefore, the UK Government would not extend regulation beyond the minimum required by the Directives.[24]

[20] *Optima Health v Secretary of State for Work and Pensions* [2025] EWCA Civ 127, para 59.

[21] On the historical context, see S Arrowsmith, 'Methods for purchasing ongoing requirements: the system of framework agreements and dynamic purchasing systems under the EC Directives and UK procurement regulations' in S Arrowsmith and J Tillipman (eds), *Public Procurement Regulation in the 21st Century: Reform of the UNCITRAL Model Law on Procurement* (West, 2010/11).

[22] Arrowsmith (n 2) 19.

[23] Cabinet Office, 'Consultation Document, UK Transposition of new EU Procurement Directives Public Contracts Regulations 2015' (undated) 3. Available at assets.publishing.service.gov.uk/media/5a7ed2bf40f0b62305b8366f/Consultation_Document_UK_Transposition_of_new_EU_Procurement_Directives_Public_Contracts_Regulations_2015.pdf.

[24] On the general approach to transposition, see Department for Business Innovation & Skills, 'Gold-Plating Review, The Operation of the Transposition Principles in the Government's Guiding Principles for EU Legislation', March 2013.

However, it is questionable whether this copy-out approach was sufficient justification for the UK Government to adopt no further substantive rules or policies on frameworks. For instance, there are certain market-related features of frameworks (and centralised purchasing) that were not explicitly regulated by the EU Directives and where domestic rules or policies might have been adopted that either did not engage EU law issues or which could have been compatible with EU law. As discussed below, the UK Government also chose not to implement further options that were available to it under the Directives.

2.3.1. Implementation of Directive 2004/18/EC

In the OGC consultation on the implementation of Directive 2004/18/EC several general observations were made about implementing Article 32 on frameworks:

> A framework agreement, in this context, is a general term for agreements with economic operators which set out terms and conditions under which specific purchases (call-offs) can be made throughout the term of the agreement. Such a framework agreement is not a contract to which the Directives naturally apply. It is only at the call-off stage that a contract is formed in EC terms. However, under Article 32, the framework agreement is, itself, treated as a contract for the purposes of advertising, selection and award procedures, so that these procedures do not have to be applied to each call-off. There are specific rules, in the new Article, for calling-off under a framework. These include rules on so-called 'mini-competitions', a situation where the basic terms of the framework are not precise enough for a particular call-off and a competition is run within the framework to find the supplier most capable of meeting the refined terms.[25]

The UK stated that it had been pressing for explicit recognition of frameworks in the Directive and felt that 'this provision fully meets our objectives and is in line with our current practice'.[26]

The above reflects the uncertainty at both the EU and domestic level as to when a contract arises in a framework. Notwithstanding, the UK clearly understood the firm conception that a framework agreement *qua* contract involves procedures for selection and award which should be complete at the point of establishment and which set precise terms; mini-competitions were possible where the basic terms of the framework were insufficiently precise and needed refinement Ultimately, as discussed in chapter three, the PCR 2006 replicated the Article 2(1) Directive 2004/18/EC definition of a framework in regulation 2(1) PCR 2006, except that it referred to 'an agreement or other arrangement' as opposed to only an 'agreement'. This seemingly acknowledged that some frameworks may not be formally legally binding from the outset but which nevertheless required an upfront competition to establish the terms for call-offs, as indicated. This can be taken as the historical reference point against which to appraise how the UK's understanding of frameworks and practice evolved. However, even in 2004, it was questionable whether the UK had clear objectives in respect of the use and regulation of frameworks. It was also not verified whether the UK's 'current practice' at that time actually reflected that conception of a regulated framework. This should be considered

[25] OGC, 'Consultation Document, The Approach to Implementation of the New Public Sector Procurement Directive', May 2004, 11.

[26] ibid.

against the backdrop of the UK's questionable use of frameworks being a catalyst for action by the Commission; as early as 2004, concerns were being raised about the involvement of CPAs and the private sector which have clearly impacted understandings of the regulated framework concept. It should also be considered in light of the fact that the UK sought reform of the rules only a decade later, calling into question whether the rules ever met the UK's objectives and practice and, if they did, what changed the UK's view in that intervening period.

Whilst the UK Government appeared content to implement the framework rules in legislation, consultation responses indicated that there was a need for additional guidance on frameworks:

> A number of the specific points raised … cover issues such as categorisation of goods and services within a framework, aspects of running a mini competition, the use of negotiation at the call-off stage, the implications of the length and size of frameworks for SMEs, the contracting out of services under framework agreements, further clarity on what constitutes 'exceptional circumstances' for agreeing a framework of more than four years, whether the four year limit provides for extension options beyond four years and difficulties in estimating potential uptake of a framework. All of these issues will be considered in drafting new guidance on framework agreements at the appropriate time.[27]

It may be added that, in another consultation document, the OGC added the need for guidance on 'the use of pricing mechanisms',[28] and the response to consultation on draft regulations identified a range of further guidance that was to be given.[29]

It appears, therefore, that stakeholders had little objection to the legal rules on frameworks but required further guidance on implementing some aspects of the rules and on the practicalities of framework set-up and operation. However, it does not appear that all of the above were ever systematically addressed in guidance, as distinct from guidance explaining basic interpretations of the rules. As discussed in Part III, many of the above issues continue to arise in practice today and in respect of which there are continuing calls for guidance. Further, the practice highlighted in Part III calls into question whether any guidance would have adequately addressed these issues and more without further legal regulation.

Further, whilst there seemed to be no major objections to the new rules on frameworks, there was continuing ambivalence about whether the legal rules were suitable and whether certain matters should be addressed by regulations as distinct from guidance. Thus, in response to another consultation on draft regulations implementing Directive 2004/18/EC, several conflicting views were expressed on the definition of framework agreements and whether a framework agreement can be a contract. This issue is discussed in more detail in chapter five. The OGC accepted that it is possible for a framework agreement to be a contract, for example, where it places an obligation

[27] OGC, 'Response to Consultation on the New Procurement Directives' (undated) 8. Available through the National Archives at webarchive.nationalarchives.gov.uk/ukgwa/20100303181810/http://www.ogc.gov.uk/procurement_policy_and_application_of_eu_rules_european_procurement_directives.asp.

[28] OGC, 'Consultation document, Draft Regulations Implementing the new Public Sector and Utilities Procurement Directives', June 2005, 15.

[29] OGC, 'Response to Consultation, Draft Regulations Implementing the new Public Sector and Utilities Procurement Directives', December 2005, 9.

on the contracting authority to purchase requirements for pecuniary interest and for it to be treated the same as any other contract under the EU rules. It considered that the Article 32 provisions were meant to apply to framework agreements which were not themselves contracts as defined by the Directive. It also acknowledged a suggestion that a framework agreement which does not place an obligation to purchase requirements for pecuniary interest could still be a contract under UK law; the OGC agreed that this is possible but stated that it may still not be a public contract for goods, works or services falling within the scope of the EU rules.[30] Thus, the circumstances in which a framework agreement gave rise to a contract and whether the general rules of the Directives or the specific rules on frameworks applied, remained unclear. Also, interestingly, certain responses suggested that guidelines on mini-competitions should be set out in the regulations rather than accompanying guidance; however, the OGC rejected this possibility as doing so 'could inadvertently reduce the flexibility within the provision represented in the Directive text'.[31] Therefore, stakeholders were alive to the possibility of introducing further hard-law rules instead of guidance, or a combination.

The OGC also made certain observations in respect of the introduction of Article 11 on central purchasing, explained in chapter three. It stated that this provision resolved doubt apparently cast on the use of CPAs by the CJEU ruling in *Teckal*[32] on 'in-house' arrangements in which it was held that contracts concluded between legally distinct bodies, one of which was controlled by the other, were subject to the Directives for their award, unless that control was similar to that exercised over internal departments and the controlled body carried out the essential part of its activities with the controlling body.[33] It also stated that:

> it is worth stressing that this particular Article only applies to central purchasing bodies, as defined in the Article. Currently contracting authorities may also be making use of agents and private sector bodies for obtaining goods and services. This Article does not change the situation or procedure with regard to these bodies i.e. the contracting authority is still responsible for ensuring compliance with the provisions of the public procurement Directives when using these other bodies.[34]

Thus, as early as 2004, the UK Government was aware of the use of private sector agents. However, whilst mentioning the contracting authority's legal responsibility, the OGC did not categorically address some of the legal and practical issues that may arise and clearly did not deter inappropriate private sector involvement in framework set-up and management. For instance, in 2008, it had been observed that non-public bodies had not been decisively prevented from acting as 'de facto' CPAs which sought to circumvent the definition of a contracting authority by being appointed as agents, amongst other means.[35]

[30] ibid 8–9.
[31] ibid10.
[32] Case C-107/98 *Teckal Srl* ECLI:EU:C:1999:562, [1999] ECR I-8121.
[33] OGC (n 25) 8.
[34] ibid.
[35] J Chard, G Duhs and J Houlden, 'Body beautiful or vile bodies? Central purchasing in the UK' (2008) 2 *PPLR* NA26, 27.

In consultation responses, no respondents expressly objected to full implementation of Article 11. However, several concerns and queries were raised, some of which were legal, some practical, and certain of which remain relevant today.[36]

First, there was confusion about the legal status of CPAs referring to 'joint ventures' and 'virtual consortiums' and about the arrangements between contracting authorities and CPAs.[37] The OGC stated that the regulations would not be able to change or broaden the Article 1(9) and (10) definitions of contracting authorities and CPAs as this would go beyond the Directives' text, and that whether a body is a CPA would depend in each case on the legal status and their activities and intended purpose, the key issue being that the CPA must be a contracting authority. It did not elaborate on how matters such as 'activities and intended purpose' might be determined.[38] As will be discussed, the PA 2023 has brought into sharper focus the essential nature of a CPA in introducing a new definition of a 'centralised procurement authority' but which is no clearer in determining a CPA's status or activities.

Second, it was questioned how should CPAs organise frameworks in a manner compliant with the rules, eg whether a contracting authority can join a CPA framework if this was not provisioned when the framework was set up.[39] It was observed that a CPA, as a contracting authority itself, must apply the rules on frameworks set out in Article 32 and that the need to identify the authorities that will make use of the framework at the time it is set up 'using generic or specific names of the authorities concerned' applies whether it is a CPA awarding the framework or another contracting authority.[40] It also noted some concern that CPA-run frameworks blurred the distinction between: (a) the selection process for the framework; (b) the evaluation process for the award of the framework; and (c) the evaluation process for the award of the contract. There was also concern that contracting authorities could not join CPA frameworks if they were not party to the arrangement when the framework was established. As indicated in chapter five and discussed in chapter seven, the issue of who can join a framework and how this is provided for was subsequently the subject of EU litigation.

Third, concern was expressed that a new provision on CPAs would mean a move towards bulk buying, compromising quality and the ability of SMEs to compete.[41] In response, it was stated that circumstances will arise where buying through CPAs is 'the best option on value for money, and the Regulations should therefore allow for this option' but that 'in other cases, an individual contract or framework awarded by the authority might be more appropriate', and that the implementation of the Directives was not an appropriate vehicle for addressing these decisions, the Directives simply allowing for all of these possibilities.[42] Relatedly, it was suggested by certain respondents that there should be a requirement to publish below-threshold contracts on a national basis to balance the disadvantage of CPAs for SMEs. In response, the OGC stated that below-threshold procurement was not addressed in Directive 2004/18/EC but noted that the

[36] OGC (n 27) 2.
[37] ibid 3.
[38] ibid.
[39] ibid.
[40] ibid.
[41] ibid.
[42] ibid.

issue of advertising below-threshold contracts was being considered generally in the context of EC Treaty obligations and in relation to support for SMEs.[43] These responses therefore indicated that if legislation was going to allow free choice between procurement options, there was a need for guidance to help make an informed choice between the use of CPA frameworks and other procurement options, as well as an early awareness of the potential for aggregated procurement to affect market access, particularly, for SMEs.

Finally, respondents suggested that Article 11 'disadvantages private sector agents' by giving CPAs 'an unfair advantage'. In response, it was stated that:

> This Article is not addressing the issue of using private sector agents which buy on behalf of contracting authorities, and for which such authorities are therefore contracting directly with the suppliers. Where a body, which is not a contracting authority, purchases on behalf of a contracting authority, it is the contracting authority which is ultimately responsible for ensuring that the EC rules are applied. This article is covering the situation in which a contracting authority is, itself, acting as a central purchasing body. It makes clear that, where contracting authorities purchase from or through such bodies, they will be deemed to have complied with the requirements of the Directive where the CPB, as a contracting authority itself, has complied with them. It is not clear why this can be seen as an advantage in relation to the use of private sector agents which are acting on behalf of contracting authorities. The two situations are different.[44]

This indicated early on a concern expressed about the legal and market implications of CPAs offering their services *vis-à-vis* private sector organisations offering the same. It is interesting to observe the apparent concern over the disadvantages for private sector agents rather than any impact on the public interest.

In another consultation document, it was acknowledged that many respondents wanted guidance on CPAs on 'the mechanics for setting up' a CPA in practice, on the need for transparency, and on whether contracting authorities 'still need to enter into direct contractual arrangements' when using a CPA.[45] As discussed below, some limited guidance on centralised purchasing was introduced in 2008.

2.3.2. UK Submissions for Reform of Directive 2004/18/EC

In 2011, the UK Government published a response to the European Commission's Green Paper on modernisation of EU public procurement policy.[46] It observed that frameworks, DPS, approved supplier lists and qualification systems (in the utilities sector) exist to achieve a similar set of objectives, namely, providing opportunities to reduce the detailed bureaucracy of applying the full set of the procedural rules in certain situations, thereby facilitating faster, more efficient and/or less costly procurement processes. However, it considered that there are many inherent problems with the design, scope or limitations imposed by the existing rules and there was a 'compelling

[43] ibid.
[44] ibid.
[45] OGC (n 29) 5.
[46] United Kingdom response to the European Commission Green paper on the modernisation of EU public procurement policy (COM (2011) 15 final).

case' for merging and simplifying the range into a smaller, more permissive and more flexible set of provisions.[47] Particular problems with framework agreements were not singled out in this regard. Instead, two broad (although not unequivocal) alternatives were suggested.

The first was a preference for a single, highly flexible 'purchasing system' enabling prospective procurement to be advertised upfront without having to be re-competed and which could bear similar hallmarks to a framework, DPS, qualification system or approved list but with 'none of the apparent defects'. More specifically, this system would include five options. The first would be to make specific contracts from the system without any further publication of notices by either competing the requirement amongst relevant suppliers on the system or by applying the contract award terms that had been agreed when the system was set up.[48] The second was to use mini-competitions for contracts where some of the award terms have been previously agreed, or more intensive competitions using any of the existing procurement procedures (including negotiated procedure and competitive dialogue) if award terms have not been previously established and if the requirement fell above the relevant EU threshold. The third would be to make the system open to new competition or closed to initially successful applicants, with the option to periodically reopen it to EU-wide competition via a notice. The fourth would be to run the system for up to seven years in the case of closed systems (as for frameworks in Directive 2009/81/EC on defence and security procurement), although open systems would not be subject to any time limits provided there was an obligation for incumbent suppliers to be reassessed periodically (eg. every seven years). The fifth was to determine whether and to what extent electronic or non-electronic means should be used to establish and make contracts under these systems.[49]

The second alternative proposal was to make qualification systems available in the public sector and remove DPS.[50]

As indicated, no specific defects were noted in respect of the rules on frameworks. Rather, it was simply stated that '[f]ramework agreements are extremely useful but have one drawback: they are closed systems, which can limit competition over the life of the framework, locking out new and potentially innovative suppliers'.[51] Therefore, the UK Government suggested that any new tool should enable (but not require) frameworks to be 'open' to new entrants over the life of the framework. It continued that any concerns the Commission might have over competition or transparency could be easily overcome by a periodic notice (eg, six-monthly or annually) which re-advertised the framework across the EU.[52]

Thus, the UK Government sought a reconceptualisation of the available purchasing systems but largely along a framework model, including the possibility of open frameworks. The above proposals are interesting when considered in retrospect given the provisions adopted under the PA 2023. The above suggested a maximum duration

[47] ibid 8.

[48] If such terms had been set up, which would make the system more like a framework agreement. Had they not, the system would be more like a qualification system or DPS. ibid 9.

[49] ibid.

[50] ibid 9–10.

[51] ibid 10.

[52] ibid.

for closed frameworks of seven years; however, the PA 2023 adopts the same four-year maximum duration rule as under the PCR 2015. No explanation was provided as to why Directive 2009/81/EC should be taken as the model for the public sector. Further, the PA 2023 introduces the possibility of setting up open frameworks but, again, the policy justification for introducing it remains unclear.

In addition, in the UK's submission, the Government expressed concern about the lack of flexibility regarding award criteria relating to the tenderer in contracts involving services where an individual or team with a specific skill set is being purchased (management consultancy, professional services etc), giving a framework for consultancy as an example.[53] The problem was that award criteria could not generally be used as a basis for assessing the tenderer (as distinct from the tender), the tenderer being assessed according to earlier selection criteria. The UK's view was that the authority would need to examine the tenderer's experience as part of the selection criteria, perhaps examining the range of skills sets of the various consultants employed by the tenderer, but when it came to making call-offs, it was imperative that the authority should be able to consider the skills of the specific individual(s) that the consultancy proposed to deliver the work, in order to ensure that they would get the best person(s) for the job. It reasoned that if authorities cannot examine skills and experience in this way, they cannot validate whether the consultancy has put forward people with relevant skills and make an objective comparison between the different tenderers' offerings. It therefore called for the skills and quality of service providers to be taken into account, where appropriate, at the award stage.[54] This appeared to be addressed by Article 67(2)(b) Directive 2014/24/EU / regulation 67(3)(b) PCR 2015 indicating that award criteria may comprise organisation, qualification and experience of staff assigned to performing the contract, where the quality of the staff assigned can have a significant impact on the level of performance.

Conversely, the UK Government did not appear to raise any specific issues of its own initiative in respect of centralised purchasing.

Thus, paradoxically, whilst the UK was prepared to make radical submissions to reform the EU regulated framework model, it was not prepared to act to improve the implementation of EU rules domestically or adopt further rules and practices to address various issues raised in consultations.

2.3.3. Implementation of Directive 2014/24/EU

Following the adoption of Directive 2014/24/EU, the UK Government further consulted on its implementation in the PCR 2015.[55] Regulation 33 PCR 2015 transposed and largely replicated Article 33 Directive 2014/24/EU on frameworks, explored in Part III of this book. The consultation did not focus on frameworks but rather on areas where there was scope for further potential implementation measures, including in respect of centralised purchasing. In this regard, Article 37(1) provides that Member States may provide that certain procurements are to be made by having recourse to CPAs or to

[53] ibid 12.
[54] ibid 13 and 23.
[55] Cabinet Office (n 23).

one or more specific CPAs. The UK Government chose not to implement the option to mandate that CPAs (or specific CPAs) must be used for certain procurements.

Early pre-consultation stakeholder feedback indicated that there was a continued need for flexibility to enable use of CPAs for particular procurements but did not offer specific reasoning in this regard.[56] It did not indicate whether there was any stakeholder feedback on the possibility of mandating that certain CPAs must be used for certain procurements. This may be contrasted with pre-consultation stakeholder feedback on whether a limit should be placed on using CPAs in other Member States, which indicated that this would have the potential to 'harm value for money'.[57] Respondents agreed that the PCR 2015 should not mandate use of CPAs, some simply objecting and others expecting that any such proposal should be subject to consultation; again, no specific reasons for these views were published.[58] The Government's response was that it would continue to provide the flexibility to use CPAs but not mandate the use of vspecific CPAs for certain procurements.[59] Importantly, it qualified, however, that as the Directive allows Member States to decide on whether to mandate the use of specific CPAs, 'it would be wrong for the Government to rule out the possibility of doing so in future in the pursuit of better value for money for the taxpayer' and would consult on any such proposal.[60] It did not appear to ever reopen this to consultation, including in the *Transforming Public Procurement* consultations.

One respondent also called for guidance on whether private bodies can act as CPAs.[61] In response, the Government gave its interpretation of the Directive as that it is not possible for anything other than a 'contracting body' to act as a CPA and that 'a private provider would not normally fall within the definition of a contracting authority'.[62] This call for guidance should be considered in light of the fact that, as discussed below, by this point, there was guidance in circulation, warning of the role of non-contracting authorities seeking to set up frameworks in 2010, ie before the 2015 consultation. This may suggest that the guidance did not provide adequate clarification. Nor was the Government's response here categorical. For instance, if its assessment was that a private provider would not 'normally' fall within the definition of a contracting authority, it did not indicate any circumstances in which it might do so.

2.4. Non-EU-derived Domestic Public Procurement Legislation

As indicated, the UK has adopted some domestic legislation that may apply to the exercise of public functions generally, of which procurement is one. As discussed, examples include the so-called best value regime and the Public Services (Social Value) Act 2012.

[56] ibid 25.

[57] ibid.

[58] Cabinet Office, 'Government Response to the Consultation on UK Transposition of new EU Procurement Directives Public Contracts Regulations 2015' (undated) 11. Available at assets.publishing.service.gov.uk/media/5a80afa8ed915d74e33fbd55/Government_Response_to_the_Consultation_on_UK_Transposition_of_new_EU_Procurement_Directives_Public_Contracts_Regulations_2015.pdf.

[59] ibid.

[60] ibid.

[61] ibid.

[62] ibid 12.

There are certain limited exceptions, however, where the Government has enacted legislation concerning procurement which does not derive from EU law. For instance, Part 4 PCR 2015 was introduced to implement a set of exclusively domestic reforms, known as the Lord Young reforms.[63] These were designed primarily to improve SME access to procurement and essentially comprised: (1) abolition of a pre-qualification stage for procurements below the EU thresholds, as well as a requirement to have regard to guidance on qualitative selection for above EU threshold procurements; (2) a requirement for contracting authorities to insert provisions in all public contracts to ensure prompt payment through the supply chain; and (3) the requirement to advertise as many contract opportunities as possible in one place (on Contracts Finder, a national portal), and publish award notices for contracts and call-offs from frameworks.[64] However, whilst seeking to introduce further transparency, this was not intended to significantly improve framework contracting.

Further, in accordance with plans to aggregate procurement by the police service, the Police Act 1999 (Equipment) Regulations 2011 were introduced to mandate use of certain frameworks by police forces when purchasing certain types of equipment.[65] The regulations were never enacted. This example is perhaps symptomatic of the lack of strategic vision for the use and regulation of frameworks and other purchasing systems in the UK.

More generally, broader legislation applies which may have some bearing on procurement, including frameworks. For instance, the Public Services (Social Value) Act 2012 introduces a statutory duty to consider social value which applies to the concluding of frameworks for services. The UK Government has issued various policies and guidance on social value that are not specifically directed at frameworks but which are included within their scope. An example is the Social Value Model published in association with PPN 06/20,[66] requiring social value to be explicitly evaluated in all central government procurement, where the requirements are related and proportionate to the subject-matter of the contract. Guidance stipulates that a framework 'should always enable users to explicitly evaluate for social value' both at framework agreement level and for all call-offs (by mini-competition or direct award).[67] However, as discussed in chapter five, concerns are expressed in the empirical research about the difficulty of trying to secure social value in frameworks.

It should be added that contracting authorities must also comply with their own organisational rules and policies on procurement. As indicated, these may be termed 'standing orders' or, alternatively, 'contract procedure rules', 'financial regulations' or 'financial instructions'. These might include policies on using frameworks, even mandating the use of certain frameworks for some requirements.

[63] Lord Young, 'Growing Your Business, A Report on Growing Micro Businesses, The second part of the report on small firms', May 2013.

[64] CCS, 'Procurement Policy Note – Reforms to make public procurement more accessible to SMEs', Information Note 03/15, 18 February 2015.

[65] SI 2011/300.The schedule to the Regulations sets out the different frameworks to be used to purchase body armour, police vehicles, IT commoditised hardware and IT commercial off-the-shelf software.

[66] Cabinet Office, 'Procurement Policy Note – Taking Account of Social Value in the Award of Central Government Contracts' Action Note PPN 06/20, September 2020.

[67] See GCF, 'Guide to Using the Social Value Model, Edition 1.1 – 3 Dec 20', 24 September 2020, 16.

3. Policy Guidance

As discussed, given the historical tendency to avoid detailed hard-law regulation of procurement, the policy preference has been to govern procurement (particularly within central government) using policy guidance. Such guidance may be designed to further broad policy agendas which may or may not be specific to procurement, to specifically implement procurement policy, to provide exposition or interpretation of legislation, or to disseminate good or best practice. Importantly, in respect of UK Regulations implementing EU Directives, whilst basic guidance was issued on the interpretation of certain provisions, including on frameworks, there had been no detailed dedicated guidance on the law and practice of frameworks, despite consistent calls for such in the consultations on implementation, as discussed.

Much of the procurement guidance has tended to be driven top-down by central government and directed to 'in-scope' central government departments but with an expectation that it sets the standard across the public sector.

It may be said that the guidance has tended to be *ad hoc*, giving effect to specific procurement policies or issues of the day and requiring certain action. By contrast, expository or interpretative guidance on the UK Regulations implementing the EU Directives was very limited and largely only issued at the point of implementation without subsequent updates.

3.1. Guidance on Frameworks

Both the European Commission and UK Government have issued interpretative guidance addressing frameworks in general terms. In 2005, the European Commission issued its Explanatory Note – Frameworks – Classic Directive.[68] In 2008, the UK Government issued its own guidance,[69] which will be considered when analysing the provisions of the PCR 2015 in later chapters. Suffice to state, the guidance is high-level and has raised its own interpretative issues. Basic updated CCS guidance was provided in 2016[70] but was not updated again before the introduction of the PA 2023.

The legal status of guidance and whether it incurs any compliance-related legal obligations has become the subject of litigation, specifically concerning policies on publication of contract awards and contracts during the COVID-19 pandemic. In one case, it was held that there is a common law duty to comply with prescribed policies unless there is good reason for departing from them.[71]

As indicated, most UK policy guidance focuses on topical issues and which often takes the form of updates rather than addressing many new areas. These procurement

[68] European Commission Explanatory Note – Frameworks – Classic Directive CC/2005/03, 14 July 2005.

[69] OGC, 'Frameworks: OGC Guidance on Frameworks in the Procurement Regulations', September 2008. Accessible at webarchive.nationalarchives.gov.uk/ukgwa/20100609095129/http://www.ogc.gov.uk/procurement_policy_and_application_of_eu_rules_guidance_on_the_UK_regulations.asp.

[70] CCS, 'The Public Contracts Regulations 2015 & The Utilities Contracts Regulations 2016 Guidance on Framework Agreements', updated October 2016.

[71] *R (Good Law Project Ltd & ors) v Secretary of State for Health and Social Care* [2021] EWHC 346 (Admin), para 132.

policy guidance documents typically take the form of very short Procurement Policy Notes ('PPNs') on a range of topical issues and which are published with increasing frequency. As they apply to procurement generally, they will often necessarily have application to frameworks. The OGC originally issued general PPNs, including both (a) information notes, which provided guidance to public sector organisations and industry on public procurement policy issues; and (b) action notes, which required a form of response.[72] CCS has also issued guidance on frameworks under the PCR 2015 although this guidance only addresses a limited number of issues.[73] As indicated in chapter two, CCS is also the main user of frameworks. Whilst it is not the case that CCS policy documents emphasise use of CCS frameworks, CCS has not drawn on its own experience in setting up and operating frameworks to disseminate extensive policy guidance on frameworks that would assist the public sector more widely.

Notwithstanding, a limited number of PPNs have sought to address certain issues specific to frameworks and their set-up. In 2010, PPNs were issued concerning frameworks. The first was Action Note 16/10[74] on ensuring that bodies permitted to use frameworks were adequately identified. This was issued because the European Commission expressed concerns about several frameworks that did not clearly identify permitted users. The second was Action Note 15/10[75] which highlighted the issues and risks of using arrangements described as frameworks but set up by private organisations. PPN 15/10 identified that there had been attempts to set up such frameworks in the energy and other sectors. It observed that compliance of such frameworks with legal requirements could not be shown simply by advertising a framework in a particular way (eg, in the OJEU) or using a particular term such as 'framework agreement' as used in the regulations.[76] It reiterated that the regulations, in particular, the definition of a framework agreement, envisaged a contracting relationship between a contracting authority and economic operators, such that one cannot be set up by an entity that is not a contracting authority.[77] It further stated that a framework could be established if the non-contracting authority was 'acting on behalf of' a contracting authority; in that instance, it would be established for use by that particular and other contracting authorities.[78] It also indicated that where a contracting authority purchased through a CPA under a framework agreement, the CPA would need to comply with the regulations and noted the risk of challenge for failure to do so.[79] However, this guidance introduced some further uncertainty in stating that:

> It is unlikely that an organisation can legitimately promote a contracting arrangement as a framework agreement, which contracting authorities can use, if:
>
> (a) the organisation is not a contracting authority acting *demonstrably* on the instructions of a contracting authority as the authority's agent;

[72] A list of PPNs issued by the OGC between 2006 and 2011 is available at webarchive.nationalarchives.gov.uk/20110405225311/http://www.ogc.gov.uk/procurement_policy_and_application_of_eu_rules_procurement_policy_notes.asp.

[73] CCS (n 70).

[74] OGC, 'Procurement Policy Note – Need to ensure that bodies permitted to use frameworks are adequately identified and clarification is issued if necessary', Action Note 16/10 8 September 2010.

[75] OGC, 'Procurement Policy Note – Use of Frameworks Set Up by Non-Contracting Authorities' Action Note 15/10 12 July 2010.

[76] ibid 2.

[77] ibid.

[78] ibid.

[79] ibid 3.

(b) the terms of any relationship of agency between it and a contracting authority are inconsistent with the requirements of the public procurement rules;
(c) the arrangement was set up at the organisation's initiative, as part of its general business activities/interests with contracting authority participation secured subsequently.[80]

This did not appear to decisively address the issue of private sector involvement in frameworks and seemed to introduce unclear tests or features not found in the regulations such as acting 'demonstrably on the instructions of a contracting authority', the concept of 'agency' and the 'terms of any relationship of agency', and some sort of assessment based on the extent to which an arrangement was at the organisation's initiative, part of a general business activity or interest and the timing at which contracting authority participation was secured. The PPN added that even if a private sector organisation acted as an authorised agent 'within specified parameters for a contracting authority', it could not act outside this scope, stating that:

> If it did so, for example, by seeking to increase its access to public sector customers or gain an advantage over other competitors without going through competitive procurement, this would be inconsistent with the public procurement rules.[81]

Therefore, there was, at least, some acknowledgement of the market exploitation potential of private sector organisations seeking to unlawfully expand the scope of frameworks when acting on behalf of contracting authorities or seeking to secure other competitive advantage. However, it is questionable to what extent this brief guidance was sufficient to deter such practices. As observed, this PPN was published before the subsequent Cabinet Office consultation on the implementation of Directive 2014/24/EU in which calls were reiterated for guidance on private sector involvement in CPAs.

It should be added that, in 2017, the Scottish and Welsh Governments published PPNs on so-called 'speculative framework agreements'[82] involving 'flag of convenience' contracting authorities, described as contracting authorities that commercial organisations may invite to act as the named lead contracting authority in a contract notice for a framework they wish to establish. Such frameworks may have even been set up without any prior consultation of contracting authorities. This raises the question not explored in this book of the extent to which there could be divergence or difference in approach to the treatment of frameworks across the nations of the UK.

In addition to basic interpretative guidance and PPNs on topical issues, the Government has published various 'playbooks' disseminating good procurement practice and intended to apply across central government.[83] Recently, guidance has

[80] ibid. Italics in the original.
[81] ibid 4.
[82] Scottish Government, Speculative framework agreements: SPPN 03/2017 and Welsh Government, Speculative Framework Agreements, Procurement Advice Note (PAN) for the Welsh Public Sector, October 2017. Scotland had earlier issued some guidance on frameworks generally: Scottish Procurement Directorate, Scottish Procurement Policy, Note SPPN 5/2010, Scottish Government Guidance on Framework Agreements, 21 May 2010.
[83] HM Government, 'The Sourcing Playbook, Government guidance on service delivery, including outsourcing, insourcing, mixed economy sourcing and contracting', June 2023; HM Government, 'The Consultancy Playbook, Government guidance on how to commission and engage with consultants more effectively, achieving better outcomes, better value for money and supporting Civil Service capability through the creation of knowledge and skills', Version 1.1 September 2022; HM Government, 'The Construction Playbook, Government Guidance on sourcing and contracting public works projects and programmes', Version 1.1 September 2022; and HM Government, 'The Digital, Data and Technology Playbook, Government guidance on sourcing and contracting for digital, data and technology projects and programmes', June 2023.

been published on how those playbooks may be used in conjunction with framework agreements;[84] however, this has been criticised as being unclear whether it simply provides guidance on good practice or actually seeks to introduce interpretations of legislation that are legally questionable.[85]

As indicated in chapter two, NAO and PAC reports have examined approaches to frameworks in the UK and expressed the view that the current guidance is inadequate. For instance, there is no clear guidance on exercising a choice between use of a framework and other procurement routes, acknowledging, of course, that much will depend on the individual circumstances and requirements of each contracting authority. Nevertheless, there is significant flexibility regarding choice even where the use of frameworks might be questionable. As a PAC report has identified, CCS has stated that it does not consider that frameworks are the 'wrong' vehicle, but 'just one vehicle that we use' and that whilst DPS are more flexible and open (inasmuch as being able to bring new suppliers in at any point), it believes that 'frameworks do the right thing in terms of competition if one uses them correctly'.[86] The PAC appeared unconvinced that any real clarity existed on the choice between purchasing tools and recommended that the Cabinet Office issue guidance, for example, a 'Framework Playbook' to provide central guidance for government buyers on key policies. It proposed that this should cover: (1) the project delivery model assessment to be carried out by government buyers to inform recommendations on whether a department should or should not use a framework; (2) effective management processes for frameworks; and (3) the collection of appropriate data to assess whether the outcomes of the framework have been achieved.[87] Similarly, a NAO report has highlighted an urgent need for the GCF to publish a playbook or good practice guidance for frameworks. In its view, this should set the standards for accrediting framework providers, ensure greater transparency over how frameworks are created and operated, and address how and when direct awards via frameworks should be permitted, and should aim to achieve fewer frameworks, lower levies and commission rates and improve the quality of frameworks and framework providers.[88]

3.2. Guidance on Central Purchasing

In addition to guidance on frameworks, in 2008, the OGC published useful albeit brief guidance on centralised purchasing bodies but did not systematically address the issues raised in consultations on implementation.[89]

[84] Information is available at www.gov.uk/government/publications/the-sourcing-and-consultancy-playbooks/using-the-playbook-in-conjunction-with-framework-agreements-html.

[85] A Millross, 'Playing with framework agreements' *(Local Government Lawyer*, 8 September 2023).

[86] House of Commons, Committee of Public Accounts, *Competition in public procurement*, Sixth Report of Session 2023–24, HC 385, 13 December 2023,13.

[87] ibid 6–7.

[88] NAO, *Efficiency in government procurement of common goods and services*, Crown Commercial Service, Session 2024-25 HC 116, 12.

[89] OGC, 'Central Purchasing Bodies, OGC Guidance on Central Purchasing Bodies in the Procurement Regulations', March 2008. Available at webarchive.nationalarchives.gov.uk/ukgwa/20100202130137mp_/http://www.ogc.gov.uk/documents/OGC_Guidance_on_Central_Purchasing_Bodies.pdf.

For instance, it reiterated that where a contracting authority acquires requirements from or through a CPA, it will be deemed to have complied with the Regulations insofar as the CPA has complied in its acquisition or award and that, if the CPA has failed to comply, the contracting authority will not have complied.[90] It further stated that whilst the regulations do not require a CPA to expressly identify that it intends to buy for others, this would need to be indicated in notice requirements.[91] It also reiterated that whilst there was no requirement for a CPA to indicate the contracting authorities on whose behalf it was acting when undertaking procurement, it must comply with requirements on frameworks including European Commission guidance on the identification of user contracting authorities.[92]

It also stated that a contracting authority could not use the CPA provisions to provide its own resources (eg, Human Resources and other) to other contracting authorities as it would not meet the legal definition of a centralised purchasing body.[93]

More importantly, it confirmed that a body which is not a contracting authority cannot act as a CPA; however, it stated that there was nothing in the Regulations preventing other bodies from acting as agents for contracting authorities, in which case, the contracting authority would remain directly responsible for ensuring compliance with the Regulations.[94] Relatedly, an agent acting on behalf of a contracting authority could acquire goods from a CPA, provided the agent was specified as a class of organisation able to access and use the CPA's facilities; the contracting authority rather than the agent would be deemed to have acquired the requirements from the CPA.[95] Therefore, there seemed to be acknowledgement of the role of private sector organisations but, again, this did not categorically address some of the legal and practical issues involved in permitting private sector organisations to manage frameworks. As indicated above, the subsequent 2010 guidance on use of frameworks set up by non-contracting authorities introduced new uncertainty and did not specifically address this in the context of CPAs.

By contrast, it provided more detailed guidance on what would happen if a contracting authority bought from or through a CPA in 'good faith' and it later transpired that the CPA had not fully complied with the Regulations. It was stated that the contracting authority would not be in compliance either but also stated that:

> it is important (if the CPB provisions are not to be undermined) for a contracting authority to be able to rely on the CPB to carry out its various obligations under those Regulations. Thus a contracting authority should not have to supervise the processes of the CPB, but it should be careful, in entering into arrangements with CPBs, to ensure that there are appropriate provisions in those arrangements to protect itself. For example, it may be sensible for provision to be included in any such arrangements to the effect that the CPB will comply with all necessary provisions in the Regulations and providing that where the CPB fails to do this (and as a result of which the contracting authority incurs legal costs or has damages awarded against

[90] ibid 3.
[91] ibid 3 and 4.
[92] ibid 4.
[93] ibid.
[94] ibid 4–5.
[95] ibid 5.

it) that the CPB will compensate the contracting authority in respect of those legal costs or damages.[96]

It continued that, even without such provision, it may be possible for the authority to recoup damages from the CPA in respect of the CPA's breach of the regulations.[97] The guidance also stated that any form of agreement or contractual arrangement between a CPA and the contracting authority procuring from or through it was a matter for the parties concerned.[98] At the very least, this aspect of the guidance indicates that the Government was alert to the problem of CPAs not undertaking their responsibilities and the issue of apportioning liability to a contracting authority when it relied on a CPA, offering some practical advice in this regard. The Government was clearly capable of providing more tailored advice of this kind which begs the question of why, for over two decades, it did not do so.

3.3. Guidance on Competition Law in the Public Sector

It is recalled from chapter three that it is important not to overlook the potential relevance of competition law in the context of frameworks and CPAs. Therefore, it should be acknowledged that the UK has published very general guidance on the implications of competition law for public sector entities, although this does not address frameworks or centralised purchasing. Thus, in 2004, the Office of Fair Trading published an assessment of the impact of public sector procurement on competition.[99] Similarly, in 2011, it published a guide to the application of the UK Competition Act 1998 to public bodies but this did not specifically consider frameworks or centralised purchasing.[100] In 2017, the Competition and Markets Authority published a report on the potential impact of local authority practices on competition including in relation to procurement.[101] However, none addressed frameworks or centralised purchasing specifically.

4. Private Sector Initiatives

Whilst this book focuses primarily on regulation of the public sector, it is important to acknowledge the part that industry can and should play in ensuring better 'self-regulation'.

Various commissioned reports have been published by independent associations on frameworks in the UK. For example, in 2012, the Lean Client Task Group published a report for Government on the 'effectiveness of frameworks' which made various

[96] ibid 5.
[97] ibid.
[98] ibid 6.
[99] Office of Fair Trading, *Assessing the impact of public sector procurement on competition*, Summary, September 2004.
[100] Office of Fair Trading, *Public bodies and competition law A guide to the application of the Competition Act 1998*, December 2011.
[101] Competition and Markets Authority, 'Local Authorities and Competition', 20 December 2017.

proposals for improving commercial processes.[102] Further, a 2018 report by the Civil Engineering Contractors Association conducted a survey on framework use in the civil engineering sector, identifying various problems and principles for 'effective frameworks'.[103] However, findings and recommendations have been at a high level or there has been limited uptake. More recently, King's College London developed a 'gold standard' for construction frameworks comprising 24 recommendations[104] which, where implemented, has led to a standard accreditation of contracting authorities and CPAs.[105] As stated in respect of this initiative, across the public and private sectors, there are currently over 2,000 active construction frameworks but a lack of clear guidance as to a preferred structure and 'best practice' features which this standard seeks to address.[106] However, such initiatives are focused on improving the practical execution of frameworks, and do not address many of the regulatory issues that have arisen, including some of the marketised behaviours explored throughout this book. It is also difficult to find many well-publicised cross-sector examples in which industry has led the way on developing more responsible and ethical ways of engaging the public sector through frameworks and CPAs.

5. Procurement Act 2023

Following Brexit, the UK decided to introduce an entirely new legislative framework for procurement. In 2020, the Cabinet Office published *Transforming Public Procurement* which consulted on proposals for reform.[107] The provisions of the PA 2023 and accompanying PR 2024 are examined in more detail in Part III. For present purposes, it suffices to briefly set out the general legislative scheme and main provisions on frameworks. It should be added that the GCF has published a range of guidance on the provisions, including on frameworks,[108] including various learning modules and an accompanying Transforming Public Procurement Learning Manual.[109] It is difficult to discern the status and function of such guidance, which is largely explanatory, sometimes interpretative, and occasionally references expectations of practice. Importantly, however, it does not address many of the issues raised in this book.

[102] P McDermott, M Dickinson, J Ioannou and K Heard, 'Effectiveness of frameworks – A report by the working group on the effectiveness of frameworks of the procurement and lean client task group', published in 'Government Construction Strategy – Final Report to Government by the Procurement/Lean Client Task Group', July 2012.

[103] CECA Frameworks Report, Directions in policy for the UK's infrastructure sector, November 2018.

[104] D Mosey, 'Constructing the Gold Standard: An Independent Review of Public Sector Construction Frameworks', Centre for Construction Law, King's College London 2021.

[105] Information is available at www.crowncommercial.gov.uk/news/news-ccs-becomes-the-first-public-sector-construction-framework-provider-to-achieve-gold-standard-status-on-government-verification-scheme-ccs.

[106] ibid.

[107] Cabinet Office, *Transforming public procurement*, December 2020, CP 353. See also Cabinet Office, 'Transforming Public Procurement: Government response to consultation', December 2021, CP 556.

[108] GCF, 'Guidance: Frameworks', November 2024.

[109] GCF, 'Transforming Public Procurement Learning Manual', Summary Documents and Learning Aids, 26 July 2024.

5.1. Scope of Coverage

The majority of the PA 2023 applies to 'covered procurement'. Section 1(1) provides that this means the award, entry into and management of a 'public contract' (as defined). As explained below, whether or not a contract falls within the definition of a 'public contract' is important because it determines whether the procurement will be subject to the section 12 statutory objectives only applicable to covered procurement (ie, procurement involving a public contract).

Section 1(3) provides for two different ways in which a contracting authority can be determined to be carrying out covered procurement. The first is on its own behalf, including where it acts jointly with or through another person (section 1(3)(a)). The second is if the contracting authority is a centralised procurement authority (i) for or on behalf of another contracting authority, or (ii) for the purpose of the supply of goods, services or works to another contracting authority. The PA 2023 therefore replaces the term 'central purchasing body' with a 'centralised procurement authority' ('CPA'). Section 1(4) provides that a CPA is defined as 'a contracting authority that is in the business of carrying out procurement for or on behalf of, or for the purpose of the supply of goods, services or works to, other contracting authorities'. In turn, section 2(1) defines a 'contracting authority' as including a 'public authority'. Section 2(2) provides that 'public authority' means a person that is (a) wholly or mainly funded out of public funds, or (b) subject to public authority oversight (as defined),[110] and does not operate on a commercial basis. Section 2(4) provides that the following are examples of factors to be taken into account in determining whether a person operates on a commercial basis: (a) whether the person operates on the basis that its losses would be borne, or its continued operation secured, by a public authority (whether directly or indirectly); (b) whether the person contracts on terms more favourable than those that might reasonably have been available to it had it not been associated with a public authority; and (c) whether the person operates on a market that is subject to fair and effective competition.

This combination of provisions is potentially significant regarding the issues examined in this book. First, a CPA must be a contracting authority (ie, a public sector entity) but which is 'in the business of carrying out procurement' for or on behalf of other contracting authorities. It is difficult to reconcile this with the notion that a CPA is essentially performing a public service function rather than a commercial activity. This choice of language may be further evidence (alongside a very broad definition of a framework) of the extent to which regulation now reflects a marketised conception of the purchasing function, ie that CPAs are acting as businesses. Second, the definition of contracting authority involves a public authority which 'does not operate on a commercial basis'. Therefore, a CPA cannot operate on a commercial basis but is in the business of carrying out procurement for other contracting authorities. Section 2(4) gives some examples of facts to be taken into account which do not appear to be exhaustive and introduces concepts that have nowhere been clearly explained, eg whether the

[110] A person is subject to public authority oversight if the person is subject to the management or control of: (a) one or more public authorities, or (b) a board more than half of the members of which are appointed by one or more public authorities.

person 'operates on a market that is subject to fair and effective competition'.[111] This is hardly likely to resolve fundamental uncertainty about the precise nature of the services a CPA provides for the purposes of determining how rules on frameworks must be interpreted and applied and the extent to which CPAs may be caught by competition law. Ultimately, *Transforming Public Procurement* only very briefly mentioned central purchasing, namely, that 'framework agreements set up by central purchasing bodies can have a very wide scope which can still result in complex process rather than a simple call off as intended (although lots can be operated within frameworks which can mitigate this)'.[112] There are no specific provisions on central purchasing in the PA 2023.

Regarding public contracts subject to the PA 2023, section 3 provides that a 'public contract' is one of three kinds, which must have an estimated value of not less than the prescribed threshold and not be exempted. The first is any contract for the supply, for pecuniary interest, of goods, services or works to a contracting authority. The second is any framework. The third is a concession contract. There are also certain types of 'special regime' contracts, namely, utilities, defence and security, concession and light-touch contracts. The fact that the *prima facie* distinction between a public contract and a framework has been removed such that a framework now has an explicit status as a 'public contract' has possible implications, discussed in chapter five.

5.2. Principles and Objectives

Whilst, as indicated, EU law provides general Treaty principles such as non-discrimination, equal treatment, transparency and proportionality, as well as specific procurement principles in the Directives, the PA 2023 prescribes its own objectives in respect of covered procurement.

Sectio n12(1) provides that a contracting authority must have regard to the importance of: (a) delivering value for money; (b) maximising public benefit; (c) sharing information for the purpose of allowing suppliers and others to understand the authority's procurement policies and decisions; and (d) acting, and being seen to act, with integrity. Further, section 12(2) provides that a contracting authority must treat suppliers the same unless a difference between the suppliers justifies different treatment. Section 12(3) provides that if a contracting authority considers that different treatment is justified in a particular case, the authority must take all reasonable steps to ensure it does not put a supplier at an unfair advantage or disadvantage. In addition, section 12(4) provides that a contracting authority must: (a) have regard to the fact that SMEs may face particular barriers to participation, and (b) consider whether such barriers can be removed or reduced. It should be added that, whilst not mentioned expressly in section 12 but, rather, in sections 90 and 91, 'treaty state suppliers' must not be discriminated against. It is notable that there is no longer any explicit principle of transparency or proportionality. Similarly, there is no explicit inclusion of any equivalent of regulation 18 concerning provision to prevent procurement being designed to

[111] LRA Butler and S Brunning, 'Scoping coverage of above-threshold contracts in the Procurement Act 2023: towards uniformity, simplification, and flexibility' (2024) 4 *PPLR* 193–267.
[112] Cabinet Office (n 107) 44.

restrict competition or a principle of 'competition' separate from any concept of value for money or any other general indications that frameworks cannot be used to restrict competition (eg, cf Recital 61 Directive 2014/24/EU).

As discussed throughout this book, it is questionable to what extent these requirements will act as a significant enabler or, more likely, constraint on how rules are applied in practice. The GCF guidance indicates that contracting authorities must 'give genuine attention and thought to each objective, considering its relevance and importance, if any, to the procurement' and 'the significance given to each objective when carrying out a procurement must be considered independently'.[113] This sends a potentially strong signal as regards the legal importance of these objectives. Equally, the Transforming Public Procurement Learning Manual states that 'they are there to be influencers rather than gatekeepers and support best practice within the procurement exercise',[114] which is characteristically vague. It should be added that certain duties are not even legally enforceable; for example, the section 12(4) duty regarding SME barriers is not enforceable in civil proceedings under the PA 2023 (section 110(5)).

Section 13 also provides that contracting authorities must have regard to the NPPS which sets out the Government's strategic priorities in relation to procurement and section 14 provides for Wales to adopt its own. It is important to note that whilst this duty will apply to the award of frameworks, it does not apply when awarding a contract *under* a framework (section 13(10)). Further, it is not enforceable in civil proceedings under the PA 2023 (section 100(5)). An earlier NPPS was published in May 2024,[115] which it was considered would be the applicable NPPS under the PA 2023. The 2024 NPPS did not expressly refer to issues arising in relation to frameworks or centralised purchasing. However, with a change of Government, a new NPPS was published on 13 February 2025,[116] stating with respect to the section 12 duty to have regard to value for money that this is 'always the overarching priority in public procurement'.[117] According to the NPPS:

> This must include consideration of outcomes and quality to avoid waste from low value, poor quality bids. This means optimising the use of public funds by balancing effectiveness, efficiency and economy over the life-cycle of a product, service or works to achieve the intended outcomes of the procurement. This includes wider socio-economic and environmental benefits and impacts. Government guidance (e.g. Managing Public Money and Best Value statutory guidance) sets out how to use public money responsibly.[118]

The reference to the priority given to value for money could suggest that there is a hierarchy of objectives. This may be contrasted with the GCF guidance on covered procurement objectives which categorically states:

> It is not the intention of the Act that any of the objectives, for example value for money, disapply, override or take precedence over the obligation on contracting authorities to have regard to the other objectives in section 12(1) or (4).[119]

[113] GCF, 'Guidance: Covered Procurement Objectives', December 2024, 3.
[114] GCF (n 109) 14.
[115] Cabinet Office, *National Procurement Policy Statement*, 13 May 2024.
[116] Cabinet Office (n 1).
[117] ibid 2.
[118] ibid.
[119] GCF, 'Guidance: Covered Procurement Objectives', December 2024, 4.

This is symptomatic of the tendency discussed in chapters three and four to state objectives without any real clarity.

A few specific albeit brief references to frameworks have been included. The NPPS states that the PA 2023 will deliver a step change in transparency that will drive value for money and singles out frameworks, stating that it 'will shine a spotlight on framework providers who charge excessive fees and help contracting authorities collaborate to deliver efficiencies through joint procurement'.[120] Further, it states that:

> Contracting authorities can often ensure value for money by using collaborative procurement arrangements established by public sector centralised procurement authorities such as the Crown Commercial Service. These agreements aggregate spend for common goods and services and enable selected suppliers to be contracted quickly on agreed terms and with competitive maximum pricing. However, there are currently too many similar agreements across the public sector, leading to unnecessary transactional costs for suppliers and confusion for contracting authorities. In addition, some agreements are operated by private companies not in accordance with procurement legislation. Contracting authorities should ensure any collaborative arrangements they use are transparent about the provider's ownership and the fees they charge and that this represents good value for money when compared to other agreements.[121]

It continues that contracting authorities should 'use collaborative procurement agreements, where appropriate for the requirement and the market, to ensure value for money (as long as those agreements are operating in accordance with relevant procurement legislation and good practice)'. The accompanying Ministerial Statement also states that 'a new online register of commercial agreements will increase visibility of frameworks and fees, curbing excessive profits'.[122] It is also stated that a further consultation is intended to inform the development of primary legislation,[123] although there is no indication whether frameworks will be the subject of consultation. In addition, it is stated in the NPPS and Ministerial Statement that a new 'public interest' test will be introduced for contracting authorities to assess, at the outset of a procurement process, whether work should be outsourced or undertaken in-house to deliver better value for money and there is reference to rigorous evaluation of in-house, outsourced or 'hybrid delivery models'.[124] It is not clear whether this will involve an assessment of contracting authority recourse to CPAs given the emphasis on appropriate use of collaborative arrangements.

It is acknowledged that the NPPS is a high-level document and will not address details. However, it limits itself to rehearsing decades-old concerns about responsible use of CPA frameworks, private sector involvement, and fees and, most importantly, does not identify any solutions. As indicated, there are no specific provisions in the PA 2023 on central purchasing. As will be discussed in chapter five, the PA 2023 does not categorically address private sector involvement in frameworks or fees. An online register may improve transparency in identifying frameworks and related information

[120] ibid 3.
[121] ibid 5–6.
[122] NPPS, Statement made on 13 February 2025, by Georgia Gould, Parliamentary Secretary for the Cabinet Office.
[123] ibid.
[124] Cabinet Office (n 1) 2, and Ministerial Statement (n 122).

but it is not a means of systematically checking and enforcing compliance of frameworks with legal requirements. Also, it is not clear where contracting authorities and suppliers can find reference to what is 'good practice'. Much of this rhetoric does not address the reality of framework marketisation in the UK.

5.3. Procedural Phases

Section 11 provides that a contracting authority may not enter into a public contract unless it is awarded in accordance with: (a) section 19 (competitive award); (b) section 41 (direct award in special cases); (c) section 43 (direct award after switching procedures); or (d) section 45 (award under frameworks).

The PA 2023 also regulates various preliminary steps. Before publishing a tender notice, a contracting authority may publish a planned procurement notice (section 15). A contracting authority may engage in preliminary market engagement with suppliers (section 16), and, if so, must publish a notice to this effect or provide reasons for not doing so (section 17). A contracting authority must also consider whether requirements could reasonably be supplied under more than one contract and by reference to lots, and either do so or provide reasons for not doing so (section 18). Chapter six considers preliminary aspects in more detail.

Regarding procedures, a contracting authority may award a public contract to the supplier that submits the 'most advantageous tender' in a competitive tendering procedure, ie the tender that it considers: (a) satisfies its requirements, and (b) best satisfies the award criteria when assessed by reference to: (i) a prescribed assessment methodology, and (ii) if there is more than one criterion, the relative importance of the criteria (section 19).

A 'competitive tendering procedure' is: (a) a single-stage tendering procedure without a restriction on who can submit tenders (an 'open procedure'), or (b) such other competitive tendering procedure as the contracting authority considers appropriate (a 'competitive flexible procedure') (section 20). A contracting authority must ensure that the procedure is a proportionate means of awarding the public contract, having regard to the nature, complexity and cost of the contract. As indicated above, otherwise, there is no general explicit proportionality principle.

A contracting authority must publish a tender notice to invite tenders or request suppliers to participate (section 21). Formerly, advertised procurements had to be notified in the OJEU but notices will now be found on an enhanced Find a Tender central digital platform.

In setting award criteria, a contracting authority must be satisfied that they: (a) relate to the subject-matter of the contract, (b) are sufficiently clear, measurable and specific, (c) do not break the rules on technical specifications (in section 56), and (d) are a proportionate means of assessing tenders, having regard to the nature, complexity and cost of the contract (section 23). In setting award criteria, a contracting authority must: (a) describe how tenders are to be assessed by reference to them and, in particular, specify whether failure to meet one or more would disqualify a tender (the 'assessment methodology'), and (b) if there is more than one criterion, indicate their relative importance by: (i) weighting each as representing a percentage of total importance, (ii) ranking them in order of importance, or (iii) describing it in another way. A contracting authority may refine the award criteria as part of a competitive flexible procedure (section 24).

It should be added that a new concept of a 'dynamic market' has been introduced (sections 34–40). This should not be confused with a DPS which has not been retained. A dynamic market is a list of qualified suppliers, ie suppliers who have met the 'conditions for membership' of the dynamic market. As discussed in chapter five, if it is possible to award a framework by reference to a dynamic market, there is a risk of blurring purchasing tools and unintended consequences.

It is also possible to make direct awards of public contracts in certain circumstances where justified (sections 41–44 and Schedule 5). As a framework falls within the definition of a 'public contract', the provisions on direct awards apply equally to frameworks and other types of public contract.

5.4. Provisions on Frameworks

The PA 2023 does not introduce specific provisions on the award of a framework but, rather, a new chapter four on 'award under frameworks'. Section 45(1) provides that a contracting authority may award a public contract in accordance with a framework. Section 45(2) provides a new definition of a framework:

> A 'framework' is a contract between a contracting authority and one or more suppliers that provides for the future award of contracts by a contracting authority to the supplier or suppliers.

As discussed further in chapter five, GCF guidance states that this is similar to the PCR 2015 definition but it clearly omits key features such as the express purpose of establishing particular terms governing contracts to be awarded. This calls into question whether there has been a conceptual shift to facilitate generic frameworks in which key aspects of call-offs are, instead, left for future determination. This is unlikely to discourage marketised behaviours. It also remains unclear the distinction between a standard public contract and a framework given that the definition of a framework refers to a 'contract' between the parties, with certain implications.

Section 45(3) provides that a framework may only provide for the future award of a public contract following a competitive selection process, that is, unless the provision providing for the possibility to directly call off from the framework applies (under section 45(4)). A framework may provide for the future award of a public contract without competition between suppliers: (a) in circumstances where only one supplier is party to the framework, or (b) if the framework sets out: (i) the core terms of the public contract, and (ii) an objective mechanism for supplier selection. The significance of these changes will be discussed in Part III.

Section 45(5) provides that the framework must include prescribed information. This includes, among other things, the price payable, or mechanism for determining the price payable under call-offs. As will be discussed in chapter seven, it is not clear to what extent certain terms such as price must therefore be firmly established when setting up the framework as distinct from calling off under it.

Section 45(7) inserts a new provision not found in the PCR 2015 regarding fees. It provides that a framework may provide for the charging of fees at a fixed percentage of the estimated value of any contract awarded to the supplier in accordance with the framework. As will be discussed in chapter five, the Green Paper proposed stricter controls on fees which were not introduced.

Section 46 introduces a new competitive selection process at the call-off stage by which a contracting authority may provide for conditions of participation if they are satisfied that the conditions are a proportionate means of ensuring that suppliers to the framework have the legal and financial capacity and technical ability to perform. A competitive selection process may also provide for the assessment of proposals, but only by reference to the award criteria against which the tenders were assessed and the award criteria may be refined. The significance of introducing a new selection phase at the call-off stage and the need to link award back to the criteria at framework award is discussed in chapter eight.

Section 47 provides that the maximum term of a framework is four years or eight in the case of defence and security and utilities frameworks but this can be extended if the contracting authority considers that the nature of the requirement to be supplied means that a longer term is required. The reasons must be set out in a tender or transparency notice. This is considered in chapter six.

Section 48 provides that it is an implied term of every framework that a contracting authority may exclude a supplier that is an excluded or excludable supplier from participating in any selection process run in relation to the award of a contract under the framework.

Finally, section 49 introduces the concept of an 'open framework'. Section 49(1) defines an 'open framework' as a scheme of frameworks that provides for the award of successive frameworks on substantially the same terms. Section 49(2) provides that an open framework must provide: (a) for the award of a framework at least once during: (i) the period of three years beginning with the day of the award of the first framework in the scheme, and (ii) each period of five years beginning with the day of the award of the second framework in the scheme; (b) for the expiry of one framework on the award of the next; (c) for the final framework to expire at the end of the period of eight years beginning with the day on which the first framework under the scheme is awarded. Open frameworks are discussed in more detail in chapter five.

As indicated, various other provisions under the PA 2023 relevant to frameworks will be considered in Part III.

6. Conclusions

Consistent with a common law tradition that avoids prescription and codification through extensive rules, the UK has generally refrained from introducing hard-law regulation of procurement. Instead, it has emphasised the importance of the professional exercise of contracting authority discretion, supported by policy directions. To the extent procurement is legally regulated, it has largely derived from EU Directives.

Overall, it has been shown that the UK has not adopted a particularly clear set of objectives for its regulated public procurement system, including in respect of frameworks. Further, it has not taken any substantial domestic initiative to develop further regulation (through laws and policies) on frameworks.

Concerning implementation of the EU Directives, consultations have shown that the UK Government took a strict copy-out approach, taking advantage of flexibilities offered and not implementing certain options that might limit flexibility (eg, mandating use of certain CPAs). However, consultations repeatedly raised concerns about certain legal and practical issues and called for further guidance. Whilst some guidance was issued, including on private sector involvement in frameworks and CPAs, this has not decisively addressed the calls for focused guidance on legally compliant framework practice on a wide range of matters.

It is difficult to avoid the conclusion that successive UK Governments bear much of the responsibility for many of the issues that have arisen, acknowledging that the EU legal framework has contributed a degree of legal uncertainty in which conditions conducive to framework marketisation have also developed. The UK has been largely content to passively implement the minimum requirements of EU Directives into UK regulations. This is not problematic in and of itself, given that to do so generally complies with EU law. Arguably, it was also prudent to do so given the risk that additional domestic rules and policies could be challenged as regards their compatibility with EU law. However, there is a sense that the UK could have done more. Perhaps paradoxically, whilst the UK put forward radical proposals for reform of the EU Directives, it has not been particularly proactive in addressing behaviours that were not explicitly addressed by EU Directives (and thus did not engage copy-out or gold-plating issues). It also did not introduce regulatory controls that were actually expressly provided for under the Directives, eg mandating the use of specific CPAs for certain forms of procurement. Whatever the legal position, the UK Government has not introduced detailed guidance on frameworks and central purchasing despite repeated calls for such. In addition, it cannot be said that the private sector has taken any initiative to ensure more responsible and ethical procurement practices. It is therefore unsurprising that the UK has witnessed an extensive and largely uncontrolled marketisation of frameworks.

Post-Brexit, there was enough experience to evidence the need for reform of the rules on frameworks and centralised purchasing. However, the PA 2023 has not taken decisive action to address many of the issues raised. Indeed, in certain respects, the PA 2023 framework provisions appear to reflect the shift in the marketised framework model that has emerged, challenging the original conception of a mechanism that establishes particular terms governing future call-offs following a competition, now with much flexibility offered at the call-off stage. As will be suggested in Part III, the PA 2023 is unlikely to sufficiently address the many issues raised.

Having provided the context for understanding the emerging marketisation of frameworks and the general regulatory approaches at the EU and UK level, Part III now turns to examine UK practice in more detail.

PART III

Practice in the UK

5

Meeting the Legal Definition, the Framework Market and Choice between Purchasing Tools

1. Introduction

This chapter and the remainder in this Part analyse empirical research findings on how the PCR 2015 framework rules have been applied, and the likely impact of the PA 2023. As will be discussed, legal uncertainty has, to some degree, both undermined objectives of regulated procurement and good practice and enabled and/or failed to address framework marketisation.

This chapter examines factors that may inform contracting authority choices about frameworks. It is recalled from chapter one that it would typically be assumed that, in an efficient system, various costs and benefits are weighed, including administrative costs, legal constraints on choice, likely participants, the result, and any delay in the event of challenge.[1] It has been suggested that the primary motivation for using frameworks is to 'increase administrative efficiency'.[2] However, whilst research has identified the likely or expected factors influencing framework use, there has been less focus on what factors actually inform decisions in practice to the extent that it is truly an informed choice, as distinct from, say, based largely on convenience. Different factors may weigh on different stakeholders (eg, legal advisers primarily concerned with legal compliance, contracting authorities concerned with operational matters).

Whilst the EU and UK have not explicitly regulated the choice between purchasing tools, it would not be unreasonable to expect that a substantial operative factor would be whether a framework meets the legal definition and the arrangement purposely aligns with it. However, this chapter argues that decisions seem to be increasingly informed by convenience and market-oriented factors. Thus, reduced regulatory pressure is placed on framework selection based on fidelity to their purpose, as regulated, and principled consideration of other factors. There is a disconnect between what the law expects (even accepting discretion afforded to contracting authorities regarding the decision to use frameworks) and practice.

[1] See generally, CR Yukins, 'Are IDIQS Inefficient? Sharing Lessons with European Framework Contracting' (2008) 37(3) *PCLJ* 545.

[2] GL Albano and C Nicholas, *The Law and Economics of Frameworks: Designing Flexible Solutions for Public Procurement* (Cambridge University Press, 2016) 22.

This chapter is divided into separate sub-topics pertaining to: (1) the legal position under the PCR 2015 on an issue; (2) a summary and analysis of the empirical evidence; and (3) a consideration of the legal position under, and likely impact of, the PA 2023. These sub-topics comprise: (a) compliance with the legal definition of a framework and the extent to which it facilitates broad arrangements; (b) perceptions of the framework market; (c) fee charging; and (d) the choice of frameworks relative to other options.

To qualify, as indicated in chapter two, given the many constraints on time and resource, stakeholders will not necessarily carefully weigh all factors in advance of use. Further, the empirical research did not test perceptions of which factors are more likely to influence certain choices. Nevertheless, many factors were repeatedly mentioned. It is therefore useful to consider all of these from the outset of this Part, as they also serve as a critical introduction to issues explored in the remaining chapters.

2. Definition of a Framework Agreement

2.1. Definition in the PCR 2015

The concept of a 'framework agreement' as defined in Directive 2014/24/EU (replicated in regulation 33(1)) is an important means of determining what distinguishes a framework from another type of 'public contract' and provides a critical reference point for assessing the extent to which frameworks that have developed in UK practice conform to their intended model. The definition under EU law indicates that a framework has a distinct purpose and certain unique features that technically differentiate it from other tools as well as standard public contracts. However, there has been confusion about the extent to which multi-supplier frameworks constitute public contracts and the empirical evidence suggests that frameworks are becoming increasingly generic, losing their sense of purpose and distinguishing features, which risks their becoming instrumentalised for other ends, including market gain.

Article 33(1) Directive 2014/24/EU expressly authorises frameworks that fall within this definition:

> an agreement between one or more contracting authorities and one or more economic operators, the purpose of which is to establish the terms governing contracts to be awarded during a given period, in particular with regard to price and, where appropriate, the quantity envisaged.

This envisages the set-up of an agreement governing the award of contracts throughout its term. It does not require the framework to impose binding obligations to purchase or supply in the absence of an executed call-off. It is recalled from chapter three that the non-obligatory multi-supplier framework was of particular concern in the early stages of developing EU regulation.

The question arises as to whether this definition applies to agreements that do impose such binding obligations. Where is the line drawn between a public contract and a framework that sets up a contracting mechanism for future purchases? The position was left unclear by two EU and UK communications.

In 2005, the European Commission issued an Explanatory Note on frameworks.[3] It distinguished between 'framework contracts' which establish all the terms for the call-off 'in a binding manner' and 'frameworks *stricto sensu*' which do not and, instead, require terms to be agreed subsequently. The Commission stated that a 'framework contract' could involve one or several suppliers. The contracting authority might not be obliged to use the agreement but 'once the decision to use it has been taken, the conditions are set out in a definitive manner'.[4] The Commission confused matters by stating that 'framework contracts' constituted 'traditional' public contracts and that they fell within the framework provisions of Article 32 of Directive 2004/18/EC. It explained that a 'framework agreement' is 'by definition incomplete' and does not include certain terms or establish in a binding way all the terms necessary, meaning that further agreement between the parties is required. It acknowledged that the original proposal for Article 32 applied exclusively to this type of agreement but highlighted changes in the wording made to the Recital on frameworks as the Directive made its way through the legislative process to justify its position that Article 32 covered both frameworks *stricto sensu* and framework contracts.[5] It is curious that the Commission described 'framework contracts' as resembling traditional public contracts and in a way that indicated that the terms are established in a binding manner as this reflected neither the wording of Article 32 nor the Recitals and conflated the concepts of a 'public contract' and a 'framework contract'. For a 'framework contract' to be a 'public contract', it would need to contain mutually binding obligations to purchase and supply (on which, see further below).

In 2008, the OGC issued guidance which stated:

> In a few circumstances it may be the case that the framework agreement itself is a contract in its own right to which the EU procurement rules apply. This would be the case where the agreement places an obligation, in writing, to purchase goods, works or services for pecuniary interest (or consideration in UK legal terminology).[6]

The OGC referred to these as 'framework contracts' that 'should be treated as any other contract under the EU rules'.[7] Whilst the OGC correctly classified such contracts as public contracts not subject to the specific provisions on frameworks, it was possibly misleading to refer to these as frameworks and use the term 'framework contract' which, when considered alongside the Commission's Explanatory Note, compounded the confusion.

2.1.1. 'Pecuniary Interest' in EU Law – The Distinguishing Feature

Regulation 2 defines 'public contracts' as:

> contracts for pecuniary interest concluded in writing between one or more economic operators and one or more contracting authorities and having as their object the execution of works, the supply of products or the provision of services.

[3] European Commission Explanatory Note – Frameworks – Classic Directive CC/2005/03, 14 July 2005, Ref. Ares(2016)810203 – 16/02/2016.

[4] ibid 3, fn 7.

[5] ibid 3.

[6] OGC, 'Guidance on Framework Agreements in the Procurement Regulations', September 2008, 3. Available at webarchive.nationalarchives.gov.uk/ukgwa/20110405225545mp_/http://www.ogc.gov.uk/documents/OGC_Guidance_on_Framework_AgreementsSept_08.pdf.

[7] ibid 12, Figure 1.

The CJEU has held that 'pecuniary interest' designates a contract whereby each party undertakes to provide a service in exchange for another.[8] Whilst this might be considered similar to 'consideration' in English contract law, use of this term in the PCR 2015 (replicating Directive 2014/24/EU) should be given a purposive interpretation in the context of the application of EU law across all Member States.[9] Therefore, some economic benefit would need to be conferred on a supplier to constitute 'pecuniary interest'. Otherwise, there is no risk of any unfair advantage being conferred, a mischief the Directives are intended to prevent.[10] The CJEU has ruled on the meaning of the term in cases where the contract subject-matter is development works. It has clarified that for a public contract, the contractor 'assumes a direct or indirect obligation to carry out the works' which is 'legally enforceable in accordance with the procedural rules laid down by national law'.[11] Therefore, where a framework does not impose binding legal obligations to supply but leaves their imposition to execution of a call-off, pecuniary interest will not be present when the framework is set up. It would need to be set up in accordance with the provisions on frameworks.

2.1.2. Multi-supplier Agreements – Mutually Binding Obligations to Purchase and Supply

It is submitted that where a multi-supplier agreement establishes at the outset mutually binding legal obligations to purchase and supply, it should be treated as a 'public contract' not subject to the framework-specific provisions, being already a complete, binding contract 'for pecuniary interest'.[12] In the multi-supplier context, this type of arrangement is likely to be set up using 'lots' (pursuant to regulation 46) under a single procurement or concluding separate public contracts pursuant to distinct procedures. For example, a single competition may be used to award a group of contracts to cover a contracting authority's entire ICT needs with separate lots for the supply of desktop hardware, peripherals, software and associated services. Arrowsmith takes the view that, at least for a single provider agreement imposing an obligation to purchase all the requirements it covers (even if only as these arise), the agreement should not be subject to the specific provisions on frameworks. This is because no contracts are placed under it and there is no need for any extra controls over and above those applicable to standard contracts. It is the non-binding nature of frameworks that gives rise to the need to limit their duration.[13]

2.1.3. Multi-supplier Agreements – Binding Obligation to Purchase Only

Whilst likely to be rare in practice, where a multi-supplier agreement imposes an obligation on contracting authorities to use the agreement for all its requirements but does

[8] Case C 606/17 *IBA Molecular Italy Srl v Azienda ULwS and Others* ECLI:EU:C:2018:843, [2007] ECR I-385, para 28.

[9] Case C-14/83 *Von Colson and Kamann v Land Nordrhein-Westfalen* ECLI:EU:C:1984:153, [1984] ECR 1891.

[10] See S Arrowsmith, *The Law of Public and Utilities Procurement: Regulation in the EU and UK*, 3rd edn, Vol I (Sweet & Maxwell, 2014) 6–12 for discussion on this point.

[11] Case C-451/08 *Helmut Müller GmbH v Bundesanstalt für Immobilienaufgaben* ECLI:EU:C:2010:168, [2010] ECR I-02673, para 63.

[12] There has been a debate over the classification of 'term contracts' in the construction industry. See PLA, 'The Use of Frameworks in Public Procurement' March 2012 and Albano and Nicholas (n 2) 92.

[13] Arrowsmith (n 10) 11–14.

not oblige any supplier to fulfil them, such an arrangement will likely fall within the definition of a 'framework agreement' rather than a 'public contract'. This is due to the lack of 'pecuniary interest' in the agreement, ie no supplier is placed under any legal obligation to supply and therefore no immediate economic benefit is conferred on them when appointed to the framework.

2.1.4. Multi-supplier Agreements – Binding Obligation to Supply Only

Where suppliers are placed under an obligation to meet contracting authority requirements but the contracting authority is under no obligation to purchase, the agreement should fall within the definition of a 'framework agreement'. As no supplier is obliged to fulfil any specific order, 'pecuniary interest' is, again, absent.[14]

2.1.5. Purpose of a Framework

It is recalled from chapter three that the 'framework agreement' definition appears to indicate that the award of the framework must be used to establish the terms of call-offs in as complete a form as possible following a competition, acknowledging that some terms may need to be finalised at the call-off stage.[15] It is not entirely clear whether, according to the PCR 2015 definition, contracting authorities could include on a framework all suppliers that submit compliant tenders, or whether it requires choosing only a limited number by comparing the different terms offered. It is submitted that limiting the number is a usual requirement. There is an exception only when the nature of the market would mean that initial selection in this way arbitrarily restricts competition, notably, in markets with volatile prices where price is a key award criterion but prices need to be reset for every order. As discussed, an arguable rationale for the apparent emphasis on establishing key aspects of a framework through a competitive procedure (rather than at the call-off stage) was partly in recognition of the need to uphold EU objectives; if the terms are not clear from the outset, the agreement of any subsequent terms that may only become (more easily) known to local suppliers could shut out foreign suppliers.

As discussed in chapter seven, the PCR 2015 also set out procedural rules to be followed when awarding call-offs. Such rules must only be applied between the original parties to the framework, effectively closing it off to new suppliers during its term. These rules cover the award of call-offs under both single- and multi-supplier frameworks, the latter being subject to more detailed rules.

Three multi-supplier framework models are allowed under the PCR 2015. The first is a complete framework. This sets out 'all the terms governing the provision of the works, services and supplies concerned' and 'the objective conditions for determining which of the economic operators that are party to the framework shall perform them', ie frameworks that only allow 'direct awards' of call-offs (regulation 33(8)(a)). The second is an incomplete framework. This does not set out all the terms. Call-offs are awarded

[14] C-300/07 *Hans & Christophorous Oymanns v AOK Rheinland/Hamburg* ECLI:EU:C:2009:358, [2009] ECR I-04779, paras 66–76.

[15] See also Arrowsmith (n 10) 11-02.

through reopening competition amongst the suppliers party to the framework ie frameworks that only allow mini-competitions to award call-offs (regulation 33(8)(c)). The third is a hybrid framework. This sets out all the terms (i) partly without reopening competition; and (ii) partly through reopening competition amongst the suppliers party to the framework ie frameworks that allow both direct awards and mini-competitions to award call-offs (regulation 33(8)(b)).

2.1.6. Parties to a Framework and Central Purchasing Authorities

The PCR 2015 definition of a framework requires the arrangement to be set up 'between one or more contracting authorities and one or more economic operators' (regulation 33(2)) and the framework procedures 'may be applied only between those contracting authorities clearly identified for that purpose in the call for competition or the invitation to confirm interest and those economic operators party to the framework agreement as concluded' (regulation 33(5)). Regulation 33(1) explicitly provides that only 'contracting authorities may conclude framework agreements'. This necessarily precludes a non-contracting authority from being party to the framework and awarding call-offs, as well as suppliers subsequently being appointed to the framework or being awarded call-offs if not originally appointed.

As indicated in chapters two and three, a 'central purchasing body' (now referred to as a centralised procurement authority or 'CPA' under the PA 2023) was identified as a type of contracting authority that may set up frameworks. Regulation 2(1) defines it as:

> a contracting authority which provides centralised purchasing activities and which may also provide ancillary purchasing activities.

Recital 69 to Directive 2014/24/EU provides that such authorities should be able to act: (a) as wholesalers by buying, stocking and reselling; and (b) as intermediaries by awarding contracts, operating DPS or concluding frameworks to be used by contracting authorities. It further states:

> Where the central purchasing body has sole responsibility for the conduct of the procurement procedures, it should also be solely and directly responsible for the legality of the procedures. Where a contracting authority conducts certain parts of the procedure, for instance the reopening of competition under a framework agreement or the award of individual contracts based on a dynamic purchasing system, it should continue to be responsible for the stages it conducts.

Recital 70 also states that:

> Contracting authorities should be allowed to award a public service contract for the provision of centralised purchasing activities to a central purchasing body without applying the procedures provided for in this Directive. It should also be permitted for such public service contracts to include the provision of ancillary purchasing activities.

These principles are reflected in Article 37 Directive 2014/24/EU and regulation 37.

The role of a CPA is usually focused on awarding frameworks with eligible contracting authorities taking responsibility for running the call-off stage. However, as highlighted by Albano and Nicholas, the role of a CPA risks creating divergent objectives between it and user contracting authorities.[16] CPAs may become more attentive to technical inputs from potential bidders and awardees rather than to the requests from final users which may tempt user contracting authorities to use alternative procurement options.[17] It will be seen that these divergent objectives are apparent in the UK.

Albano and Nicholas also describe two emergent CPA 'business models': (a) funding through general taxation; and (b) funding through fees paid by suppliers appointed to frameworks (usually a percentage of actual purchases) with some hybrid models.[18] It will be seen below that UK multi-supplier frameworks generally follow model (b). As they further highlight, this carries the risks of CPAs not being incentivised to foster competition and reduce prices in order to generate more revenue, being motivated to market suppliers' offerings, and encouraging aggressive sales tactics.[19] As explained below, it appears that these risks have materialised in the UK.

In the UK, most CPAs act as an 'intermediary'. Despite the legal reference to 'centralised purchasing activities', there are no explicit central government mandated controls on the type or volume of frameworks that can be set up, who can set them up and use them, and how CPAs may operate eg the conditions on which a CPA may grant access to frameworks through access agreements, any instruction by contracting authorities to the CPA, or their income-generating mechanisms.

In addition, contracting authorities may award a public service contract for provision of centralised purchasing activities including ancillary purchasing activities directly to a CPA without following any competitive procedure. It will be seen that this is important in the UK as some CPAs provide various consultancy support services as part of their framework offerings. Without any explicit regulation or proper oversight, there is scope for such activities to expand beyond subsidiary or supporting public service provision to a principal commercial offering to public sector 'customers' – a marketised service. This may call into question both the appropriateness and legality of the provision of such activities, particularly where a private sector entity is also involved in their provision.

For CPA-established frameworks, the question arises as to which entity (the CPA or user contracting authority) holds the legal compliance risk for breaches of the PCR 2015. Regulation 37 provides a degree of clarity in stating that a contracting authority fulfils its obligations where it acquires works, supplies or services by using a CPA-concluded framework (regulation 37(5)). However, it will be responsible in respect of any parts of the procedure it conducts itself, such as conducting a reopening of competition or determining which suppliers shall perform a given task (ie, use of the direct award call-off procedure) (regulation 37(6)(b) and (c)).

Notwithstanding, it is arguably unclear where legal responsibility lies if both a CPA and another contracting authority are implicated in a breach. For example, who would be liable if a contracting authority applied the call-off procedures or award criteria

[16] For a discussion on demand aggregation through centralised procurement and the challenges faced by CPAs, see Albano and Nicholas (n 2) ch 11.

[17] ibid 282.

[18] ibid 284.

[19] ibid.

formulated in a CPA-concluded framework that did not comply with regulation 33? What is the position if the framework does not set out all the terms and conditions for the direct award of call-offs and a contracting authority makes a direct award by supplementing them with its own? Given the short time limit for bringing a legal challenge,[20] the practical risk of challenge against the CPA is likely to be negligible, leaving the user contracting authority exposed. Some CPAs provide support services to user contracting authorities, even running a mini-competition on their behalf. This raises the question of whether a CPA bears or should bear the regulatory compliance risk if it provides such support.

These regulation 37 provisions on apportionment of liabilities between CPAs and other contracting authorities differ from those in regulation 38 in respect of occasional joint procurement, which Recital 71 describes as 'less institutionalised and systematic common purchasing or the established practice of having recourse to service providers that prepare and manage procurement procedures on behalf and for the account of a contracting authority and under its instructions'. Regulation 38 is likely to apply in circumstances where a few contracting authorities collaborate to set up a framework for their joint requirements. Regulation 38(2) provides that:

> Where the conduct of a procurement procedure in its entirety is carried out jointly in the name and on behalf of all the contracting authorities concerned, they shall be jointly responsible for fulfilling their obligations under this Part.

Regulation 38(3) provides that:

> Such joint responsibility applies also in cases where one contracting authority manages the procedure, acting on its own behalf and on the behalf of the other contracting authorities concerned.

Regulation 38(4) provides that it is only where the conduct of a procurement procedure is 'not in its entirety carried out in the name and on behalf of the contracting authorities concerned' that:

> (a) they shall be jointly responsible only for those parts carried out jointly; and (b) each contracting authority shall have sole responsibility for fulfilling its obligations under this Part in respect of the parts it conducts in its own name and on its own behalf.

Therefore, whereas a CPA will bear sole legal responsibility for setting up the framework with each user legally responsible for the parts it conducts itself, regulation 38 envisages joint liability between those contracting authorities in whose name or on whose behalf a procedure has been conducted to set up a framework. This is so even if just one manages the procedure acting on behalf of the others. The only exception is when the procedure is 'not in its entirety carried out in the name and on behalf of the contracting authorities concerned' (eg if a particular lot of the framework concerns just one contracting authority that will enter into the resultant contract in its own name and on its own behalf).

Given the diverse range of joint procurement and CPA models in the UK, it may not always be clear whether a framework has been set up by a CPA or on an occasional joint procurement basis and, therefore, who bears the legal responsibility.

[20] Thirty days from the date when the supplier first knew or ought to have known that grounds for starting the proceedings had arisen: reg 92(2) PCR 2015.

2.1.7. Applying the Definition of a Framework Agreement in Practice under the PCR 2015

2.1.7.1. Non-binding Nature

Interviewees generally recognised the utility of a multi-supplier framework model, avoiding a fully-fledged procurement process each time a contracting authority wants to source a requirement. Further, it was generally understood that until a call-off has been entered into, there are no binding obligations to purchase or supply. Whilst several highlighted the binding nature of some single-supplier frameworks, none gave examples of a multi-supplier framework imposing binding obligations without concluding a separate legally binding call-off.

A few queried whether the PCR 2015 definition of a framework agreement was truly representative of the types of agreement that purport to fall within this definition in the UK. It will be seen throughout this Part that many definitional elements are absent from many purported frameworks. Some legal advisers mentioned that the UK Government's recent post-Brexit Green Paper consultation[21] provided little engagement on important aspects such as the defining characteristics of a framework. According to one, '[t]he UK Government is not yet seizing the opportunity to design more bespoke rules for the UK public sector'.[22] This is discussed in more detail in chapter ten.

2.1.7.2. Lack of Rigour in Framework Award Process

Legal advisers apart, few interviewees mentioned the significance of the definition and purpose of a framework as requiring a full upfront competitive procurement process to establish clear terms for future awards. This is possibly symptomatic of the reality that many multi-supplier ICT frameworks in the UK may involve little to no substantive competition, particularly where no limit is placed on the number appointed, as discussed below.

A further indication of a lack of focus on the purpose of a framework may be evidenced by a discernible elision of the distinction between a framework and a DPS, with one legal adviser commenting that 'some recent frameworks appear to be an amalgam of a DPS and a framework'.[23] Many cited a specific pan-public sector ICT framework (considered in chapter eight) which appoints an unlimited number of suppliers based on limited pass/fail selection criteria and very limited tender requirements. It therefore effectively operates as a standing list pursuant to which future procurements may be conducted. Call-off awards can be made directly using an online filtering mechanism and clarification process.

It is therefore significant that the stated purpose and distinguishing features of a framework have partly been lost in practice and are only properly acknowledged by legal advisers rather than contracting authorities. Whilst the EU Directives and UK Regulations have not imposed specific regulatory controls on the choice between a

[21] Cabinet Office, *Transforming Public Procurement*, December 2020, CP 353. See also Cabinet Office, 'Transforming Public Procurement: Government response to consultation', December 2021, CP 556.

[22] LA15.

[23] ibid.

framework and other tools, the expectation implicit in the definition of a framework is that its use would reflect its essential purpose and that there would be a clear consciousness of this purpose when setting up and using it, not least to ensure legal compliance. This is not a trivial observation. It risks contracting authorities potentially focusing largely or solely on the outcome, ie what they ultimately want to procure as opposed to whether, based on its legally stated purpose, a framework is the best means of attaining it. It can lead to the creation of frameworks which are ultimately unsuitable for procuring certain types of requirements (eg, complex requirements) or which may meet needs but on less suitable terms than might have been the case had other options been considered. In which case, frameworks are instrumentalised to become just one indistinguishable route to procuring whatever is needed.

2.2. Definition in the PA 2023

Section 45(2) includes the following definition of a 'framework':

> a contract between a contracting authority and one or more suppliers that provides for the future award of contracts by a contracting authority to the supplier or suppliers.

The GCF guidance states that this is 'generally similar' to the PCR 2015 definition, other than referring to 'frameworks' rather than 'framework agreements'.[24] However, this is questionable. Even if this were the case as a matter of law (and which is debatable), the guidance risks overlooking the semantic signals it sends. At the risk of pedantry, the old combination of 'framework' and 'agreement' embodied the idea of a firmly established basis at stage one for making future contracts at stage two. By contrast, the absence of reference to an agreement and identification of both a framework and call-offs as 'contracts' somewhat elides or lessens the distinction between the stages. Conceptually, it effectively becomes a broad umbrella term: a contract 'providing for' (rather than firmly establishing) the future award of the same. It is difficult to refute that the essence of a framework has been removed. As will be discussed, section 45(5) prescribes what a framework must contain but this is not the same as stating its very purpose. By contrast, the new Health Care Services (Provider Selection Regime) Regulations 2023 refer to the concept of a 'framework agreement' as an agreement 'which establishes the terms based on which the provider will enter into one or more contracts for the provision of relevant health care services with a relevant authority in the period during which the framework agreement applies' (regulation 16(1)(a)).

Following Brexit, it has been interesting to see how the Government has rejected EU terminology and invented new terms to mark a conceptual break whilst purporting that this is not a change of substance. If legal language can be politicised in this way or have this effect, it can equally become a signal or 'nudge' to markets to act in a certain way. It is suggested that the new definition risks giving the impression that highly generic, non-descript frameworks are generally suitable. This may not necessarily have been the intention; perhaps, instead, such a definition intended to emphasise the flexibility

[24] GCF, 'Guidance: Frameworks', November 2024, 2.

of this purchasing tool. However, as discussed in chapter ten, combined with certain other messaging describing them as 'commercial vehicles' and absent certain regulatory controls, the definition is unlikely to deter behaviours identified in this book. Thus, the new definition of a 'framework' could arguably represent the influence of marketisation on legislative reform, seemingly reflecting the proliferation of highly generic multi-supplier frameworks. This chapter now turns to consider some of the remaining uncertainty in the definition.

2.2.1. Public Contracts and Frameworks

First, it remains unclear the distinction between a public contract and a framework by reference to binding obligations. Section 3(3) defines a 'public contract' as including a 'framework'. Further, the section 45(2) definition of a framework refers to 'a contract between a contracting authority and one or more suppliers'. The term 'contract' is not further defined.

The singular reference to a contracting authority (rather than plural) could be an acknowledgement that the tendency in the UK is not to conclude an agreement between contracting authorities (ie signing the same agreement) but rather that one single contracting authority signs the agreement but is subject to other arrangements entered into regarding framework use. Thus, this tends to take the form of: (a) a CPA (under section 1(4)) acting on behalf of other contracting authorities with 'access agreements' sometimes entered into between the CPA and user contracting authorities; (b) a lead contracting authority acting on behalf of others who enter into back-to-back agreements with the lead contracting authority; or (c) each contracting authority acting separately with the appointed framework supplier(s).

As before the PA 2023, frameworks have the potential to differ in terms of the extent to which the parties enter into binding commitments to purchase and/or supply on establishment. The GCF guidance on frameworks acknowledges that 'in most cases a framework will not commit a contracting authority to enter into a call-off' although it recognises that 'it is possible that some do'.[25] As indicated above, most in the UK are non-obligatory arrangements that facilitate rather than necessitate the future award of public contracts. A framework that imposes an obligation on a contracting authority to enter into a call-off is most likely to arise in the single-supplier context where a strategic partnering-type arrangement is set up. A supplier is unlikely to commit to upfront investment in that partnership without the guarantee of at least some work.

By denoting a framework as both a 'contract' (s.45(2)) and a 'public contract' (s.3(3)), the question arises as to whether the PA 2023 provisions on frameworks have similar application to the PCR 2015 provisions on framework agreements regarding different types of contractual arrangement. The PCR 2015 definition of a 'framework agreement' referred to an 'agreement' between one or more contracting authorities and one or more suppliers and a framework agreement did not fall within the EU-derived definition of a 'public contract'. The definition of a 'framework' in the PA 2023 refers to a 'contract' instead of an agreement which might suggest that the definition covers all agreements

[25] ibid.

that have the essential ingredients of a 'contract' as understood by English contract law principles and therefore has broader application than the PCR 2015 definition. However, 'pecuniary interest' is still referred to in the definition of a public contract in the PA 2023. Section 3 requires there to be 'pecuniary interest' present for one category of public contract, namely a public contract for goods, services or works but, interestingly, not for the other category of public contract, namely, frameworks. 'Pecuniary interest' is not explained further but this distinction between public contracts for goods, services and works and frameworks might indicate that a similar approach to that under the PCR 2015 should be adopted when considering which types of agreement fall subject to the provisions on frameworks. Adopting the logic above, this would mean that agreements that impose binding obligations to purchase and supply should be treated as standard public contracts and not subject to the provisions on frameworks. This analysis would make sense but is called into question because of the GCF's guidance stating that in most cases a framework will not commit a contracting authority to enter into a call-off but 'it is possible that some do'.

The categorisation of a framework as a public contract in the PA 2023 has other possible implications. The GCF guidance states that 'frameworks that are public contracts are most likely to be awarded following a competitive tendering procedure'.[26] However, the guidance also states that contracting authorities are permitted to directly award a framework under sections 41 or 43.[27] Presumably, this is because the rules on both types of procedure refer to a 'public contract'. The guidance states that as frameworks are awarded either following a competitive tendering procedure or, where permitted, directly, the provisions in the PA 2023 relating to both generally apply to the award of a framework.[28]

The guidance has not distinguished between single-supplier and multi-supplier frameworks in this regard; it is easier to conceive of a direct award of the former as opposed to the latter. Section 49(10) also provides that a framework under an open framework may not be awarded under sections 41 or 43.[29] As an open framework necessarily involves more than one supplier, this seems sensible. However, the logic behind permitting the direct award of a multi-supplier closed framework whilst prohibiting the direct award of an open framework is difficult to comprehend. The ability to make a direct award of a framework also contrasts with the position for health services in The Health Care Services (Provider Selection Regime) Regulations 2023, under which a relevant authority must follow a competitive process to conclude a framework agreement (regulation 16(3)).

Another possible implication of frameworks constituting public contracts and their likely award following a competitive tendering procedure is the risk of conflating frameworks and other purchasing tools. As a framework will generally be awarded following a competitive tendering procedure, provisions on the competitive flexible procedure will apply to its award. Those provisions also apply to 'dynamic markets', a new tool introduced under the PA 2023. Section 34(1) states that a competitive flexible procedure may

[26] ibid 3.
[27] ibid.
[28] ibid.
[29] ibid.

provide for suppliers that are not members of an appropriate dynamic market (or part of one) to be excluded from participating in, or progressing as part of, the procedure. Thus, if a competitive flexible procedure is used to award a framework, participation in that procedure may be limited to members of an appropriate dynamic market (or part of one). This risks conflating the tools, with possible undesirable consequences. For example, section 38(1) provides for the possibility of charging fees to suppliers awarded a contract by reference to their membership of a dynamic market and section 45(7) provides that a framework may provide for the charging of fees to the supplier; thus, there may be a double incursion of fees when being admitted to a framework awarded by reference to a dynamic market and when being awarded a contract under the framework.

2.2.2. Provides for the Future Award of Contracts but No Reference to Purpose

Second, as indicated, the PA 2023 definition of a framework omits express reference to its purpose. The GCF guidance interestingly states that a framework 'sets out the provisions under which future contracts' are to be awarded.[30] In the absence of any emphasis on establishing terms for future contracts through competition at the first stage, there is a risk that this definition may signal much flexibility to address key aspects of call-offs in the 'future'. The references in the definition and guidance risk the impression that whilst a framework is a 'public contract', it is not a contract in any real sense because there is no emphasis on agreeing much at the start except to enter into future contracts; the suggestion is that it is largely a facilitative mechanism ie 'providing' the basis for future awards. This change in wording calls into question the extent to which a substantive competition needs to be held to set up the framework and establish the terms of call-offs, in particular, pricing terms.

As indicated above, the purported emphasis on establishing the key aspects of a framework agreement through a competitive procedure was partly in recognition of EU objectives. The PA 2023 is built on a different set of objectives, as explained in chapter three, including the need to have regard to value for money (section 12). The definition of a 'framework' in the PA 2023 and the specific provisions on set-up and use therefore need to be considered against this different teleological construct. It is thus not necessarily clear whether there is now less, the same, or, indeed, more emphasis on using competition to formalise the framework.

That the new definition does not indicate any particular emphasis on the importance of using a competition to establish key terms, in particular on price, is further suggested by the fact that a framework is also a 'public contract', and may, therefore, be awarded by either a competitive tendering procedure or by making a direct award. The PA 2023 does not include any provisions explicitly stating that a competitive tendering procedure is the default in preference, albeit a direct award of a framework can only be made in certain limited circumstances.[31] Notwithstanding, as discussed above, the GCF

[30] ibid 2.

[31] See s 19 on competitive tendering procedures and ss 41–43 on direct awards.

guidance has provided a further indication towards the general importance of awarding frameworks in competition with direct awards being exceptional.[32]

There do not appear to be any other controls to ensure that the award of a framework is more selective than simply providing for 'future awards' and which could otherwise imply that much can be left to be determined in those future awards rather than upfront. For example, it is at least arguable that whilst the EU Directives and PCR 2015 did not expressly require any limit to be placed on the number that could be appointed, it is submitted that some limit was implied in a way that encouraged a substantive competition when awarding the framework and to use award criteria to establish a minimum number. For instance, regulation 33(5) provides that call-off procedures may be applied only between those contracting authorities clearly identified 'for that purpose' in the call for competition or the invitation to confirm interest and those suppliers party to the framework 'as concluded'. This link between the framework terms and parties involved could suggest some limitation on numbers. Otherwise, if all suppliers are appointed, it is difficult to see what purpose is served by requiring the establishment of terms governing the contracts to be awarded, in particular, with regard to certain factors (price or quantity). By nature, it seems to assume that it is only through some form of limitation that meaningful terms can be determined to govern contracts to be awarded. Further, not imposing a maximum limit on numbers would not have seemed logical considering the closed nature of a framework ie a prohibition on appointing suppliers after framework award (regulation 33(5)). Considering domestic objectives, it is questionable whether a framework that provides broad terms and admits many suppliers will secure value for money, for example.

It is therefore curious that the above loose definition appears to allow for the possibility of setting up both closed and open frameworks with an unlimited number of suppliers. Section 49(4) PA 2023, which sets out the process for awarding a framework under an open framework to an existing supplier, states 'there is no limit on the number of suppliers that can be party to a framework'. An unlimited number also seems possible for closed frameworks as the list of information that needs to be included in a tender notice advertising both closed and open frameworks includes 'whether the intention is to award the framework to […] an unlimited number of suppliers' (regulation 20(2)(i)(iii) PR 2024).

Relatedly, whereas proportionality-related requirements have been incorporated in some PA 2023 provisions (eg section 46(1) on setting conditions for participation when using a competitive selection procedure under a framework), the ability to set up a framework with an unlimited number has not been made subject to any proportionality considerations; consistency with other provisions would support such a reference. It is also not clear to what extent, if at all, the section 12 objectives may bear on determinations about the number admitted.

Thus, by removing reference to the core 'purpose' of establishing the terms of call-offs awarded under the framework and permitting the appointment of an unlimited number, whether intentionally or not, by definition, a new type of framework is being facilitated which is arguably a hybrid of the framework agreement and DPS tools, the

[32] GCF (n 24) 61.

rationale for which is unclear. As discussed below, when considered alongside the new flexible procedures for awarding call-offs, this new formulation could potentially encourage further marketised behaviours.

Another aspect explicitly absent from the new definition concerns the importance of undertaking a competitive process for the award of the framework on price. Indeed, as discussed in chapter seven, it is only in the context of section 45(4), which provides that a framework may provide for the future award of public contracts without competition between suppliers, that there is any reference to the framework setting out the 'core terms of the public contract', one of which must, presumably, be price howsoever 'core terms' is construed. It is then only in the subsequent provision in section 45(5)(b) concerning information to be contained in a framework that there is reference to 'the price payable, or mechanism for determining the price payable, under such contracts'. Neither of those provisions alone actually expressly requires the *procurement process* used to set up the framework to include a competition to establish pricing and other terms. Also, whilst, as discussed below, a framework is a public contract and, therefore, when following a competitive tendering procedure must be awarded to the 'most advantageous tender' or tenders (s.19(1)), the provisions on award criteria do not specify that 'price' must always be one of those criteria.

It is conceivable that a contracting authority's duty to have regard to the importance of 'delivering value for money' (s.12(1)(a)) would mean that in practice, some competition on price and key commercial terms will usually be necessary to award the framework but it would have been preferable to include this as an explicit requirement if that was the intention. As discussed in more detail in chapter seven, it is submitted that for both closed frameworks and open frameworks awarded pursuant to a competitive tendering process and which involve the appointment of a limited number, some competition on price should normally be required.

Whilst, as will be discussed in other chapters, there are other controls in the PA 2023 that could be considered to act as appropriate constraints on this new framework model, it is submitted that such controls are unlikely to be sufficiently strong to change practice. This is because some of these controls are linked to requirements only to 'have regard' to the importance of certain 'objectives' (eg value for money). These are not hard-edged obligations like the procurement principles written into regulation 18 discussed in chapter three which, it will be seen, have not been successful in preventing the distortion of the framework agreement model in the UK notwithstanding the clear requirements of the definition of a framework agreement in the PCR 2015.

3. The UK Framework Market

3.1. The UK Framework Market under the PCR 2015

As indicated, the PCR 2015 definition of a framework agreement deriving from the EU Directives was fairly broad. This has, in turn, at least partially contributed to the facilitation of similarly broad framework models, the most prevalent in the UK being a multi-supplier framework that imposes no legally binding obligations to purchase or supply. In addition to this broad definition, as indicated in chapter three, the EU Directives did not impose detailed regulatory controls on the set-up and operation of these arrangements. Moreover, as indicated in chapter four, no further detailed domestic rules were introduced. As will be discussed, the empirical research identified that this 'light-touch' approach to regulation has, to some extent, contributed to enabling significant variances in practice and marketised behaviours, albeit that some behaviours have also emerged in disregard of fundamental, well-established rules. Ultimately, a confident framework market has been allowed to flourish subject to few disciplined constraints.

3.1.1. General known Features of the Framework Market

Chapter two identified certain features characteristic of the framework agreement market. This Section considers these in more detail. As the empirical research confirmed, many interviewees are acutely aware of such features, their impact on practice and, in some instances, the limitations of the regulatory framework in addressing them, all of which inform choices about framework use.

A first characteristic feature is market choice ie the availability of many different types of framework. It is not known how many frameworks there are or to what degree they overlap, and with what effects. As indicated, the PCR 2015 definition of a framework agreement did not place explicit definitional controls on the type of framework that could be created. Further, although the EU Directives and PCR 2015 have required reporting or registers in respect of certain procurement activity, under the PCR 2015, there was no requirement to create a single, centrally controlled UK- or EU-wide repository of frameworks. In conducting research for this book, attempts were made to identify lists of frameworks for use[33] and some companies have established subscription services for contracting authorities and suppliers which identify suitable frameworks and appointed suppliers.[34] However, the lack of central coordination means that it has been very difficult to create an all-encompassing list.

As discussed below, the proliferation of many general public sector-wide frameworks suggests certain behaviours that were, to some extent, corroborated by the empirical research. The very fact that so many frameworks have been established indicates that the tendency now is not for contracting authorities to individually set up frameworks strategically to address their requirements over a projected duration; rather, it is often a case of using frameworks set up by other contracting authorities as a quick and easy route to market. Moreover, this proliferation has begun to have implications in terms of the resource required to shop around the framework market and make a business case for the framework selected.

A second characteristic feature, no doubt coinciding with the proliferation of multi-supplier frameworks, is the growth of CPAs. Again, attempts have been made to provide a

[33] See eg www.nhsx.nhs.uk/key-tools-and-info/procurement-frameworks/procurement-framework-strategy-recommendations/ and www.gov.uk/government/publications/ministry-of-defence-framework-library-list-of-purchasing-agreements.

[34] See eg www.framespan.com/.

list of the most well-known, but no comprehensive list exists.[35] It is recalled from chapters three and four that whilst the EU Directives provide definitions of central purchasing activities, the rules did not place particular controls on the establishment of CPAs and their role in the set-up and operation of frameworks. In 2010, the NAO and the Audit Commission noted that there were nearly 50 professional buying organisations, as well as individual public bodies, running commercial and procurement functions, many operating frameworks for similar goods and services, incurring unnecessary administration costs by duplicating activity and paying a wide range of prices for the same commodities.[36]

A third characteristic feature is the advent of private sector organisations active in the set-up and management of frameworks.

3.1.2. *Volume and Overlap of Frameworks*

All interviewees relayed a vast array of public sector frameworks for ICT requirements, including a mix of single-supplier and multi-supplier frameworks overlapping in scope. It was observed that these lacked homogeneity in terms of the application process to join the framework and the call-off procedures.

Regarding overlapping frameworks, it is recalled from chapter three that research has considered 'parallel framework agreements'.[37] It has been observed that Directive 2014/24/EU 'neither directly allows nor prohibits the creation of parallel frameworks'[38] and entry into them 'constitutes a grey area in the framework agreement practice'.[39] However, it has also been suggested that a choice made between parallel frameworks could violate the former Article 32(2) Directive 2004/18/EC, namely, that contracting authorities may not use frameworks improperly or in such a way as to prevent, restrict or distort competition.[40] It is recalled that Arrowsmith has suggested that an obligation is arguably implied to show objective commercial grounds for choosing one particular framework, to ensure that the discretion to choose is not abused for illegitimate reasons, such as to favour national providers.[41] In response, it has been questioned whether this approach is feasible and, if so, what are the legitimate grounds for such a choice. In this regard, it has been considered by analogy that there may be a precedent for a justificatory rule predicated on choice between framework options on the basis that Article 33(4) Directive 2014/24/EU provides that where a choice is to be made between a direct award and a mini-competition at the call-off stage, it must be based on objective criteria governing the choice.[42] It has been suggested that there is room for such an interpretation if read in accordance with Article 18(1).[43] However,

[35] See eg NAO, 'A review of collaborative procurement across the public sector: List of professional buying organisations', May 2010.

[36] NAO and Audit Commission, *A review of collaborative procurement across the public sector*, May 2010.

[37] M Socha, 'Competitive landscape of parallel framework agreements' in C Risvig Hamer, K-M Halonen and M Socha (eds), *Public Procurement: Centralisation and new trends* (Djøf, 2024).

[38] ibid 132.

[39] ibid.

[40] ibid 134 and citing at fn 13 a view expressed in Denmark.

[41] Arrowsmith (n 10) 11–101.

[42] Socha (n 39) 140.

[43] ibid 141.

even if there were a requirement to specify objective criteria as regards the choice between frameworks and which could increase transparency, it would still be difficult to determine what criteria may be legitimate. Applying such objective criteria to the choice would 'considerably limit flexibility' and even, paradoxically, limit competition were their application to result in required use of a framework concluded with large market players that prevents procuring outside the framework, thereby enabling market concentration and preventing SME market access.[44] It has also been argued that the reporting requirements under the Directive could require such a choice to be justified. Article 84(1)(g) requires that for every framework, contracting authorities must draw up a written report which must include 'where applicable, the reasons why the contracting authority has decided not to award a contract or framework agreement' and Article 84(2) requires documented progress of all procedures, which should necessarily include the motivation for certain choices. However, again, it has been observed the difficulty of relying on such a report if matters are documented in a procedure for one framework but not the other.[45]

The above suggests that there is legal uncertainty regarding the extent to which a choice between frameworks is subject to particular legal constraints. Whilst research has proposed including criteria regarding the choice between overlapping frameworks at the point of establishing the framework, it has been proposed that clarification in the Directives would be useful.[46]

By contrast, this issue does not appear to have been raised in the UK. The intimation has been that contracting authorities have considerable flexibility to choose between procurement options and between frameworks. Thus, in the UK OGC consultation on implementation of Directive 2004/18/EC, it was stated that:

> There was a concern that contracting authorities, which award framework agreements as defined in the new Article, do not have to use them for all their needs. The point is that, as defined, a framework agreement normally places no obligation on the authority to purchase. It simply sets out the terms and conditions which apply if it does purchase. This gives the authority the scope to go elsewhere if it can achieve better value for money in that way. If that flexibility is not required, a framework agreement may not necessarily be the best option.[47]

Thus, this might tend to suggest that it is implicit in the definition of a framework that places no obligation to purchase, that there is free choice between purchasing tools without having to particularly justify selection between options. It appears from the OGC guidance that if another framework or other alternative offers better value for money, it can do so without any explicit justification. Similarly, in response to consultation on draft regulations, such reasoning was identified in respect of a scenario in which a contracting authority awarded a framework but then decided to contract outside the framework for its requirements. It was stated that assuming the framework was not in itself a contract, this approach was entirely legitimate on the basis that the obligation

[44] ibid 141–42.
[45] ibid 146–47.
[46] ibid 150.
[47] OGC, 'Response to Consultation on the New Procurement Directives' (undated) 8. Available through the National Archives at webarchive.nationalarchives.gov.uk/ukgwa/20100303181810/http://www.ogc.gov.uk/procurement_policy_and_application_of_eu_rules_european_procurement_directives.asp.

is to secure the best value for money, meaning contracting authorities are free to use frameworks when these provide it and to go elsewhere if they do not.[48] There was no indication in the consultation or responses that, when choosing between frameworks and other options or between frameworks, objective grounds for the decision are required or that constraints applied on this choice because of the risk that it might restrict, prevent or distort competition. In any event, the UK's experience indicates that this issue does not appear to have been categorically addressed through policy guidance.

Whilst, as discussed below, there is evidence of contracting authorities preparing 'business cases' to justify as a commercial proposition the selection of a particular framework, there is little indication that they are applying objective grounds for choosing between frameworks.

In practice, interviews confirmed that a contracting authority considering using a framework is likely to face a choice of options from different CPAs. The lack of homogeneity between different frameworks has had an impact on the resource required to support decision-making processes when considering whether to use one, and which may vary among stakeholders. Contracting authorities described the framework 'market' being 'fragmented and complex' with no central catalogue.[49] Other general comments included:

> There are so many frameworks with blurred boundaries and lots of overlap in scope. For us to join a framework, we now have to prepare a decent business case. There is a heavy maintenance and reporting burden for being on a framework and we are concerned about wasting time and money.[50]
>
> There is a lot of confusion amongst purchasers when it comes to deciding which framework to use (there is a lot of overlap between national and local frameworks) and how to use them. Whereas frameworks were originally designed to make purchasing easier and simpler, they now often constitute just another barrier of bureaucracy and admin.[51]
>
> There are a lot of conflicting frameworks such that it has resulted in frameworks competing against each other for business. I would like to see more consolidated frameworks and a centralised database of frameworks available. At present, I have to write option papers for internal approval weighing up the pros and cons of different frameworks I could use.[52]

A few legal advisers referred to the 'framework shopping'[53] phenomenon whereby contracting authorities search for a framework that includes the supplier they want to use. Some turn to frameworks precisely because they have small procurement teams and thus frameworks are intended to save procurement capacity, but which does not always appear to be the case. Interviewees noted that contracting authorities 'cannot compete a framework against a framework and it is simply not feasible to run multiple mini-competitions simultaneously'. In other words, as frameworks are self-contained but may co-exist, there is the practical constraint that it is not possible to compete and

[48] OGC, 'Response to Consultation, Draft Regulations Implementing the new Public Sector and Utilities Procurement Directives', December 2005, 10.
[49] CA12.
[50] EO1.
[51] LA8.
[52] CA3.
[53] LA16, LA4.

compare suppliers across frameworks. This can lead to contracting authorities searching for frameworks that permit direct awards and ensuring that their preferred suppliers are admitted to them. It is submitted that this is a poor consequence of the development of the framework market and may represent 'improper' use of a framework if contracting authorities are effectively seeking to match frameworks to their suppliers. Given the above, it is certainly questionable, not least from a value for money perspective, as to whether the resource required in selecting a framework is proportionate to the outcome.

As discussed in chapter ten, it is submitted that more guidance is needed to support choices between frameworks and other procurement options and between frameworks.

Some interviewees queried whether frameworks could be centrally coordinated and controlled and whether mandatory use of specific frameworks could be introduced in legislation.[54] It is recalled from chapter four that this had been raised in consultations on implementation of the Directives as early as 2004 concerning mandating use of certain CPAs but which was rejected. This issue is briefly revisited in chapter ten.

A few interviewees remarked that some central government departments and others are already mandated as a matter of internal policy to use a particular central government CPA framework in the first instance.[55] This corroborates the 'framework first' policy documents produced in sectors such as the NHS and ICT, as discussed in chapter two. One interviewee described their organisation's policy of using a framework if they can identify a suitable one and having to record the reasons for not. They stated that 'this framework first approach can be problematic as it stops us from running independent standalone competitions for low-value requirements on Contracts Finder and establishing more appropriate, tailored terms and conditions'. They were also concerned about being mandated to use the frameworks of a particular CPA when the same organisation was also issuing the central government mandates and guidance on using its frameworks, thereby leveraging their conflicted position to gain a market advantage over other CPAs. In their words, this organisation 'is a market operator of frameworks and therefore cannot be an independent enforcer'.[56]

It follows that truly centralised purchasing is not present in the UK due to the number of CPAs in competition with each other and frameworks running in parallel. Indeed, the above interviewee comment suggests that a disincentive towards further centralisation arises precisely because of the sheer market and institutional dominance of a particular central government CPA in setting policies on frameworks and the conflict that this creates, a matter discussed in chapter ten. Arguably, much of the above may also be an instantiation of a wider uncertainty at the heart of UK public procurement policy, namely, the extent to which procurement should be centralised and driven by central government.

Similarly, on the supply side, most interviewees mentioned the significant work involved in identifying which frameworks they should apply to join. It was explained

[54] CA1 referred to mandatory frameworks in other countries eg Norway. CA12 referred to a previous mandate in place in Wales.

[55] NHS England introduced a policy of 'expected commercial adherence' to using several specific frameworks in its guidance, 'Guidance for trusts when buying digital and IT goods and services in the NHS'. Information is available at transform.england.nhs.uk/key-tools-and-info/procurement-frameworks/procurement-framework-strategy-recommendations/.

[56] CA15.

that some suppliers have specialised framework teams tasked with this work, with one supplier revealing that they have appointed a 'business administrator' whose main role is to identify all framework opportunities and monitor framework market developments.[57] There is also an indication that some suppliers are discriminating or discerning in their choices about which frameworks to join and, indeed, may be put off if the contracting authority operates too much like a business. One interviewee commented, 'I see [redacted] as a pseudo-commercial organisation and I am more selective now in terms of which frameworks we join'.[58] There is also evidence of some suppliers building their entire business model around managing supplies through frameworks on behalf of other suppliers. An interviewee described their business model as being based on it acting as a specialist 'thin prime' contractor on behalf of other suppliers seeking work through frameworks. It has built up significant expertise in accessing frameworks for ICT products and services and acting as an intermediary between the public sector and ICT companies for many years.[59] It is not clear to what extent the resource that is being invested by suppliers may be reflected in prices charged through frameworks, again, raising questions about the impact on value for money.

3.2. Centralised Procurement Authorities

3.2.1. Competition, Collaboration and Market Effects of Centralised Purchasing

As discussed in chapter three, under EU law, in the absence of explicit rules on CPA activities, questions have arisen as regards the market dominance of CPAs and whether the central purchasing activities (and ancillary activities) offered constitute a market for the provision of those services on the basis that they may compete against other contracting authorities or the private sector to provide them. It is therefore perhaps unsurprising that, considering the range of other factors and conditions conducive to marketisation of frameworks, CPAs increasingly compete against each other to a greater extent than they collaborate as contracting authorities in the public interest.

As indicated in chapter two, as early as 2008, various market-related issues were identified concerning CPAs in the UK. One article identified two implications of CPAs that merit particular focus. The first is their potential effect on the markets in which they are involved, in particular, on the structure of the market, without necessarily having legal consequences. The second is the extent to which they may create or increase the risk of a legal challenge to their activities, particularly under competition law.[60] The legal aspects were considered in chapter three and further examples are identified throughout this Part.

Focusing on consideration of the market effects of CPAs, that article observed that procurement via CPAs generally involves moving away from frequent but small

[57] EO2.
[58] EO1.
[59] EO3.
[60] J Chard, G Duhs and J Houlden, 'Body beautiful or vile bodies? Central purchasing in the UK' (2008) 2 *PPLR* NA26, 28.

procurements and towards less frequent but larger competitions.[61] The short-term result may be expected to be savings by increasing buyer power, minimising collusion through Buggins' turn (ie rotation) often found in frequent and small purchases in markets with few suppliers, and securing economies of scale through simplified procedures and channelling procurement expertise.[62] It was noted that some of the clearest examples of supplier collusion are fines on small construction sector roofing contracts which is, perhaps, prescient given that, in 2025, the Competition and Markets Authority[63] announced an investigation into school roofing contracts.[64] By contrast, it was observed that infrequent, one-off procurements encourage participation by large suppliers that do not wish to 'miss the boat' and be locked out for a period which may encourage submission of better offers. However, it was suggested that, in the long-term, the benefits to the purchasers of their cooperation may be reduced as their exercise of buyer power may have unintended negative consequences on market structure. The example was given of a contrast between one scenario in which a CPA is one of many purchasers (from the public and private sectors) of a product and another in which a CPA is a purchaser of a specialist service but there are few other private sector purchasers of that service. Whilst a single large procurement through a CPA may secure a favourable deal for a particular supplier in the short term, the fact that others may be locked out for that period may lead to market exit and contracting authorities being faced with reduced choice, in turn, reducing buying power because of a lack of innovation and diversity in the sector and reduced availability of supply.[65]

Further, it was suggested that central purchasing may disadvantage and discourage participation by SMEs due to the greater emphasis on being able to offer goods and services on a bigger scale and in more parts of the country favouring larger suppliers able to 'deal better with a feast and famine cycle, and who can assuredly offer a one-size-fits-all service'.[66] Smaller businesses may have preferred tendering frequently, for smaller orders, in a less homogenous market with opportunity to grow organically.[67] That said, it was also acknowledged that 'there are mitigating factors'; for example, the fact that CPAs may have a greater ability than individual contracting authorities to encourage new suppliers to enter markets.[68] It was ultimately stated that:

> In the end the extent to which CPBs can have positive effects on competition on markets depends on whether they seek to encourage competition through their procurement practices, or rather whether they focus on short-term gains which may reduce competition. In this context it is worth noting that government bodies are under increasing strain to minimise expenditure. This is unlikely to foster an environment where contracting authorities are willing to forego short-term savings in procurement expenditure in order to nurture healthy markets.[69]

[61] ibid.
[62] ibid.
[63] Information is available at www.gov.uk/government/news/cma-probes-possible-bid-rigging-in-relation-to-school-improvement-fund.
[64] Chard, Duhs and Houlden (n 60).
[65] ibid 29.
[66] ibid.
[67] ibid.
[68] ibid.
[69] ibid 29–30 (footnotes omitted).

This last observation is pertinent because it speaks to the likely reality of contracting authority recourse to CPA-led frameworks in the UK. Whilst research has tended to place emphasis on the need for competition, the reality is that contracting authorities, including CPAs, under increasing short-term pressure to reduce expenditures, are unlikely to be focused on the long-term fostering of markets to ensure 'healthy competition' even if that could lead to greater efficiencies and reduced expenditures.

Considering these wider market effects in light of the empirical research, there was agreement across all categories of interviewee that CPAs are competing against each other both for key suppliers and contracting authorities. One interviewee expressed concern that there was too much competition between CPAs and that this might be having a distortive effect on competition between suppliers considering which frameworks to apply to join.[70] They queried whether the 'aggregation of demand' driver that has been used by the UK Government to encourage framework use was actually having any positive effects, alluding to a 'waterbed effect', whereby the ability of some CPAs to secure lower prices for some aggregated demand may, paradoxically, be resulting in higher prices being paid on other frameworks and when using other procurement routes.[71] As indicated in chapter ten, such effects indicate a need for a closer examination of the economics of frameworks in the UK.

Another interviewee questioned whether it would generate better economies of scale if there was a single UK-wide framework provider, noting that 'there are just too many frameworks out there and too much choice' with most frameworks now available for use by all contracting authorities. They referred to a dispute with a CPA that occurred when they decided to set up a new framework rather than collaborate with the CPA.[72] This interviewee and many others acknowledged, however, that the suggestion of a single CPA was not feasible because of the way in which the framework market has developed with so much competition between CPAs.

It appears that such competition is only intensifying and marketisation is clearly playing a role. One interviewee who had previously worked for a CPA had experienced 'a push to adopt a more commercial approach to risk and purchasing and to achieve more commercial outcomes' and adopt a 'market strategy' for frameworks. Design workshops focused on the need to generate profit to fund the 'business' and analyses were undertaken to determine the extent to which each framework was likely to penetrate the market. To become a more 'commercial organisation' and 'win business across the public sector', this organisation had introduced sales teams, regional account managers and marketing and promotional resources.[73] This commercialisation had even extended to marketing frameworks as being locally based when this was not the case. Another interviewee reported how some frameworks advertised in the name of a localised CPA were actually frameworks set up and run by a larger, dominant organisation, but the name of the local organisation was used to facilitate 'buy-in' from local contracting authorities.[74] An interviewee from another CPA referred to a particular central government department

[70] CA15.
[71] ibid.
[72] CA12.
[73] CA1.
[74] CA12.

CPA as the 'dominant framework provider in the market' and said, 'we do not consider it sensible to compete with them'. They described trying to build good relations with the organisation and had even promoted some of its frameworks with their own public sector customers so as not to 'reinvent the wheel and establish a duplicate framework'.[75]

It is not only that CPAs are competing against each other, but also that contracting authorities that may have formerly collaborated see relationships break down and each set up separate frameworks. For instance, one interviewee said they previously collaborated closely with a particular contracting authority but 'found this to be increasingly difficult due to [redacted] adopting an overly rigid approach and not listening to their suggestions'. This CPA has, therefore, since opted to set up ICT frameworks independently.[76] Further, another interviewee from a CPA was aware that they operated in a highly contested market, viewing a particular CPA as their main competitor and preferring to work with smaller CPAs.[77]

There was also a sense that the public service driven mission is being increasingly subordinated to profit-making considerations. Thus, whilst it is possible to see how some CPAs may be remote or divorced from immediate service user needs and may not necessarily put those needs above other objectives, it appears that this has also started to occur among regional CPAs that might have been expected to put local service priorities first. An interviewee expressed surprise at how independent regional procurement 'hubs' (meaning separate regional entities set up to act as CPAs) established specifically to meet local public sector needs have been allowed to turn into profit-making commercial entities by setting up frameworks in contrast to the cost recovery basis upon which local authorities tend to set up their own frameworks. They thought there should be central and regional hubs supporting each other to drive best practice and align central and local government agendas, with the hubs acting as 'centres of excellence' with different specialisms in a supportive rather than a competitive way.[78]

As indicated in chapter three, whilst this book does not examine matters from a competition law perspective in detail, interviewees are clearly speaking using the 'dominant' market terminology of competition law. As discussed in chapter ten, this further confirms the need for research into the competition law implications of the framework market, particularly whether some CPAs have evolved into 'economic entities' at risk of engaging in anti-competitive practices.

However, whilst there was a general perception amongst regional CPAs that they were in competition with the perceived dominant central government framework provider, and, to a lesser extent other regional CPAs, these organisations sometimes also collaborate. One interviewee had observed 'more collaboration [...] than there used to be'[79] and another gave an example of three separate regional CPAs that had informally agreed not to compete against each other but instead concentrate on separate

[75] CPB5.
[76] CPB3.
[77] CPB7.
[78] CA9.
[79] CA7.

requirements that did not overlap.[80] The degree of collaboration appears to vary from sector to sector. For example, it was indicated that there appears to be a significant amount of collaboration in the further and higher education sectors with the emergence of several university consortia collaborating in joint purchasing and acting as CPAs.[81] However, it remains unclear to what extent collaboration could become collusion leading to anti-competitive practices contrary to competition law.

It should be added that contracting authority choice as regards the use of CPAs may be informed by factors that have little to do with sound procurement practice. Some interviewees from contracting authorities alluded to certain CPAs in which they are stakeholders. Naturally, such contracting authorities seek to use the frameworks established by such organisations in the first instance as their procurement officers are more familiar with using their terms and conditions. One interviewee commented that 'using a different provider brings added risk and requires additional resource to review all the terms and conditions' and therefore their approach is to 'stick to what you know'.[82] Therefore, parochialist attitudes to the use of frameworks cannot be excluded.

3.2.2. CPA Marketing of Framework Flexibility

As discussed in chapters six, seven and eight, much interview data was collected on procedures used to set up frameworks and call-off procedures. However, it is important to highlight certain salient findings that demonstrate the consequences of competition between CPAs regarding set-up and operation.

Interviewees indicated that market competition has led to CPAs introducing features in their frameworks to make them as attractive as possible to both contracting authorities and suppliers and which is considered by contracting authorities when selecting a framework to use. Many observed CPAs introducing progressively lighter requirements for suppliers to satisfy at the framework award stage. Examples were given of no limit on the number of suppliers appointed, low economic and financial standing and technical and professional ability thresholds, and limited requirements for tender submissions. In respect of one well-known pan-public sector ICT framework one interviewee expressed surprise at 'how little we had to do to get on to the framework which didn't actually fill me with much confidence' and that 'there are a huge amount of suppliers on it and we haven't received any work from it all'.[83] At the call-off stage, there was a noticeable trend of framework documents allowing significant flexibility to contracting authorities when using direct award or mini-competition call-off procedures. Examples were also given of frameworks that allow significant scope for introducing new terms or making changes to framework terms at the call-off stage. As one CPA interviewee explained, customers 'do not like to be dictated to with regard to terms and conditions'. For this reason, the organisation used a 'pretty light' standard set of terms for its call-off templates and allowed contracting authorities to use their own terms 'providing they do not breach the procurement rules'. They also referred to a need to allow contracting authorities and

[80] CA14.
[81] CPB9.
[82] CA13.
[83] EO4.

suppliers 'to sort out the terms and conditions between them' because many suppliers acting as resellers 'will need to apply third party terms (eg end user licence agreements) that are simply non-negotiable'.[84] As another interviewee observed, 'the reality is that you don't want to fix things too much at the framework level'.[85]

Again, these examples reflect how competition in the framework market has developed. CPAs are seemingly introducing more flexibilities in attempts to win business. However, it must also be acknowledged that CPAs are responding to imposed pressures from contracting authorities and suppliers. This is an important qualifier that it is not simply CPAs that are driving such behaviours for market gain; contracting authorities and suppliers are also demanding flexibilities which result in poor procurement practice. Notwithstanding, it is reminded that the purpose of a framework should be to frontload a process by setting out the terms governing the award of call-offs, as opposed to the emerging reverse trend of frameworks being set up without settling the terms or call-off procedures at the outset.

3.2.3. Monitoring and Enforcement by CPAs and Legal Responsibility

The PCR 2015 do not include explicit rules on enforcement and monitoring of frameworks by contracting authorities, in particular, CPAs. Interviews indicated that the extent of effective enforcement and monitoring by CPAs is a relevant consideration informing framework use. This aspect also has various market dimensions. As will be discussed, the private sector generally has a better customer service driven ethos (mainly given the profit incentive), which is perceived as a particular benefit of private sector managed frameworks. Further, by taking a hands-off approach to how the framework terms will operate at the call-off stage, it may be hardly surprising if a CPA does not then offer robust monitoring, oversight and enforcement. In other words, a consequence of a marketised approach to frameworks may be reduced oversight and accountability.

A question raised by many interviewees was whether the legal rules placed enough onus on CPAs to monitor and enforce compliance with the PCR 2015 and the terms of their frameworks. The level of management, support, monitoring and enforcement activity undertaken by CPAs varies, depending on factors such as: the capacity and resources available; a CPA's strategic and operational priorities; its perceived legal responsibilities; and allocation of legal and commercial risk.

Some CPAs provide ancillary support services to contracting authorities which can result in higher rebates and other fees chargeable. One interviewee stated, 'customers regularly ask for advice on whether their proposed call-off route is legally compliant' and that they willingly provided guidance. They 'hand-hold customers quite a lot now as they have the capacity to do so' and that 'it is in their interest to make sure that the call-offs are compliant'. More than one interviewee stated that they offered a service whereby they could run mini-competitions on behalf of contracting authorities, if desired.[86] Another described how they helped with 'completing documents and answering

[84] CPB3.
[85] LA7.
[86] CPB3, CPB6.

questions'.[87] Other examples were given of 'stakeholder meetings' where common issues experienced by contracting authorities are raised.

Notwithstanding, most contracting authority interviewees considered that support was insufficient, especially on the largest pan-public sector frameworks. One gave the example of a supplier refusing to sign a call-off unless the contracting authority agreed an amendment that its terms took precedence. Despite this being in flagrant breach of the framework terms, the CPA seemed 'disinterested' or 'powerless' and declined to intervene. This interviewee considered CPAs to be 'all relatively unhelpful' and that 'they can clarify but they don't fix!'.[88]

There was also consensus that CPAs are not policing the use of their frameworks and that 'framework owners are not holding suppliers to account'.[89] One interviewee had come across frameworks where the maximum values were exceeded with no action taken. Their view that 'framework providers should be held more responsible for managing a framework properly throughout its life' echoed many other contracting authority views.[90] Another questioned, 'does anyone raise a red flag when a framework is being abused, if for example too much is being charged under a framework? Where are the audit controls?'[91] One legal adviser commented that their contracting authority clients complain of the 'hands-off' culture.[92]

An interviewee from a CPA stated that they did not have visibility of supplier behaviours because they lacked 'the capacity or inclination to police every use of its frameworks'. There was a risk of suppliers not declaring all the work generated through the framework with the CPA, relying solely on suppliers providing accurate management information. This problem appears to have been exacerbated throughout the COVID-19 pandemic during which there was little to no visibility of how its frameworks were being used.[93] Another interviewee gave examples of 'inaccurate (sometimes grossly inaccurate) management information' being sent by suppliers and rebate figures being manipulated and the lack of audits being carried out by the CPA.[94] An interviewee from a supplier disclosed that they had approached a well-known CPA with a 'what-if' proposal to scrap all management information reporting requirements and instead for the supplier to pay a fee upfront to cover the framework running costs.[95] Another interviewee from a large CPA stated that they did not have capacity to proactively oversee use of their frameworks and that whilst they required suppliers to provide a limited amount of 'management information' regularly, they did not have sight of the final call-off documentation. They were aware that 'suppliers often breach the requirements of the frameworks by agreeing special terms seeking to override the main framework terms' and that penalties could be imposed. However, they said, 'it is unlikely that anyone is going to shame the big suppliers' and 'usually, it is handled by a phone call [...] but is not

[87] CPB10.
[88] CA18.
[89] CA2.
[90] CA10.
[91] LA17.
[92] LA9.
[93] CPB2.
[94] CA11.
[95] EO1.

taken any further'.[96] Several interviewees from contracting authorities called for more and better internal coordination within CPAs in this respect.

Concerning legal responsibility, some interviewees acknowledged that contracting authorities are saddled with the responsibility for complying with the PCR 2015 in respect of the stage of the framework procedure they conduct themselves ie the call-off stage (under regulation 37(6)). One interviewee felt that 'there is no rhyme nor reason to this'.[97] Several interviewees queried whether additional legal obligations should be placed upon those setting up frameworks instead. One objected to the lack of transparency-related obligations on framework providers and thought that 'they should have a role to play on data reporting'.[98]

Some CPAs require contracting authorities to sign undertakings to comply with the procurement rules or enter into access agreements which include indemnities that shield them from any liability arising from any breach in making a call-off. The terms 'buyer beware' and '*caveat emptor*' were mentioned by several interviewees to describe their understanding of risk allocation.[99] Some legal advisers explained that their clients frequently sought advice on whether a framework they wished to use had been set up in compliance with the PCR 2015 and the associated legal risks. As one interviewee stated, 'if the framework does not provide a solid basis of contracting in accordance with the rules, there is a risk that each call-off award constitutes an unlawful contract award'.[100] Another stated, 'contracting authorities should really be looking for indemnities from the framework provider instead of the other way around!' and highlighted that alongside legal risks, there were 'reputational risks' that accompanied using a non-compliant framework.[101]

It appears that the allocation of legal risk is not fully understood by all contracting authorities, however. A legal adviser described being asked by clients about who bears the liability risk if a framework has not been set up properly.[102] For many contracting authorities, declarations of legal compliance are required prior to awarding public contracts, including call-offs from frameworks. One interviewee highlighted that in local government, monitoring officers are required to report where it appears to them the local authority has done, or is about to do, anything that would contravene the law.[103]

These issues emphasise the uncertainty regarding the allocation of legal responsibilities between CPAs and contracting authorities using their frameworks and some indication of attempts to shift risk allocation but subject to few clear controls or guidance and which must be addressed, as discussed in chapter ten. Nevertheless, whilst this creates uncertainty and additional burdens, there remains a perceived low risk of challenge, as discussed in chapter nine.

[96] CPB1.
[97] CA12.
[98] CA15.
[99] CPB5.
[100] LA6.
[101] LA15.
[102] LA12.
[103] LA16. See generally, s 5 Local Government and Housing Act 1989.

3.3. Private Sector Framework Providers and Managers

It is recalled from chapter two the increasing involvement of private sector organisations in the set-up of frameworks. An NAO report has noted several instances of small contracting authorities (health trusts or academies) 'hosting' frameworks operated by the private sector and 'marketed to a wide range of public sector buyers as a convenient route to market with proactive customer service'.[104] The NAO states that '[t]hese frameworks operate separately from central initiatives to aggregate demand and improve category management and have not been subject to oversight or accreditation' and notes commissions charged to suppliers (and in some cases, buyers) for using these frameworks as high as 5 per cent to 6 per cent (compared with the average of 0.7 per cent for CCS frameworks).[105] In some instances, those commissions may have incentivised direct awards over competition at call-off stage and 'profits generated from commissions are not available to improve the public procurement system'.[106] It has also noted that public bodies which agree to host frameworks may receive income from these private sector partners.[107]

The NAO has observed: a lack of transparency about the allocation of risk and benefits between framework provider and host; possible delays or omissions in the reporting of the procurement procedures and the value of call-off activity; and the unknown extent to which frameworks are being used as a route for direct awards instead of competition at the call-off stage.[108] In its report, the NAO looked at five private sector companies offering frameworks to public sector buyers. Three generated a combined annual operating profit of around £26 million; the other two published abbreviated accounts,[109] raising questions about how those frameworks contribute to value for money.[110]

It is clear from the definitions of a 'framework agreement', 'contracting authority' and 'central purchasing body' in the PCR 2015 that a private sector organisation cannot be a party to a framework in place of a contracting authority. Such organisations might also be providing procurement consultancy services to contracting authorities but these may not necessarily be awarded in accordance with procedures under the PCR 2015.

Notwithstanding, as discussed in chapter four, private sector involvement has only grown. It is recalled that as early as July 2010, the OGC issued a PPN warning against the use of frameworks set up by such organisations. The Procurement Lawyers' Association ('PLA') had also highlighted that even when a 'framework' set up by a non-contracting authority (whether purporting to be a CPA or not), has been subject to full advertisement, the award of specific contracts under that agreement could constitute an illegal direct award if the agreement in question cannot satisfy the definition

[104] NAO, *Efficiency in government procurement of common goods and services*, Cabinet Office, Session 2024–25 HC 116, 8.

[105] ibid.

[106] ibid.

[107] ibid 18.

[108] ibid.

[109] ibid 41.

[110] ibid 8.

of a framework.[111] It is further recalled, however, that much of that guidance was not categorical in prohibiting such arrangements.

Many interviewees mentioned the emergence of private sector organisations, relaying responses ranging from the extremely negative to the relatively positive. The variation of attitudes is an important reminder that regulating effectively in this area may not be as simple as precluding any and all private sector involvement. This should not detract, however, from a more searching enquiry into its impact on framework contracting.

Concerning the framework models used, various examples of both the purported 'agency' and 'neutral vendor' models were given. In relation to agency models, an interviewee from a private sector organisation described how their organisation had been set up to take over a public sector purchasing consortium and had invested heavily into building the business. An agreement is in place between it and a contracting authority pursuant to which it is delegated wide-ranging powers and acts as a CPA for a variety of customers. In contract notices advertising frameworks, it describes itself as a CPA acting as an agent for that contracting authority.[112] Another interviewee stated that these frameworks involved 'doing a deal' with a contracting authority mentioned in the Contract Notice on an apparent 'agency' basis but where the contracting authority is not closely involved. Another described 'very loose hosting arrangements'.[113] It was queried whether the relationship between the private sector entity and the 'sponsoring' contracting authority is a true agency relationship[114] if the contracting authority is not truly acting as a principal. A legal adviser stated that this relationship needed closer scrutiny, questioning whether a relationship similar to the so-called CJEU *Teckal*[115] in-house public-public cooperation principles should apply.[116] It is recalled from chapter four that the conceptualisation of CPA-led frameworks as involving an in-house arrangement was raised early on and is considered again in chapter ten.

In relation to neutral vendor models, some interviewees described arrangements that they initially perceived to be multi-supplier frameworks run by private sector organisations but which were revealed as single-supplier frameworks set up to allow the procurement of an unlimited scope of supplies, services and works by contracting authorities. The private sector organisation awarded the framework would source a suitable supplier or suppliers through a network at the sub-contract level. Such frameworks are explained in more detail in chapter eight. This has caused confusion and concern for contracting authorities. Several instances were recounted of procurement departments being approached by their internal IT teams seeking to use such routes to contract to appoint a supplier of their choice swiftly and easily. Interviewees regularly grappled with difficult questions about whether the private sector organisation was even permitted to operate the framework and whether the contracting authority would be permitted to use it. Several interviewees referred to a 'fixed fee phenomenon' whereby frameworks set up by one private sector organisation had been 'bought' by suppliers.[117] The call-off

[111] PLA (n 12) 21–22.
[112] CPB12.
[113] CA15.
[114] CA14. CA1.
[115] Case C-107/98 *Teckal Srl* ECLI:EU:C:1999:562, [1999] ECR I-8121.
[116] LA3. See generally reg 12 PCR 2015.
[117] CA10.

procedures operated by some private organisations were also called into question. One interviewee referred to the 'rather dubious ranking systems' adopted when appointing suppliers[118] and another mentioned 'very dubious call-off methods', expressing concern about whether these provided value for money.[119] Examples were given of direct award and mini-competition procedures that allow unlimited discretion when choosing a supplier for a particular requirement or formulating mini-competition award criteria and weightings.

Concerning legal liability, a legal adviser noted that 'there can be difficulties for a claimant wishing to bring a legal claim under the PCR 2015 as it may not be clear who the defendant is' and reiterated that 'under the PCR 2015, claims can only be brought against the contracting authority'.[120] Relatedly, an interviewee complained that such organisations usually disclaim all liability to contracting authorities seeking to use their frameworks and were not acting as lawful CPAs at all.[121] A few legal advisers said that the definition of a CPA in the PCR 2015 might need to be revisited to address this issue.

Again, as a balanced perspective, interviewees did identify certain benefits of private sector management of frameworks. They were considered by some to offer better and more professionally organised purchasing and ancillary support than that offered by CPAs. Two interviewees from suppliers stated that they were attractive because they were 'very flexible' offering user-friendly 'direct award' options. One described how they have a greater understanding of market-acceptable contract terms.[122] Another stated that they are 'set up purposefully for the customers'.[123] An interviewee from a private sector organisation explained how their business model and the charges they levy are predicated on them acting on a professional basis and offering wide-ranging support from pre-market engagement to running the call-off procedure.[124] One interviewee indicated how 'customers take comfort from the fact that lots of other public sector buyers are using them'.[125]

The fact that private sector organisations are being 'purposefully' set up for customers who 'take comfort from' the fact that others are using them is a concern given that it is categorically not the case that the PCR 2015 provides a clear legal basis on which such arrangements can be adopted.

Whatever the perceived advantages and disadvantages of introducing private sector involvement in the set-up and management of frameworks, the fact remains that their legal status and liability as contracting authorities is questionable. Such organisations may effectively be generating profits by providing procurement consultancy and support services to CPAs as well as running frameworks without any effective procurement process being used to appoint them, thereby potentially circumventing the PCR 2015. More fundamentally, it introduces private sector objectives and mentalities into the public sector. Some might argue that this is objectionable in principle. Even for those

[118] CA3.
[119] CA1.
[120] LA9.
[121] CPB1.
[122] EO2.
[123] EO5.
[124] CPB12.
[125] CPB6.

who consider it is not (after all, there has been a drive for public sector procurement to become more 'commercial' in delivering outcomes), it is hard to overlook the fact that there is little oversight of the potential effects of those objectives and mentalities on the cost and delivery of public services.

3.4. ICT Market-specific Factors

In choosing to use a framework, any factors specific to the sector will need to be considered. As the interviews focused on frameworks for ICT requirements, inevitably, certain responses related to issues specific to this sector. As will be discussed, these provided an important perspective on an aspect that is likely to be overlooked in legal research, namely, considerations external to the framework itself and which are not explicitly regulated but which may have a direct bearing on its operation and may well raise legal issues. Two recurring issues were raised, namely, the 'reseller' market and central government memoranda of understanding ('MoU') that set prices and commercial terms.

3.4.1. Resellers

For context, many interviewees highlighted the distinct characteristics of the software and commoditised ICT hardware markets, in particular, the distinction between original software and hardware suppliers and suppliers that act in a 'reseller' capacity. One interviewee explained that, whilst the original suppliers might be inclined to join some of the large, high-value frameworks, they tended to refrain from joining the lower-value frameworks for standard 'off-the-shelf' items, choosing instead to rely on resellers who are expected to join.[126] Several interviewees raised concerns about the suitability of framework procedures for sourcing such products through resellers.

First, one interviewee highlighted that using a framework to purchase off-the-shelf software can result in a competition between the resellers on the profit margins they are charging but that the real control on pricing is determined externally by the original supplier, giving a contracting authority little ability to verify whether the prices offered represent value for money.[127] Interviewees indicated that original suppliers appeared to have significant control over their respective distribution channels with resellers sometimes applying very low profit margins to their onward sales. When a particular requirement under a framework arises, these resellers tend to deal outside the frameworks with the small number of large, global, original software suppliers. One interviewee reported that business relationships can be 'incestuous' with resellers having employees outsourced from the original suppliers.[128] Another alluded to this having 'always been a problem with lots of resellers on a framework relying on the same supplier to price a requirement under a framework'.[129] An interviewee from a contracting authority thought that the large original suppliers were 'running the show'

[126] CPB5.
[127] CA3.
[128] CPB1.
[129] CPB2.

with contracting authorities having 'little power' over supplier activity and 'with no knowledge if they are obtaining value for money'.[130]

Second, relatedly, to some extent, it is original sellers not contracting authorities who effectively determine which suppliers should be rated the best and be given the best prices according to the application of their own criteria and ratings *outside* the framework, rendering a mini-competition on price redundant. Some interviewees referred to 'preferred reseller arrangements' that have been established through 'deal registrations'. These seemingly involve the original supplier grading resellers using ratings such as 'platinum', 'gold' and 'silver' or even awarding 'partner' level and applying preferential pricing to its products based on the reseller's rating, determined by the revenue generated or their qualifications. Reference was made to 'exclusivity deals' being arranged between original suppliers and resellers which enable a reseller to secure better pricing terms.[131] The experience of one interviewee was that the proposals from resellers in response to the framework were usually focused on emphasising any 'special' or 'preferred' relationships with key original suppliers. One interviewee thought that pricing on frameworks fails where deal registrations are involved because 'whichever reseller registers a deal first gets the best discount' and 'a mini-competition is ridiculous in this context'.[132] They described a call-off opportunity whereby an original supplier only allowed three deal registrations for a particular tender which, in their opinion, signified that 'work was being done on the opportunity before the tender was actually released'. They stated that whilst deal registration occurs at the sub-framework level, some frameworks require certain partner levels and customers needed to check the market to assess partner levels and whether the costs of running a mini-competition outweigh the potential benefits.[133] One interviewee referred to resellers as the 'sales and marketing arms' of the original suppliers and mentioned a 'dynamic' framework under which the original suppliers have been permitted to nominate four resellers annually to allow flex to reflect the dynamic realities of the market and to allow more 'partnering'-type arrangements to be set up with the original suppliers through the framework.[134]

Therefore, original sellers can directly impact the functioning of the framework model, even rendering call-off procedures nugatory. This also raises issues in respect of transparency of pricing. According to one interviewee, original suppliers selling to different resellers obviates any transparency of the prices given by the original supplier to the different resellers. One interviewee had experienced a difference of over £1 million between the lowest and the highest bid when supplying substantially the same solution.[135] Further, another interviewee sought to call off from a framework when they received identical bids (in terms of pricing, product and support) from resellers using the same original supplier. They saw the mini-competition as being 'futile' and opted to use the first reseller on the framework list instead.[136]

[130] CA2.
[131] CA3.
[132] CA10.
[133] EO2.
[134] CPB9.
[135] CPB5.
[136] CA6.

This lack of transparency may also render it difficult to verify offers made by a reseller purporting to be the 'preferred reseller' which, according to one interviewee, has necessitated further checks with the original supplier, incurring additional administrative costs and time.[137] Another interviewee reported that contracting authorities may have to conduct additional due diligence on the prices offered by resellers, giving an example in which they received a very high price from a reseller which prompted them to approach the original supplier, only to discover that the reseller was imposing a very high margin to align with prices offered to private sector customers.[138]

The ICT market has also witnessed the emergence of 'value-added resellers'. These do not simply pass through the product but try to differentiate their offering by providing ancillary support services as part of a wider package.[139] One interviewee had observed some resellers applying a 0 per cent margin on software products sourced from original suppliers, relying instead on the revenue generated from the value-added services to make a profit.[140]

Interviews also revealed that, in contrast, some original suppliers will not work through resellers or frameworks at all, seemingly because they are concerned about price transparency, claiming that if they have to publish their pricing in a framework catalogue, they will not be able to offer the same individual deals and prices will be forced up.[141]

To offer a balanced perspective, one interviewee identified such 'reseller frameworks' as useful for sourcing ICT items where 'good savings can be made' as 'it often leads to some limited negotiation with a supplier on price which can result in a lower price after the reseller has negotiated further with the supplier'. They referred to resellers as 'intermediaries' who do much of the commercial work for customers by going to the market and managing supplier issues, giving an example in which an original supplier could not provide a requirement under the framework terms so the reseller took the risk contingency on behalf of the supplier and accepted the terms of the framework. A reseller might charge a higher 'mark-up' in such circumstances, but this interviewee considered this to be justified because of the added value they bring by managing original suppliers.[142]

3.4.2. Central Government Memoranda of Understanding

The UK Government has also entered into MoUs with large original software suppliers. These are agreed independently of frameworks and set pricing and commercial terms under which the original suppliers will supply to central government departments. Whilst such MoUs are not specific to supplies through frameworks and can be invoked when using other procurement procedures, one interviewee observed how they have been used to underpin pricing provided through frameworks. They stated that MoUs

[137] CPB6.
[138] CA7.
[139] CPB1.
[140] CPB7.
[141] CPB5.
[142] ibid.

could be used as a tactic by central government 'to lure big suppliers to do business with them', and that some customers would be aware of discounts that had been agreed through MoUs and would refer to these when agreeing call-offs.[143] A few interviewees used the term 'dominant' when referring to original suppliers benefitting from such MoUs and viewed these as unfair for smaller suppliers and with the potential to distort competition. Another interviewee from a supplier mentioned a framework with only two resellers appointed to supply the software of a particular original supplier and which were the only resellers permitted to offer the 'special pricing' pursuant to a special MoU, resulting in those suppliers being automatically appointed to the framework whenever it is re-issued.[144]

One interviewee referred to the 'power and clout' that a particular central government department-run CPA was likely to have over other CPAs in putting such MoUs in place and the resulting advantages. None of the other CPAs appeared to have enough bargaining power to agree such arrangements.[145]

Another interviewee thought that the pricing secured through such arrangements did not offer value for money and led to expensive pricing in frameworks because of the amount of risk built in (ie uncertainty in customer demand), giving an example of where they had managed to secure better pricing by approaching the original supplier independently.[146]

The reseller and MoU arrangements raise a host of legal and practical questions beyond the scope of this book. One legal adviser opined that 'the software vendor market is juxtaposed with the public sector purchasing market and it is very difficult to get both to work together'. They highlighted that there may be some competition law issues to address particularly with the use of MoUs. This is because, as raised by another interviewee, a central government department is driving these whilst also acting as a CPA. In addition, new market entrants might face difficulties when seeking to compete with the products of large original suppliers on frameworks because of the MoU arrangements in place to secure large volume discounts. As indicated above, in respect of reseller arrangements, there is concern about the lack of effective control by the contracting authority over pricing and other terms given the power of the original seller, and even the suggestion that original suppliers and resellers were working on opportunities before tenders were released. As reiterated in chapter ten, the reseller phenomenon and the use of MoUs in the context of frameworks are clear instantiations of the impact of marketisation and evidence the need for more systematic sector-specific research into wider arrangements and behaviours that impact on frameworks both from a procurement regulation and competition law perspective.

3.5. The UK Framework Market under the PA 2023

The PA 2023 focuses primarily on processes for the award of contracts. It does not generally explicitly regulate wider aspects of market behaviour associated with procurement.

[143] CPB1, CPB7.
[144] EO2.
[145] CPB5.
[146] CA10.

However, it cannot be said that the PA 2023 does not acknowledge such issues; as discussed below, section 45(7) introduces an express rule permitting the charging of fees to suppliers. Technically, this does not concern the award of contracts. It is more a feature of the organisation of the procurement function (ie the financing of a framework operation), although it could be argued that such fees may limit market access to procurement for suppliers. The fact that the PA 2023 has, for the first time, extended provision on frameworks to cover fees, raises the question of how far *procurement* legislation should extend in regulating the wider market implications of frameworks, quite apart from other areas eg competition law. If procurement legislation is considered the appropriate mechanism by which to also regulate these market aspects, it is submitted that the PA 2023 otherwise clearly fails by its omission. Consequently, the trends identified in this book are only likely to continue.

Notwithstanding, it should be acknowledged that certain of the transparency-related reforms could, at least, provide a means of better understanding aspects of the framework market. Thus, one potentially positive development is a centrally held register of purchasing tools. In this regard, the 2020 Green Paper *Transforming Public Procurement* which precipitated the PA 2023 stated that a central register would make it easier to find and compare frameworks and that additional transparency would be required in contract awards, with all award notices being visible in the new central platform and linked to the framework from which they were procured.[147] The Government also stated that it 'should reduce the current duplication of frameworks'.[148]

However, it is not clear how such a register will, by itself, prevent the proliferation and duplication of frameworks. There are no additional rules limiting the volume or type of frameworks that can be set up, which contracting authorities can set them up, and which can or should use particular frameworks. It is also not clear what, if any, due diligence will be carried out on each framework before it is entered onto the register or whether any assurance will be provided about its legality. This may be considered in light of the fact that, as indicated in chapter four, a February 2025 Ministerial statement states that 'a new online register of commercial agreements will increase visibility of frameworks and fees, curbing excessive profits'.[149] It is not clear how simply providing a register will curb excessive profits, not least given that the PA 2023 does not provide any significant controls on fees.

Other transparency-related reforms include an increase in the amount of information to be included in tender notices advertising frameworks (regulation 20 PR 2024), frameworks themselves (section 45(5)), and new contract award notices to be published before entering into frameworks and call-offs (regulation 27 PR 2024), as well as contract details notices after concluding frameworks and call-offs (regulations 33 and 34 PR 2024). These provisions should provide useful data to build up a picture of frameworks but do not directly address many of the issues raised in this book. The following is an illustrative list of issues that should be addressed.

[147] Cabinet Office, *Transforming Public Procurement* (n 21) 47.

[148] Cabinet Office, 'Transforming Public Procurement: Government response to consultation' (n 21) 49. Green Paper Response para 215.

[149] NPPS, Statement made on 13 February 2025, by Georgia Gould, Parliamentary Secretary for the Cabinet Office.

First, there are insufficient controls on the establishment of (parallel) frameworks. CPAs are actively competing between themselves and are unlikely to be deterred from setting up a framework just because another CPA has already commenced a framework covering similar subject-matter or is in the process of doing so. On the contrary, if a CPA considers it could set up a framework to win business from another, it may do so.

Second, there is a lack of effective guidance for contracting authorities on whether they should set up or use a framework and, if so, which framework they should use. The GCF guidance gives very limited advice in this regard, simply stating that where a contracting authority wishes to award a call-off established by another, it must ensure that it is 'suitable for the contract it intends to award'.[150] Given that there seems to be concern within the EU about the legality and impacts of parallel frameworks, there is a need for more tailored guidance on selection of the most appropriate frameworks.

Third, there are insufficient controls and guidance on the involvement of private sector organisations in framework set-up and operation. The GCF guidance only briefly highlights that '[t]he Act does not regulate entities that are not contracting authorities (for example private companies)' and refers to frameworks established by a person that is not a contracting authority as 'third party frameworks'.[151] It states that such frameworks 'must have been set up in the name of a contracting authority or authorities; the non-contracting authority entity would have to be acting as the agent of the named contracting authority (or authorities) (the 'principal contracting authority') if it sets up and administers the framework'.[152] By referring to the ability of private companies to establish frameworks without clarifying what conditions must be satisfied for such an agency relationship, the Government has failed to address this issue. It is reasonable to interpret the guidance as confirming that the position under the PA 2023 is the same as under the PCR 2015 in that a private company might run the process to establish a framework and be involved in administering it but a contracting authority must itself enter into the framework with the supplier(s) ie the private company must be acting as an agent as understood in legal terms. It would have been preferable, however, for this issue to be addressed more directly, as discussed in chapter ten.

Fourth, guidance has not addressed inappropriate framework use in certain sectors such as ICT, where large ICT suppliers have already agreed bespoke pricing and commercial terms with central government or dictate prices outside the framework.

4. Charging Fees for Use of Frameworks

4.1. Charging Fees under the PCR 2015

The PCR 2015 are silent on the charging of fees to suppliers and/or contracting authorities under frameworks. It is not clear to what extent this was considered by the EU based on, for example, their impact, if any, on ensuring non-discrimination and removing

[150] GCF (n 24) 3.
[151] ibid 3.
[152] ibid 4.

market access barriers to create an internal market (eg in particular for SMEs).This may be contrasted with the fact that Article 34(9) Directive 2014/24/EU in respect of DPS which provides that 'no charges may be billed prior to or during the period of validity of the dynamic purchasing system to the economic operators'.

This is significant in the UK context because, as indicated in chapter two, it has been questioned whether the charging of fees or commissions (particularly by CPAs) actually extends beyond merely covering operational costs in running a framework into the generation of 'surpluses' or profit, and where it is not necessarily clear if such are being reinvested back in public services. Suppliers may not necessarily consider fees as a market access barrier as they may simply accept them as a cost of doing business and which, in theory, is only incurred once the contract has been awarded, such that it might be argued that fees are not an 'access' issue per se. Nevertheless, the fact remains that such fees can be profit-generating tools. They may also potentially compromise value for money where suppliers pass on the cost of those fees to contracting authorities using the framework through charging higher prices. It is submitted that the charging of fees is an archetypal example of marketisation because it clearly involves a basis of exchange (ie, payment for access) and is a business model for CPAs.

4.1.1. Charging Fees in Practice under the PCR 2015

There has been a growth in the use of business models to generate revenue and support the establishment, promotion and administration of frameworks. The types of model used varies depending on the size, ownership, organisational and business objectives of the contracting authority or private sector entity. This can have negative effects as the actual costs associated with procuring through a framework may lack transparency, vary significantly from framework to framework and be difficult to factor into a value for money assessment of whether to use a framework.

A common and widely used method for generating revenue for a CPA is the imposition of 'rebates' (also known as 'levies', or 'management charges'). These are charged to a supplier usually based on a percentage of call-off value. When known, the applicable rebate can influence a contracting authority's decision on which framework to use as there is a perception that rebates are recharged to the customer procuring through the framework. As an NAO report has observed, some organisations have indicated that the levy paid by suppliers is embedded in the price,[153] that 'this transfers funds from buyers to framework providers and it is an incentive for the framework provider to maximise the flow of procurement spend and open their frameworks for other public authorities to access'.[154] CCS informed the NAO that it explicitly requires suppliers not to invoice customers separately for the cost of the levy.[155]

It is recalled from chapter two that the NAO has reported on CCS's use of the levy model, which is double the rate it requires to achieve its return on capital employed.[156] The majority of CCS's income levies on suppliers are paid as a proportion of the value of

[153] NAO (n 104) 41.
[154] ibid.
[155] ibid.
[156] ibid 11.

the business they win through CCS frameworks.[157] In 2015–16, 28 per cent of CCS's income came from charging departments a fee for its services, including buying goods and services on their behalf, which fell to 11 per cent in 2016–17, and to less than 1 per cent by the end of 2017–18. CCS has stopped charging most departments a fee, with only two still paying a small fee for managed services in 2022–23.[158] CCS's levy, which is an average of 0.7 per cent, generated income of £177 million in 2022–23, nearly twice CCS's operating cost (£94 million).[159] CCS informed the NAO that it has been asked to pay a larger dividend to the Cabinet Office.[160] In 2022–23, CCS doubled the annual dividend to £36 million (20 per cent of the levy collected), but still retained a substantial surplus, 'somewhat to the dissatisfaction of some of the CCS customers'.[161]

The NAO also found limited evidence that framework providers have used the surplus income to make procurement more efficient, although noted CCS's claim that it was able to fund certain improvements in commercial capability on behalf of customers.[162] The report further observed that CCS is introducing a payment scheme in 2024–25 to return part of its surplus to some of its customers following approval from the Cabinet Office and HM Treasury. HM Treasury also asked CCS to consider reducing the levy rate if surpluses continue to grow but the NAO noted that this had not yet been done. Further, there was no guarantee that future payments would accurately reflect the usage of CCS frameworks.[163] It was indicated that funding pressures meant that commercial directors are happy to receive cash payments from CCS, but they also felt that a wider review of the levy system could identify a more efficient way to distribute CCS's surplus.[164] The NAO suggested that the levy could be cut by 50 per cent with public sector organisations avoiding over £500 million in costs.[165] However, it ultimately concluded that CCS has insufficient incentives to reduce the levy.[166]

Interviews for this book revealed some uncertainty as regards the motives for charging fees. Two interviewees representing different CPAs run by different groups of local authorities stated that the rebates were used to cover the CPA's overheads, with one interviewee stating 'any profit remaining is returned to the member local authorities'[167] and another describing its organisation as 'non-profit-making' with the relatively low rebates charged set on a cost recovery basis only.[168] However, the NAO has reported that some framework providers owned by local authorities may generate a surplus from other public sector buyers that use their frameworks.[169] By contrast, an interviewee from another CPA described its organisation as 'self-funding' with a 'sales-orientated focus' and that 'it aims to generate as much spend as possible through its frameworks

[157] ibid 40.
[158] ibid.
[159] ibid. CCS generally sets the levy at 1% but alternative rates can be used, if justified.
[160] ibid 11.
[161] ibid 41.
[162] ibid.
[163] ibid 42.
[164] ibid.
[165] ibid.
[166] ibid 11.
[167] CPB5.
[168] CPB3.
[169] NAO (n 104) 41.

in order to make profit'. They also revealed that 'the vast majority of frameworks are routinely re-let based mainly on how they have performed commercially'.[170] Another interviewee mentioned 'other purchasing organisations popping up from nowhere which are focused solely on being profit-making/securing huge margins' which they viewed as 'very wrong'. They compared rebates of less than 1.5 per cent being charged on some frameworks with 5–7 per cent being charged on others and queried the purported justification of covering operating costs.[171] Another CPA interviewee was aware of accusations that such mechanisms result in 'milking the taxpayer' because of the way in which the charges are passed to customers. Reference was also made to frameworks being 'nice little earners'.[172] One legal adviser referred to the 'commercialisation of frameworks'.[173]

Even more fundamentally, interviewees called into question whether such fee arrangements undermined the purpose or objectives of frameworks and may compromise value for money on the basis 'that organisational objectives are not encouraging the right behaviours'[174] and CPAs are 'too concentrated on attracting the big suppliers rather than meeting the needs of the user authorities'.[175] This view was echoed by some legal advisers, one observing 'a mismatch' between the objectives of setting up a framework for public service provision and the commercial incentivisation of CPAs, and that 'they need contracting authorities and suppliers to use their frameworks to fund their commercial operations'.[176]

The commercial objectives of some CPAs seem to contrast with the objectives of contracting authorities who set up frameworks for their own use or for the use of a limited group of contracting authorities. In the local authority context, one interviewee highlighted the legal limitations that apply to their commercial activities eg the legal requirement to set up a company to conduct commercial activities (under section 95 Local Government Act 2003) (which they did not consider to be attractive or appropriate for operating frameworks) and requirements to act in accordance with local authorities' powers granted by legislation. They highlighted the focus of local authorities on providing value for money for local citizens and being more sensitive to public policy goals.[177]

From a contracting authority perspective, there is sometimes limited transparency on fees and their use. It is important that contracting authorities are made aware of fees and what they cover in order to conduct a value for money assessment. However, an interviewee expressed their frustration at the revenue generated by rebates on a particular framework being retained by the CPA and not shared with customers.[178] There may also be arrangements for refunding or offsetting charges but which, again, are not always transparent. Thus, one interviewee stated that some frameworks might provide for a contracting authority to receive a percentage refund based on their use of the framework.[179]

[170] CPB1.
[171] CPB9.
[172] CA15.
[173] LA3.
[174] CA5.
[175] CA4.
[176] LA8.
[177] CA9.
[178] CPB8.
[179] CA3.

Relatedly, some interviewees expressed concern that the revenue generated by CPAs does not translate into the provision of better support to, and engagement with, contracting authorities or suppliers,[180] although one legal adviser who had observed high rebate percentages on some frameworks considered it did, commenting that 'purchasing bodies ought to be doing more for their money'.[181] An interviewee from a private sector organisation acting as a CPA also described how many contracting authorities preferred to use their frameworks over those of other CPAs for this reason.[182]

This variance between the revenue generating mechanisms used, the objectives of different CPAs and the ancillary services provided across different frameworks makes it difficult for contracting authorities to assess which framework to use. An interviewee described how they assess the different percentage rebates payable and whether any 'payback provisions' are included.

However, these charges do not appear to be a deterrent to suppliers considering which frameworks to apply to join. An interviewee described how they do not look closely at the applicable rebate percentages as 'they are simply viewed as a cost of business' and that 'account managers add these to their costs'.[183] Another interviewee explained how 'we tend to be guided by our customers as to which frameworks we need to be on to win business from them and that is the most important factor'.[184]

As explained, some CPAs collaborate with each other in certain respects. Rebate sharing arrangements are sometimes put in place for pipelines of work that one refers to the other. There can be an ongoing dialogue between these 'friendly competitors' to agree such arrangements. One interviewee discussed a rebate agreement by which they receive a percentage of the rebate for business that they direct through the other's frameworks, acting as 'an extension' of the other.[185] Again, such arrangements raise questions as to their compatibility with competition law.

By contrast, one interviewee stated that the Scottish Procurement and Property Directorate does not impose rebates with costs instead being 'top-sliced' from the Scottish Government's budget.[186] This also raises a broader issue, namely, to what extent there is any divergence across the devolved nations as regards framework set-up and use.

Given the above, questions arise as to the appropriateness of charging fees, or, at the very least in ways that are largely unregulated.

4.2. Charging Fees under the PA 2023

The *Transforming Public Procurement* Green Paper included a brief section on 'charging', stating that 'a fee or levy can be charged on a supplier for participating in a commercial vehicle' but 'only when it results in a contract being awarded and the supplier submitting

[180] CA10, EO3.
[181] LA2.
[182] CPB12.
[183] EO2.
[184] EO4.
[185] CPB5.
[186] CPB8.

an invoice'.[187] It also qualified that 'any charges recovered by the contracting authority must be proportionate, used solely in the public interest and be transparently described on the central register of commercial tools'.[188] Further, these must reflect a percentage of the maximum estimated value of the call-off and be set out in the framework.[189] Whilst not explained, this proposal could be an acknowledgement that fees may not have not been proportionate or transparent, or may have been used for profit. This also appeared to be an attempt to firmly restore a link between the charging of fees and their reinvestment in public service provision. However, the final policy position reflected in the PA 2023 is much less decisive.

Section 45(7) clarifies that '[a] framework may provide for the charging of fees at a fixed percentage of the estimated value of any contract awarded to the supplier in accordance with the framework'. However, this provision does not appear to go as far as the Green Paper proposal, and introduces uncertainty.

Regarding the type of charges permitted, it appears that only one type is possible against suppliers, namely, payment corresponding to a contract awarded to the supplier. This is not explicit because section 45(7) only states that a framework 'may' provide for the charging of such fees, not that it may 'only' charge such fees and which might not otherwise preclude charging other fees in respect of set-up, access or management. However, in parliamentary debate, it was stated that:

> There is no 'pay to play'. Fees can be charged only where a supplier is awarded work under the framework. That is a very important point: if you get the work, you pay the fee; if you do not get the work, you do not pay the fee.[190]

Further, it appears from the remaining wording of section 45(7) in specifying the nature of the charge and the fact that it is applicable only to the supplier, that it is only that type of fee that can be applied. The GCF guidance also states that fees can only be charged to suppliers that have been awarded a call-off.[191] Therefore, it does not appear to be possible to charge fees directly to contracting authorities. However, there is no express provision addressing the risk of a supplier passing on fees through an increase in the price payable by the contracting authority.

The GCF guidance also confirms that it is not permissible to charge suppliers to gain access to a framework or any other fees associated with the management of the framework.[192] Thus, CPAs that have historically charged other fees to suppliers and contracting authorities for framework management and support services may need to reconsider their business models. It cannot necessarily be excluded that this could potentially result in CPAs using the only charging mechanism available ie charging a fixed fee percentage in certain ways, such as charging different fixed fee percentages to suppliers depending on the level of service provided. However, this creates certain risks, including lack of transparency, regarding the basis on which these are set or fairly administered among different suppliers.

[187] Cabinet Office, *Transforming Public Procurement* (n 21) 47.
[188] ibid.
[189] Cabinet Office, 'Transforming Public Procurement: Government response to consultation' (n 21) 49.
[190] Grand Committee (Sixth Sitting), Hansard, 24 October 2022.
[191] GCF (n 24) 4.
[192] ibid 5.

As indicated, the basis for charging the fee is a fixed percentage of the estimated value of any contract awarded. However, the rationale for such is not clear. A discrepancy often exists between the estimated value of a contract and the actual value recovered by suppliers, meaning that either: (a) suppliers could be required to pay a fee on an amount they have not actually recovered if the estimated contract value exceeds the actual contract value, or (b) the fee could be lower than expected where the estimated contract value is lower than the actual contract value. Framework fees have traditionally been based on invoiced values and it is submitted that this would have made more sense. This may be a point of dispute in practice, particularly where the estimated value of a call-off differs from the actual, agreed invoiced value. It also appears that it is not possible to vary the fee during the lifetime of the framework. The GCF guidance states that the reference to fees being a 'fixed' percentage means that the fees may not change during the lifetime of the framework.[193]

Creditably, there is an attempt to ensure at least some transparency of fees. According to regulation 20(2)(k) and regulation 26(2)(w) PR 2024, fees can only be charged if the details are set out in the framework (section 45(7)) and the tender or transparency notice. However, as indicated, it is difficult to see how providing transparency of fees will necessarily curb excessive profits.

More fundamentally, the PA 2023 does not appear to have gone as far as requiring fees to be proportionate and used solely in the public interest. This is means that there are no explicit controls on the level of fees chargeable. For instance, as the percentage is not uniformly fixed, it is conceivable that a contracting authority may set one that is, by any objective measure, unreasonably high. Whilst it is appreciated that the fee may need to differ depending on various factors (eg, nature and complexity of contracts), there is no explicit means of ensuring the reasonableness of the fee charged. Further, a contracting authority might arbitrarily set fixed percentages; for example, on two similar contracts, a different percentage fee may be applied to each and vice versa. Different contracting authorities may also apply different percentages. Clarity will also be required as regards information on fees. As indicated, regulation 20(2)(k) on tender notices requires the provision of 'any other information needed in order to enable suppliers to understand how fees will be charged'. This would need to be consistent with the section 12 objective on sharing information. However, regulation 26(2)(w) on transparency notices does not contain an identical requirement in this regard. Notwithstanding, contracting authorities setting up frameworks will still need to have regard to the section 12 statutory objectives when setting framework fees.

This should be considered in light of the February 2025 *National Procurement Policy Statement*. This identifies that the step change in transparency to be delivered under the PA 2023 'will shine a spotlight on framework providers who charge excessive fees'.[194] However, it is one thing to increase the transparency of fees, another to determine whether they are excessive and to address this. The PA 2023 provides no mechanism for preventing the charging of excessive fees. As discussed in chapter ten, this is another aspect in need of reform.

[193] ibid 4.

[194] Cabinet Office, *National Procurement Policy Statement*, 13 February 2025, 2–3.

5. Surveying the Procurement Options

5.1. Surveying Options under the PCR 2015

Another relevant consideration is whether to use a framework as against other options.

5.1.1. Framework Agreements, Dynamic Purchasing Systems and Qualification Systems

As discussed in chapter two, there are various advantages and disadvantages of frameworks, and which are not rehearsed in detail here. Albano and Nicholas have demonstrated the main potential benefits in reducing transaction costs and time by aggregating purchases, thereby improving procedural efficiency, particularly for repeat purchases of standard items and for urgent requirements.[195] However, it has also been qualified that 'procedurally efficient procurement does not guarantee overall value for money'.[196] The call-off stage may involve 'the use of considerable discretion and is not always fully transparent and competitive which may result in higher prices exceeding administrative savings'[197] and frameworks of long duration may limit market access.[198] As discussed below, interviewees generally concurred in identifying the same benefits and drawbacks.

Another similar tool that has been referenced in this book but not considered in detail is the DPS, which has been gaining popularity since the legal rules on its use have become more user friendly under the PCR 2015. Directive 2004/18/EC introduced the concept, defined in Article 1(6) as:

> a completely electronic process for making commonly used purchases, the characteristics of which, as generally available on the market, meet the requirements of the contracting authority, which is limited in duration and open throughout its validity to any economic operator which satisfies the selection criteria and has submitted an indicative tender that complies with the specification.[199]

In essence, a contracting authority runs the selection phase of a restricted procedure to set up a DPS. When admitting suppliers, the contracting authority does not invite tenders that are then used as the basis for the award of call-offs (as under a framework); rather, suitable suppliers are identified to meet future requirements. The tender stage under a DPS for award of a contract only begins when a contracting authority decides to award a call-off. Further, a contracting authority must keep the DPS open for suppliers to join throughout its lifetime rather than being closed to only those appointed. Under a DPS, the contract award phase only commences when a contracting authority conducts a subsequent procurement procedure inviting admitted suppliers to tender for a specific

[195] Albano and Nicholas (n 2) 5.
[196] ibid.
[197] ibid 6.
[198] ibid.
[199] See generally, Arrowsmith (n 10) 19-99–19-123.

contract. All contracts must be awarded pursuant to a competitive tender process as there is no facility to make direct contract awards.

Under the original form of a DPS, a supplier would submit an indicative tender and be admitted if it satisfied the selection criteria and the indicative tender was compliant. Any admitted supplier was allowed to improve its indicative tender at any time. When awarding a contract under the DPS, the contracting authority had to publish a simplified contract notice inviting any potential suppliers to submit an indicative tender within at least 15 days. The indicative tenders received then had to be evaluated for admittance to the DPS before any invitations to submit tenders for a call-off could be issued. The contracting authority had to invite all admitted suppliers to submit a tender within a specified time limit and would award the contract applying the award criteria specified in the original contract notice as may be more precisely formulated in the invitation to submit tenders (regulation 20(11)–(14) PCR 2006).

In 2011, the Commission noted 'some lack of clarity in the original provisions on DPS' and that 'the actual use of the procedure has been marginal, and in most cases seems to demonstrate a misunderstanding of the provisions'.[200] The UK Government's response to the Commission's Green Paper on modernisation stated that DPS were 'virtually unused in the UK and elsewhere because of flawed and unnecessarily onerous procedural rules'.[201] Eyo has highlighted the various academic criticisms levelled at the DPS provisions in Directive 2004/18/EC and PCR 2006.[202] Article 34 Directive 2014/24/EU improved the DPS. CCS[203] referred to the new rules as 'more useable and useful' as: (a) suppliers no longer have to submit an 'indicative tender'; (b) contracting authorities do not need to publish a further simplified advertisement each time they wish to award a call-off; and (c) the default four-year limit on the duration of a DPS has been removed.

Under regulation 34, contracting authorities may use a DPS for commonly used purchases (regulation 34(1)) and the DPS may be divided into different categories of products, works or services objectively defined based on the characteristics of the procurement to be undertaken (eg, maximum size of contracts or specific geographic areas) (regulation 34(3)–(4)). The fact that a tender stage under a DPS only begins when a contracting authority decides to award a call-off can be attractive when procuring ICT requirements subject to dynamic changes in technology and pricing where awards based on tenders submitted some time ago may not be relevant or up to date. As indicated, a version of the restricted procedure must be used to set up the DPS, modified to the extent that the selection phase cannot be used to limit the number of suppliers on the DPS. Throughout its term, any supplier must be allowed to apply to be admitted and all that satisfy the specified selection criteria for each category under the DPS must be admitted (regulation 34(6)–(7)). For each call-off, contracting authorities must invite

[200] European Commission, Staff Working Paper, Evaluation Report: Impact and Effectiveness of EU Public Procurement Legislation, SEC (2011) 853 final, Part 1 June 2011, 106.

[201] United Kingdom response to the European Commission Green Paper on the modernisation of EU public procurement policy (COM (2011) 15 final), 10.

[202] A Eyo 'Evidence on use of Dynamic Purchasing Systems in the United Kingdom' (2016) 6 *PPLR* 237–48. See also, S Arrowsmith, 'Dynamic Purchasing Systems under the New EC Procurement Directives – a not so dynamic concept' (2006) 1 *PPLR* 16–29.

[203] CCS, 'The Public Contracts Regulations 2015 & The Utilities Contracts Regulations 2016, Dynamic Purchasing Systems', updated October 2016, 2.

all admitted suppliers to submit a tender (regulation 34(21).[204] Each contract must be awarded to the bidder that submitted the best tender based on the award criteria set out in the call for competition, with the possibility of formulating such criteria more precisely in the invitation to tender (regulation 34(23)–(24)).

Another tool is a mandatory supplier list which requires suppliers to register on the list as a condition of participating in a procurement. As highlighted by Arrowsmith, however, frameworks are distinguished by the fact that they 'establish to a significant extent the terms of future contracts'.[205] Mandatory supplier lists usually involve the admission of suppliers based on whether they meet certain eligibility criteria relating to their technical expertise, experience, financial standing and other due diligence requirements. They tend not to involve the submission of tenders for future contracts and the terms of such contracts are usually established later. Such mandatory supplier lists are not defined or provided for in the PCR 2015[206] but are available for utilities. Under Article 77 Directive 2014/25/EU (as implemented in the Utilities Contracts Regulations 2016), a 'qualification system' allows utilities to limit participation in contract award procedures to candidates registered to a relevant supplier list that has been set up.[207] A competition under the qualification system is conducted only between registered candidates.

5.1.2. Comparison of Frameworks and Dynamic Purchasing Systems under the PCR 2015

A single contracting authority can set up either a framework or DPS for its own use or use by multiple contracting authorities (regulation 37(2) but there are important differences between these tools, certain of which were highlighted above). Regarding scope, a DPS can only be used for 'commonly used purchases' whereas the rules on frameworks impose no such restriction. The rationale for this distinction is unclear. For example, it might reasonably be considered that 'commonly used purchases' are the types of requirement most suited for procurement by way of direct award but these are not available under a DPS, only frameworks.

In respect of set-up, unlike a framework, for a DPS set up for use by other contracting authorities no identification of user contracting authorities (either by name, class or category) is required in the original call for competition. The call for competition must simply mention this fact (regulation 46(3)), although CCS guidance recommends that CPAs who set up a DPS clearly identify the permitted and potential user base.[208]

Concerning market access, a DPS is an open system allowing suppliers to join throughout its period of validity and is not restricted to four years, unlike a framework. A supplier unsuccessful in its application to be admitted to the DPS can re-apply,

[204] Where the DPS is divided into categories, contracting authorities must invite all suppliers admitted to the category corresponding to the specific procurement to submit a tender: reg 34(22).

[205] Arrowsmith (n 10) 11–15.

[206] ibid 12–171 and Case C-74/09 *Bâtiments et Ponts Construction v Berlaymont 2000* ECLI:EU:C:2010:431, [2010] ECR I-07271.

[207] Achilles' Utilities Vendor Database is a qualification system used by UK utilities. See 'Guide to Utilities Procurement in the UK', CMS Law Tax, July 2018, see www.achilles.com/community/uvdb/.

[208] CCS (n 203) 13.

whereas there is only one chance to be appointed to a framework after which it is closed for its duration. Further, a DPS, unlike a framework, cannot restrict the maximum number to be appointed and therefore needs to consider the administrative burden of managing applications to join throughout its term.[209] In addition, in contrast to the rules on lots applicable to frameworks which allow a contracting authority to limit the number of lots that a supplier can apply for or be awarded (regulation 46), a DPS can be set up involving different categories of goods, services or works where suppliers can apply for as many categories as they wish and must be admitted to categories where they meet the selection criteria.

In respect of the structure of the process, for a DPS, the substantive competition occurs at the second stage when a contracting authority invites suppliers on the DPS to submit a tender whereas a framework is intended to involve a substantive competition at the first stage for award of a place on the framework with a view to future call-offs. Also unlike frameworks, there is no ability to award a contract directly to a DPS supplier without running a competitive tender (unless, presumably, there is only one supplier appointed to the DPS or a particular category under it). This reflects the nature of the DPS in that the award stage is still to be completed. As CCS guidance has explained, 'the decision on the best value-for-money offering can only be decided at the tender stage for each individual requirement, and equal treatment requires that all suppliers on the DPS (category) have the opportunity to bid'.[210]

In respect of the end of a DPS process, contracting authorities can set up a DPS without having to run a standstill period either before appointing suppliers or awarding a call-off. Further, the provisions requiring a contracting authority to send a contract award notice to bidders do not apply (regulation 86(5)(c)). By contrast, these rules do apply to the set-up of a framework (regulations 86 and 87).

Finally, whilst the PCR 2015 is silent on the issue of charging suppliers on the framework, regulation 34 provides that no charges can be billed to suppliers interested in or party to a DPS.

Previous empirical research has revealed that DPS have been used increasingly since the coming into force of the PCR 2015.[211] The Local Government Association has issued some practical advice on use, highlighting key benefits such as generating cost savings through increased competition, providing an opportunity to stimulate markets and increasing access for SMEs.[212] However, it also noted barriers to using a DPS including the administrative burden.[213] It has been surmised that the removal of the requirement in the PCR 2015 to issue a contract notice for each order under a DPS may mean that the cost-benefit balance will more often favour using a DPS over a framework, particularly when a DPS is used together with an electronic catalogue where tenders could merely

[209] There are arguably ways to mitigate this risk. See discussion in L Edwards, 'Dynamic Purchasing Systems and the Death of Frameworks', 26 February 2016. Available at www.procurious.com/procurement-news/dynamic-purchasing-systems-and-the-death-of-procurement-frameworks.

[210] CCS (n 203) 10.

[211] Eyo (n 202) 237–48.

[212] The Local Government Association, 'A Guide to Dynamic Purchasing Systems in the Public Sector: Is it right for you and your suppliers?' May 2017, 4.

[213] ibid 11.

require confirmation of catalogue information (under regulation 36(12)).[214] However, the DPS still remains 'fairly cumbersome and complex' due to the requirement to invite and evaluate tenders from all admitted suppliers and, so, the extent to which DPS may take over frameworks for common purchases remains to be seen.[215]

For the purposes of the empirical research, interviewees were asked to comment on how they arrived at the decision to use a framework over other tools.

5.1.3. Surveying Options in Practice under the PCR 2015

5.1.3.1. Perceptions of the Dynamic Purchasing System under the PCR 2015

When explaining the process for deciding whether to use a framework, many interviewees mentioned the DPS as an alternative, alongside a plea for more guidance on which tool to use. There was general acknowledgement that an increasing number of DPS have been set up since the rules were changed by Directive 2014/24/EU and that 'a few arrangements that were previously frameworks are now being iterated in DPS format'.[216]

DPS were considered by some interviewees to be useful for maintaining competitive tension on the basis that, 'suppliers are aware that any number of other suppliers can join which keeps them on their toes'.[217] One thought they were useful for markets with a regular stream of new entrants as they can facilitate SME access.[218] This could raise doubts about the utility of mini-competitions in frameworks, particularly where these involve a competition on most terms. Except where mini-competitions are used to a limited extent to 'complete' the original competition, a DPS may be more appropriate to use from a value for money perspective given its dynamic nature.

A few interviewees highlighted the benefit of suppliers being able to propose new technologies when responding to invitations to submit tenders. As indicated, a supplier is not required to submit a tender to join the DPS and its offering is not therefore fixed on joining in the same way as under a framework. One interviewee had set up a DPS for 'Internet of Things' solutions under which new technologies were regularly added.[219] Another said the choice between using a framework or a DPS was usually based on the relevant product market as 'the IT market is very innovative and some clients like a DPS as they can still benefit from market innovations when using one'.[220]

Some interviewees mentioned that DPS are not very useful for procuring urgent requirements or commoditised, low-value items that require a quick turnaround and do not merit running a full competitive procedure. As indicated, unlike frameworks, DPS do not permit direct awards and so it is not possible to choose a solution directly from a supplier's catalogue.[221] This suggests that frameworks that allow direct awards may be

[214] Arrowsmith (n 10) 19–101.
[215] ibid.
[216] LA18.
[217] LA11.
[218] EO4.
[219] CPB8.
[220] LA12.
[221] CA3.

more appropriate for 'commonly used purchases', even though the DPS tool has been designed for such purchases.

The biggest drawback identified is the active management, resource and additional cost required given the obligation to keep it open to new suppliers.[222] One interviewee stated that they only opened a DPS at six-monthly intervals and did not view DPS as being useful 'if there is a large saturated market'.[223] Another discussed the possibility of keeping frameworks open like DPS (possibly prevising the introduction of the new open framework under the PA 2023) but explained that the increased management burden would make them less attractive.[224] Even though it is not possible to limit the number on a DPS, the management burden might be less for some product and service markets than others. One interviewee described how they were in the process of setting up a DPS for academic database tools which was a specialised market and were thus confidence that they would not be overwhelmed with suppliers asking to join as they had engaged with the market and developed specialised selection criteria for admission.[225]

From the supplier perspective, it was mentioned that a framework might be seen as more attractive where the supplier is one of a small number of appointed suppliers. One interviewee saw 'frameworks as being much more beneficial to SMEs as they have a much better chance of success'. They compared a supplier being one of six on a framework to being one of thousands on a DPS,[226] although, of course, the same observation would not necessarily apply in respect of a large multi-supplier framework. A few interviewees viewed a DPS as an approved supplier list and could not see any significant benefits in setting one up for large markets. Contracting authorities are far more familiar with using a framework that appeared to offer more certainty of business. A properly scoped framework with a limited number (as their purpose was originally conceived) may, therefore, still be preferable to using a DPS for some requirements.

It should be added that one interviewee observed that the PCR 2015 prohibit CPAs imposing any charges on suppliers under a DPS but said 'there is a bit of uncertainty around whether this includes a prohibition on charges based on the value of goods/ services supplied or if it just prohibits general charges on joining/remaining a member of the DPS', observing that they had come across a DPS that includes such charges.[227] Another thought that the Green Paper proposals which envisaged such charges being levied under a DPS-type arrangement might result in CPAs establishing more DPS in the future.[228]

5.1.3.2. Perceptions of the Advantages and Disadvantages of Using a Framework under the PCR 2015

In respect of advantages, despite the original rationale for introducing rules on frameworks being to address purchasing of indefinite or uncertain requirements over a longer

[222] CPB10, LA12.
[223] CA9.
[224] CPB3.
[225] CA6.
[226] CA15.
[227] LA16.
[228] LA4.

duration, as discussed in chapter three, a key attraction of using a framework in practice is that it provides a quick and cost-effective route to contract particularly for frequent sustained purchases of commoditised items. Several interviewees highlighted a perception that frameworks are advantageous 'in terms of ease of governance, there being less bureaucracy and knowing that commercially acceptable contracting arrangements have been established in advance'.[229] A legal adviser explained that frameworks are generally considered convenient and provide an opportunity to take advantage of a CPA's purchasing power and ability to agree favourable terms and conditions on behalf of contracting authorities.[230] Interestingly, one interviewee couched this in slightly different terms, stating that using a framework is a 'sticking plaster to avoid having to run full-blown procurements that take a long time and attract a higher risk of challenge'.[231]

Many interviewees perceived benefits rather than criticisms of creating a closed marketplace of suppliers that can meet similar requirements. One interviewee observed that 'it makes it easier to buy from capable and credible suppliers by establishing a sensible and validated micro-market'.[232] Several interviewees mentioned the cost and time savings that can be achieved when using a framework. One interviewee highlighted that a substantive competition should have already been carried out to appoint suppliers to a framework which should make call-off orders quicker and easier in the knowledge that key terms have already been established pursuant to a competitive process.[233] Another attraction appears to be the finite number of suppliers that can bid for a call-off, making the procurement process more manageable.[234] However, some frameworks have emerged in recent years that place no limit on the number of suppliers. Where this results in an excessive number, it may not be practicable to run a mini-competition. As discussed in chapter seven, even when a framework provides for the ability to make direct awards of call-offs, it is likely to be difficult to apply 'objective conditions' to identify which of many suppliers should be awarded the call-off.

Concerning the ICT sector, several interviewees considered frameworks useful for procuring ICT requirements, providing a ready-made route to contract established by those with technical expertise often lacking in contracting authorities. By using a framework, they do not need to worry about the need to negotiate complex matters (eg software escrow arrangements) and can take comfort that they have been addressed upfront. They saw the use of frameworks for ICT requirements as attracting less risk than running a standalone procurement.[235] A legal adviser similarly commented that 'ICT is seen to be a very complex area and it is perceived to be easier and safer to use a framework for such requirements'.[236] Another interviewee thought that frameworks helped prevent suppliers attempting to impose their own terms on customers and found it appealing that the call-off terms were already established and accepted by framework

[229] CA3.
[230] LA16.
[231] CA15.
[232] CPB1, CPB6.
[233] CA3.
[234] CA6.
[235] CA13.
[236] LA9.

suppliers.[237] This places an onus on CPAs setting up frameworks to employ sufficient technical, legal and commercial expertise, albeit at a cost that may be factored into the rebates charged to suppliers.

In respect of disadvantages, fundamentally, there was a perception amongst some interviewees that frameworks have not achieved the original objectives that supported the introduction of this regulated contracting model. One legal adviser said frameworks were originally intended to make it easier and simpler to make repeat purchases of goods and services which could be aggregated but that 'they have become a barrier to doing business with the public sector now'. They stated that much uncertainty and caution pervades, particularly amongst overseas ICT suppliers looking to break into the UK market.[238] Similarly, as alluded to in chapter three, one legal adviser took issue with the 'one-size-fits-all approach adopted by the European Commission for all Member States when setting the procurement rules'. They viewed the rules 'as a failure of the principle of subsidiarity' and felt frameworks were being used in practice as a tool 'to circumvent public procurement discipline, transparency and a proper regulated competition'.[239] However, as indicated in chapters three and four, it is arguable that the UK bears some responsibility for failing to take decisive action in respect of the regulation of frameworks.

Concerns were also raised about a lack of control over the procurement process when using a framework. If contracting authorities have not been involved in the award to set-up the framework, they will not have directly inputted into the scope of procurable requirements, call-off procedures or contract terms. Thus, a contracting authority might face difficult decisions about the extent to which they can adapt a framework to meet their specific needs. Common issues include inflexible terms on intellectual property ownership, software licensing and the sharing of information. This can lead to suppliers entrench their position early on, rendering any competition for a follow-on contract futile. Obsolescence issues were also reported due to frameworks not incorporating sufficient change control mechanisms to enable variations to reflect advances in technology.[240]

The absence of key suppliers can also be a deterrent to using a framework. A contracting authority may want its incumbent to be able to compete for a new contract. There are certain ICT product markets comprising only a few key suppliers that contracting authorities would expect to see on a framework but which may not be included. Some may also want to ensure that a framework includes enough SMEs to allow sufficient opportunity to contract directly with them. This partly explains 'framework shopping' to identify an acceptable group of suppliers. Some interviewees gave examples of frameworks that failed to attract key suppliers which can result in no, few or poor tender responses when running a mini-competition. Unsurprisingly, this deters such contracting authorities from using those frameworks again.

Some interviewees also expressed frustrations about frameworks not incorporating the ability to factor in wider policy objectives when making call-offs. Two interviewees

[237] CA14.
[238] LA8.
[239] LA11.
[240] CA2.

mentioned uncertainty encountered when seeking to include social value award criteria in a call-off procedure, due to the absence of any such award criteria being factored into the award of the framework.[241] Award criteria (including on social value) must be related to the subject-matter of the contract (regulation 67(2)) which therefore requires a bespoke approach for each call-off. For a multi-user framework, it might be difficult to specify social criteria that could be applied to all call-offs and this is, therefore, an example of where only high-level award criteria should be applied at the framework award stage, to be refined at the call-off stage.

Interviewees also reported some unintended consequences of using frameworks. A legal adviser described how a single supplier can be favoured by a contracting authority which has distortive effects on subsequent contract awards. It was explained that a framework supplier might perform well on the first call-off and be given the subsequent call-off as a result. When the framework is re-iterated, however, other suppliers will decrease prices to try to win more work whereas the supplier who won the work under the previous framework may not. It then stops receiving contracts from that customer. Ultimately, 'all parties end up unhappy and annoyed!'.[242]

5.2. Use of Frameworks for Commoditised, Bespoke and Complex ICT Requirements under PCR 2015

Given the sectoral focus of the empirical research, it is important to acknowledge sector-specific factors that may influence framework choices.

Interviewees discussed the extent to which frameworks were considered suitable across the spectrum of needs eg commoditised items, bespoke requirements and complex ICT solutions. From the outset, it should be observed that a range of frameworks are in operation covering this full spectrum. It is apparent from the interviews that contracting authorities consider the nature of the requirement to be important in determining the suitability of a framework as against other options.[243]

These choices must also be put in context. A framework to supply ICT peripherals for a single local authority may differ substantially in structure, content and call-off procedures from a framework providing 'enterprise resource planning'[244] solutions for all central and local government bodies. Further, the degree to which the terms of call-offs are agreed at the framework award stage and the type of call-off procedure(s) required are likely to depend on such factors as the technical complexity of the subject-matter, the price volatility of the relevant market and the number of contracting authorities and suppliers that will use and supply through the framework, which may all involve different needs and priorities. There is resulting scope for considerable variation in how frameworks are used for different types of requirement.

[241] CA14.
[242] LA8.
[243] CPB5.
[244] 'Enterprise resource planning' refers to software that organisations use to manage day-to-day business activities such as accounting, procurement, project management, compliance and supply chain.

Regarding commoditised items, most interviewees agreed that frameworks are most suitable for 'common', 'commoditised', 'off-the-shelf' ICT requirements and are not appropriate for highly complex, bespoke ICT requirements. The PCR 2015 has provided certain facilitative tools to more effectively procure commoditised requirements. Regulation 36(1) provides that 'contracting authorities may require tenders to be presented in the format of an electronic catalogue or to include an electronic catalogue'. Further, regulation 36(6) provides that where a multi-supplier framework has been set up in this way, mini-competitions may take place 'on the basis of updated catalogues'. Regulation 36(7) provides that a contracting authority can invite suppliers to resubmit their electronic catalogues, adapted to the requirements of the contract in question, or notify them that they intend to collect from the electronic catalogues which have already been submitted the information needed to constitute tenders.

Interestingly, however, few interviewees mentioned the use of such electronic catalogues and they do not appear to feature in a significant number of ICT frameworks. For such a standardised approach to be successful, it would likely require a decent uptake of this option by CPAs to justify suppliers investing the time to prepare such catalogues. One interviewee considered frameworks to be more useful than DPS for standardised ICT items using a catalogue-based system as they can offer a very quick turnaround with the substantive competition having already been carried out.[245] Notwithstanding the lack of evidence on the use of electronic catalogues, there was a consensus that frameworks can usefully provide a group of 'assured' or 'accredited' suppliers of commoditised ICT items (peripherals, desktops, laptops, etc) and can reduce procurement timescales and costs compared with running standalone procurements.

Frameworks also appear to have been useful for the procurement of commoditised ICT items in urgent circumstances. Several interviewees mentioned that frameworks had 'come to the rescue'[246] during the COVID-19 pandemic for laptops and associated support to work from home that could be procured quickly on agreed prices and terms.[247]

Regarding more bespoke requirements, there was a consensus that the more a framework is tailored to a contracting authority's requirements, the more useful it will be.[248] Specific case management or finance system requirements were given as examples where it makes sense to pre-select a number of suppliers to bid for particular opportunities.[249] Broadly scoped frameworks intended for pan-public sector use are generally viewed to be less useful.

By contrast, several interviewees mentioned the difficulties of using frameworks for complex ICT projects. One interviewee thought that these should be procured using a standalone procedure allowing negotiation to establish a strategic partnering relationship with a single supplier. The benefits of a single-supplier framework were mentioned alongside the 'grey area' of when a strategic partnering arrangement constitutes a

[245] CA3.

[246] CA8.

[247] For detailed analyses of procurement through the COVID-19 pandemic see S Arrowsmith, L Butler, A La Chimia and C Yukins (eds), *Public Procurement in (a) Crisis – Global Lessons from the Covid-19 Pandemic* (Hart Publishing, 2021).

[248] CPB8.

[249] EO3.

framework or a standard public contract under the PCR 2015,[250] an issue discussed above. Another interviewee stated that for complex requirements it had been necessary to run standalone procurements as the available frameworks did not offer the required flexibility and considered single-supplier frameworks to be the preferred route for complex requirements that require much investment.[251] Whilst single-supplier frameworks are outside the scope of this book, several interviewees highlighted the difficulties encountered in practice when using them, eg setting the scope of the framework and the permissibility of making changes to the arrangement over the life of the framework with a dynamic and evolving ICT market. One interviewee said 'if frameworks are allowed to be used for such requirements, there should be more flexibility allowed in terms of dialogue, engagement, and negotiation with suppliers' and that 'at the moment, it is not clear to purchasers how far they can go in this respect'.[252] Unease was expressed about the foreclosure of the market to all but one supplier during the life of a single-supplier framework.[253] Valid concerns were also raised that the same set of rules on frameworks applied to all types of products and services, with one interviewee stating, 'it does not seem sensible that the same set of rules on frameworks applies to both the procurement of commoditised items and long term strategic partnering arrangements'.[254]

Notwithstanding these concerns, many multi-supplier frameworks purport to allow contracting authorities to procure an entire complex ICT solution. These might be divided into 'lots' covering different product and service areas. One interviewee gave the example of a framework consisting of 10 lots which could be used to procure a whole networking and telecommunications solution, with a single lot allowing the procurement of an integrator for the entire solution. However, they observed that unless the entire management of the project was outsourced, 'you end up with multiple contracts and providers without one throat to choke', referring to the dissemination of risks and liabilities when multiple suppliers are involved in providing a single solution.[255] Similar 'integrator' models were mentioned by others.[256] A legal adviser also referred to the difficulties of using this approach, highlighting the interoperability and interface issues that may arise from appointing different suppliers for different elements of a complex ICT project.[257]

The general view from legal advisers was that, although it is at least technically possible to set up a framework for virtually any type of ICT requirement, it can be difficult to use a framework effectively for complex ICT projects. One generally advised clients to avoid using frameworks for complex requirements, given significant legal risks although this advice was not always heeded.[258] Several others referred to 'workarounds' where 'perceived flexibilities in the rules are exploited to their maximum potential in practice and often go beyond what is expressly permitted in the black-letter law',[259] for example,

[250] CPB1.
[251] CPB4.
[252] CA4.
[253] CPB2.
[254] CA11.
[255] CPB1.
[256] CA7.
[257] LA2.
[258] LA1.
[259] LA3.

significant numbers of contract amendments at the call-off stage.[260] In the opinion of another:

> if you cannot carry out a proper test of the market at the appointment stage through a meaningful competition and then make a direct linkage to that competition at the call-off stage, then a framework is not an appropriate purchasing mechanism for that requirement.[261]

Another legal adviser agreed that frameworks work well for commoditised items but that they had:

> never come across a multi-supplier framework for complex services/software requirements that works well. They just result in locking out the market bar a few appointed suppliers which can lead to borderline abuse. The customers cannot specify what they really want – they just state the desired outputs and the mini-competitions are pretty meaningless as the suppliers are in control.[262]

Other legal advisers held similar views, with one revealing that they 'rarely see a framework that does not breach regulation 33(6) for complex procurements. The rules on material change are being breached all the time but risk mitigation strategies are adopted to address the practical risks'.[263] Relatedly, one legal adviser suggested having a separate set of framework rules for complex ICT and construction projects which could be tailored and act as a legal 'safe harbour' for the strategic partnering-type arrangements that such projects usually require. In their view, there were 'likely to be lots of issues that need to be resolved at the call-off stage and therefore more flexibility is required for changes both when awarding the call-off and throughout the project'.[264] Another thought that some partnering arrangements should be permitted using a bespoke, flexible framework model, perhaps by having a high-level general scope defined at the outset and mechanisms to add detail and flex within certain boundaries.[265]

Ultimately, multi-supplier frameworks involving a broad range of requirements and a wide range of users are very different animals from single-supplier frameworks and standard public contracts. For instance, it is questionable whether it is appropriate to apply the same set of rules on making contract modifications (ie those under regulation 72) to all these types of agreement. As discussed in chapter ten, this invites consideration whether a separate set of rules on modifications could be devised that apply specifically to the multi-supplier framework context.

5.3. Surveying Options under the PA 2023

The PA 2023 has changed the procurement options available, retaining closed frameworks and adding the possibility of an 'open framework'. The DPS has been removed and a new 'dynamic market' introduced.

[260] LA4.
[261] LA2.
[262] LA11.
[263] LA4.
[264] LA3.
[265] LA8.

As regards the choice between these options, the Cabinet Office in its response to the Green Paper consultation indicated that it planned to issue guidance 'which will provide suggestions on selecting the best tool for different requirements' and 'advice on designing framework agreements so that they contain all of the relevant terms and, where appropriate, mechanisms for direct award'.[266] At the time of writing, such guidance has not yet been provided, although some high-level comparisons and guidance on the various tools is available in an accompanying Transforming Public Procurement Learning Manual.[267]

5.3.1. Dynamic Market

As discussed, despite having distinct legal rules, the line between a framework and a DPS has become blurred in practice as some frameworks admit unlimited suppliers and adopt light-touch procedures for appointing suppliers not dissimilar to the first stage of a DPS, thereby resulting in a closer comparison between the two options when a contracting authority is considering which option to use.

Under the PA 2023, the DPS option has been removed and replaced with the 'dynamic market' tool (under sections 34–40). This appears to differ substantially from the EU-derived DPS concept and bears a vague correlation to a so-called 'DPS+' first proposed in the *Transforming Public Procurement* Green Paper.[268] The main point of diversion is the fact that a dynamic market involves the establishment of a standalone supplier list that contracting authorities can reference when running their own competitive flexible procedures to award a public contract ie an above-threshold (only) non-exempt contract. This differs from a DPS which uses a modified restricted procedure to award both above- and below-threshold contracts pursuant to the procedures established when the DPS was set up. Whilst this change of direction has not been explained, the dynamic market concept in the PA 2023 bears a closer resemblance to the 'qualification system' provided for in Directive 2014/25/EU for utilities. It is therefore more akin to a supplier list and, it is assumed, has been used to preserve the flexibilities historically enjoyed by utilities. A dynamic market can also be used for all types of requirements ie it is not restricted to commonly used goods and services as is the case with a DPS.

The dynamic market concept is, therefore, a novel one for the public sector and it is not yet clear if it will prove to be popular. There are a few factors that might discourage its use. These include: the requirement to publish a notice whenever a contracting authority wants to use a dynamic market (as one can only be used when running a competitive flexible procedure under the PA 2023), the prohibition on using a dynamic market to award below-threshold contracts, and the fact that fees may be chargeable to suppliers that are awarded a public contract by reference to a dynamic market (which impact on the price payable by contracting authorities). The ability to charge fees puts dynamic markets on a similar commercial footing to frameworks. This may mean that dynamic

[266] Cabinet Office, 'Transforming Public Procurement: Government response to consultation' (n 21) 49.

[267] GCF, 'Transforming Public Procurement Learning Manual, Summary Documents and Learning Aids', 26 July 2024, Module 5.

[268] Cabinet Office, *Transforming Public Procurement* (n 21) 45.

markets could become commercially attractive to profit-driven CPAs in contrast to DPS which prohibit such fees (regulation 34(29)).

5.3.2. *Open Framework*

The PA 2023 also introduces an 'open framework'. Section 49(1) defines an 'open framework' as 'a scheme of frameworks that provides for the award of successive frameworks on substantially the same terms'. Section 49(2) identifies the essence of the open framework model. It provides that:

An open framework must provide:

(a) For the award of a framework at least once during –
  (i) the period of three years beginning with the day of the award of the first framework in the scheme, and
  (ii) each period of five years beginning with the day of the award of the second framework in the scheme;

(b) for the expiry of one framework on the award of the next [...]

(c) for the final framework to expire at the end of the period of eight years beginning with the day on which the first framework under the scheme is awarded.

Thus, an initial framework is established but which must subsequently be reopened by providing for the award of another framework at least once within three years of the award of that first framework. Further, once that second framework is awarded (which results in the expiry of the first), there must be another award of at least one more framework within five years of the award of that second (each expiring on a new award). Ultimately, the final framework must expire within eight years of the award of the first.

As discussed in chapter ten, the policy justifications for the open framework are difficult to discern, particularly given the limits that apply to its use and the mechanics for reopening it.

For instance, it is difficult to see why a contracting authority would opt for an open framework in preference to a series of closed frameworks or some other procurement route. The maximum term of the first framework before it needs to be reopened is actually shorter than the maximum four-year term applicable to a closed framework. In addition, it is difficult to conceive of many instances in which such open frameworks will be desirable. Reopening any shorter than a three- to four year term is likely only to be appealing for commoditised, straightforward procurements with a manageable number of suppliers in the market. Otherwise, contracting authorities may be reluctant to reopen frameworks frequently, in particular, as often as annually, as suggested by GCF guidance.[269] A contracting authority would also be exposing itself to the risk of challenge each time it opens the framework. It is also difficult to see what administrative reductions there will be. On the assumption that an open framework has an estimated value above the applicable financial threshold (which comprises the value of all frameworks under it: Schedule 3, paragraph (2)) and is not exempted, each framework under

[269] GCF (n 24) 6.

the open framework will be a public contract that needs to be awarded by publishing a tender notice and conducting another competitive tendering procedure.[270]

It is also questionable whether open frameworks are particularly flexible compared with closed frameworks. Each framework must be on 'substantially the same terms'. Section 49(9) provides that 'a reference to an award on substantially the same terms is a reference to an award that could be made by reference to the same tender or transparency notice without substantial modification'.[271] The GCF guidance states that this means that the 'successive tender or transparency notice' must allow the same suppliers to submit requests or tenders as did the original tender or transparency notice and that there can be no substantial amendment to the award criteria for the award of the framework.[272] The Transforming Public Procurement Learning Manual goes slightly further in stating that this means that the 'scope of the open framework, award criteria and the terms and conditions should remain substantially the same'.[273] This does appear to mean, then, that it is nevertheless possible to modify a framework in the scheme provided it is not a substantial amendment. No such restriction, however, applies to the award of successive closed frameworks.

From a supplier perspective, for open frameworks that limit the number, in the majority of circumstances it is submitted that the existing framework suppliers will likely want to update their tender at each iteration to improve their offering to ensure they stand the best chance of being reappointed and awarded a call-off. Indeed, surely, this ought to be the expectation on a contracting authority's part – if a supplier is offering identical terms to previously and feels secure enough to do so, this hardly encourages behaviour likely to improve value for money.

Considering the potential unattractiveness of these other options in the PA 2023, a standard closed framework under the PA 2023 may become even more popular than previously.

Finally, contracting authorities setting up and using frameworks will need to have regard to the importance of the section 12 statutory procurement objectives and certain other considerations. However, just as the requirement to comply with the regulation 18 procurement principles in the PCR 2015 does not appear to have prevented the misuse of frameworks in the UK, it is submitted that the requirement for contracting authorities to have regard to the importance of the statutory procurement objectives when awarding, entering into and managing above-threshold non-exempt frameworks and above-threshold call-offs will not have a major impact on frameworks in practice for reasons explored in the remainder of Part III.

6. Conclusions

This chapter has demonstrated the range of factors that may inform choices about framework use.

[270] See ss 11(2), 49(10) and reg 20(2)(f)–(h) PR 2024.
[271] Cross-referencing to s 31 on modifying a s 19 procurement.
[272] GCF (n 24) 6.
[273] GCF (n 267) 265.

The most common type of multi-supplier framework in the UK is one that does not impose any legally binding obligations to purchase or supply. In the absence of any general regulatory controls on the volume and usage of such frameworks and if organisations setting them up are being encouraged to operate more commercially, the creation and exponential growth of a market for such purchasing tools is perhaps unsurprising. Filipon has termed broadly scoped frameworks set up for use by a large group of contracting authorities 'generic frameworks', an apposite description of many in the UK.[274]

The replacement of the definition of a 'framework agreement' in the PCR 2015 with a new definition of a 'framework' in the PA 2023 represents a potentially seismic change. This arguably reflects the influence of marketisation on legislative reform because, rather than address the instances of non-compliance with the PCR 2015 rules in a more systematic way, the PA 2023 seems to align with, and in some cases expressly legitimate, certain emergent market practices (eg, in the case of fee charging).

There is an unwieldy market for the supply of frameworks which is impacting heavily on the resources and expertise of users and suppliers. There are also numerous organisations (both public and private) competing for contracting authorities to channel their purchasing needs through their frameworks and for suppliers to join their frameworks. This raises the question whether more targeted regulation is required to address the proliferation of CPAs and private sector participation, especially given that some private sector organisations are purporting to act as a CPA notwithstanding not legally constituting contracting authorities. Thus, it is not just a case of a light-touch, permissive regulatory framework creating grey areas susceptible to exploitation; practices are emerging in clear disregard of categorical rules.

This competition between CPAs has led to them adopting business models and behaviours that are arguably inconsistent with the ethics and principles underpinning public sector purchasing howsoever defined. Even if it is accepted that the public sector must be more 'commercial' (whatever this means) to deliver public services, there is a sense that some practices are losing sight of the public service mission of securing the best goods and services for the taxpayer. Further, CPAs are introducing increased flexibilities in frameworks to attract business in ways that, whatever the ethics, are arguably unlawful. There is a lack of visibility, monitoring and enforcement of the use of framework procedures and little impetus for organisations to police compliance with the internal 'rules' of their frameworks and the applicable legal rules. As indicated, given the focus of this book on procurement regulation, the competition law implications have not been examined in detail but it is questionable to what extent CPAs might be acting as 'undertakings' and frameworks might be having a detrimental effect on competition between suppliers in the market.

The empirical research has revealed the commercial behaviours that CPAs are adopting in competition with public and private sector entities. This includes the development of market and business-winning strategies and revenue generating tools. The percentage rebate chargeable has even become a metric factored into the decision-making process

[274] S Filipon, *Framework Agreements, Supplier Lists, and Other Public Procurement Tools: Purchasing Uncertain or Indefinite Requirements* (Bloomsbury, 2023), ss 1.1 and 5.3.2.3.3.

of contracting authorities when considering which framework to use. It is also an indicator of how much support and advice ('customer service') is provided and justified in those terms. There is a lack of transparency of fees and the use to which they are put.

Sector-specific issues have also been revealed which bring into question the utility of frameworks for certain requirements and raise competition law issues that may require further investigation, especially in relation to reseller markets and MoUs. Such market forces as exist within the wider framework contracting ecosystem compromise the very basis and integrity of the regulated framework model.

Moreover, a framework is not the only two-stage ongoing purchasing arrangement available. The most obvious alternative has been a DPS. A framework remains a very different contracting model but there are indications that clear distinctions between frameworks and DPS are eliding as generic multi-supplier frameworks increasingly resemble appointed supplier lists from which future awards are made rather than awarded agreements in which future requirements are simply called off. It remains unclear to what extent new purchasing tools such as dynamic markets and open frameworks will impact the longstanding preference for the use of closed frameworks.

Ultimately, frameworks are considered to offer many benefits when set up properly. This must be the case by reason of their ubiquity in practice. It cannot simply be that they are being used for convenience or for other motives when other options are available. They can offer a quick, efficient and cost-effective route to contract particularly for commoditised items. Whilst they might be considered less attractive for complex solutions, there are many multi-supplier frameworks used for such requirements. However, the empirical research indicates that the legal rules are sometimes circumvented and poor procurement practices adopted where frameworks are used inappropriately to procure them.

Importantly, whilst the PA 2023 introduces new rules on frameworks, they do not address many of the issues raised in this chapter. Further, there is little indication from the supporting policy infrastructure of how to guide contracting authority and supplier choices in using frameworks. The following chapters now turn to examine how some of these choices play out in practice and may do so in future.

6

Preliminary Market Engagement and Advertising a Framework

1. Introduction

Following the decision to use a framework, a procurement procedure for award will be commenced. This may involve preliminary engagement with the market to help prepare for the procurement and inform the market of the proposals.

When ready to commence a procurement procedure, various decisions must be made in respect of framework scope. It will be necessary to advertise the contract opportunity by publishing a notice. However, as will be discussed, the level of detail to include in the call for competition and associated procurement documents is a legal grey area. Notwithstanding, contracting authorities tend to take a broad-brush approach to scoping frameworks in notices to reserve as much flexibility as possible. It will be argued that this appears to have been exploited to the greatest extent in the case of the set-up of pan-public sector multi-supplier frameworks that seek to attract large and/or diverse user contracting authorities and where, due to the number of potential users, it may be difficult to estimate the value of the framework. This approach is generally considered to attract a low risk of legal challenge. It is an approach that can lack transparency, however, particularly if the framework being advertised has not been scoped properly or supported by informed estimations of throughput and which may have any number of implications in terms of achieving value for money and other objectives.

This chapter examines the following aspects: preliminary market engagement (Section 2); the choice of procurement procedure and formulating a call for competition (Section 3); identifying users of a framework (Section 4); estimating and disclosure of framework value (Section 5); setting the duration of a framework and call-off contracts (Section 6); and use of lots (Section 7), before offering conclusions (Section 8).

2. Preliminary Market Engagement

2.1. Preliminary Market Engagement under the PCR 2015

A contracting authority might engage with the market before commencing a procurement procedure and will need to do so sufficiently in advance. Preliminary market engagement ('PME') constitutes good procurement practice, providing a transparent means by which a contracting authority can inform the market of its plans as well as its own understanding of requirements and how to meet them. It can investigate market capability and, in the case of ICT requirements, advances in technology, and test the appropriateness of specifications, proposed lotting structures, and proposed contract terms relating to, for example, software licensing, maintenance and support, cyber security, data protection and apportionment of liabilities. A contracting authority also might want to identify the potential estimated total value and usage of the framework. However, market factors may also influence the motives for PME, particularly where the contracting authority is looking to attract user contracting authorities and suppliers to the framework. As will be discussed below, interviewees were asked to comment on the amount and type of PME carried out.

There are certain risks in using PME that have necessitated regulation. PME may be used to pre-select a preferred supplier before conducting the procurement process and tailor it to favour them. Further, a supplier may unduly influence a contracting authority through preliminary discussions. There is also the potential for a conflict of interest if certain participants are involved in PME who are then involved in the conduct of the procurement procedure. Also, information disclosed at this stage may be provided to some bidders in the subsequent procurement process but not others. All create risks of discrimination and unequal treatment. However, this is a delicate balance given that suppliers should not be excluded from procurement processes because of their involvement in informing the procurement; the whole point of PME is to enable suppliers to feed into a procurement process. Therefore, an important concern is to ensure that a supplier involved in PME is permitted to participate in a procurement process provided it can be demonstrated that there is no risk of discrimination, unequal treatment or some other unfair competitive advantage accruing or other distortion of competition.

Article 48 Directive 2014/21/EU / regulation 48 provides that contracting authorities may make known their intentions of planned procurements through the publication of a prior information notice ('PIN') up to 12 months before formal commencement of the procurement process. Whilst a contracting authority is not required to publish a PIN, it enables it to put the market on notice of a forthcoming contract opportunity with a view to potentially attracting more and/or better prepared tenders. Further, Article 40 Directive 2014/24/EU / regulation 40 provides that contracting authorities may conduct 'preliminary market consultations' with a view to 'preparing the procurement and informing economic operators of their procurement plans and requirements'. Regulation 40(2) and (3) included examples of seeking advice 'from independent experts or authorities or from market participants' which may be used 'in the planning and conduct of the procurement procedure, provided that such advice does not have the effect of distorting competition and does not result in a violation of the principles of non-discrimination and transparency'.

Article 41 / regulation 41(1) provides that if a participant in a procurement process or a related undertaking has advised a contracting authority or been involved in the preparation of the procurement procedure, the contracting authority must take 'appropriate measures to ensure that competition is not distorted' by their participation. Regulation 41(2) provides that such measures shall include communicating all relevant information with the other bidders and fixing adequate time limits for submitting tenders. Regulation 41(5) provides that these measures shall be documented in a report (under regulation 84(1)). Importantly, regulation 41(3) provides that the contracting authority cannot exclude a participant from a procurement procedure unless there are 'no other means to ensure compliance with the duty to treat economic operators equally'. Regulation 41(4) provides that the participant must be given the opportunity to prove that their involvement is not capable of distorting competition.[1]

In 2016, the Government issued a PPN describing market engagement as 'essential good practice [which] helps to maximise value for money and encourage appropriate innovation'.[2] The Government's 'Digital, Data and Technology Playbook'[3] also provides that market engagement should be used to assess the health and capability of the market early on and to develop clear, outcome-based specifications that enable innovation. This should include 'consideration of the available skills, capabilities, size and capacity of the market, and an assessment of barriers to entry and market concentration'.[4] There has therefore been a reasonable push from central government to use PME effectively.

2.1.1. *Preliminary Market Engagement in Practice under the PCR 2015*

2.1.1.1. Relevance of Expertise and Capacity

According to many interviewees, despite central government encouragement, little PME has been undertaken historically by contracting authorities when setting up frameworks. Further, the amount carried out varied depending on capacity, experience and expertise, the complexity of the subject-matter, the urgency attached to establishing the framework and whether the framework was for a new set of requirements or a new iteration of an existing framework. Notwithstanding, interviewees were conscious of the harm to procurement outcomes that could result from establishing and operating a poorly conceived framework without having undertaken proper PME.

For non-CPA contracting authorities or which did not have a specialised procurement division focused on setting up frameworks, PME was limited by a lack of expertise and capacity. Several interviewees expressed a desire to obtain information such as indicative spend from potential user contracting authorities but this was usually a 'secondary consideration' due to the lack of resources.[5] A legal adviser gave an example of where, due to lack of PME, the specification for an ICT system was drafted specifically for one supplier, mentioning certain products provided by it by name, having not investigated what competing suppliers could provide.[6] This raises the question whether

[1] See Case C-21/03 *Fabricom v Belgium* ECLI:EU:C:2005:127, [2005] ECR I-1559 and S Arrowsmith, *The Law of Public and Utilities Procurement: Regulation in the EU and UK*, 3rd edn, Vol I (Sweet & Maxwell, 2014) 7-60–7-65 for discussion on pre-procurement market engagement.

[2] CCS, 'Procurement Policy Note – Onerous Practices in Procurement and Contracting' Action Note PPN 10/16, December 2016. See also previous guidance: Office of Government Commerce, 'Early Market Engagement Principles and Examples of Good Practice', 2009; and guidance issued by Crown Commercial Service, 'How to carry out early market engagement successfully – Procurement Essentials', June 2022.

[3] The Cabinet Office, 'The Digital, Data and Technology Playbook', March 2022.

[4] ibid 3.

[5] CA9.

[6] LA14. See reg 42 on specifications.

multi-supplier frameworks should generally be allowed to be set up without some effective PME being demonstrated beforehand.

Some contracting authorities were wary of proceeding without PME due to past failures. One interviewee considered 'the lack of maturity and planning to be endemic' and flagged a specific example of an ICT educational framework where the failure to consult with and address the specific needs of the relevant local authorities and schools resulted in a framework that was largely unusable.[7] One legal adviser highlighted that some CPAs assumed that a framework that had not been challenged was working well and therefore did not need to be changed when next reiterated.[8]

Some CPAs and other contracting authorities with the relevant expertise and capacity used PME in various ways, including: incorporating PME in their procurement strategies to determine whether a framework represented the best contracting model; recruiting people into roles focused on understanding and managing the expectations of the market; use of external consultancies to conduct market research and run PME events on their behalf; use of focus groups and workshops; use of ICT subject-matter experts to prepare PME; use of supplier engagement events to relay publicly available pipeline information;[9] and hosting annual conferences open to ICT manufacturers and resellers.[10] There was some awareness of the need to engage contracting authorities and suppliers equally 'to keep both sides of the market on board, to ensure that the framework design was efficient and effective and to manage the expectations of suppliers'.[11] However, it should be emphasised that whilst such developments could be beneficial in setting up effective frameworks, the practices were limited to a handful of CPAs with the resources to carry out such activities.

Further, one well-resourced organisation active in setting up and managing frameworks described the additional marketing services it provided to suppliers that were successfully admitted to its frameworks. These included hosting 'meet the supplier' events at which a supplier could set up a stall to market its goods and services to potential customer contracting authorities in return for a fixed fee paid by them.[12] However, this example calls into question the purpose of PME. The conventional understanding is that it is to engage with the market to enable contracting authorities to better understand *their* own requirements and how to achieve them or to forecast demand by ultimate users of the goods and services procured. The above example suggests that PME may be used by a CPA not only to scope the requirements of user contracting authorities but also to scope the commercial potential of the framework ie how many contracting authorities and suppliers it can attract through marketing its services and even providing suppliers with an opportunity to market their services in return for additional fees. This gives a whole new meaning to 'market engagement'. It is one thing for PME to potentially better understand likely operational costs and resource in administering the framework but quite another to determine its revenue potential.

[7] CA7.
[8] LA13.
[9] CA10.
[10] CPB9.
[11] CPB1.
[12] CPB11.

This raises a broader question of whether existing rules and policies provide a sufficiently clear steer as to the nature and function of PME. This should be considered in light of the fact that, historically, regulation of PME has been justified, in part, because of the risk of distortions of competition. It is conceivable that additional arrangements for marketing services for remuneration may create such risks.

Some interviewees referred to their use of PINs to provide the market with advance information about the framework and details of any planned PME. However, interviewees expressed concern that contracting authorities used PINs tokenistically to demonstrate compliance with the PCR 2015 without conducting any useful PME at all.

More generally, one interviewee stated that, in respect of the use of PINS and PME, 'lots of feedback may be generated but it is often not used or incorporated in the procurement process' and that 'contracting authorities need to follow a better implementation exercise and not continue based on a pre-determined end result'.[13] This poor use of PINs and the information obtained from the market at the preliminary stages may reflect the lack of capacity, expertise, and resources but also an element of 'pre-determination' in the result which raises concerns about legal compliance.

2.1.1.2. Purpose and Effectiveness of Market Engagement

As indicated, PME can be used to identify contracting authorities that are likely to use the framework and, thus, estimate the total financial value of the requirements to be put through it. The degree of PME undertaken is linked to the legal obligation to disclose the value of a framework in the call for competition. As one legal adviser explained, however, 'it is not clear how rigorous a contracting authority needs to be in engaging with the potential framework user base'.[14] Most CPA interviewees mentioned that one of the biggest challenges in setting up a framework was determining the expected usage and degree to which 'buy-in' or commitment from contracting authorities could be obtained. One interviewee noted that, 'commitment is only usually possible where a framework is being set up specifically for one main organisation' because 'the framework will reflect the requirements of that particular organisation'.[15]

The degree to which contracting authorities were consulted by CPAs when setting up frameworks varied substantially depending on the CPA and its relationships with them, the framework scope, the size of the potential user group and the CPA's market engagement strategy. A few interviewees noticed increased and more effective, proactive market engagement by some CPAs in recent years, although several complained about the lack of PME. One commented that they were 'sceptical as to whether those setting up a framework have actually tried to place themselves in the shoes of users about to embark on the procurement of an IT system'. In their opinion, 'a lot of frameworks appear to be rolled out as a matter of course and can be difficult to use if they are not sufficiently tailored to the needs of users'.[16]

[13] LA9.
[14] LA12.
[15] CPB1.
[16] CA4.

Sometimes, contracting authorities were closely involved in the development of the framework from the outset. Interviewees gave examples of 'partner' frameworks set up by small groups of contracting authorities, with collaborative engagement in advance of the formal procurement, pursuant to formal collaboration agreements. Such frameworks were common in the higher education sector where university purchasing consortia have been established. It seems that frameworks in this sector tend to be tailored more to the niche requirements of universities and are therefore more likely to provide attuned solutions that effectively address the needs of such purchasers.

A few interviewees highlighted engagement as useful in informing the structure of the framework including whether to split the framework into lots and, if so, how such lots should operate. Regulation 46 expressly provides for the ability to separate a contract into lots. There seemed to be some awareness of how lotting structures could impact competition with one interviewee giving an example of specialist software suppliers that did not provide hardware and 'so to set up a framework that required the joint purchase of hardware and software would freeze out such suppliers'.[17] The use of lots in frameworks may therefore be beneficial to facilitate access for SMEs who provide specialist products and services and was one of the rationales for introducing division into lots under the EU Directives.

The extent to which PME was used to test the suitability of proposed framework terms from buyer and supplier perspectives seemed to vary depending on the maturity of the organisation, the perceived acceptability of terms used in past frameworks and its capacity and expertise. An interviewee from a well-resourced, higher education-focused organisation stated that they had worked very closely with in-house and external lawyers and suppliers to ensure their call-off contracts are 'concise, user friendly and fit for purpose'. They stated that after spending 12 months conducting PME on the proposed framework terms 'the supply market has expressed their appreciation with this as the contracts are seen as mutually agreeable and as a result there is a lot less pushback from suppliers in practice'.[18] On the whole, however, there appeared to be insufficient PME on the proposed framework and call-off contract terms and conditions. This could lead to problems at the call-off stage as suppliers sought to agree acceptable terms.

The supplier community had also witnessed increased PME in recent years, albeit some complained that they were rarely approached directly by CPAs, being reserved for large ICT suppliers already appointed to frameworks. Whilst some suppliers monitored the market engagement activity of CPAs, small suppliers did not have the capacity for such, one interviewee admitting that 'the first time we hear of a new framework is usually when the contract notice is published'.[19] Some stated that good market engagement practice was not shared between teams within CPAs working on the same product categories leading to a 'siloed organisational structure' within the same ICT category of a single organisation with very different framework structures, procedures and content being adopted by different teams.[20] It was observed that 'overlaps' and 'gaps' could occur in the scope of ICT supplies and services covered by the frameworks of the same CPA

[17] CPB5.
[18] CPB9.
[19] EO4.
[20] EO1.

as teams were perceived not to be aligned and not adopting 'a single architecture'.[21] This is an important reminder that, as CPAs grow and expand into different categories, it is essential that good practice is shared to ensure the consistent development of frameworks.

2.2. Preliminary Market Engagement under the PA 2023

Section 16 includes provisions on 'preliminary market engagement', a slight difference in wording from preliminary market 'consultations'. The provision is similar to that in the PCR 2015; however, it includes examples of the purpose of PME such as: developing the authority's requirements and approach to the procurement; designing a procedure, conditions of participation or award criteria; preparing the tender notice and associated tender documents; identifying suppliers; identifying likely contractual terms; and building capacity among suppliers. This list will be a useful reminder to contracting authorities of the core purpose of PME when setting up frameworks.

A more significant change, however, is the introduction in section 17 of an obligation to publish a PME notice if a contracting authority carries out PME. This is to be used to invite suppliers to participate in PME or notify the market that PME has taken place. GCF guidance states that this is intended to help ensure a level playing field and serve to attract new entrants.[22] Section 17(1) provides that this notice must be published before publishing a tender notice, or reasons for not doing so must be provided in the tender notice. It is recalled that under the PCR 2015, a PIN was often used to publish a contracting authority's plan for conducting market engagement, but this was not compulsory. By introducing mandatory notification of PME, there will be increased transparency of any PME conducted prior to commencing the procurement process for a framework. The requirement to give reasons for not having conducted any PME should prompt consideration of whether any should be conducted.

Another PA 2023 notice that could provide more transparency of frameworks is the new section 93 requirement to publish a pipeline notice. Strictly speaking, this requirement only applies in relation to any contracting authority that considers that in the coming financial year it will pay more than £100 million under non-exempt contracts for goods, services or works. Such a contracting authority must publish a pipeline notice within 56 days of the first day of the financial year setting out specified information about any public contract with an estimated value of more than £2 million in respect of which the contracting authority intends to publish a tender notice or transparency notice during the reporting period.[23] Whilst the PA 2023 does not require a CPA to publish details of all its frameworks, GCF guidance indicates that a CPA that is planning to establish a framework valued over £2 million (based on the total value of the contracts to be awarded under it) should publish a pipeline notice in order to provide visibility to the market.[24]

[21] EO3.
[22] GCF, 'Guidance: Preliminary Market Engagement', updated 14 January 2025, 1–2.
[23] Section 93(1)–(3).
[24] GCF, 'Guidance, Pipeline Notice', updated 9 December 2024, 8.

More generally, the Government proposed to introduce a Register of Commercial Tools which is intended to be a publicly available, searchable resource that contracting authorities can use in order to determine whether a framework or other commercial purchasing tool currently provides the goods, services or works they seek.[25] Whilst this should increase visibility and transparency, making it easier to find and compare active frameworks and the relevant fees, it is also likely to provide a useful tool for CPAs to identify competing frameworks and the fees charged to suppliers under them. In a sense, therefore, this new register could be viewed as a market-information tool.

Further, sections 1 and 11 indicate that the PME phase before commencing a procurement for a framework that is a public contract is part of a 'covered procurement'. This means that contracting authorities setting up frameworks will need to have regard to the section 12 statutory objectives when carrying out PME. It is unclear, however, whether this will significantly affect behaviours when setting up frameworks. Section 100(3) provides that a supplier bringing a legal challenge under the PA 2023 for breach of the obligations relating to these objectives would need to be able to demonstrate that they have suffered or are at risk of suffering loss or damage as a result of the breach. It is also important to note that the obligation to have regard to the fact that SMEs may face particular barriers to participation and consider whether such barriers can be removed or reduced is not legally enforceable (section 100(5)).

Neither the PA 2023 nor accompanying guidance directly address the marketised behaviours discussed above. Therefore, it is questionable whether the new regulatory regime and accompanying guidance under the PA 2023 adequately address some of the marketisation risks that may arise at the preliminary market engagement stage and should be considered for reform.

3. Choice of Procurement Procedure and Formulating Call for Competition

3.1. Choice of Procurement Procedure and Formulating Call for Competition under the PCR 2015

As explained in chapter five, regulation 33(1) left open the possibility of using any prescribed procedure to award a contract to appoint suppliers to the framework thereby establishing it. The 'open' (single tender stage) and 'restricted' (two-stage) procedures were freely available to use.

Whichever competitive procedure was used, a contracting authority had to formulate a call for competition, usually by publishing a regulation 49 contract notice containing prescribed information (set out in Part C of Annex 5 to Directive 2014/24/EU).

Regulation 53(1) required contracting authorities to offer free, unrestricted and full direct online access to the 'procurement documents' (defined in regulation 2(1)) from the date of the publication of the call for competition. Whilst 'procurement documents'

[25] See Module 5 of GCF, 'Transforming Public Procurement Learning Manual', 22 April 2024, 8.

were defined widely in the PCR 2015, CCS guidance takes a purposive view of this definition. It stated that the meaning of that wording changes based on the different stages of the process reached and that as the process crystallises it expected more of the documents falling within that wide definition to be generated and supplied. In contrast, at very early stages, fewer of the documents, if any, would be included.[26]

3.1.1. Choice of Procurement Procedure and Formulating Call for Competition in Practice under the PCR 2015

Concerning the choice of procedure, interviewees were virtually unanimous that the open and restricted procedures were generally appropriate for setting up a framework, others being impractical given the volume of bidders involved. One CPA interviewee highlighted that the open procedure had become the default for setting up frameworks but that this had imposed a 'huge burden' due to the requirement to evaluate tenders and address all clarification questions submitted by bidders. They had recently been tasked internally with researching whether using the competitive procedure with negotiation would be a lawful and useful procedure for more complex ICT requirements.[27] However, it is difficult to see how this would be appropriate for a multi-supplier framework as it would require a significant amount of resource and would attract significant costs for both contracting authorities and bidders. It is suggested that if there are matters relating to a proposed framework that are uncertain, or require clarification or testing with the market, these can more effectively be addressed through PME, as discussed above. This may be an example of internal marketisation in that contracting authorities have to become more efficient in establishing frameworks as quickly as possible given the large supply market seeking to meet demand and pressure from other contracting authorities competing to set up frameworks.

Concerning the formulation of the call for competition, procurement teams within contracting authorities commonly take control of drafting the advert for a framework, obtaining internal stakeholders' input as necessary. Interviewees suggested that many procurement teams viewed the disclosure requirements for most frameworks as attracting low legal risk although a few legal advisers commented that they are regularly asked to advise on how to communicate certain information in the advert, such as the estimated total value of the framework.

Regarding the level of detail provided in an advert, interviewees suggested that different approaches were taken, with some including more detail than others depending on the complexity of the framework. For most interviewees, however, a broad, high-level approach was adopted to retain flexibility. As already intimated in chapter five, CPAs that habitually issue frameworks for wide use do not want their frameworks to become unnecessarily restrictive, resulting in limited usage. The more bespoke a particular framework, the harder it is for a wide range of contracting authorities to use it to procure different requirements. A few interviewees expressed some nervousness about setting

[26] CCS, 'The Public Contracts Regulations 2015 & The Utilities Contracts Regulations 2016: Guidance on Electronic Procurement & Electronic Communication', updated October 2016.
[27] CPB1.

the framework scope and how much detail to include, with one providing 'more of a general output-based statement as there is always a concern that a vital element is not included'.[28] Practice indicated that long lists of CPV codes[29] might also be inserted into adverts to try to ensure that the full framework scope is covered. Another interviewee explained they 'adopt a very flexible approach in setting broad scopes for frameworks and allowing products to be added by suppliers throughout the framework providing they fall within the overall scope'.[30]

It is submitted that this is an example of where practice has not been sufficiently transparent and where some contracting authorities are gearing frameworks to market needs, allowing suppliers as much flexibility as possible to amend their offering during the framework term. Frameworks set up in such a generic way may not be attuned to specific requirements of user contracting authorities. By not providing accurate information about the specific services required, the estimated value of purchases and scope and regularity of use, bidders might need to include various assumptions and exclusions and price various risks into their tenders and may not therefore be able to submit the best tenders.

Not all frameworks are set up in such a flexible manner, however. One interviewee complained about a rigid framework with a limited scope of ICT products. This seemed to be an example of where poor market engagement might have resulted in a framework that did not adequately service the range of requirements held by contracting authorities.[31]

Interestingly, supplier perspectives called into question the utility of an advert, albeit that, as indicated above, where there had been poor or no PME, the contract notice advertising the procurement was the first time they would have heard about the opportunity. The reality is that ICT suppliers are generally aware of the most popular frameworks on which they need to secure a place. One interviewee explained, 'we have to be on frameworks, or we would not have a business' and 'some frameworks are more essential to be on than others'.[32] Suppliers do not appear to be preoccupied with the content of adverts or whether PCR 2015 requirements have been satisfied. Ultimately, it cannot be expected that formal legal requirements on notification will be the only means by which information becomes known but the fact that suppliers do not perceive advertisements to be an important means of informing their decision of whether to bid may indicate the impact of framework marketisation. Suppliers find other ways (no doubt aided by proactive marketing of frameworks by framework providers) to identify the most suitable frameworks to join. This reduces the advertisement to a mere formality, perhaps of greatest relevance only to those without the resources to scope out the most suitable frameworks. Further, if advertisements are highly generic, suppliers are not sufficiently informed of the opportunity, impacting the quality of tenders.

Notwithstanding, interviewees agreed that there are a few important legal requirements. All interviewees whose role involves drafting adverts agreed that they must include the proposed framework duration including any optional extensions. Some acknowledged that for frameworks with longer than the standard maximum four-year

[28] ibid.

[29] The common procurement vocabulary ('CPV') codes establish a classification system to standardise the references used to describe contract subject-matter. See simap.ted.europa.eu/cpv.

[30] CPB6.

[31] EO3.

[32] EO5.

term, they would need to set out adequate reasons for this duration in the advert. Other issues that must be addressed, particularly the value of the framework and the scope of the user base, are explored further below.

Regarding other procurement documents, it has been common practice to issue a comprehensive set of documents at the outset. This can include, for example, the selection questionnaire, draft invitation to tender and template tender response documentation, evaluation guidance, specifications, framework contract, call-off contract, customer lists and framework guidance. Experienced CPAs reiterating previous versions of frameworks can easily produce and collate standardised documentation. This is helpful from a transparency perspective to inform potential bidders about the tender process, potential usage and the applicable contract terms but only if such documents are sufficiently complete and include all key information. However, as discussed in chapter five, certain information may not be transparent; for example, the rebate percentage chargeable in respect of call-offs.

3.2. Choice of Procurement Procedure and Formulating Call for Competition under the PA 2023

As discussed in chapter five, there is no explicit rule or leaning prioritising the use of competitive procedures over direct awards.[33] However, if the framework is to be awarded following a competitive tendering procedure, the contracting authority can choose whether to follow an 'open' procedure (single tender) or a 'competitive flexible' (two or more stages) procedure. Whichever choice it makes, section 20(3) requires that the procedure is 'a proportionate means of awarding the public contract, having regard to the nature, complexity and cost of the contract'. Therefore, it appears that more flexibility is provided to design a procedure used to award a framework than under the PCR 2015. For instance, contracting authorities may consider incorporating some supplementary processes when using the competitive flexible procedure, provided they are proportionate (eg, a negotiation stage, demonstrations, preferred supplier stages etc). However, it is not clear that such increased flexibility will be seen as beneficial to the set-up of frameworks when concerns over speed, efficiency and cost savings are often paramount.

Regulation 20 PR 2024 sets out information required in the section 21(1) tender notice for a framework. It is questionable whether it is permissible to set out some of this information in the 'associated tender documents' (sections 21(3) and (4)) published alongside a tender notice. The information required to be disclosed is the same as required when advertising a public contract using the open or competitive flexible procedures (under regulations 18(2) or 19(2)), plus additional information. Some of this information replicates that required when publishing a contract notice under PCR 2015 but some represents increased transparency. It includes:

- details of the selection process to be applied on the award of contracts;
- the term of the framework;

[33] See Directive 2014/24/EU Recital 50, which provides that 'negotiated procedures without prior publication of a contract notice should be used only in very exceptional circumstances'.

- the contracting authorities entitled to award contracts in accordance with the framework (whether by listing the names of those authorities or by describing categories of authorities);
- whether the framework is being awarded under an open framework;
- where the framework is being awarded under an open framework, the unique identifier for the procurement of the last framework awarded under the open framework (unless no framework has previously been awarded under the open framework);
- where the framework is being awarded under an open framework, the estimated end date of the open framework;
- whether the intention is to award the framework to—
  - a single supplier;
  - a maximum number of suppliers; or
  - an unlimited number of suppliers;
- where the intention is to award the framework to a maximum number of suppliers, the maximum number of suppliers;
- whether the framework provides for the charging of fees in accordance with section 45(7), and, if so, the fixed percentage of the estimated value of any contract awarded to a supplier in accordance with the framework and any other information needed in order to enable suppliers to understand how fees will be charged; and
- where the framework is being awarded by reference to suppliers' membership of a dynamic market—
  - the unique identifier for the dynamic market against which the public contract is being awarded;
  - a statement that the tender notice is for the award of a public contract which is to be awarded by reference to suppliers' membership of a dynamic market, and
  - where the public contract is being awarded under an appropriate part of a dynamic market—
    - the title of the part, and
    - the distinct number given to the part by the person who established the dynamic market.

In Parliamentary debate, it was stated that '[t]he provisions ensure that all frameworks will contain basic information about the scope and estimated value of the framework to clearly set out the parameters in which the framework can be used, and to avoid frameworks being used in a manner that unduly or unfairly closes off markets to competition'.[34]

Some of the disclosure requirements are welcome from a transparency perspective. In particular, the requirement to disclose in the tender notice 'any other information needed in order to enable suppliers to understand how fees will be charged' will, for the first, increase visibility on fee-charging arrangements which may inform decisions about framework use. It will also enable the collation of data across different frameworks in order to assess whether frameworks are offering value for money.

[34] HC Deb 7 February 2023, vol 727, cols 129–166.

However, the value of some of the other information requirements is questionable and unlikely to stem the tide of generic pan-public sector frameworks.

Whilst there is a long list of information that must be included in the tender notice for a framework. the requirements are vaguely worded and are not adequately expanded on in the GCF guidance. For example, it is not specified what level of information relating to the chosen selection process needs to be disclosed. As discussed below, the guidance provides little clarification on the identification of eligible user contracting authorities. Further, it remains possible to set up a framework appointing an unlimited number of suppliers.

Confusingly, section 45(5) separately requires certain information to be included in the 'framework', including:

- a description of goods, services or works to be provided under contracts awarded in accordance with the framework;
- the price payable, or mechanism for determining the price payable, under such contracts;
- the estimated value of the framework;
- any selection process to be applied on the award of contracts;
- the term of the framework;
- the contracting authorities entitled to award public contracts in accordance with the framework;
- whether the framework is awarded under an open framework.

However, a contracting authority will likely provide a copy of the framework as part of the associated documents when publishing the tender notice in any event. It is not therefore clear why the legislator has provided for two separate lists of information, some of which is duplicative The Explanatory Notes to the PA 2023 explain that the information to be included in the framework is required 'to ensure it is set up correctly and there is adequate transparency when the framework is awarded' and that 'these matters determine the scope of the framework and, as a result, the nature, type and value of future public contracts that can be awarded under it'.[35] It is assumed that this is to further increase transparency by ensuring that certain information is provided in the framework documents rather than just in the original tender documents. It is noted, however, that no proportionality requirements appear to apply to the disclosure of such information which, in terms of volume, could be considered excessive.

The information requirements that apply to the framework itself, some of which duplicate the information required in the tender notice, are also vague and, it can be argued, give an implied licence to, or at least do not deter, the establishment of generic frameworks. In particular, the requirement to include 'the price payable, or mechanism for determining the price payable' under call-offs raises a fundamental question about the extent to which the pricing of call-offs needs to be established at the framework award level, if at all, an issue discussed in more detail in chapter seven.

[35] Explanatory Notes to the Procurement Act 2023, para 290.

Thus, whilst there is now more flexibility in the use of a procedure to award a framework (although it is questionable whether this is desired) and some increased transparency, the PA 2023 provisions do little to discourage contracting authorities looking to set up generic, pan-public sector frameworks.

4. Identifying the Users of a Framework

4.1. Identifying the Users of a Framework under the PCR 2015

Another significant issue that has been litigated in EU courts is the need to ensure a clear identification in the call for competition of the potential users of a framework. This is important for various reasons, including verification of whether a particular entity is legally entitled to use it given that it is restricted to use by contracting authorities and may be legally responsible in respect of that use, and enabling suppliers to identify users when planning whether or not to tender for admission.

Regulation 33(5) provides that the call-off procedures can only be applied:

> between those contracting authorities clearly identified for that purpose in the call for competition or the invitation to confirm interest and those economic operators party to the framework as concluded.

Recital 60 Directive 2014/24/EU further explains that:

> framework agreements should not be used by contracting authorities which are not identified in them. For that purpose, the contracting authorities that are parties to a specific framework from the outset should be clearly indicated, either by name or by other means, such as a reference to a given category of contracting authorities within a clearly delimited geographical area, so that the contracting authorities concerned can be easily and unequivocally identified.

In the Commission's Explanatory Note on Frameworks,[36] it was explained that when a framework is to be used by several contracting authorities, they 'must be identified explicitly in the contract notice, either by naming them directly in the notice itself or through reference to other documents (eg the specifications or a list available from one of the contracting authorities etc)'.[37] The Commission stated, for example, that it would not be sufficient to state that the framework could be used by 'contracting authorities' established in a Member State, because of the difficulties that may arise in determining whether an entity was a contracting authority by virtue of meeting the definition of a 'body governed by public law'. It indicated that a description permitting immediate identification of the contracting authorities concerned – for example 'the municipalities of x province or of y region' – would be sufficient, however.[38] The Commission gave the example of a 'list of contracting authorities that have the right to use frameworks concluded by a central purchasing body', provided that 'such lists … indicate the

[36] European Commission Explanatory Note – Frameworks – Classic Directive CC/2005/03, 14 July 2005, Ref. Ares(2016)810203 – 16/02/2016.

[37] ibid 5.

[38] ibid.

date from which the contracting authorities obtained this right', begging the question whether such lists must be fixed at the point of advertising the framework or can be updated during the framework term eg where new municipalities emerge. This was not conclusively resolved.

The UK OGC guidance seemed to adopt a slightly broader view. In the UK's response to consultation on implementing Directive 2004/18/EC, the OGC stated that the contract notice must state the contracting authorities entitled to call-off and that 'these authorities can be either named individually, or a generic description may be used – for example, government departments, health authorities, all contracting authorities in a particular region and so on'.[39] However, it then noted that '[c]ontracting authorities not covered by the original OJEU notice may not make use of the framework agreement; therefore, it may often be worth drawing the description in generic terms, to enable maximum take-up across the public sector' and 'we would recommend that where generic terms are used the notice should include a reference to where details of the authorities can be found'.[40] This would appear to suggest that UK policy actively encouraged use of generic descriptors to maximise public sector-wide uptake. In its 2008 guidance,[41] it repeated the above regarding the type of authority described; however, it referred to the Commission's guidance that the description of classes should enable 'immediate identification of the contracting authorities concerned', noting that '[i]t is not considered to be sufficiently precise to refer to all contracting authorities in a particular region'. The OGC advised that a reference to where details of the contracting authorities covered can be obtained should be included in the notice eg if there is an accessible list of contracting authorities in a relevant 'class', or an organisation with responsibility for maintaining details of the members of a 'class', that list or organisation should be quoted in the contract notice.

In September 2010, the OGC issued an action note[42] in response to concerns expressed by the Commission about several frameworks that only generically identified permitted users. It recommended that 'where the identification of permissible users of an existing framework is currently insufficiently precise, the owner of the framework should issue clarification to relevant suppliers and potential users' to avoid any extension of the scope of a framework. It warned against 'circular or contingent identification' such as referring to 'bodies which undertake a particular function or activity' as 'there must be adequate information to enable unambiguous identification of the bodies which undertake that function or activity'. As for identifying users by 'class', the OGC stated that the framework should be 'limited to those bodies which are already identified as members of the 'class' at the time of the procurement but acknowledged that 'during the lifetime of a framework the identity of members of a class may change and evolve, owing to bona fide changes of function, reorganisation and restructuring'. It therefore

[39] OGC, 'Response to Consultation, Draft Regulations Implementing the new Public Sector and Utilities Procurement Directives', December 2005, 10.

[40] ibid.

[41] OGC, 'Guidance on Frameworks in the Procurement Regulations', September 2008.

[42] OGC, 'Procurement Policy Note – Need to ensure that bodies permitted to use frameworks are adequately identified and clarification is used if necessary', Action Note 16/10, 8 September 2010, accessible at webarchive.nationalarchives.gov.uk/20110405231446/http://www.ogc.gov.uk/documents/PPN_1610_Identifing_and_confirming_bodies_able_to_call_off_from_framework_agreements.pdf.

clarified that such changes could be legally permissible, provided 'the scale and scope of the framework is not materially altered, and details of these changes are made available to interested parties'. It also stated that 'changes to the identity of class membership must not extend the size of scope of the user base beyond that originally existing at the time the framework was put in place'. As a condition of allowing such changes, the OGC provided that 'any bodies which purport to join a framework as a result of such a reorganisation must be able to demonstrate a direct continuation of scope and functions from their predecessor body/bodies which had been rightful beneficiaries of the framework and therefore entitled to use it'. The information on any changes to the members of a 'class' should also be kept up to date and made available to interested parties.

Cabinet Office guidance on the PCR 2015 framework provisions,[43] confirming the principles in Recital 60 to Directive 2014/24/EU, stated, '[w]here possible a link to a list of relevant authorities should be provided'. In accordance with the OGC's previous guidance, it provided that 'potential framework users may be identified by reference to a specific class of contracting authorities in a defined region that can be identified on the internet'.

Whilst the guidance helps to clarify the level of detail required to be included in a call for competition, it is questionable whether merely referring to specific classes or lists of contracting authorities met the requirements of the EU transparency principle. This is because the guidance did not extend to requiring a precise indication of those contracting authorities that intended to use the framework and, therefore, suppliers are not aware of the extent to which the framework may be used during its term.[44]

In *Autorità Garante*[45] one question the CJEU had to address was whether Directive 2004/18/EC allowed a framework under which a contracting authority acts on its own behalf and other contracting authorities not direct parties to the framework. The case concerned the use of a single-supplier framework by an Italian regional health authority not signatory to the framework. However, the tender specifications included an extension clause allowing the possibility of extending the framework to several health authorities identified in that clause. The CJEU considered Article 32(2) which provided that the procedures used for awarding contracts under a framework can only be applied 'between the contracting authorities and the economic operators originally party to the framework'. It applied a contextual and purposive approach to interpreting this provision.[46] The CJEU held that only economic operators are required to be 'original parties' to the framework, and it was not necessary for a 'secondary' contracting authority be a signatory in order for it to be able to award a contract under it. Although this case concerned Directive 2004/18/EC, the CJEU noted the second subparagraph of Article 33(2) Directive 2014/24/EU.[47] This provides more clarity, stating that the procedures used for awarding contracts under a framework can only be applied 'between those contracting authorities clearly identified for this purpose in the call for

[43] CCS, 'The Public Contracts Regulations 2015 & The Utilities Contracts Regulations 2016: Guidance on Framework Agreements', updated October 2016.

[44] See Arrowsmith (n 1) 11–25, for discussion on this point.

[45] Case C-216/17 *Autorità Garante* ECLI:EU:C:2018:1034.

[46] ibid paras 49–56.

[47] ibid paras 49–56 referring at para 54 to the Opinion of AG Campos Sánchez-Bordona at para 62.

competition or the invitation to confirm interest and those economic operators party to the framework as concluded'.

Even though user contracting authorities are not required to be parties to the framework, the question arises as to what other preliminary steps, if any, the primary contracting authority setting up the framework must take to identify other user authorities in the call for competition. The AG stated:

> it will suffice if a party seeking that status has agreed to be bound by the terms and conditions of that agreement;

and

> if the conclusion of the framework is preceded by a collective decision, in which a number of contracting authorities agree to make group purchases of certain goods or services, that prior collective decision can be used as the basis for a framework signed by just one of those authorities on behalf (or with the consent) of them all.[48]

It could be argued that it is a necessary implication of this case that the primary contracting authority should obtain the express consent of user contracting authorities before identifying them in the call for competition.[49] Without communicating their consent alongside their estimates of their likely volumes of purchases, the advert will not be able to provide a meaningful estimate of value and volume of spend.

Given the uncertainty about whether it is permissible under each national legal regime for a contracting authority to conclude a framework on behalf of another contracting authority (as each Member State has its own administrative and contract law regimes), it is not surprising that the CJEU adopted a legal interpretation that avoids prescriptive contractual or consent requirements.

In terms of how to identify the user contracting authorities in the procurement documents, the CJEU stated:

> It is sufficient that such a contracting authority appear as a potential beneficiary of that framework from the date on which it is concluded by being clearly identified in the tender documents with an explicit reference that makes both the 'secondary' contracting authority itself and any interested operator aware of that possibility. That reference can appear either in the framework itself or in another document, such as an extension clause in the tender specifications, as long as the requirements as to advertising and legal certainty and, consequently, those relating to transparency are complied with.[50]

Whilst the above statement confirms that a contracting authority must be clearly identified by an explicit reference in the tender documents used to advertise the framework, it provides no further guidance on the level of precision required for the explicit reference. The legal position is not completely clear, therefore, and contracting authorities may encounter practical difficulties when faced with links to poorly defined lists and lists subject to regular change.

[48] ibid paras 67–68 of AG Opinion.

[49] See eg www.eversheds-sutherland.com/global/en/what/articles/index.page?ArticleID=en/Competition_EU_and_Regulatory/framework-agreements-110219.

[50] Case C-216/17 *Autorità Garante* (n 45) para 56.

4.1.1. Identifying the Users of a Framework in Practice under the PCR 2015

Notwithstanding the legal requirements described above, interviewees confirmed that a broad-brush approach to advertising eligible user contracting authorities has developed in practice. It cannot be excluded that in some instances, this may constitute an attempt by CPAs to broaden the contracting authority customer base, assuring suppliers that their target customers are eligible. This is a prime example of the exploitation of legal uncertainty with a view to maximising market scope, an aspect of the marketisation of frameworks.

It has become attractive for CPAs to set up frameworks for ICT products and services accessible by a wide user base. It is common to come across a contract notice for an ICT framework that states it is for use by the entire UK public sector, the voluntary sector and third sector without providing any detailed lists of such users. Several interviewees were cynical of this development on the basis that 'framework providers want the framework to be accessible to the widest possible user base as they see it as a money-making opportunity'.[51] One interviewee had come across several arm's length bodies that did not meet the definition of a contracting authority but were actively using frameworks to procure their requirements.[52]

Two interviewees reported that some frameworks in the health sector were seemingly being opened out for use by private sector customers eg private sector hospitals. It is recalled that the PCR 2015 provide that frameworks are only intended to be used by contracting authorities (regulation 33(5) and regulation 37(10). From a legal perspective, such use is questionable on grounds of transparency. It has implications for such duties as estimating the maximum value of a framework and might result in higher prices being charged under frameworks than if the customer base were limited to the public sector. It is unlikely that the estimated requirements of such non-contracting authorities are considered when calculating the estimated value of the framework. The real value of the supplies or services to be procured through the framework is therefore very unclear, and which may affect the way in which suppliers seeking a place on the framework price their tenders. It also raises the issue of whether this is in the spirit of Recital 62 Directive 2014/24/EU to the effect that frameworks should not be used improperly or in such a way as to prevent, restrict or distort competition. One interviewee raised a concern that such private sector customers are unjustifiably taking advantage of pricing agreed with public sector customers and that this raises issues from a competition law perspective.[53] More generally, from a regulatory policy perspective, permitting a mix of contracting authorities and non-contracting authorities to use a framework creates a regulated and non-regulated environment when using the same framework. This bifurcation may lead to poor behaviours, and problems in ensuring effective oversight and enforcement. For example, non-contracting authorities might

[51] LA12.

[52] CA15.

[53] LA10 – this interviewee queried whether such organisations are subject to competition law if facilitating the purchase of goods for use in connection with an economic activity. Case C-205/03 *FENIN v Commission* ECLI:EU:C:2006:453, [2006] ECR I-6295.

adopt very flexible call-off methods which could impact on supplier behaviours when dealing with contracting authorities. The opening up of frameworks to non-contracting authorities could also explain the high-level, ultra-flexible call-off procedures that are now incorporated in some frameworks.[54]

Concerning an indication of the likely usage or frequency of usage of the framework by the eligible customer base, most interviewees concurred that this was not something that was usually disclosed in the advert because of the difficulties highlighted above and the non-binding nature of the majority of frameworks in the UK. The likely usage of a framework might be explored through the PME process and information gathered from an examination of call-off contract values put through previous iterations of the framework (where applicable). It was indicated that CPAs looking to identify potential usage might take some assurance in instances where a contracting authority has a 'framework-first' policy mandate that may require use of that particular CPA-led framework.

4.2. Identifying the Users of a Framework under the PA 2023

As indicated, section 45(5)(f) provides that a contracting authority must set out in the framework 'the contracting authorities entitled to award public contracts in accordance with the framework'. Regulation 20(2)(e) PR 2024 provides that when running a competitive tendering procedure to award the framework, the contracting authority must set out in the tender notice 'the contracting authorities entitled to award contracts in accordance with the framework (whether by listing the names of those authorities or by describing categories of authorities)'. The same information is required in a transparency notice where a direct award of a framework is being made (regulation 26(2)(w)(iii)). The GCF guidance expands on the above only slightly by indicating that '[t]his can be done either by listing the names of those authorities, or by describing categories of authorities, for example 'all local authorities within Norfolk', or 'all central government authorities as defined in the Procurement Act 2023', or 'all NHS Foundation Trusts'.[55]

Therefore, it remains unclear what level of precision is required when identifying eligible user contracting authorities, whether prior consultation of users is required, or whether is it necessary to obtain details of their estimated usage. The absence of clearer controls seems to implicitly acknowledge an accepted practice of scoping multiple generic, pan-public sector frameworks that lack sufficient transparency. A potential challenge based on a lack of transparency was conceivable under the PCR 2015. However, under the PA 2023, a challenge might seem more difficult given the wording of the legislation and the absence of an explicit transparency principle. Notwithstanding, there may be public law arguments (eg, on the ground of irrationality) where a framework has been set up on an opaque basis with overly broad or nondescript references to potential users but which do not appear likely given that there have been no previous challenges to such scoping practices in the UK previously.

[54] See chs 5 and 7 for further explanation of such call-off procedures.
[55] GCF, 'Guidance: Frameworks', updated January 2025.

5. Estimation and Disclosure of Framework Value

5.1. Estimation and Disclosure of Framework Value under the PCR 2015

Similar to the need to identify the permitted user contracting authorities, it is also important for the expectant framework value to be clear. However, as will be discussed, this becomes complicated where a multi-supplier framework involves many user contracting authorities whose requirements are not necessarily known.

Regulation 5(1) provides that the rules implementing Directive 2014/24/EU apply in their entirety to a framework only when its total estimated value exceeds the relevant applicable financial threshold. Regulation 6(7) provides that for competitive procurements, this calculation must be made 'at the moment at which the call for competition is sent'. Regulation 6(8) provides that for frameworks 'the value to be taken into consideration shall be the maximum estimated value, net of VAT, of all the contracts envisaged for the total term of the framework'.[56]

This estimation exercise is likely to be most challenging where there are multiple permitted user contracting authorities, all with varying requirements. The same rules on calculation apply to all frameworks irrespective of the number of permitted users, the framework term, or whether the framework contains any exclusivity obligations mandating its use. Therefore, even for a framework with many permitted users under no obligation to use it, the contracting authority setting up the framework is required to consider all the call-offs envisaged.[57] The legislation does not provide any further clarification on this calculation, therefore a contracting authority would need to rely on applying general procurement principles (particularly transparency and equal treatment) when estimating the framework's total value. Given the uncertainties involved, over-estimations of values may be likely.

Use of a contract notice to advertise a framework requires a standard form which contains the information required in Annex V, Part C10(a) of Directive 2014/24/EU.[58] This includes an:

> indication of the planned duration of the framework, stating, where appropriate, the reasons for any duration exceeding four years; as far as possible, indication of value or order of magnitude and frequency of contracts to be awarded, number and, where appropriate, proposed maximum number of economic operators to participate.

Thus, neither Directive 2014/24/EU nor the PCR 2015 explicitly require that a maximum value be stated in the contract notice, only 'as far as possible' an 'indication of value or order of magnitude and frequency of contracts to be awarded'. However, the contract notice template includes a section for estimated values which refers to the 'estimated total maximum value for the entire duration of the framework'.[59]

[56] The Public Procurement (Agreement on Government Procurement) (Thresholds) (Amendment) Regulations 2021 made the thresholds inclusive of VAT from 1 January 2022.

[57] This interpretation was adopted by Arrowsmith (n 1) 11-18–11-19), the OGC (n 42) and the PLA, 'The Use of Framework Agreements in Public Procurement' March 2012, 4.3–4.4.

[58] Regulation 49.

[59] Section II.1.5, simap.ted.europa.eu/documents/10184/99173/EN_F02.pdf.

In *Autorità Garante*[60] and *Simonsen*,[61] the CJEU has held that there is an obligation to publicise at the outset the total maximum value of the framework. In *Autorità Garante*, the CJEU referred to the provisions in Directive 2004/18/EC on the methods for calculating the estimated value of frameworks and the requirements for the content of a contract notice and held:

> a framework must, at the outset, determine the maximum volume of supplies or services that may form the subject of subsequent contracts.[62]

In support, the CJEU noted the requirement in Article 32(3) for single-provider frameworks that call-offs must be awarded within the limits of the terms laid down in the framework[63] and the importance of observing fundamental principles governing award of public contracts.[64] The CJEU considered transparency given that contracting authorities are not bound to send a notice of the results of the award procedure for each call-off and the risk that the framework could be used to divide a contract up artificially so that it remains below threshold. It also rejected the argument that a reference to the 'usual' requirements of contracting authorities specifically indicated in the framework would suffice, as this would not be sufficiently explicit for suppliers from other Member States; if known, it should not be difficult to publish the total quantity of usual requirements to observe the principles of transparency and equal treatment. It also stated that the requirement to disclose the framework's maximum value was a manifestation of the prohibition on using frameworks improperly or in such a way as to prevent, restrict or distort competition under Article 32(2).[65]

In *Simonsen*, the CJEU analysed the relevant provisions of Directive 2014/24/EU (Annex V Part C) and considered the principles of equal treatment and transparency in holding that:

> a failure by the contracting authority to indicate, in the contract notice, a maximum value of the supplies under a framework cannot be accepted.[66]

The CJEU clarified that 'the indication of the maximum quantity or the maximum value of the supplies under a framework can appear in either the contract notice or the tender specifications',[67] on the basis that, pursuant to Article 53(1) Directive 2014/24/EU, contracting authorities must allow unrestricted and full direct electronic access, free of charge, to the procurement documents from the date of publication of a notice (under Article 51). Where the maximum value is stated in the tender specifications, it would not be sufficient, however, if suppliers looking to access them were required to express, in advance, any interest whatsoever to the contracting authority.[68]

The CJEU in *Autorità Garante* and *Simonsen* effectively confirmed that lead contracting authorities need to include the requirements of all users when publicising

[60] Case C-216/17 *Autorità Garante* (n 45).
[61] Case C-23/20 *Simonsen & Weel A/S v Region Nordjylland og Region Syddanmark* ECLI:EU:C:2021:490.
[62] Case C-216/17 *Autorità Garante* (n 45) para 60.
[63] ibid para 61.
[64] ibid paras 62–68.
[65] ibid para 69.
[66] Case C-23/20 *Simonsen & Weel* (n 61) para 54.
[67] ibid para 71.
[68] ibid para 73.

the maximum value of the framework. The CJEU did not, however, give any guidance on how this requirement be complied with in practice. It would seem that consultation with all proposed user authorities would need to be carried out before issuing the call for competition so that their requirements can be factored into its estimation.

This also raises the question of what happens if the maximum is exceeded. Regulation 72 sets out the circumstances in which a framework can be modified without having to conduct a new procedure, including 'where the modifications, irrespective of their value, are not substantial' (regulation 72(1)(e). It would seem correct that the principles in regulation 72, which are based on the relevant case law of the CJEU on making 'material changes',[69] and which enshrine the equal treatment, transparency and proportionality principles, should be applicable to assess whether a contracting authority is allowed to award a call-off where this would result in exceeding the estimated maximum value of the framework stated in the original call for competition. This analysis is supported by regulation 33(6) under which call-offs cannot entail substantial modifications to the terms laid down in the framework and CCS guidance indicating that the terms of the framework should first be considered but if these are silent and regulation 33 does not prevent the amendment, the rules in regulation 72 should be considered.[70]

Therefore, where the value of call-offs only marginally exceeds the stated estimated value and no other changes to the scope or nature of the framework is made, this might be a permissible non-substantial modification (under regulation 72(8)). However, where the additional value awarded significantly exceeds the stated estimate such that, had it been incorporated in the original contract notice, it would have attracted a different group of suppliers, the call-offs risk being unlawful.[71]

However, the CJEU in *Autorità Garante*,[72] *Simonsen*[73] and *EPIC Consulting*[74] cast some doubt on the application of these principles. In the first case, it was held that where a framework is concluded with a single supplier, contracts based on that agreement must be awarded within the limits of the terms laid down in the agreement and it followed that:

> the contracting authority that is an original party to the framework can make commitments on its own behalf or on behalf of the potential contracting authorities that are specifically indicated in that agreement only up to a certain quantity and once that limit has been reached the agreement will no longer have any effect.[75]

The CJEU reiterated this principle in *Simonsen* but clarified that:

> in accordance with the third subparagraph of Article 33(2) and Article 72 Directive 2014/24, modifications to a framework that are not substantial are allowed, it being understood that,

[69] Recital 107 to Directive 2014/24/EU.

[70] CCS, 'The Public Contracts Regulations 2015 & The Utilities Contracts Regulations 2016: Guidance on Amendments to Contracts During Their Term', updated October 2016.

[71] Regulation 72 provides safe harbours under which a modification to a framework will not be substantial.

[72] Case C-216/17 *Autorità Garante* (n 45).

[73] Case C-23/20 *Simonsen & Weel* (n 61).

[74] Case C-274/21 *EPIC Financial Consulting Ges.m.b.H. v Republik Österreich and Bundesbeschaffung GmbH* ECLI:EU:C:2022:565.

[75] Case C-216/17 *Autorità Garante* (n 45) para 61.

> by definition (as the case concerned a single-supplier framework), such a modification is consensual in nature and, accordingly, the agreement of the successful tenderer is required.[76]

In the more recent *Epic Consulting*, the CJEU added clarity by stating:

> Article 33(3) of Directive 2014/24 must be interpreted as meaning that a contracting authority may no longer rely, for the purpose of awarding a new contract, on a framework in respect of which the quantity and/or maximum value of the works, supplies or services concerned laid down therein has or have already been reached, unless the award of that contract does not entail a substantial modification of that framework, as provided for in Article 72(1)(e) of that directive.[77]

Despite the strict earlier position, it appears that there has been a relaxation to permit non-substantial modifications.

These three cases concerned single-supplier frameworks but the same principles should apply to multi-supplier frameworks. The UK High Court in *Consultant Connect*, when considering the lawfulness of using a multi-supplier framework, distinguished the *Simonsen* case with the judge commenting 'I would not necessarily agree that a contract to deliver value above a stated estimated total framework value is ipso facto void'.[78]

Nevertheless, practical difficulties may arise when trying to determine whether the maximum value of the framework is exceeded, particularly where there are multiple users and multiple suppliers with little transparency or record of the values of call-offs entered into.

5.1.1. Estimation and Disclosure of Framework Value in Practice under the PCR 2015

As indicated, PME might be used to estimate framework value but engagement levels tend to vary. There was a consensus amongst interviewees that this is probably the most difficult information to provide in the advert, especially when the framework will permit many users.

A range of views was presented concerning what information to insert in the advert. Some thought that only a rough estimate was required (or a range of values was acceptable) whilst others thought that the estimate must be as accurate as possible based on the information derived from PME. One legal adviser advised clients to insert in the call for competition the estimated total value based on what that contracting authority itself intended to purchase but also to insert a higher value to cover use by others.[79] This is obviously applicable only when the contracting authority intends to use the framework for its own requirements and is not acting solely in the capacity of a CPA. Other interviewees considered it necessary to insert a maximum value in the advert, with some indicating that this can lead to over-estimates to mitigate risk of exceeding it. As one interviewee explained, 'it is a balancing act' as 'it needs to be sufficiently large so that it is

[76] Case C-23/20 *Simonsen & Weel* (n 61) para 70.
[77] Case C-274/21 *EPIC Financial Consulting* (n 74) para 68.
[78] *Consultant Connect v NHS Bath and others* [2022] EWHC 2037, paras 171, 205.
[79] LA16.

unlikely to be exceeded but not so high as to mislead the market'.[80] Another commented that flexibility is required to accommodate any potential changes during the framework's lifetime and that this can be a 'fudge'.[81] It appears that when legal advisers advise on estimation the contracting authority is more likely to conduct further due diligence to better inform the values to be inserted into the advert based on that advice. One legal adviser disclosed that 'as a rough rule of thumb, exceeding the framework value by up to 20% is usually considered to be fairly low risk'.[82] Another highlighted the *Autorità Garante*[83] case, however, and that the CJEU seemed to take a 'harsher view' when it indicated that a framework ceases to be valid once the maximum value is breached.[84] In practice, a case-by-case risk-based approach is usually taken by legal advisers advising on this point. Some CPAs also assess competitor frameworks and the values inserted in their adverts. If a framework is a reiteration of a previous one, some will look at the value of the previous iteration and make an educated guess for the new iteration.

Many interviewees reported that high framework values and wide value ranges are commonplace which, as one legal adviser explained, 'can result in a framework losing its meaning'.[85] Legal advisers tend to encourage their clients to keep an audit trail of the engagement and decision-making process used to decide on the value(s) to insert in the advert.

From the supplier's perspective, it was generally accepted that the values in the adverts are indicative only and are not to be relied upon heavily, particularly where the framework is made available to a wide range of contracting authorities. One interviewee said they no longer paid much attention to frameworks with excessively high values inserted in the adverts, as they 'are not very indicative and usually so high to be meaningless'.[86]

Therefore, despite the legal requirements, it is questionable to what extent there is certainty and transparency in the estimation of framework values. This is likely to impact on suppliers' preparation of tenders, including their proposed pricing under the framework, as the information in an advert is not being treated as an accurate indicator of framework activity.

5.2. Estimation and Disclosure of Framework Value under the PA 2023

Section 4(1) provides that when estimating the framework value, the contracting authority must estimate its value 'for the time being'. It is unclear how this should be interpreted but it suggests a degree of flexibility. According to Schedule 3, paragraph 2(1), the estimated framework value must include all contracts that have been or may be awarded.

[80] CPB6.
[81] LA10.
[82] LA15.
[83] Case C-216/17 *Autorità Garante* (n 45).
[84] LA16.
[85] LA12.
[86] EO4.

Further, section 49 introduces an 'open framework', which is scheme of successive frameworks on substantially the same terms that can be opened to admit suppliers at various intervals. Schedule 3, paragraph 2(2) provides that open frameworks must be valued by including the value of all frameworks that could be awarded under it (ie the *estimated* value of all contracts that could be awarded under each of the frameworks in the scheme). The GCF guidance does not elaborate on this estimation exercise. The position under the PA 2023 is therefore similar to that under the PCR 2015; however, as there is no transparency principle, the position is arguably even more flexible. This would appear to permit a speculative estimate for generic, pan-public sector frameworks, the set-up of which has not been informed by any likely throughput values provided by potential users.

The 'estimated value' of the framework is required to be disclosed in the tender notice and framework under the PA 2023. It is noted that the Cabinet Office has not proceeded with its original proposal in its consultation response to the *Transforming Public Procurement* Green Paper for contracting authorities to be required 'to identify in the tender notice or in the procurement documents the … overall maximum estimated value of the contracts that may be awarded under the framework'.[87] This reference to 'maximum estimated value' would have aligned with the EU case law above. The legislator has presumably resiled from this proposal on the basis that it is unnecessarily restrictive (and likely difficult to enforce for many generic, pan-public sector frameworks in the UK). Further, given the above case law, the Cabinet Office might have taken up the opportunity to include an explicit rule that exceeding the maximum value would mean that the framework would no longer have any effect. Instead, it appears to have opted to rely on the application of the general provisions on making contract modifications. The GCF guidance confirms that if the estimated value of the framework or, if relevant, an individual lot, is about to be exceeded, the contracting authority may wish to consider whether it is possible to modify the framework to amend the estimated value under section 74.[88] The Transforming Public Procurement Learning Manual module on frameworks and dynamic markets indicates even further flexibility, stating:

> There is no longer a need to assign a value to the contracts that may be awarded under each individual lot, category or part of a framework […] Now it is only the value of the potential contracts for the framework […] as a whole that need to be stated.[89]

This implies that to reserve flexibility, contracting authorities may wish to refrain from indicating the estimated value of individual lots under a framework and state the total estimated value of the framework instead.

Similar to the lack of clear controls on identifying eligible user contracting authorities, the absence of controls on framework value estimation is unlikely to deter contracting authorities, in particular CPAs, from scoping frameworks intended to appeal to the broadest customer base. As with many other obligations in the PA 2023 in respect of frameworks, decisions such as estimating the value of a framework are to be considered

[87] Cabinet Office, 'Transforming Public Procurement – Government Response to Consultation', December 2021, 213.
[88] GCF (n 55) 18.
[89] Module 5, 'Transforming Public Procurement Learning Manual' (n 25).

against the requirements to have regard to the section 12 procurement objectives. However, it is questionable whether these will have a significant impact in practice.

6. Setting the Duration of a Framework and Call-off Contracts

6.1. Setting the Duration of a Framework and Call-off Contracts under the PCR 2015

Another issue concerns setting the appropriate framework duration. As a framework under the PCR 2015 is already closed for its duration, it should be ensured that it is not closed for any longer than necessary to avoid further restriction on market access.

Regulation 33(3) imposes a maximum four-year term 'save in exceptional cases duly justified, in particular by the subject-matter of the framework'. The policy justifications underpinning this rule are examined in chapter three. A justification suggested by the PLA is where 'the desired outcomes of the framework (for example, savings through aggregation of purchaser demand) will only be achievable if the framework subsists for a longer term than four years'.[90] It suggested that one example is 'where the subject-matter of the contract requires much upfront investment to be made by the appointed supplier, and where it may take a substantial period before any kind of return on that investment (for both supplier and customer) is to be felt'.[91] In response to consultations on draft implementing regulations in relation to Directive 2004/18/EC, the exceptional circumstances justifying extension was repeatedly identified as in need of further guidance, the only example given by the OGC of when extension may be justified being 'large scale refurbishment and improvement programmes' and simply advising that legal advice should be sought before letting a framework beyond four years, particularly if 'significantly greater' than four years 'which would call into question whether a framework agreement is the most suitable form of procurement'.[92] As discussed in chapter three, when applying this 'exceptional circumstances' rules, contracting authorities have had to consider the duty under regulation 18(2) to comply with the principles of equal treatment, non-discrimination and the prohibition on designing a procurement with the intention of 'artificially narrowing competition'. Recital 61 Directive 2014/24/EU also includes reference that '[f]rameworks should not be used improperly or in such a way as to prevent, restrict or distort competition'. Under Annex V Part C10(a) Directive 2014/24/EU, contracting authorities are required to state in the contract notice 'the reasons for any duration exceeding four years'. This aligns with the principle of transparency. Contracting authorities therefore need to be able to formulate their justifications in advance of advertising the framework and include these in the contract notice (or PIN if one is used for the call for competition).

[90] PLA (n 57) 7.2.
[91] ibid.
[92] OGC (n 39) 10.

In *Autorità Garante*[93] the contract at issue was for a term of nine years. One of the grounds put forward to argue that the reference to the CJEU for a preliminary ruling was inadmissible was that the initial contract exceeded four years and therefore did not qualify as a 'framework' within the meaning of the 2004 Directive.[94] The CJEU noted that no explanation was offered justifying why the maximum period had not been complied with[95] but stated that it had not been established in any event that a public contract cannot be classified as a 'framework' solely on the basis that its term was greater than four years and the contracting authority had failed duly to justify why the term exceeds that limit.

By contrast, neither Directive 2014/24/EU nor the PCR 2015 specify any maximum length of a call-off. Nor do they expressly prohibit a call-off whose term continues beyond the length of the framework itself. The OGC in consultation on the implementation of Directive 2004/18/EC stated that the time limit or contract length 'should reflect what is reasonable for the product or service being procured and the contracting authority's normal approach to the length of such contracts'.[96] Recital 62 of the 2014 Directive states:

> the duration of the individual contracts based on a framework does not need to coincide with the duration of that framework, but might, as appropriate, be shorter or longer. In particular, it should be allowed to set the length of individual contracts based on a framework taking account of factors such as the time needed for their performance, where maintenance of equipment with an expected useful life of more than four years is included or where extensive training of staff to perform the contract is needed.

This provided helpful clarification, especially when it is considered that the Commission had suggested in its 2005 Explanatory Note that call-offs, like the framework itself, should be limited to a duration of four years.[97]

Consistent with the position on framework duration, a contracting authority has also needed to consider the prohibition on using a framework 'improperly or in such a way as to prevent, restrict or distort competition' in setting call-off contract durations.

6.1.1. *Setting the Duration of a Framework and Call-off Contracts in Practice under the PCR 2015*

Most interviewees stated that adhering to the four-year term was standard practice for multi-supplier frameworks with little need for extension.[98] One interviewee described their organisation's policy of 'comply or explain' when setting the duration.[99] Several interviewees highlighted the differences in practice between the durations of multi-supplier and single-supplier frameworks, however, in that the latter regularly last for far longer than four years particularly where a strategic partnering arrangement is envisaged. One interviewee gave examples of terms between 10 and 20 years.[100]

[93] Case C-216/17 *Autorità Garante* (n 45).
[94] ibid para 45 Opinion of AG Campos Sánchez-Bordona.
[95] ibid para 35.
[96] OGC (n 39) s 10.
[97] European Commission (n 36) 5.
[98] Set out in reg 33(3).
[99] CA15.
[100] LA3.

6.1.1.1. Duration of a Framework

In the multi-supplier context, the four-year period was generally considered to be a reasonable maximum term, which was 'necessary to minimise the lock-out effect on the rest of the market'.[101] The '2+1+1' model is commonly used whereby the framework is set up for a fixed period of two years with options to extend for two further periods of 12 months. An interviewee thought that a four-year framework term was 'probably reasonable considering the length of time it takes to go through the procurement process', and incorporated a break point at two years to decide whether to continue with the incumbent suppliers based on their original proposals.[102]

For commoditised ICT requirements, some interviewees expressed their preference for short framework durations due to the dynamic nature of the market.[103] One interviewee had witnessed an increase in legal challenges to framework awards in the ICT market and felt a two-year term for many ICT requirements would address supplier concerns about being locked out of a market for too long.[104]

Some contracting authority interviewees said longer framework terms would: undermine the UK Government's SME agenda by closing off the market to new and developing companies in the ICT space; not take advantage of the fluid ICT market;[105] and 'discourage innovation and creativity and not lead to reduced prices'.[106] Longer terms were considered particularly inappropriate for dynamic and complex ICT requirements on multi-supplier frameworks.[107]

Among suppliers, the four-year term was also considered reasonable for most requirements. One interviewee commented that 'it can take a long time to get a project moving', that 'you usually find that the first year of a framework has little revenue put through it as customers are not used to it,' and 'there is not much throughput until the framework is nearing its end', and that this explained why many frameworks are generally refreshed and reiterated on similar terms.[108] There was some support for longer durations because of the bid costs and resource burdens associated with applying to join frameworks. It was acknowledged, however, that this was unlikely to be practical 'due to the frameworks being overtaken by advances in technology and the commercial environment'.[109]

However, for some, four years was considered too short. Interviewees considered that once a framework was let, it was not long before preparation for its next iteration began so that all internal governance and procedural requirements could be met; it could take up to 12 months to procure a new iteration; and there could be a drop in spend during the first three months of a reiterated framework as all parties needed time to adjust to the procedures and requirements of the new iteration.[110]

[101] CPB1.
[102] CPB8.
[103] CPB2.
[104] LA5.
[105] CA5.
[106] CA6.
[107] LA8.
[108] EO3.
[109] EO1, EO2.
[110] CPB 1, CPB 2, CPB9.

A few interviewees mentioned the *Transforming Public Procurement* Green Paper[111] which first suggested allowing both 'closed' and 'open' frameworks to be set up in future. Many interviewees who were in favour of allowing longer framework durations were generally in favour of the proposed 'open' framework which can be set up for up to eight years and allow contracting authorities to open the framework to new suppliers during its term subject to certain conditions. One interviewee did not view the framework itself to be a 'contract' as such and thought that 'there should be flexibility around adding and removing suppliers' with some 'refresh' options.[112] Some interviewees, however, did not see the need to change the four-year rule given the possibility to extend in exceptional cases.[113] Some views expressed that the Green Paper proposals did not seem to advance or improve things and only appeared to be tackling 'perception problems'.[114]

Several interviewees were concerned that the 'open framework' proposal did not materially improve the position as it seemed to require re-running the appointment stage just as under the PCR 2015 for successive iterations of closed frameworks. A few interviewees queried whether some other type of mechanism in a framework could be introduced whereby suppliers could be added to the list of suppliers during the life of the framework; for example, 'if one of the framework suppliers is removed for some reason or terminates its involvement in the framework'.[115] As a legal adviser explained, however, 'the framework should be robust enough to withstand the vagaries of the market and delivery capacities of suppliers'.[116] This interviewee highlighted the importance of appointing a large enough pool of suppliers in the first instance, albeit a finite number that is not too large to deter purchasers and suppliers.

As discussed in chapter three, the four-year maximum rule and the ability to exceptionally exceed it raises the question of the extent to which a contracting authority must consider the effect on competition when setting it. It is recalled that it has been suggested that EU law requires a contracting authority to consider the effects on competition when setting a framework term even when this is below or up to the maximum four-year duration. Ultimately, however, it may be difficult to make a prospective assessment of such effects. Most importantly, the UK has not introduced further regulatory controls or guidance on how to set a framework duration in consideration of the effects on competition.

The above nevertheless raises an important point relating to setting regulatory policy on frameworks more generally. Most interviewees considered a four-year rule to be reasonable, but it is not clear why a four-year term has been set as distinct from some other term (eg three years or five years). Further, the interview data necessarily gave no indication of what effect setting certain framework durations may have on competition. It is therefore difficult to understand what evidence base supports the setting of particular framework requirements. This is without even considering that maximum terms effectively double the length can be set for defence and utilities contracts.

[111] Cabinet Office, Green Paper: *Transforming Public Procurement*, December 2020, ch 5.
[112] CA3.
[113] LA3.
[114] LA8.
[115] CA5.
[116] LA4.

Fundamentally, the above is important for understanding whether and to what extent *procurement* legislation should include positive legal requirements to consider the effects on competition. This is particularly relevant in debate on frameworks given that there are various claimed impacts of frameworks and the application or non-application of rules on frameworks on competition. For instance, concern is expressed about closed frameworks because they close off the market to competition for their duration. Equally, it appears that stakeholders appear to take no major issue with the fact that frameworks are closed off for the maximum duration permitted. If there is no clear objective of the regulated procurement system overall, for example, to maximise competition, and no clear understanding of what impacts procurement regulation has on competition, it is difficult to make credible arguments about the way procurement rules, including those on frameworks, should be interpreted and applied or reformed. In any event, what is clear for present purposes is that EU law and UK law and policy have not unequivocally addressed these matters.

The interviews also seem to allude to the influences of marketisation in setting framework durations. Creditably, some contracting authorities look to impose short durations to limit incumbent lock-in or advantage and refresh competition. However, others forward plan to the next framework iteration by assessing the fluidity of the market, whether it will be subject to dynamic pricing changes and the impact that any new iteration could have on the 'revenue' put through the framework as contracting authorities and suppliers adjust to new terms. It might be thought that such forward planning is designed to ensure a smooth transition and continuity of provision under successive framework iterations. Equally, it may be seen as thinking ahead to mitigate the impact of any transition to a new iteration on that future revenue.

6.1.1.2. Duration of a Call-off Contract

Notwithstanding the apparently clear legal position on setting the duration of call-offs, several contracting authority interviewees were under the mistaken impression that the maximum call-off term must correspond to the maximum framework term set. and assumed that this restriction was imposed by the PCR 2015.

Many CPAs have expressly limited the maximum duration of call-offs. One interviewee referred to 'the real risk of lock-out being at the call-off level'[117] and revealed that they had seen call-off terms for up to 10 years and long call-offs being entered into on the final day before the expiry of the framework. It is not uncommon, therefore, to see maximum call-off terms set at four years, sometimes replicating the 2+1+1 model adopted for the framework term. Encouragingly, this suggests evidence of responsible behaviours guided by regulatory baselines set elsewhere under the regime. Another interviewee described how they limited the maximum call-off term depending on the subject-matter and relevant market.[118] One gave examples of frameworks that provide for fixed maximum call-off terms but which can be extended by the parties for up to 25 per cent of the original call-off term.[119]

[117] CPB1.
[118] CPB8.
[119] CA8.

Not all CPAs restrict the duration of call-offs, however, particularly for complex requirements, given the roll-out time necessary.[120] Some interviewees expressed frustration that maximum call-off terms seem to have been imposed as a matter of policy and identified terms of seven years, for example.[121] Suppliers expressed similar views.[122]

Whether or not a maximum duration is imposed, contracting authorities still need to consider the risk of using the framework 'improperly or in such a way as to prevent, restrict or distort competition' (Recital 61 Directive 2014/24/EU). The setting of call-off durations should not, therefore, be driven by improper or anti-competitive objectives. In practice, a more consistent approach to setting call-off durations throughout the length of the framework has arguably been required with such durations set by reference to the subject-matter of the contract eg preventing a contracting authority from unjustifiably entering into a call-off for a period of 20 years on the last day of the framework when the framework was set up for the entry into short term call-offs (eg two to three years) and all previous call-offs were for such short terms.

6.2. Setting the Duration of Closed Frameworks and Call-off Contracts under the PA 2023

Concerning framework duration, section 47(1) retains the standard maximum term of four years for a public sector closed framework with a longer maximum term of eight years for defence and security frameworks and utilities frameworks. No policy justification appears to have been given for this four-year maximum and which, it is presumed, is intended to ensure continuity.

As with the PCR 2015, section 47(2) provides for frameworks to be established for longer durations where justified. However, it is no longer the case that 'exceptional circumstances' need to be demonstrated. In parliamentary debate, examples were given where 'investment is required by suppliers under the framework that will take longer than four or eight years to recoup, or where contracts have a long lead time and therefore cannot be awarded within the requisite time period'.[123] This appears to provide some flexibility to set longer terms. If so, section 74(3) requires the contracting authority to set out its reasons in the tender or transparency notice for the framework. It is recalled that under Directive 2014/24/EU, various considerations were put forward as justifications and the position may be similar under the PA 2023, although it is not clear how such considerations aligned with the objectives behind the EU regime or whether they were based on domestic objectives of value for money and efficiency. As to whether such considerations could be justified under the PA 2023, it may be that having regard to the importance of the value for money objective could lead a contracting authority to justifying a longer framework term.

Regarding call-offs, the GCF guidance confirms that it is for the contracting authority to consider whether the nature of the goods, services or works to be supplied means

[120] CPB3, CPB5, CA3.
[121] CA6.
[122] EO2.
[123] HC Deb 7 February 2023 (n 34).

that a longer term is required. It gives examples of 'large construction or infrastructure projects where a variety of call-offs are awarded throughout the life of a development. Contracts may need to be awarded, for example, for initial professional services, such as design, as well as for various aspects of the construction/development, which may be undertaken in phases, through to completion'.[124] Whilst not completely clear, this example implicitly endorses use of a single framework for large projects that usually attract significant complexity. The guidance does not explain why it is considered that a single framework with an extended term should be used for such a project. One may be required for a single-provider framework where that single provider is called upon to meet all the requirements of the project but many construction and infrastructure projects require the appointment of different suppliers who will each provide different elements of the project. In such circumstances, it may be possible to adopt a range of procurement approaches (eg using more than one framework) to fulfil the requirements of the project rather than just using a single, extended term framework. The guidance gives two more examples of when a longer-term framework may be required. The first is where the framework requires an upfront investment by a supplier to deliver the call-offs, for example an IT system development, and the return on that investment would require call-offs to be awarded over a longer term than the maximum. The second is where the funding cycle for the project (ie the contracting authority's ability to pay for the project) exceeds the maximum term (assuming the development of the project to be provided under the framework was tied to the funding cycle).[125]

The guidance clarifies that once a framework has been awarded, it might be possible to rely on section 74 to extend the term of a framework, as with any other public contract. However, section 47(2) must still be complied with, meaning that any extension beyond the maximum term must be justified in the relevant notice under section 47(3). The guidance recommends that this justification is set out in the relevant contract change notice.[126]

It is recalled that neither Directive 2014/24/EU nor the PCR 2015 specify any maximum length of a call-off. Nor do they expressly prohibit a call-off whose term continues beyond the length of the framework itself.[127] The PA 2023 is similarly silent on the maximum duration of call-offs entered, as is the GCF guidance which merely confirms that call-offs may extend beyond the framework term. As discussed, under the PCR 2015, the principle that frameworks cannot be used 'improperly or in a way that risks distorting competition' has acted as a constraint. Even though this principle does not feature in the PA 2023, contracting authorities will need to consider the importance of the section 12 procurement objectives when making decisions relating to call-off terms, particularly the objective of delivering value for money. However, it is by no means clear that the need to comply with these will act as effective restraints.

For completeness, it should be noted that the rules on setting the maximum term of a framework do not apply to an open framework (since separate rules apply under section 49) nor do they apply to frameworks awarded by private utilities or a framework that is a light-touch contract (under section 47(5)).

[124] GCF (n 55) 24.
[125] ibid 25.
[126] ibid 30.
[127] See Recital 62 Directive 2014/24/EU.

Ultimately, therefore, the PA 2023 retains maximum durations for frameworks but provides even more flexibility to exceed them where justified; although, as indicated by the interviewees with experience of applying the PCR 2015, there has been little general appetite to extend beyond the maximum. There is similarly continued flexibility in respect of the duration of call-offs. However, there remains the outstanding issue of the underlying policy justifications for setting the maximum durations based on competition related considerations. This is an instantiation of a wider problem: it is not particularly clear what are the effects of frameworks (and the rules that regulate them) on competition and how regulation (laws and policies) should address those effects.

Whilst regulation 18(2) required contracting authorities to consider the duty to comply with the principles of transparency, equal treatment, non-discrimination, proportionality and the prohibition on designing a procurement with the intention of 'artificially narrowing competition', there is no such express rule under the PA 2023. More generally, when setting the framework term, contracting authorities will need to have regard to the importance of the section 12 procurement objectives. However, as repeatedly observed, it is not clear to what constraints these will have on setting framework or call-off durations.

7. Use of Lots

7.1. Use of Lots under the PCR 2015

A framework may be subdivided with suppliers appointed to different lots for different products and services. A main driver behind the 2014 EU reforms was improving access for SMEs to procurement markets.[128] Recital 78 Directive 2014/24/EU states:

> contracting authorities should in particular be encouraged to divide large contracts into lots. Such division could be done on a quantitative basis, making the size of the individual contracts better correspond to the capacity of SMEs, or on a qualitative basis, in accordance with the different trades and specialisations involved, to adapt the content of the individual contracts more closely to the specialised sectors of SMEs or in accordance with different subsequent project phases.

Article 46(4) Directive 2014/24/EU provides that Member States may render it obligatory to award contracts in the form of separate lots but the UK Government did not take up this option. Instead, regulation 46(1) provides that a contracting authority may decide to award a contract in lots. Further, regulation 46(2) provides that where a contract is not subdivided into lots, the contracting authority must provide the main reasons for that decision in the procurement documents or the regulation 84 written report.[129]

[128] European Commission, 'Green Paper on the modernisation of EU public procurement policy: Towards a more efficient European Procurement Market', 2011.

[129] For discussion on the extent of this duty, see MA Raimundo, 'Aiming at the market you want: A critical analysis of the duties on division into lots under Directive 2014/24/EU' (2018) 4 *PPLR* 167–87 and M Trybus, 'The division of public contracts into lots under EU Directive 2014/24/EU: Minimum harmonisation and impact on SMEs in public procurement?' (2018) 43(3) *ELR* 313–42.

Regulations 46(3)-(4) provide that in the call for competition, contracting authorities must indicate whether tenders may be submitted for one, several or all the lots advertised and may limit the number awarded to one bidder provided it indicates the maximum number per bidder. Regulation 46(5) provides that where the application of the award criteria would result in one bidder winning more lots than the stated maximum, the contracting authority must apply objective and non-discriminatory criteria or rules to determine the allocation of lots, such criteria and rules to be set out in the procurement documents. Regulation 46(6) provides that a contracting authority may also award a contract combining lots where it has specified this in the call for competition and indicated the lots or groups of lots that may be combined.

More generally, it has been suggested that division into lots is 'a good counterweight to ensure that tools such as centralised purchasing do not endanger competition'.[130] By separating a framework into lots, a contracting authority may be able to increase access to procurement for different suppliers, in particular, SMEs who may lack the resources to fulfil the single requirements of a large framework but may be able to propose specialist products, skills and expertise to fulfil specific requirements under individual lots. However, it has also been observed that Directive 2014/24/EU has reinforced the aggregation regimes in particular relating to frameworks, DPS and centralised purchasing and the introduction of joint procurement provisions and that particularly in times of economic crises and tightened budgets, '[t]he division into lots regime might prove to be too soft to counteract the effects of the reinforced and extended aggregation regime with a smaller share of the procurement pie for SME as a result'.[131]

7.1.1. Use of Lots in Practice under the PCR 2015

In practice, CPAs and other contracting authorities setting up frameworks seem to assume much discretion in establishing lotting structures. However, whilst there are several ICT frameworks with many SMEs appointed to them, a few interviewees mentioned some frameworks set up with just one or a small number of large ICT providers that were seen as barriers to SME participation. There was a perception that some frameworks could have been disaggregated into lots to facilitate direct contracting with SMEs and provide the public sector with access to innovative ICT solutions provided by SMEs.[132] This suggests that the option to divide into lots subject to a justification for not doing so could be improved in some way; for example, by introducing an explicit *prima facie* duty to divide, or, perhaps more likely, strengthening the provision on justification and/or providing further guidance on how to develop effective lotting structures.

7.2. Use of Lots under the PA 2023

The PA 2023 includes a section titled 'Duty to consider lots'. Section 18 provides that before publishing a tender notice in respect of a public contract, a contracting authority

[130] Raimundo (n 129).
[131] Trybus (n 129).
[132] EO4.

must consider (a) whether the goods, services or works to be supplied under the contract could reasonably be supplied under more than one contract, and (b) whether such contracts could appropriately be awarded by reference to lots. If so, the authority must arrange for the award of the contract(s) by reference to lots, or provide reasons for not doing so.[133]

Whilst the corresponding provision in the PCR 2015 stated only that contracting authorities 'may decide to award a contract in the form of separate lots', under both the PCR 2015 and the PA 2023 a contracting authority is required to provide an explanation of any decision not to subdivide a contract into lots and so a 'duty to consider' arguably also applied under the PCR 2015. The explicit 'duty to consider' in the PA 2023 may have more of an impact than its predecessor, however, if one also takes into account the related requirement section 12 requirement to have regard to the fact that SMEs may face particular barriers to participation and consider whether such barriers can be removed or reduced. One way of removing barriers to the participation of SMEs in frameworks may be to divide frameworks into lots, using proportionate conditions of participation and transparent call-off procedures under each lot. However, again, the duty to comply with the section 12 duty to have regard to SME barriers is not enforceable in civil proceedings under the PA 2023 (section 100(5)), rendering it unclear how far this is likely to significantly improve SME access in reality.

8. Conclusions

This chapter has revealed several grey areas in the law that have led to certain questionable practices when setting up frameworks.

At the beginning of the procurement lifecycle, PME is encouraged. However, the level of market engagement undertaken is largely dependent on resources, experience and expertise. Further, PME is used by some CPAs as a marketing tool to attract both contracting authorities and suppliers, including generating fees from enabling suppliers to market their offerings, calling into question whether PME is being used in the ways intended. The PA 2023 will increase transparency of early planning to some extent, particularly by introducing requirements relating to the publication of a pipeline notice, a PME notice and the register of commercial tools. However, neither the PA 2023 nor the GCF guidance address specific market engagement behaviours.

The most common procedures used to award frameworks under the PCR 2015 were the open and the restricted procedures. The PA 2023 provides more flexibility, including a new competitive flexible procedure that can be adapted to include various stages. It is not apparent that such increased flexibility substantially benefits the setting-up of frameworks, however, particularly considering CPAs focused on streamlining procedures for quick and efficient use and user contracting authorities and suppliers looking to limit use of resources.

When advertising a framework, there has been uncertainty regarding the identification of user contracting authorities and estimation and disclosure of the framework

[133] Section 18.

value. There are no strict legal requirements for a CPA to obtain prior consent of potential users. It is not unclear what level of PME should be undertaken and which would surely be prudent to effectively scope the framework subject-matter and value. A common occurrence is a contract notice providing a wide description of potential users including references to long lists, and very high estimated values or wide value ranges principally with the aim of encouraging maximum possible usage. It is difficult to reconcile such practices with the transparency principle in the PCR 2015 but this is not considered to be a high legal risk in terms of challenge. Whilst the PA 2023 introduces increased information requirements for tender notices and associated tender documents, the precise requirements remain vaguely worded such that the prospect of generic, broadly scoped frameworks that lack transparency are likely to continue.

Concerning framework and call-off duration, interviewees suggested that the maximum four-year duration seems to be appropriate for ICT frameworks due to the dynamic nature of this market. Contracting authorities seem to be acutely aware of the impracticalities of renewing frameworks at short intervals due to the associated time and resource implications. Category management teams are also likely to consider external developments, in particular, the existing and future frameworks of other CPAs and levels of fluidity and dynamism in the relevant markets when setting the framework duration.

Finally, contracting authorities have exercised their discretion when choosing whether to use lotting structures, there being some evidence that lots could be used more effectively in practice. Under both the PCR 2015 and the PA 2023, a contracting authority is required to provide an explanation of any decision not to subdivide a contract into lots but it may be that this decision is given greater consideration under the PA 2023 when considering whether SMEs face barriers to participation in frameworks.

7

Appointment of Framework Suppliers

1. Introduction

The nature of frameworks dictates that the exact requirements to be fulfilled and when cannot necessarily be stated at the outset. It can be difficult to determine the number of suppliers to appoint, what selection and award criteria to use to award the framework, the extent to which the call-off contract terms can be settled at the outset, the design of the call-off procedures, and whether there can or should be a competition on price when awarding the contract, incomplete prices be agreed, or pricing left for determination at the call-off stage. When awarding the framework, tenders might be invited based on projected requirements or using hypothetical specifications, quantities and timeframes. The framework terms and specifications will usually be established using a combination of the terms in the procurement documents and the tenders received. The degree to which the terms are settled when awarding the framework will vary depending on the type of framework being set up. Thus, there are many considerations to be made when setting up the framework.

This chapter examines: limiting the number of framework suppliers to appoint (Section 2); use and application of selection criteria for appointment (Section 3); formulation and use of award criteria and weightings for appointment (Section 4); establishing call-off procedures for direct awards and mini-competitions (Section 5); and establishing pricing terms (Section 6), before offering conclusions (Section 7).

2. Limiting the Number of Suppliers

2.1. Limiting the Number of Suppliers under the PCR 2015

Neither Directive 2014/24/EU nor the PCR 2015 place any express limit on the number appointed to a multi-supplier framework. It is not entirely clear whether the concept of a framework means that contracting authorities could include all who submit compliant tenders or requires choosing only a limited number by comparing the different terms offered. However, it seems expected or usual to impose some limitation based on the terms offered and complete as much of the competition as possible at the appointment stage.

It has been suggested that it should only be in exceptional situations that the number should not be reduced; for example, where price is a significant award criterion but the volatile nature of prices means that binding prices can only realistically be submitted when placing the order. In that instance, it may make sense to exclude price as an award criterion for choosing between suppliers at the appointment stage and to admit all suppliers that submit compliant tenders, with actual prices determined at the call-off stage.[1]

As highlighted by Arrowsmith, the framework provisions in Directive 2014/24/EU are designed to encourage as much competition as possible to take place at the appointment stage and to use the award criteria to establish a minimum number of suppliers.[2] If all that meet the award criteria are appointed, the effectiveness of the procedure and criteria used for appointment may be questioned, given that the purpose of a framework is not to produce a standing list of suppliers but rather a 'framework agreement'. This would not enable a substantive competition and may not achieve value for money. Further, it would seem incongruent with other aspects of the legislative scheme, eg the regulation 33(5) PCR 15 prohibition on appointing suppliers after the framework has been awarded; the emphasis should be on making focused appointments, not least because there will be no further opportunity to appoint others.

Annex V, Part C Directive 2014/24/EU provides that the contract notice must include the 'number and, where appropriate, proposed maximum number of economic operators to participate'. This could imply the appointment of some, not all, although it appears the number may be stated as a range, allowing some flexibility. In practical terms, for a framework providing for mini-competitions, the contracting authority would need to ensure that it does not appoint too many, otherwise it would become impractical to manage. This is especially since regulation 33(11)(a) provides that all appointed suppliers 'capable of performing the contract' must be invited to bid in the mini-competition. This further signals the importance of robustly assessing supplier capability at the appointment stage, which, if done properly, should filter out suppliers for appointment. Further, even for frameworks that provide for the direct award of call-offs, it is likely to be difficult to apply the requirement in regulation 33(8)(a)(ii) to use 'objective conditions' to determine which supplier should be awarded each call-off if excessive numbers have been appointed.

2.1.1. Limiting the Number of Suppliers in Practice under the PCR 2015

Practically, the issue of how many suppliers to appoint is divergent. In interviews, examples were given of frameworks advertised based on: (a) appointing an unlimited number; (b) appointing a minimum number with no specified maximum; (c) providing an indicative number with some flexibility reserved depending on the tenders received; and (d) appointing a fixed number with little to no flexibility reserved.

Concerning the factors informing such choices, one interviewee noted the 'misconception that more suppliers results in more competition on the framework', preferring a 'sweet spot' that gives 'enough capacity to satisfy demand but also gives suppliers

[1] S Arrowsmith, *The Law of Public and Utilities Procurement: Regulation in the EU and UK*, 3rd edn, Vol I (Sweet & Maxwell, 2014) 11-35-36.

[2] ibid.

credible expectations of business'.[3] Interviewees suggested between five and 15 being appropriate for each framework or lot, with one commenting that 'interest wanes from contractors where there are lots of places and lots of work to be done to complete the bid documentation'.[4] Another stated that 'each framework is different' and 'it depends on the market and whether they are looking to reduce the size of the market'.[5] There were concerns that appointing too many makes it unfeasible to run mini-competitions unless the framework has a sophisticated filtering and mini-tender process. As indicated in chapter two, it is not particularly clear how a 'sweet spot' is objectively determined, other than perhaps through experience and/or trial and error, reinforcing observations made in this book that few decisions appear to be predicated on rigorous market analyses. Consequently, it is difficult to accurately assess the effects of frameworks on competition. Further, it is one thing to limit numbers to ensure that competitions are manageable (eg for capacity or other issues) but another if the framework provider is 'looking to reduce the size of the market' by deliberately trying to eliminate certain suppliers, for example. This is an important reminder of the control that contracting authorities can exert on the demand side in determining the size and shape of markets.

Many interviewees commented on the emergence of frameworks that do not place any limit. An interviewee from a CPA that has set up such frameworks justified them on the basis that 'if everyone is let on to the framework then no one will challenge'. They indicated that 'one benefit of having so many suppliers on the framework is that you are more likely to have both small and large suppliers on it and therefore it is likely to be more SME friendly'.[6] It is submitted, however, that such frameworks do not align with the underlying purpose and objectives of the EU framework model (as discussed in chapter three). Rather, they bear a closer resemblance to the DPS model (discussed in chapter five) which neither limits the number nor requires a tender competition at the set-up stage.

It is submitted that the admission of suppliers to avoid the risk of challenge (whilst simultaneously providing a means of generating significant revenues) is a clear indication of both the increasingly limited regulatory pressure exerted on frameworks and the extent of marketisation. In such an environment, it is unsurprising that the potential reputational harm on the market following a successful challenge increases the perceived importance of this factor when setting the framework terms.

2.2. Limiting the Number of Suppliers under the PA 2023

In contrast to the PCR 2015, the PA 2023 explicitly authorises appointment of an unlimited number of suppliers, evidenced by requirement for a tender notice to include 'whether the intention is to award the framework to […] an unlimited number of suppliers' (regulation 20(2)(i)(iii) PR 2024). Relatedly, whereas proportionality-related requirements have been incorporated in some provisions (eg section 46(1) on setting

[3] CPB1.
[4] CA5.
[5] CPB5.
[6] CPB1.

conditions of participation when using a competitive selection procedure under a framework), determination of the number of suppliers for appointment is not subject to express proportionality considerations; consistency with other provisions might have supported such a reference. It is also not clear what bearing, if any, the section 12 objectives may have on determinations about setting the number to be admitted to the framework.

As discussed in chapter five, a new looser definition of a framework, together with the express ability to make direct awards of frameworks, suggests that a new regulatory conception of a framework has emerged. It no longer appears to be based on use of a substantive competition to establish the terms of future contracts with a limited group of suppliers; instead, borrowing a feature that has hitherto been appropriate only for DPS which, as also discussed in chapter five, allows for the appointment of an unlimited number of suppliers and where competition between tenders is delayed until a later stage. The absence of regulatory controls and guidance on appointing an appropriate number of suppliers means that the highly marketised generic pan-sector multi-supplier framework model is likely to continue. As discussed in chapter ten, there is a need for guidance to assist in determining the appropriate number of suppliers to invite.

3. Use and Application of Selection Criteria

3.1. Use and Application of Selection Criteria under the PCR 2015

In awarding any contract, a contracting authority must assess whether a supplier has the requisite economic and financial standing and technical and professional ability to deliver, which is distinct from (but related to) the goods, services or works they offer to meet the requirement. This stage focusing on the tenderer (rather than its tender) need not always be completed before the evaluation of tender stage, but it will be done before award. By contrast, the selection process for a framework is potentially less straightforward because of a separation between the award of the framework which involves a selection process to appoint suppliers and the subsequent call-off stage in which a contracting authority awards individual contracts. This separation can be particularly acute if one contracting authority applied a selection process for appointing suppliers to the framework but a different contracting authority awards individual call-offs but where it may wish to verify that the supplier can perform according to the set selection criteria or even apply its own. As discussed below, this has proven to be problematic.

Regulation 27(3) effectively provides that when a contracting authority uses the open procedure to award a framework, they may use selection criteria to set certain minimum levels of suitability that tenderers must meet. Regulation 28(4) and regulation 65 provide that when using the restricted procedure (or any other multi-stage procedure), in addition to using such minimum levels, the contracting authority is able to use selection criteria to shortlist tenderers who are then invited to submit a tender.

It can be challenging to devise selection criteria at the appointment stage to identify the most suitable suppliers when each call-off may require different levels of suitability depending on, for example, its technical scope and financial value. Separating a framework into lots based on different technical requirements and/or different call-off contract values may help address this issue. Different selection criteria might be applied to each lot according to the likely scope and value of call-offs under each lot.

3.1.1. Use and Application of Selection Criteria in Practice under the PCR 2015

As alluded to above, there is a risk in practice of a disconnect between the initial approach to supplier selection at the framework award stage and any subsequent approach to call-offs. One interviewee highlighted that 'the economic and financial risk lies with the contracting authority and so the timing for economic and financial assessments is wrong and inappropriate'. This is because the framework provider (eg, CPA) sets the selection criteria but there are perceived legal restrictions on the ability of user contracting authorities to undertake additional checks at the call-off stage other than confirming that suppliers still meet the criteria used to award the framework. They explained how the selection stage does not easily transpose to the call-off stage when a framework has many different suppliers and users. They queried whether, as requirements only crystallise at the call-off stage, it would be lawful for a CPA to undertake a general financial health check at the framework award stage using one set of ratios and then for a contracting authority to undertake a more forensic economic and financial assessment at the call-off stage using a bespoke set of ratios, providing they are published in the procurement documents issued to award the framework and comply with EU transparency and equal treatment principles.[7]

The above is not explicitly provided for under Directive 2014/24/EU and PCR 2015. The suggestion of using a bespoke selection process at the call-off stage is understandable but would be problematic. The criteria used to assess economic and financial standing and technical and professional ability form part of the procedure used to award a framework. Once a framework is established, the selection stage is complete and the call-off phase is used to award a public contract. Of course, a contracting authority should be allowed throughout the life of a framework to assess whether each of the suppliers continues to meet the original selection criteria prior to awarding a call-off, but the application of different selection criteria at the call-off stage would reopen the selection phase in a way that does not seem to be permitted and risks undermining the result of the original framework award. The introduction of new criteria could constitute an unlawful modification of the procurement process. An obvious solution might be to take steps early in the framework award stage to ensure appointment of suitable suppliers eg through a careful specification of the requirement(s), limiting the potential user contracting authorities (given that this also increases the chance that each will approach selection processes differently and have different views about suitable suppliers), and limiting the number of suppliers through a robust selection stage. In these instances, it may be questioned why the contracting authority should not instead run a standalone procurement and benefit from the additional flexibilities this might provide.

[7] CA16.

Interviewees raised concerns that a supplier that met the selection criteria to be appointed might cease to meet those criteria at the call-off stage; for example, due to a deterioration in its financial health. It was stated that, to mitigate this risk, a tiered lotting structure is sometimes used to appoint suppliers, involving using a single set of selection and award criteria to appoint a priority group of suppliers to one lot and a reserve group of suppliers to another. A supplier appointed to a priority lot can be removed, suspended or relegated to the reserve lot and a supplier on the reserve lot promoted to take their place (based on the results and ranking established in the original competition and checking the reserve supplier still meets the required selection criteria).[8] One interviewee queried whether the legal rules should expressly incorporate 'an early warning system' to limit the risk of awarding contracts to framework suppliers on the verge of insolvency which could mandate 'regular, repeated due diligence requirements' and 'putting more concrete obligations on framework owners to provide assurance of suppliers'.[9]

Regulation 72(1)(a) and (d) provide for the possibility to lawfully modify contracts in certain circumstances. It could conceivably be argued that those provisions provide a facility to replace a framework supplier pursuant to a 'clear, precise and unequivocal review clause'.[10] It is submitted, however, that such a strict requirement makes this provision difficult to apply generally to the replacement of suppliers on multi-supplier frameworks except in corporate restructurings under regulation 72(1)(d)(ii).[11]

As considered in chapter ten, the perceived need for the ability to remove and replace suppliers on frameworks raises the question of whether the legal rules should expressly build in such a mechanism specific to frameworks. This might be useful in practice to provide for the admission of new suppliers in certain limited circumstances and subject to certain conditions.

Yet another issue concerns ongoing poor performance. In a typical public contract, a sanction may be applied or contract terminated in response to poor performance. In a future procurement for a different contract, this may be considered in assessing the suitability of that supplier at the selection stage. By contrast, a framework may involve the award of more than one call-off to the same supplier under an ongoing framework. This raises how the scenario should be addressed whereby a supplier has been awarded more than one call-off and performed poorly but will continue to bid for call-offs under that framework. Some interviewees queried whether sanctions could be imposed during the life of the framework where suppliers no longer meet the original technical and professional ability standards set. One interviewee noted suppliers being scored based on call-offs performed and 'sin-binned' (ie temporarily excluded from being awarded further call-offs) for poor performance (with rules written into the framework

[8] LA10, LA17.

[9] CA15.

[10] See generally, M Andrecka 'Framework agreements, EU procurement law and the practice' (2015) 2 *Procurement Law Journal* 127–49.

[11] Also, see *R (on the application of) Redwood Health Limited v NHS Purchasing and Supply Agency* [2009] EWHC 2511 (an application for permission to apply for judicial review) in which a court rejected the argument that a standard assignment/novation clause in a framework could be relied upon to effect the replacement of a contractor by another entity in the contractor's group due to a group re-organisation where the conditions set out in Case C-454/06 *Pressetext Nachrichtenagentur GmbH v Austria* ECLI:EU:C:2008:351, [2008] ECR I-4401, para 54 were not satisfied.

to provide for this).[12] Another described substituting in a reserve supplier, effectively using past performance as an ongoing exclusion criterion.[13]

It is submitted that under a standard procedure in the PCR 2015, it is possible to rescind a qualification decision before the award of a contract if a supplier ceases to meet the qualification conditions and there is no reason why this should not apply in respect of a framework.[14] However, if such suspension or exclusion practices go beyond checking that a supplier still meets the original qualitative selection criteria used to award the framework, this would involve a reopening of the selection phase post-award which is not explicitly or possibly impliedly permitted under Directive 2014/24/EU. The OGC's guidance on frameworks confirms this point:

> It should be noted that there is no scope, at this stage, to run a selection procedure, based on technical ability, financial standing etc. This will have been carried out before the framework itself had been awarded and should not be repeated at the further competition stage.[15]

Concerning the nature of, and approach to, the selection process at the framework award stage, many interviewees referred to a specific pan-public sector ICT framework established by a CPA that appoints an unlimited number of suppliers at each iteration and which involves little rigour in terms of assessing economic and financial standing and technical and professional ability.[16] This framework requires suppliers to complete a 'supplier declaration' setting out minimum requirements for appointment but which relate to such matters as agreeing to the proposed terms, taking full responsibility for their work, and confirming that they have not broken any laws that could constitute a mandatory exclusion ground. It is understood that the customer guide for this framework indicates that a supplier's financial status is not checked when they apply to join on the basis that this presents an unnecessary barrier to entry but is monitored during the framework term by reference to credit check scores. Customers are advised to conduct their own financial assessments of shortlisted suppliers prior to awarding a call-off.

If robust economic and financial standing assessments are not conducted until the call-off stage, questions arise as to whether this can be reconciled with the PCR 2015. Such frameworks bear a closer resemblance to approved or qualified supplier lists of the kind explained in chapter five that do not involve substantive competition between tenders at the appointment stage. Of course, on one hand, extensive checks early in the selection stage could be perceived as a market access barrier and deter suppliers but, on the other, this is the reality of doing business with the public sector. Nevertheless, it should be expected that a selection process is undertaken at the framework award stage, albeit this may leave verification checks until later, as opposed to leaving the selection process to be done at the call-off stage or through ongoing monitoring which may or may not be done.

According to interviewees, many contracting authorities feel uncomfortable about using frameworks comprising very light selection criteria for appointment. Where capacity

[12] LA6.

[13] LA17.

[14] Arrowsmith (n 1) 11–85.

[15] OGC, 'Frameworks: OGC Guidance on Frameworks in the Procurement Regulations', September 2008, 9. Accessible at webarchive.nationalarchives.gov.uk/ukgwa/20100609095129/http://www.ogc.gov.uk/procurement_policy_and_application_of_eu_rules_guidance_on_the_UK_regulations.asp.

[16] In particular, EO4.

and expertise permit, some will repeat selection questionnaire checks at the call-off stage. As one interviewee explained, 'those involved in setting up and using frameworks are not making full use of the tools available in the Regulations to do adequate checks on framework suppliers'.[17] It must be acknowledged that one of the purported benefits of a framework is that a selection process has already been completed once in establishing the framework; further administrative burden is incurred if aspects of this process have to be repeated.

3.2. Use and Application of Conditions of Participation under the PA 2023

Similar to the use of selection criteria under the PCR 2015, under the PA 2023, a contracting authority can set minimum levels of suitability that tenderers must meet in their tenders for the framework now termed 'conditions of participation'. Section 22(1) provides that these conditions must represent a proportionate means of ensuring that suppliers have the legal and financial capacity or technical ability to perform the contract. When using the competitive flexible procedure, in addition to such minimum levels, a contracting authority can use criteria to shortlist tenderers who are then invited to submit a tender for award of the framework.

However, there appears to be a significant change in the PA 2023. There no longer seems to be a conceptual understanding that the selection phase is central to award of the framework, with the call-off stage only being used to check compliance against the selection criteria used in the original procurement to award the framework. Section 46 introduces a new flexibility at the call-off stage for contracting authorities to apply different conditions of participation when using the competitive selection process to award a call-off, as discussed below. Whilst it is possible to see how, in exceptional circumstances, it may be necessary to undertake supplemental selection decisions at the call-off stage, section 46 suggests that there is general flexibility to conduct the selection process at this stage. This may be a further indication of the extent to which the regulated framework model has been changed to accommodate the marketised multi-supplier framework model, in which it is seen as marketable to be able to gain easy admission to a framework and determine other matters at the call-off stage.

4. Formulation and Use of Award Criteria and Weightings to Appoint Suppliers

4.1. Formulation and Use of Award Criteria and Weightings to Appoint Suppliers under the PCR 2015

Regulation 67(1) requires contracting authorities to base the award on 'the most economically advantageous tender assessed from the point of view of the contracting

[17] LA12.

authority'. Regulation 62 provides that this shall be identified on the basis of the price or cost, using a cost-effectiveness approach (such as life-cycle costing), and may include the best price-quality ratio, assessed on the basis of criteria, such as qualitative, environmental and/or social aspects, linked to the subject-matter of the contract.[18] Regulation 67(5) provides that award criteria shall be considered linked to the subject-matter of the contract 'where they relate to the works, supplies or services to be provided under that contract in any respect and at any stage of their life cycle'. Regulation 67(9) provides that the relative weightings for each of the award criteria must be specified in the procurement documents either as a range or, if weightings are not possible for objective reasons, 'in decreasing order of importance'.

4.1.1. Formulation and Use of Award Criteria and Weightings to Appoint Framework Suppliers in practice under the PCR 2015

This formulation of award criteria and weightings can prove challenging when setting up frameworks because, whereas in the award of a typical public contract, the award criteria are a means of assessing a supplier's tender against an actual requirement, in a framework they are a means of assessing a supplier's tender against requirements known only at the point of call-off. Notwithstanding, contracting authorities will want to ensure that they appoint the most suitable suppliers, considering the likely scope and size of the requirements that will be subject to subsequent call-offs.

For rapidly evolving ICT requirements, it can prove difficult to devise award criteria that reflect the current state of technological development and contemplate potential changes during the framework term. One interviewee was concerned that they lacked experience in the marketplace and might be using 'outdated criteria' and was 'constantly looking for up-to-date models'.[19] This may, in part, explain the trend of formulating award criteria in generic terms to allow contracting authorities to formulate award criteria and sub-criteria tailored to their requirements using the mini-competition call-off procedure. It is regularly the case that award criteria used at the appointment stage are broken down only into 'price' and 'quality', with 'quality' possibly divided into three or four further sub-criteria at most. A corresponding set of high-level weightings is also typically used. One interviewee gave an example of a framework under which contracting authorities are provided with the quality-related questions that suppliers were evaluated against at the appointment stage and allowed to either use these questions again at the call-off stage or devise their own bespoke criteria and questions.[20]

Whilst such flexibility might seem necessary, similar to the discussion of the use of selection criteria above, this supplementation of award criteria at the call-off stage raises a concern about whether an effective competition based on a tailored framework specification is being held to award the framework.

[18] The requirement that award criteria be 'linked to the subject-matter of the contract' was established by the CJEU in Case C-513/99 *Concordia Bus Finland Oy Ab, formerly Stagecoach Finland Oy Ab v Helsingin kaupunki and HKL-Bussiliikenne* ECLI:EU:C:2002:495, [2002] ECR I-07213.

[19] CPB10.

[20] CPB5.

4.2. Formulation and Use of Award Criteria and Weightings to Appoint Suppliers under the PA 2023

Contracting authorities establishing frameworks under the PA 2023 are likely to face similar challenges when formulating award criteria and weightings to use when awarding a framework.

Section 19 provides that when running a competitive tendering procedure to award a framework, the overall basis of award is now the 'most advantageous tender' ('MAT'), rather than the 'most economically advantageous tender' ('MEAT') under the PCR 2015. The GCF guidance confirms, however, that this is not a policy change but rather reinforces that tenders do not have to be awarded on the basis of lowest price/cost, or that price/cost must always take precedence over non price/cost factors.[21] It is notable, however, that the provisions on award criteria do not specify that 'price' must always be one of those criteria. Notwithstanding, when formulating the criteria, contracting authorities must have regard to the section 12 objectives, including value for money. This could conceivably mean that, in most circumstances, pricing criteria will need to be used at the framework award stage. It is not clear that these changes will change behaviours regarding award unless they lead to the formulation of more transparent award criteria better attuned to achieving value for money and which do not create barriers to participation for SMEs, for example. Concerning frameworks specifically, it is not clear that such provisions will address the challenges of adapting criteria at the call-off stage.

5. Establishing Call-off Procedures for Direct Award and Mini-competitions

5.1. Establishing Call-off Procedures under the PCR 2015

The degree to which call-off terms are settled when awarding the framework can vary depending on whether it is complete, incomplete or hybrid, as explained in chapter five.

Regulation 33(8)(b) provides that for hybrid frameworks ie those setting out all the terms governing provision of works, services and supplies (i) partly without reopening competition; and (ii) partly through reopening competition, the possibility of using (i) or (ii) must be stipulated in the procurement documents for the framework. Regulation 33(9) provides that the procurement documents must also set out the objective criteria that will be applied to choose between (i) and (ii) and specify which terms may be subject to the reopening of competition. It is not clear why this requirement to specify in the procurement documents which terms may be subject to mini-competition has been included for hybrid frameworks but not for incomplete frameworks (ie that only allow mini-competitions). Regulation 33(10) provides that the ability to include both call-off procedures in a single framework also applies for each 'lot' in a framework.

[21] ibid.

Recital 61 Directive 2014/24/EU states that the objective criteria for choosing between each call-off procedure in a single framework (or lot of a framework) may, for example, 'relate to the quantity, value or characteristics of the works, supplies or services concerned, including the need for a higher degree of service or an increased security level, or to developments in price levels compared to a predetermined price index'. It is understood that there has been a recent trend for hybrid frameworks to reserve much discretion to contracting authorities regarding which call-off procedure to apply. Most interviewees from contracting authorities acknowledged this trend but highlighted the legal uncertainty in using such frameworks. Some legal advisers gave examples of contracting authorities seeking advice on which procedure could be used under a particular hybrid framework because of the lack of clarity in the framework documentation or because of a perceived conflict between the framework documentation and the black-letter law.[22] However, even if the framework includes objective criteria, it will be seen below that further conditions must still be satisfied to use the direct call-off procedure.

5.1.1. Direct Call-off Awards without Further Competition (Complete and Hybrid Frameworks) under the PCR 2015

Regulation 33(8)(a) provides that the direct call-off method requires a contracting authority to follow the framework terms and conditions without reopening competition. The framework must set out all the terms of supply, meaning that these need to be determined in the original competition to award the framework. This method may be appropriate for standardised products where it is relatively straightforward to devise a complete set of contract terms applicable to all purchases. The framework must also set out the 'objective conditions' for determining which supplier shall perform a particular requirement.

The policy underpinning Directive 2004/18/EC and the transposing PCR 2006 informed the relevant provisions on direct awards in the PCR 2015 and are explained briefly below.

5.1.1.1. Position under Directive 2004/18/EC and PCR 2006

Article 32(4) Directive 2004/18/EC and regulation 19(7)(a) PCR 2006 referred to the award of a specific contract 'by application of the terms laid down in the framework without re-opening competition' but did not explicitly state that the choice between appointed suppliers must be made based on 'objective conditions' as explicitly required under Directive 2014/24/EU and the PCR 2015.

The Commission's Explanatory Note observed that for multi-supplier frameworks that establish all the terms, the choice between the different suppliers was not specifically regulated by Directive 2004/18/EC.[23] According to the Commission, this choice could be made simply by using 'objective criteria' and complying with the equal

[22] LA5.
[23] European Commission Explanatory Note – Frameworks – Classic Directive CC/2005/03, 14 July 2005, 8.

treatment, transparency and non-discrimination principles.[24] It gave the example of the 'cascade method' by which the contracting authority would contact the supplier whose original tender for the award of a framework was considered the best for the framework as a whole and turn to the second-placed bidder where the first was not capable of, or interested in, performing the call-off. Arrowsmith has highlighted that 'such a policy is important to allow contracting authorities to obtain value for money without disproportionate costs'.[25] This method does not seem any different from the ranking of tenderers according to the criteria used to identify the MEAT when using a standard procedure to award a public contract. Guidance issued by the OGC in 2008 similarly referred to such a possibility but did not state that this was the only direct call-off method permitted.[26]

In 2012, the PLA observed that case law had not established whether the general requirement to award contracts based on MEAT applies to the criteria used to make direct call-offs, but considered this to be consistent with general principles of procurement law.[27] It remarked, however, that the criteria used to appoint suppliers to the framework need not be the same as those used to award the call-off, provided that the respective criteria are clearly communicated.[28] In addition, the PLA identified other call-off methods which, it claimed, are 'commonly deployed', namely: (a) rotation between suppliers under which each takes a turn in being awarded a call-off; (b) percentage allocation of call-offs between suppliers; or (c) random selection of a supplier for each call-off.[29] It acknowledged that their legitimacy had not been tested but would likely be upheld providing the criteria are objective, transparent, non-discriminatory and 'potentially identify the most economically advantageous tender for the particular contract being called off'.[30] It did not appear to reach any definitive view on what methods were permissible and whether any criteria used should comply with the requirement to identify the MEAT.

Arrowsmith has noted the two possible views that could be used to choose between the suppliers when using a direct call-off method:

(a) the criteria of lowest price or MEAT relating to the specific call-off contract must be used in accordance with Directive 2004/18/EC's usual rules on award; or
(b) it is merely necessary to comply with the general principles so that any transparent criteria complying with the equal treatment principle could be used.[31]

Arrowsmith favoured (a) as 'more logical in light of the policy of the directive as a whole'.[32] Arrowsmith has also argued that rather than base the award on the lowest price or MEAT overall from the appointment stage, the award of a call-off should be based on the best tender for the order in question.[33] If the supplier with the lowest price

[24] ibid.
[25] Arrowsmith (n 1) 7-296.
[26] OGC (n 15) 8.
[27] PLA, 'The Use of Frameworks in Public Procurement', March 2012, 35–36.
[28] ibid.
[29] ibid 35.
[30] ibid.
[31] Arrowsmith (n 1) 11-51.
[32] ibid.
[33] ibid 11-52.

or MEAT for a particular order was unable or unwilling to meet it, the next-ranked would be given the opportunity, as would be the case in an ordinary award of a contract. The view described in (b) aligns with the Commission and UK Government interpretations. Arrowsmith considers that the Commission may have taken this view based on its assertion that a framework setting out all the terms of the contract and envisaging that orders will be placed on the basis of original tenders is itself a 'public contract' and that the orders do not constitute separate public contracts.[34] It is therefore unnecessary to revisit the application of award criteria originally applied to award the framework; other criteria can be used at the call-off stage, provided compliant with EU Treaty principles.

The Commission's view is questionable because if a framework contains mutually binding obligations to purchase and supply, it is difficult to see how it should not be treated as a standard public contract and, thus, not subject to the provisions on frameworks at all. Further, as Arrowsmith points out, 'the purpose of the directive is to control the allocation of work' and it would seemingly undermine the directive's effectiveness if a call-off under which work is allocated to a supplier under a multi-supplier framework arrangement is not the fully regulated 'public contract'.[35] The Commission's view is also difficult to reconcile with the fact that regulation 19(9)(d) PCR 15 indicates that different rules on the use of award criteria apply to making orders by means of a mini-competition. Moreover, as Arrowsmith has noted, this concept is incompatible with the fact that a single framework can include both direct awards and mini-competitions to place orders and 'to have special rules on award criteria for orders placed under certain frameworks entails a significant inconsistency of principle within the directive'.[36] Thus, it made more sense if the same rules on use of award criteria (ie the use of price or MEAT under Directive 2004/18/EC) applied to the award of call-offs both with or without competition.

5.1.1.2. Position under Directive 2014/24/EU and PCR 2015

Notwithstanding the apparent uncertainty, Directive 2014/24/EU adopted the Commission's approach, such that any transparent and non-discriminatory criteria complying with general Treaty principles can be used. For the reasons indicated above, it is not clear why the Commission took this approach and how this can be reconciled with the requirement for the use of award criteria based on the MEAT when using other procedures.

Replicating Directive 2014/24/EU, regulation 33(8)(a) provides that a framework may be performed 'following the terms and conditions of the framework, without reopening competition, where it sets out: (a) all the terms governing the provision of the works, services and supplies concerned; and the objective conditions for determining which of the economic operators that are party to the (b) framework shall perform them, which conditions shall be indicated in the procurement documents for the framework'.

Regulation 33(8)(b) provides that the same conditions apply to direct call-offs made under hybrid frameworks. In accordance with the transparency and equal

[34] ibid 11-53.
[35] ibid.
[36] ibid.

treatment principles, such 'objective conditions' must be disclosed in the procurement documentation when the contracting authority advertises the opportunity to join the framework.

Regarding the meaning of 'objective conditions', Recital 61 Directive 2014/24/EU elaborates by stating:

> The objective conditions for determining which of the economic operators party to the framework should perform a given task, such as supplies or services intended for use by natural persons, may, in the context of frameworks setting out all the terms, include the needs or the choice of the natural persons concerned.

The 'needs or the choice' of individuals who are to use the supplies or services being procured may be relevant; for example, for social care contracts where a user's preference is to be considered when choosing a care provider. However, general clarification would have been welcome on what precisely is meant by 'objective conditions'.

As indicated, regulation 33(8)(a) provides that the objective conditions to determine must be stated in the procurement documents for the framework. As noted by Arrowsmith,[37] even though these objective conditions do not appear to be covered by the specific provisions on 'award criteria' (regulation 67), the disclosure obligations in relation to objective conditions should, by analogy, be interpreted in the same way, as a logical application of the transparency principle. It is submitted that any sub-conditions, weightings and evaluation methodologies to be applied when using the direct call-off method also need to be disclosed in the procurement documents.

5.1.2. Establishing Direct Call-off Procedures in Practice under the PCR 2015

Concerning the circumstances in which a direct call-off will be used as against a mini-competition, there was consensus amongst interviewees that direct awards are most appropriate for commoditised ICT items and mini-competitions for complex ICT solutions requiring further agreement of contract terms. One interviewee described how they considered direct awards to be appropriate when the contract terms were complete and the customer wanted to rely on an existing, trusted relationship or had an urgent requirement;[38] they did not highlight that such considerations should comply with the 'objective conditions' requirement.

Regarding how conditions for making direct call-offs are devised, in respect of hybrid frameworks, some CPAs allow significant flexibility when applying conditions to make a direct call-off. Interviewees reported that previously, most frameworks would have set clear, strict conditions and processes for making direct awards but there is now significant discretion as to which call-off procedure to use and how to select a supplier. One interviewee stated that they 'used to apply thresholds for making direct awards off frameworks but these were not practicable and prevented some direct awards from being made when they were most needed'.[39] Many ICT frameworks now leave it to user

[37] ibid 11-81.
[38] CPB5.
[39] CPB2.

contracting authorities' discretion to decide which call-off route to use without any 'hard and fast rules'.[40] Another interviewee stated that some CPAs allow complete discretion in deciding whether to make direct awards from complete and hybrid frameworks 'on the basis that contracting authorities will be liable if they get it wrong'.[41] There is a risk of such methods being incompatible with the PCR 2015, especially given the apparent lack of emphasis on using objective criteria for determining which call-off procedure to use in a hybrid framework. There is confusion about the legality of this approach,[42] and clarification may be required, as discussed in chapter ten.

From a supplier perspective, one interviewee stated that 'very flexible practices have developed to allow suppliers and customers to achieve a 'win-win' situation' and which have arisen 'despite the rules instead of because of them'.[43] Another commented that 'if there is a direct call-off route available on a framework then we pretty much assume that we can direct a customer to use it as a route to contract with us'.[44] Understandably, suppliers who have received lots of business through direct awards are in favour of this approach, but as one interviewee noted, 'the rules around direct awards is a very grey area'.[45] Those who have not received business through direct awards tend to be more critical, with one interviewee commenting that 'customers are lazy when they use direct awards and know who they want before they pick up the framework'.[46] This risks the assumption by some contracting authorities seeking to contract with a specific supplier, in the absence of sufficient legal scrutiny, that the procedure offers a lawful route to contracting with that supplier.

Nevertheless, there is some evidence of CPAs adopting stricter approaches to direct call-offs. One interviewee considered the direct award route to be feasible only where it is possible to fix pricing when awarding the framework. However, they did not want to force a competition unnecessarily and so allowed direct awards where the call-off value was below the applicable financial threshold that would usually trigger the PCR 2015 'as customers would not have had to run a competition for such requirements anyway'.[47] Another described the strict approach they had taken whereby the first ranked supplier from the original competition was the only supplier to whom a direct award could be made.[48]

Many frameworks also use 'ranking' systems based on the results of the original competition. However, one interviewee highlighted a framework managed by a private sector entity that used a 'dubious' system that allowed the top-ranked supplier to market their 'preferred' status under the framework to customers.[49] This is an example of where a framework provider may be more attuned with the interests of a supplier than user contracting authorities with the objective of generating maximum revenue.

[40] CPB8.
[41] CA1.
[42] CPB9.
[43] EO1.
[44] EO4.
[45] EO5.
[46] EO6.
[47] CPB3. This does not appreciate that the award of all call-offs (above and below threshold) are subject to the framework rules in the PCR 2015.
[48] CPB9.
[49] CA3.

It also appears that direct awards on a rotational basis are common. One interviewee described a framework where this was permitted for call-offs below £500,000, with mini-competitions required for each call-off above.[50] It is submitted that whilst the courts have not ruled on the lawfulness of rotational direct awards, they may result in awarding a contract to a supplier which does not offer the MEAT. As one interviewee put it 'if there were six suppliers on a framework, you would have to award every sixth contract to the worst supplier'.[51]

In the ICT sector, the ability to make direct call-offs can be appealing to contracting authorities who have simple but urgent requirements and want to reduce procurement costs and timescales. However, it is sometimes the case that contracting authorities have a particular supplier in mind and are looking for a compliant route to access them without running a full procurement (due to, for example, the perceived need to contract with an incumbent systems provider or to access unique software only supplied by one provider). One supplier described some frameworks that allow direct awards if the contracting authority has an existing ICT system in place and needs to upgrade it. An example was given of one permitting a direct award if an 'intrinsic link' to an existing service provision could be established. They assumed these were legally permitted based on applying the same principles authorising use of the negotiated procedure without prior publication of a contract notice in regulation 32 or the rules on substantial modifications in regulation 72.[52] However, it is submitted that this conflates the rules on direct call-offs in frameworks with those applicable to direct awards and modifications outside of the framework context. In the absence of clearly prescribed circumstances permitting direct call-offs in this way, this read-across cannot necessarily be assumed.

A few interviewees described a 'desktop calculator' call-off method whereby contracting authorities can change the weightings for criteria used to award the framework depending on their perceived priorities and apply these revised weightings to the results of the original competition. One explained how suppliers are informed about this method at the appointment stage and are presented with hypothetical scenarios where they can use the desktop calculator tool to test their pricing and see how their bid would change under different scenarios. At the call-off stage, contracting authorities are permitted to change each weighting by up to 10 or 20 per cent. Another acknowledged that this mechanism is not widely used and may be seen as a 'cheat' or a 'loophole' as some 'might just fiddle with the desktop calculator until it results in the supplier they want winning'.[53] Another interviewee acknowledged that this exercise potentially undermined the original competition as bidders were not given the opportunity to revise their prices to reflect the different weightings being used.[54]

Recognising that there are instances of more innovative practices, one legal adviser described a 'dynamic direct award tool' which allows direct awards using a dynamic 'ranking' of suppliers based on each supplier's performance in previous call-offs from the framework and the application of certain performance criteria. It is a live

[50] LA10.
[51] CA13.
[52] CA3.
[53] CPB9.
[54] CA6.

tool whereby the ranking of suppliers, the priority order of which can be awarded a contract directly, can change throughout the framework term.[55] This tool highlights the difference between the conditions that are used to make direct awards and the award criteria in a mini-competition. Whilst 'past experience' might arguably constitute an 'objective condition' under the rules for making a direct award, it would not satisfy the requirements for criteria designed to identify MEAT when using a mini-competition procedure.[56]

Given the variability of some of the direct award methods, a few legal advisers queried whether 'objective conditions' need to comply with the requirement to award contracts based on MEAT as with any other public contract. Some acknowledged that flexibility is allowed when making a direct call-off but questioned whether this was the Commission's intention when drafting the rules and the correct legal approach. One interviewee suggested that direct awards could be distinguished from mini-competition awards as direct awards merely involved applying the terms of the framework already established using MEAT criteria.[57] However, other legal advisers observed some frameworks allowing direct awards when there had not been a substantive competition based on MEAT criteria at the appointment stage and where not all contract terms were fully settled in the framework. One commented, 'it has become accepted that different direct award methods have different variations of subjectivity, and some are legally questionable'.[58] Another thought the rules in the PCR 2006 on direct awards were preferable to those in the PCR 2015, as the express reference to 'objective conditions' under the PCR 2015 gave contracting authorities almost a free choice of criteria. They had observed 'a fig leaf of compliance' as frameworks failed to incorporate any such objective conditions.[59]

Therefore, it appears that the express reference to 'objective conditions' for direct awards has created a grey area and led to some poor practices and even potential deliberate circumvention of the rules. For a framework that has not been awarded pursuant to a procedure which has held an effective competition between tenders using MEAT award criteria, it is difficult to justify the use of direct award call-off procedures that are not based on objective conditions that reflect MEAT award criteria. In practice, however, it appears that some CPAs are flexing their frameworks to permit direct awards to be made by reference to the user contracting authority's discretion with no rigorous application of MEAT-compliant award criteria either at the framework award or call-off stage.

5.2. Direct Call-off Awards without Further Competition (Complete and Hybrid Frameworks) under the PA 2023

Unlike under the PCR 2015, under the PA 2023 there are no general rules on 'awarding contracts based on a framework agreement', ie governing the exercise of choice of call-off

[55] LA19.
[56] Case C-532/06 *Lianakis v Municipality of Alexandroupolis* ECLI:EU:C:2008:40, [2008] ECR I-251.
[57] LA7.
[58] LA9.
[59] LA16.

method. It is submitted that this is a helpful development. The requirement for 'objective criteria' was arguably superfluous given that, as indicated, a separate set of strict conditions must regardless be satisfied to use a direct call-off process. Further, anecdotally, it is understood that this requirement has not always been met in many frameworks. The PCR 2015 requirement to specify 'which terms may be subject to reopening of competition' was also incoherent as there was no equivalent for frameworks that only allow mini-competitions.

By contrast, section 45(3) simply provides that 'unless subsection 4 applies, a framework may only provide for the future award of a public contract following a competitive selection process'. Section 45(4) provides that a framework may provide for the future award of a public contract 'without competition' between suppliers: (a) in circumstances where only one supplier is party to the framework, or (b) if the framework sets out (i) the core terms of the public contract, and (ii) an objective mechanism for supplier selection. The PA 2023 does not, therefore, include an express default presumption that a competitive selection process should be included in a framework, although it could arguably be implied. The GCF guidance merely reiterates that call-offs may be awarded with or without competition between suppliers on the framework.[60] However, the reference to 'only' in section 45(3), together with the section 45(3)–(4) provisions and the absence of any requirement to set out in a framework that allows both competitive selection and direct award call-off procedures the 'objective criteria' to apply to determine which call-off procedure to use, could be construed as implying such a presumption in favour of competition with direct awards being the exception. Of course, the provisions on award without competition also come after the rule on a competitive award process. The general observation stands, however, that the PA 2023 does not send out clear policy signals or steers emphasising the importance of competition but simply provides flexibility of choice.

It follows that, in the absence of provisions governing how a contracting authority decides which call-off method(s) to incorporate in its framework design, the PA 2023 appears to permit frameworks which allow (a) only the competitive selection procedure (which seems to be the implicit preference, as above); or (b) only a direct call-off procedure; or (c) both, although section 45 is not explicit as regards (c).

A contracting authority will also need to have regard to the importance of the section 12 procurement objectives when designing the framework. A contracting authority will probably need to consider whether to incorporate a competitive selection process as part of its value for money assessment, although, in some instances, a direct call-off may represent better value for money. It is therefore unclear what impact section 12 may have as a constraint.

Whereas the PCR 2015 provided that in a direct call-off scenario the framework must set out all the terms governing provision of requirements and objective conditions for determining which supplier must perform, section 45(4)(b) provides that a framework must set out (i) the core terms of the public contract, and (ii) an objective mechanism for supplier selection.

Concerning 'core terms', this apparently represents a relaxation of 'all the terms' and is, perhaps, unsurprising. In practice, it may be difficult to anticipate at the point of

[60] GCF, 'Guidance: Frameworks', November 2024, 9.

setting up the framework all possible terms and changes to them which may eventuate at the call-off stage (unless purchasing commoditised items subject to stable pricing and standard market terms). Therefore, it can be practical to leave the determination of specific terms for the call-off stage. If there is a strict insistence on setting out all the terms in a CPA-led framework, for example, there may be reduced scope for possibly better placed individual user contracting authorities to address particular risks or specifics at the call-off stage through revised terms.

The PA 2023 does not define 'core terms'. The Explanatory Notes to the PA 2023 indicate that this is 'intended to cover key terms such as deliverables, standards, charges and pricing mechanism and basic terms such as warranties, indemnities, termination rights, confidentiality, disputes, variations etc'.[61] However, it is also stated that this allows 'additional terms on matters which are specific to the contract to be awarded to be included at the time of award, for example a detailed specification, prices and detailed performance requirements'.[62] The Explanatory Notes are not particularly helpful in this regard in inclusively referencing subsets of 'key terms' and 'basic terms' as well as a category of 'additional terms'. In the absence of any clear indication to the contrary, there is not a requirement to set the additional terms out in the framework itself. It is also unclear to what extent additional terms must relate to the core terms. The GCF guidance similarly gives the following examples: 'deliverables (ie the basic requirements that the supplier has to deliver under the call-off contract, such as compliance with the authority's requirements, the supplier's framework tender, standards, policies and timeliness), warranties, charges and pricing mechanism, record keeping, indemnities, termination provisions, variation mechanism'.[63] As no further guidance is provided on 'core terms', it is not clear how this requirement will be met. There is a potential risk of frameworks being set up which only include very limited 'core terms' that can be supplemented by the contracting authority's other terms, which could potentially increase recourse to call-off awards without competition.

To give one example of possible uncertainty, the reference to 'pricing mechanism' indicates that prices do not necessarily need to be fixed completely when awarding the framework. Rather, some flexibility is allowed to devise a pricing mechanism that can be applied to determine the price of a call-off without the supplier being able to propose revised or different pricing at the call-off stage. The reference to 'charges and pricing mechanism' without any further detail potentially permits a wide range of call-off pricing mechanisms to be incorporated in frameworks without any explicit requirements on how rigorous these need to be and how they should relate to any pricing submitted at the framework award stage.

Concerning an 'objective mechanism for supplier selection', as explained above, under the PCR 2015, the term 'objective conditions' was used instead. This reference to 'mechanism' is not defined, although it is used elsewhere in the PA 2023 (eg section 23(4) on the award of lots) and there is limited GCF guidance on this aspect. This reference may be intended to reflect the diverse range of direct call-off processes that have developed in practice but this is not clear. As under the PCR 2015, the formulation of an

[61] Explanatory Notes, Procurement Act, ch 53, 35.
[62] ibid.
[63] GCF (n 60).

'objective mechanism' does not appear to need to comply with the rules on formulating 'award criteria' ie there is no need to use criteria that comply with the section 23 award criteria requirements to identify the MAT. The rationale behind this approach is unclear, and which was questioned above in respect of Directive 2014/24/EU.

Again, it is not clear what will suffice to meet the requirement for an 'objective' mechanism. A considered approach will be needed because section 45(5)(d) provides that the selection process must be set out in the framework. The GCF guidance simply states that an objective mechanism may, for example, be a 'taxi-rank' system where call-offs are awarded on a rotational basis, or a 'highest ranking' system with a limitation on the number or value of call-offs to be awarded to any one supplier.[64] It explains that once the supplier submitting the highest ranking tender reaches the cap, the next call-off would be awarded to the supplier with the next highest scoring tender.[65] However, as indicated above, such methods may be questionable. An opportunity was therefore missed to provide guidance on how to configure a mechanism that supports contracting authorities in identifying the MAT for their specific call-off requirement. The above and many other selection mechanisms have been developed in practice, some of which, although objective, might not necessarily ensure value for money or even make commercial sense. In addition, contracting authorities will need to consider their broader obligations under section 12 including the requirement to 'treat suppliers the same unless a difference between the suppliers justifies different treatment'. Relatedly, again, there is no explicit requirement for proportionality in call-off design and which might have been useful in guiding the use of direct call-off mechanisms for different types of requirement.

Given the above, it appears that there will continue to be significant flexibility to develop call-off procedures for direct awards without competition concerning which there will be ongoing legal uncertainty. The PA 2023 provisions are therefore unlikely to discourage extensive use of direct call-offs in large multi-supplier frameworks and may offer opportunity for further market exploitation of this route to contract.

5.3. Mini-competition Call-off Procedure (Hybrid and Incomplete Frameworks) under the PCR 2015

Another way in which call-offs may be awarded under the PCR 2015 is by reopening competition amongst suppliers party to the framework. As explained, this is possible both for incomplete and hybrid frameworks. Regulation 33(11) provides that competition shall be based on the same terms as applied for the award of the framework and, where necessary, more precisely formulated terms and, where appropriate, other terms referred to in the procurement documents for the framework. Accordingly, one option is to run a mini-competition based on the same contractual terms established in the framework. This would allow suppliers to revise their original tender, eg the method statements originally submitted or the original pricing. As indicated, the contracting authority may, 'if necessary', run the mini-competition based on 'more precisely

[64] ibid.
[65] ibid.

formulated terms' than those established in the framework or, 'if appropriate', on 'other terms' referred to in the framework. The inclusion of 'if necessary' and 'if appropriate' indicates that a contracting authority is not given complete freedom to change the terms of the framework for all mini-competitions. Neither Directive 2014/24/EU nor the PCR 2015 provide any guidance on the extent to which the call-off terms need to be settled when appointing suppliers to the framework. The PLA has referred to the EU *Telaustria*[66] case and the transparency principle when arguing that 'the framework must specify the terms of future call-off contracts sufficiently clearly so as to enable economic operators contemplating submitting tenders both to understand the nature of the opportunity and to review the impartiality of the process'.[67]

As discussed in chapter five, as the purpose of a PCR 2015 framework in regulation 33(2) 'is to establish the terms governing contracts to be awarded during a given period', the appointment stage should be used to establish the terms as completely as possible, whilst acknowledging that some terms may need to be finalised or refined at the call-off stage. Further, regulation 33(6) provides that call-offs 'may under no circumstances entail substantial modifications' to the original terms laid down in the framework.

It is possible to envisage the need to formulate more precise contract terms for certain requirements at the call-off stage. For example, under a framework for IT training services, it might make sense to reserve such matters as course design and content, delivery plan and the quality of personnel delivering the training to be covered at the call-off stage when the contracting authority has a clearer idea of the nature and timing of its requirements. The exact pricing for some large ICT projects may also need to be determined at the call-off stage as the project requirements materialise. However, as indicated, it can be difficult to determine how precisely terms should be formulated at the point of establishing the framework rather than at the call-off stage.

5.3.1. Mini-competition Procedure

Regulation 33(11) sets out the required procedure when running a mini-competition. This requires the following.

5.3.1.1. Written Consultation with Suppliers Capable of Performing

Regulation 33(11)(a) provides that for every contract to be awarded, contracting authorities shall consult in writing the economic operators capable of performing the contract. The OGC consultation on implementation of Article 32 Directive 2004/18/EC addressed the point raised in consultation of whether this wording meant that the purchaser can select which suppliers they want to include in the mini-competition. In response, it was stated that:

> The answer is that you cannot 'select' in the sense of inviting, say, four out of ten suppliers simply because four is a reasonable number. The test is 'capable of performing the contract'.

[66] Case C-324/98 *Telaustria Verlags GmbH and Telefonadress GmbH v Telekom Austria and Herold Business Data AG* [2000] ECR I-10745.

[67] PLA (n 27) 36.

> Thus, if all ten were capable of meeting the specific requirement, as indicated in their bids at the time the framework was awarded, then they should all be invited.[68]

All suppliers qualified to perform must therefore be invited to participate in the mini-competition. The European Commission has given the example of a framework for a range of office supplies divided into lots and clarified that there is no obligation to consult those suppliers not covered by the framework for the type of supplies subject to the particular call-off.[69] Arrowsmith notes that the transparency principle probably requires contracting authorities to set out in advance, so far as possible, which suppliers are qualified for particular sizes and types of orders under the framework.[70] This would be determined at the appointment stage.

Arguably, a contracting authority may use the framework award stage to appoint suppliers more generally to the framework, leaving the decision on which suppliers are qualified to fulfil a particular requirement and should be invited to participate in a mini-competition until the call-off stage. This may be desirable where, for example, the nature of the requirement makes it difficult to determine in advance which of the appointed suppliers will be qualified to fulfil a specific order. It appears that the transparency principle would require the procurement documents for the framework to include details of how this further qualification process is to be conducted. For example, a short questionnaire might be sent to the suppliers at the call-off stage asking them to confirm they are capable of fulfilling the requirement and want to receive an invitation to participate in the mini-competition.[71] Electronic filtering systems have become common in recent years which allow contracting authorities to apply certain criteria to identify capable suppliers on a framework.

As with any procurement procedure under the PCR 2015, it should be possible to revisit (and potentially revoke) the qualification decision at any point prior to the award of a call-off. In *Harmon*[72] it was held (when considering a qualification decision made in the context of a restricted procedure) that a qualification decision can be revisited based on facts which had occurred since or which were 'not apparent or not reasonably discoverable' when the decision was made, or for reasons arising later.[73] There is an even stronger case for being able to revisit the qualification decision in a framework as contract awards may take place at any time during its term. This could potentially result in an appointed supplier being removed from the framework.

As explained above and mentioned by Arrowsmith,[74] when using standard procurement procedures, performance of previous contracts can be considered when deciding whether a supplier is qualified to perform a particular contract. It should be

[68] OGC, 'Response to Consultation on the New Procurement Directives' (undated) 8. Available through the National Archives at webarchive.nationalarchives.gov.uk/ukgwa/20100303181810/http://www.ogc.gov.uk/procurement_policy_and_application_of_eu_rules_european_procurement_directives.asp.

[69] European Commission Explanatory Note (n 23) 9.

[70] Arrowsmith (n 1) 11-84.

[71] There is evidence that this process has been adopted in practice. See, for example, Ministry of Defence Framework for Technical Support / 5 (FATS/5).

[72] *Harmon CFEM Facades (UK) Ltd v The Corporate Officer of the House of Commons* (2000) 2 LGLR 372.

[73] See discussion in Arrowsmith (n 1) 7-146.

[74] Arrowsmith (n 1) 11-85.

permissible, therefore, to consider execution of previous orders under a framework when deciding whether a framework supplier remains qualified to fulfil future orders under that framework. The PCR 2015 include a discretionary exclusion ground for past poor contract performance (regulation 57(8)(g)).[75] This only applies where deficiencies in performance have 'led to early termination of that prior contract, damages or other comparable sanctions'. It is submitted that past performance can be considered more generally to assess whether a framework supplier remains qualified to perform a call-off and is relevant when considering the obligation to consult in writing the suppliers that can perform the call-off in question.[76]

This ability to reassess whether a framework supplier remains qualified under the framework must be distinguished from introducing a further selection stage at the call-off stage. This will have already been carried out when appointing the suppliers to the framework and which was confirmed in the 2008 OGC guidance.[77]

5.3.1.2. Fixing a Sufficient Time Limit to Allow Tenders for Each Specific Contract

Regulation 33(11)(b) provides that contracting authorities must fix a suitable time limit to allow tenders for each specific contract to be submitted, taking into account factors such as the complexity of the subject-matter of the contract and the time needed to send in tenders. A contracting authority has discretion to decide an appropriate timeframe for suppliers to submit a tender.[78] This contrasts with the position under the regulation 27 open and regulation 28 restricted procedures where a minimum number of days must be allowed for tenders to be submitted. In its Explanatory Note, the Commission stated that 'a short time limit could be sufficient', for example, where electronic means of communication are used and only a single aspect in the specific tender remains outstanding (eg price).[79] If the call-off concerns a complex requirement with various aspects still to be resolved, clearly a longer timeframe should be considered.

5.3.1.3. Tenders to be Submitted in Writing and not Opened Until Time Limit for Reply has Expired

Regulation 33(11)(c) provides that tenders must be submitted in writing and must not be opened until the stipulated time limit for reply has expired. Since 18 October 2018, communications have had to take place by electronic means at all stages of the procedure, including the transmission of requests for participation and e-submission of tenders (regs 1(3) and 22(1)). All tenders must remain confidential and their content not accessed until the submission deadline has passed.

[75] This exclusion ground can apply when a contracting authority becomes aware, at any time during a procurement procedure, that the supplier is in this situation: reg 57(10).

[76] See argument put forward by Arrowsmith (n 1) 12-106.

[77] OGC (n 15) 9.

[78] Where the contracting authority uses an e-auction it is required to allow at least two working days between the date on which the invitation to participate in the e-auction is sent out and the start of the e-auction: reg 35(16).

[79] European Commission Explanatory Note (n 23) 9.

5.3.1.4. Awarding Each Contract to the Framework Supplier that has Submitted the Best Tender Based on the Award Criteria Set Out in the Procurement Documents

Regulation 13(11)(d) provides that contracting authorities must award each contract to the tenderer that has submitted the best tender on the basis of the award criteria set out in the procurement documents for the framework.

This means that the award criteria on the basis of which the mini-competition is to be held should be disclosed at the same time as the call for competition for the framework is published.

As explained above, for complete and hybrid frameworks using the direct call-off method, under the PCR 2015 'objective conditions' will be used to determine which supplier will perform a particular call-off. Such objective conditions need not comply with the requirements of award criteria to determine the MEAT (under regulation 67). As recalled, the rationale for this, which seems to be based on the Commission's logic that such frameworks are a type of public contract, is questionable considering the requirement in regulation 67(1) under all other procedures in the PCR 2015 to use contract award criteria based on MEAT to award public contracts. The position is different for incomplete frameworks and hybrid frameworks where the term 'award criteria' is used to describe the basis upon which it will be determined which supplier will perform a particular call-off.[80] The drafting in the legislation is equally questionable as it refers to awarding the call-off to the supplier that has submitted the 'best tender on the basis of the award criteria set out in the procurement documents for the framework'; there is no reference to the award criteria needing to comply with regulation 67 to identify the MEAT. However, the reference to 'best tender' almost certainly necessitates such an interpretation. When using the mini-competition procedure, the tender stage which commenced when the framework was awarded is only part-complete and so award criteria compliant with the requirements of regulation 67 must be used to complete the tender phase for a particular call-off.[81] It is important to note Recital 92 Directive 2014/24/EU in this regard which states:

> The chosen award criteria should not confer an unrestricted freedom of choice on the contracting authority and they should ensure the possibility of effective and fair competition and be accompanied by arrangements that allow the information provided by the tenderers to be effectively verified.

Whilst references to 'effective and fair competition' are unclear given the absence of such clearly stated objectives in Directive 2014/24/EU (as discussed in chapter three), the above nevertheless supports the notion that some parameters apply to the choice of award criteria.

5.3.2. Changing the Award Criteria and Weightings at the Call-off Stage

As indicated, regulation 33(11)(d) requires the mini-competition to be based on the award criteria set out in the procurement documents. However, it does not explicitly

[80] The distinction was not so apparent in Directive 2004/18/EC Directive and PCR 2006 as the term 'objective conditions' was not used to describe the basis of award for direct call-offs.

[81] Arrowsmith has commented that the OGC's 2008 Note is ambiguous as it states that 'the contracting authority should award the call-off to the economic operator which has submitted the most economically advantageous tender on the basis of the award criteria set out in the framework' not making it clear whether the word 'should' refers to the legal position or just best practice. See Arrowsmith (n 1) 11-64, fn 184.

state that the award criteria used at the mini-competition stage need to be the same as those used at the appointment stage.

It is submitted that the equal treatment and transparency principles require the award criteria used at the mini-competition stage to replicate or at the least link closely to the framework award criteria. Otherwise, an award based on different criteria could undermine the result of the original competition. As Arrowsmith has observed, there would be an increased risk that suppliers that were not appointed to the framework might have been able to fulfil the order on better terms applying those criteria and there could be a violation of the requirement not to act in an anti-competitive manner, considering Recital 61 Directive 2014/24/EU.[82] The Commission's Explanatory Note stated 'the award criteria do not have to be the same as those used for the conclusion of the framework itself' providing the criteria were set out in the specifications for the framework.[83] The OGC's 2008 note stated that 'criteria used for mini-competitions may differ from the award criteria used to set up the framework if they are related to (ie, derive from) the original award criteria'.[84] It also stated that 'new award criteria may be added as long as they relate to the award criteria set out in the framework and weighting may be varied to reflect the particular requirement'.[85]

The legislation is silent on whether it is permissible, when running a mini-competition, to alter the weightings of award criteria used to appoint the suppliers. It is submitted, however, that the same legal principles that apply to use of award criteria apply to use of weightings.

Regarding whether new award criteria may be included, as indicated, the OGC seemed to suggest that this is permissible. However, this needs to be considered against the rules on disclosure of award criteria and general procurement principles, as discussed below.

There may be circumstances in which it would make commercial sense and even be necessary for a contracting authority to vary the award criteria and weightings at the mini-competition stage to address the specific requirements of a call-off. For example, for an urgent IT service procurement to address a gap in service, a contracting authority might need to increase the weighting allocation for the delivery period, introduce more specific technical criteria eg a mobilisation plan, and consequently reduce the weighting allocation given to price.

Whilst the Commission and OGC guidance envisage the possibility of varying the award criteria and weightings at the mini-competition stage, the extent to which such variations are permitted is not clear. As discussed below, to comply with the transparency principle, the permitted list of award criteria and range of weightings should be provided when setting up the framework so that it is clear what parameters apply at the mini-competition stage. A contracting authority should not be permitted, therefore, to introduce its own separate award criteria if they do not relate to those which have been disclosed in the procurement documents for the framework.

As Arrowsmith has stated, 'the greater the difference between the two stages, the greater the legal risk involved'.[86] Using criteria and weightings which diverge significantly

[82] ibid.
[83] European Commission Explanatory Note (n 23) 9.
[84] OGC (n 15) 7.
[85] ibid 10.
[86] Arrowsmith (n 1) 11-78.

from those used at the appointment stage is likely to be harder to justify under the equal treatment principle and the requirement in Recital 61 Directive 2014/24/EU not to use frameworks improperly or in a manner which distorts competition. This is one of the most difficult areas that contracting authorities grapple with in practice.

5.3.3. Disclosing Award Criteria and Weightings

Award criteria and weightings must be disclosed in the procurement documents for the framework (regulation 67(9)).

The requirement for the award criteria to be set out in the procurement documents indicates that even if different award criteria and weightings are to be used at the call-off stage pursuant to a mini-competition, these must still be formulated in advance and the parameters of use clearly explained and disclosed at the same time as the framework is advertised.

If setting a range of weightings, regulation 67(10) indicates that the contracting authority must set an 'appropriate maximum spread'.[87] Arrowsmith notes that setting a range will need to be 'exercised in good faith in accordance with the general transparency principle' and therefore 'a very broad range that indicates a lack of good faith and/or does not provide reasonable guidance' would be unlawful.[88]

Regulation 67(11) provides that there is a limited exception to the obligation to state weightings in the procurement documents, namely, where 'weighting is not possible for objective reasons' in which case 'the contracting authority shall indicate the criteria in decreasing order of importance' in the procurement documents instead. Recital 90 Directive 2014/24/EU indicates that this exception is only available 'in duly justified cases for which they must be able to give reasons [...] in particular because of the complexity of the contract'. From a transparency perspective, it is submitted that such reasons should also be set out in the procurement documents.

There is some scope for using different weightings at the mini-competition stage from those at the appointment stage and, given the unpredictable nature of requirements under frameworks, it may be more appropriate to state a range of weightings in the procurement documents to allow more flexibility for weightings to be adapted to the specific requirements of a contracting authority at the mini-competition stage.

5.3.4. Application of Transparency Principle to Disclosure of Sub-criteria, Sub-weightings and Evaluation Methodologies

Although not explicitly provided for in Directive 2014/24/EU or the PCR 2015, when formulating award criteria and weightings, contracting authorities may decide to divide these into sub-criteria and sub-weightings to evaluate tenders. The contracting authority may also devise an evaluation methodology and other materials to score tenders. The extent to which such information should be disclosed in advance has been the subject of case law at the EU and UK level. The legal position at the time of writing is that such

[87] See also *Mclaughlin and Harvey Limited v Department of Finance and Personnel No2* [2008] NIQB.
[88] Arrowsmith (n 1) 7-206.

materials should be disclosed in advance if knowledge of them could affect the conduct of tenderers when preparing their bids.[89] The rules established by this line of case law apply equally to tenders being submitted seeking admission to a framework.[90] As noted by Arrowsmith, they probably also apply to the call-off stage of a framework under the general principle of transparency.[91] Therefore, when inviting mini-tenders, the contracting authority should disclose to suppliers in advance of the mini-competition any sub-criteria, sub-weightings and evaluation methodologies where these could affect the preparation of such mini-tenders.

5.3.5. Establishing Mini-competition Procedures in Practice under the PCR 2015

Similar to the trend regarding direct call-off procedures, significant flexibility can be detected in recent mini-competition procedures incorporated in frameworks. Whilst some frameworks exist that specify the precise award criteria and weightings to be used at the call-off stage, these are generally considered to be inappropriate for procuring bespoke ICT solutions. Most frameworks for ICT requirements acknowledge that different customers have different priorities and requirements and allow award criteria and weightings to be changed or supplemented at the call-off stage. Some frameworks limit the extent to which award criteria and weightings can be amended or supplemented; for example, by capping the degree of variation allowed to the weightings. However, some leave it to contracting authority discretion to determine what award criteria and weightings to use at the call-off stage. This is difficult to reconcile with the regulation 33(11)(d) requirement to set out the award criteria in the original procurement documents for the framework but, as with other developments in respect of frameworks, may reflect the way in which market-led objectives are given priority in practice over strict compliance with the applicable legal rules.

However, the need to deliver value for money was a slightly more prominently consideration when interviewees discussed use of the mini-competition procedure. A few interviewees mentioned that, from a value for money perspective, this procedure is usually preferable to the direct award procedure except potentially for the procurement of highly commoditised ICT items with little price volatility. One interviewee commented that the mini-competition procedure not only secures value for money but 'mitigates against the customer re-using the same supplier all the time'.[92] By contrast, as discussed in chapter five, for ICT requirements that involve resellers relying upon the same original software or hardware supplier, a mini-competition can be a futile process and difficult to justify from a value for money perspective, leading many contracting authorities to use direct call-offs instead. It is recalled that reseller frameworks require further investigation because even if it is deemed that frameworks are

[89] *Varney & Sons Waste Management Ltd v Hertfordshire County Council* [2011] EWCA Civ 708 which confirmed the ruling in Case C-331/04 *ATI EAC v ACTV Venezia* [2005] ECR I-10109.

[90] Confirmed in *Mclaughlin and Harvey Limited v Department of Finance and Personnel (No2)* [2008] NIQB 91 and [2011] NICA 59.

[91] Arrowsmith (n 1) 11-82–11-83, noting support for this view in OGC (n 15) 7.

[92] CPB10.

appropriate tools for such requirements, the incomplete framework model which only allows mini-competitions may be unsuitable where requirements are sourced through such intermediaries.

The use of award criteria in mini-competitions was also discussed by many interviewees. One legal adviser queried whether the regulation 33(11)(d) requirement to award call-offs to the best tender on the basis of the framework award criteria means that MEAT criteria are not required for mini-competitions and stated that opposing arguments from an EU or UK perspective could be made due to this 'sloppy drafting'.[93] As explained above, it is submitted that a mini-competition is an extension of the original competition and is used to complete a call-off, such that criteria should be based on MEAT.

A CPA interviewee explained how they inform the user contracting authority of the award criteria and weightings used to award the framework and the scores achieved, and allow mini-competitions to be run using bespoke criteria and weightings to address specific requirements. This is subject to setting some parameters around changes to certain criteria eg social value.[94] Again, it is submitted that any such criteria would need to relate to, and be based on, the original award criteria.

CPAs usually issue guides for contracting authorities using their frameworks, which might advise what flexibility is allowed to change the award criteria or weightings at the call-off stage. One interviewee usually states in the guidance that the award criteria need to link back to the award criteria used at the appointment stage.[95] Not all CPAs include this limitation, however. It also appears that the guides issued for some frameworks do not provide sufficient clarity on the amount of flexibility permitted.[96] Another highlighted the significant differences between frameworks and that it was necessary to read each guide in detail, observing that 'some require you to stick to original criteria and weightings, some allow criteria to be changed, some allow weightings to be changed from 10–90%! It can be very time consuming to figure out what is and is not permissible for a particular framework'.[97]

By seeking to make frameworks more appealing to user contracting authorities through flexible award criteria and weightings, CPAs risk creating the spectre of legal uncertainty for user contracting authorities who are exposed to the risk of a legal challenge if they award a contract in breach of the PCR 2015. This uncertainty can result in contracting authorities incurring additional legal costs as they seek advice on the legality of call-off procedures as well as administrative costs in familiarising themselves with different approaches to award criteria and weightings.

Some poor evaluation practices have also developed. An interviewee had come across a framework for non-commoditised ICT requirements under which the 'quality' criteria at the call-off stage was to be assessed on a pass/fail basis only which resulted in all suppliers in the mini-competition passing this aspect of the evaluation and the award being determined by an assessment of price only. They expressed concern that 'quality'

[93] LA11.
[94] CPB3.
[95] CPB10.
[96] CA4, CA10.
[97] CA12.

criteria are not, therefore, being assessed properly.[98] This was a surprising example as it would seem that such an approach would only be appropriate for highly commoditised items where there are very few differences in the quality of products across suppliers.

When legal advice is sought by a CPA on the formulation of award criteria and weightings, a nuanced approach is more likely to be adopted. One legal adviser explained that if a client wanted to set up a framework with a flexible mini-competition procedure, they advised to 'try to lay down some principles that tell a story as to how you might flex the criteria and weightings'. However, they acknowledged the risk associated with writing in such principles if they were not followed in practice and the perception of frameworks being misused where too much flexibility was permitted. In their experience, 'the more flex allowed, the more likely it is that people will be cynical of your use of the framework'.[99]

Some interviewees expressed frustration about the limited options available in some frameworks to address wider issues such as social value at the call-off stage. One observed that social value criteria are sometimes not featured in the award criteria at the appointment stage and are not specified in the framework documentation as permissible award criteria that can be used at the call-off stage, perceiving this as a disincentive to using such frameworks.[100] Other research has also identified other factors in this regard.[101]

As indicated, if a framework has many suppliers with no clear groupings based on capabilities, it might not be feasible to run mini-competitions between them all. Interviewees have reported that for large frameworks this can result in a 'supplier minefield and the potential of having to evaluate hundreds of responses'.[102] Filtering mechanisms have emerged to address this issue. For example, a contracting authority might issue an 'expression of interest' request to all appointed suppliers to identify those interested in bidding for an opportunity. One interviewee argued that a further short-listing process at the call-off stage should be expressly permitted in the rules as there was considerable uncertainty around using bespoke selection criteria at the call-off stage to identify suitable suppliers.[103] Further 'capability assessments' are provided for in some frameworks to narrow the pool of suppliers invited to participate in a mini-competition. According to another interviewee, some frameworks allow mini-competitions only with a few selected suppliers, with other appointed suppliers retained for 'back-up' purposes.[104] It is submitted that all framework suppliers capable of meeting a call-off requirement should be invited to participate in a mini-competition and, so, unless such reserve groups of suppliers have been established at the point of framework award (eg via the use of lots), such practice of inviting only certain capable suppliers to submit a mini-tender could be unlawful under the PCR 2015.

[98] EO3.
[99] LA6.
[100] CA14.
[101] B Awuzie, F Farag and P McDermott, 'Achieving social value through construction frameworks: the effect of client attributes' (2018) 171(1) *Proceedings of the Institution of Civil Engineers – Management, Procurement and Law* 25–31.
[102] CA3.
[103] CPB4.
[104] LA6.

Two supplier interviewees expressed scepticism about the use of award criteria and weightings by contracting authorities at the call-off stage and criticised the degree of subjectivity allowed when operating frameworks. One had noticed identical tender questions being asked by different user contracting authorities but with vastly differing evaluation results which they attributed to the amount of subjectivity at play and the customers knowing their desired outcome already.[105]

Questionable practices are also sometimes adopted by suppliers to win work through mini-competitions and further indicate the extent of the marketisation of frameworks in the UK. An interviewee revealed that they had helped customer contracting authorities to write capability questions to ensure that they would be 'shortlisted' for the mini-competition. They complained that 'lots of SMEs cannot get shortlisted due to capability requirements such as demonstrating lots of previous government experience'.[106]

5.4. Competitive Selection Call-off Procedure (Hybrid and Incomplete Frameworks) under the PA 2023

Section 45(3) provides that if the conditions for an award without competition are not satisfied, a framework may only provide for the future award of a public contract following a competitive selection process. Section 46(10) defines a 'competitive selection process' as 'a competitive selection process for the award of a public contract in accordance with a framework'. Section 45(5)(d) provides that this process must be set out in the framework. The GCF guidance states that 'there is some flexibility in that whilst the selection process must be set out, the level of detail is not specified in the Act and this may be in high level or more detailed terms'.[107] The absence of detail is perhaps unsurprising given that there is similarly little detail on how to run a full section 20 competitive tendering procedure.

The provisions in the PA 2023 on running a competitive selection process differ from the rules in the PCR 2015 in two fundamental respects, considered below.

5.4.1. *Use of Supplementary Conditions of Participation*

The PA 2023 introduces a new flexibility to apply conditions of participation when using the competitive selection process to award a call-off. This is another example of how the framework concept in the PA 2023 has moved away from the PCR 2015 concept. Under the PCR 2015, the call-off stage was used to complete the 'award' of a call-off under the framework, the 'selection' phase having been completed at the framework award stage. Under the PA 2023, it is permissible to introduce new conditions of participation when using the competitive selection process at the call-off stage, providing the contracting authority is satisfied that they are a proportionate means of ensuring that suppliers have the legal and financial capacity or technical ability to perform the contract.

[105] EO1.
[106] EO7.
[107] GCF (n 60) 9.

It is not clear to what extent contracting authorities should rely on the conditions of participation set for the award of the framework in the first instance or should set their own at the call-off stage and, in the latter case, to what extent they need to relate to those used at the framework award stage, if at all. Without any such linkage, suppliers could find themselves excluded from tendering for call-offs because of new conditions being introduced which they were not made aware of, and could not prepare for, under a framework on which they had been pre-qualified to contract.

5.4.2. Assessment of Proposals by Reference to Award Criteria for Awarding the Framework

The other main difference between the provisions in the PA 2023 on running a competitive selection process and those in the PCR 2015 on reopening competition relates to the evaluation of tenders. As indicated, under regulation 33(11)(d), it was not clear to what extent call-off award criteria had to be the same as, or based on, the original framework award criteria, it being argued that they should replicate or at least link closely back to the original award criteria.

Section 46(8) provides that a 'competitive selection process may provide for the assessment of proposals, but only by reference to one or more of the award criteria against which tenders were assessed in awarding the framework'. In parliamentary debate, it was stated that '[t]his is to ensure that suppliers that have already been admitted to a framework do not have to meet entirely different criteria later'.[108] It is now, therefore, an explicit requirement that the award criteria used to award a call-off must relate back to that used to award the framework. This is a helpful clarification and a somewhat stricter approach than applies in respect of conditions of participation under section 46(1)–(7), as discussed above. Section 46(9) further provides, however, that '[t]he award criteria may be refined'. This confirms that the award criteria used at each stage do not have to be identical but the permitted extent to which award criteria can be 'refined' is not clear. The GCF guidance states that 'additional sub-criteria may be included or the criteria explained further'.[109] Therefore, the refinement of award criteria by splitting the original award criteria into sub-criteria would likely be permissible but the replacement of the original award criteria with completely different, unrelated award criteria would not.

The PA 2023 appears to take different approaches in respect of call-offs made with and without competition. The PA 2023 clarifies the need for a linkage between the award criteria used to award the framework and those used to award a call-off when using the competitive selection process but no such explicit linkage applies between the award criteria used to award the framework and the objective mechanism used to select a supplier without further competition. This approach might have seemed logical under the PCR 2015 which, for direct call-offs without competition, requires all the terms of the call-off to be set out in the framework together with the objective conditions for selecting a supplier. However, the logic is not so readily apparent under the PA 2023.

[108] HL Deb, 24 October 2022, vol 824, col 331GC.
[109] GCF (n 60) 9.

This is because a framework does not need to set out all the terms of the call-off for a direct award without further competition to be made. Under the PCR 2015, objective conditions need to comply with equal treatment and transparency principles but do not need to align with MEAT on the basis that a direct award just involves the application of the terms of the framework to enter into a call-off. It is not necessarily clear that this is the position under the PA 2023.

6. Establishing Pricing Terms

6.1. Establishing Pricing Terms under the PCR 2015

As discussed below, many interviewees expressed uncertainty about the extent to which there is a need to use the framework award stage to agree prices that can be charged under a framework as distinct from being left to be determined at the call-off stage.

As explained, regulation 33(2) defines a framework agreement such that its purpose 'is to establish the terms governing contracts to be awarded during a given period, in particular with regard to price'. Whilst not unequivocal, some competition on price would appear to be required when awarding a framework to establish such terms. However, in its Explanatory Note, the Commission stated 'the Directive does not require certain aspects to be established at the beginning: as regards the price in particular, it should be emphasised that this aspect does not need to be established in the framework itself'.[110] It is unlikely that the Commission intended this statement to mean that price did not need to feature in the competition[111] to award the framework at all. It is the nature of a framework that further steps may be needed to determine the price for each call-off, albeit perhaps by applying the mechanism established in the framework.

At one extreme, it might be argued that there should be a complete competition at the appointment stage extending to determining the mechanism by which the price for call-offs will be fixed (eg by setting out a schedule of rates that must be used to determine the relevant price at the call-off stage) to ensure the award has been made on a most economically advantageous basis. The PLA gave the hypothetical of a mini-competition for professional services, where suppliers have fixed their hourly rates at the appointment stage but are unable to give a price for any particular project until further details are known.[112] Once the project details have been finalised, the suppliers may propose different ways of staffing the project and make their own estimates of the time required to carry it out. A mini-competition can be used to elicit a specific price for that project from each supplier which uses the predetermined hourly rates, but yields different prices.

At the other end of the spectrum is a framework under which price does not feature prominently as an award criterion at the appointment stage and is left almost completely to be determined at the mini-competition stage without any reference to a pre-agreed

[110] European Commission Explanatory Note (n 23) 6.
[111] ibid.
[112] PLA (n 27) 39.

pricing mechanism.[113] This, however, risks discrimination and unequal treatment and could facilitate collusion between appointed suppliers. The PLA has suggested that such a framework could be justified on the basis that the essence of a framework is the establishment of a closed class of suppliers amongst whom business may be awarded flexibly and that the general procurement principles still apply, but between the members of the framework. Therefore, competition on price should be permitted as part of mini-competitions, provided it does not contravene those principles.[114] Contracting authorities have the option of establishing the price for any call-off by means of an e-auction[115] and it could be argued that such option is redundant if the price competition cannot be left to the call-off stage.[116] However, Arrowsmith has argued that this position is not sound as e-auctions can be used in a framework which set out the pricing mechanism to be used to establish prices at the call-off stage (eg by giving appointed suppliers the opportunity to improve their prices where maximum prices only have been submitted at the appointment stage).[117]

It is submitted that, generally, a framework under which price is left to be determined at the mini-competition stage without any reference to the price or at least a pricing mechanism established at the appointment stage is not consistent with the general EU procurement principles and the purpose underpinning the regulatory provisions on frameworks. It risks having a distortive effect on the market notwithstanding the fairly limited duration of a framework. Arrowsmith highlighted under Directive 2004/18/EC that it would be illogical to allow a closed market in which a substantial part of the competition (including on price) only takes place at the mini-competition stage with only with a few firms whereby substantial terms are then set (effectively constituting a mandatory list of select suppliers), but at the same time precluding the possibility of using mandatory qualification lists.[118] This view must now be considered in light of the rules on DPS under Directive 2014/24/EU but it is still the case that under Directive 2014/24/EU and the PCR 2015, the award of public contracts must be based on the MEAT identified on the basis of the price or cost and may include the best price-quality ratio (regulation 67(1)–(4)). As indicated, perhaps a limited exception to conducting a substantive competition on price at the framework award stage would be where the requirement is procured from a market with very volatile prices such that it would not be sensible or in keeping with the procurement principles to hold a competition on price at this stage.[119] In its guidance based on Directive 2004/18/EC and the PCR 2006, the OGC, contemplating energy or fuel procurements subject to price fluctuations, stated that:

> Even though it would be possible to award the framework itself on the basis of quality criteria alone, with prices being offered at a mini competition, this is unlikely to be consistent with value for money and is generally only considered appropriate in a few limited circumstances

[113] ibid 38.
[114] ibid 39–41. Recital 11 Directive 2004/18/EC was referred to as possible justification.
[115] ibid. The PLA referred to reg 21(2) PCR 2006. See also reg 35(5)(a).
[116] ibid 41.
[117] Arrowsmith (n 1) 11-37–11-39.
[118] ibid 11-39.
[119] Arrowsmith (n 1) 11-61–11-62.

> where it is not possible to determine price or a pricing structure at the time the framework is established.[120]

For most procurements that do not attract volatile prices, if price did not feature as a criterion at the appointment stage at all, a contracting authority could restrict the competition on a major award criterion to a closed group of suppliers, risking offending against Recital 61 Directive 2014/24/EU, which states that frameworks 'should not be used improperly or in such a way as to prevent, restrict or distort competition'.

Arrowsmith suggests that a further determination on price may take place at the mini- competition stage where this is appropriate given the subject-matter of the contract and providing there is compliance with the general procurement principle. This is likely to be appropriate where the further specification of a project at the mini-competition stage may determine the prices offered by suppliers based on the pricing mechanism contained in the original competition.[121]

Support for the above can be gleaned from *Henry Bros*[122] in which the High Court in Northern Ireland rejected the notion that when awarding admission to a framework, a contracting authority was entitled to omit criteria relating to price or cost altogether. It noted the court's view in *Harmon*[123] that in determining which tender is the most economically advantageous, 'price is the starting point for the exercise' due to the framework definition which refers to establishing the terms of the subsequent contract, 'in particular the terms as to price'. The court had to consider whether it was sufficient to establish a 'pricing mechanism' (in the form of fee percentages) at the appointment stage which might later be applied to determine overall cost when awarding individual call-offs. This argument was rejected on the facts but the court refrained from holding that fee percentages could never be legitimately used as a pricing mechanism when setting up a framework. Instead, it was held that fee percentages could only be so used where prices for individual call-offs were established competitively at the call-off stage. This is unlikely to mean that merely setting out in the framework the type of pricing to be used at the call-off stage would be sufficient (eg fixed, firm target pricing, cost-plus or some other type of pricing methodology). Some degree of substantive competition on price is surely required for the reasons given above.

It may also be questioned whether the apparent exception regarding contracts that attract volatile pricing is still sound and whether, for such requirements, a DPS might be more appropriate given the award stage is carried out entirely when putting a specific contract out to competition, as explained in chapter five, leaving any competition on price to the second stage of the process. However, the closed nature of a framework is such that it may remain easier to manage in terms of the number of appointed suppliers and the ability to undertake the substantive part of the competition (which would at least allow the qualitative aspects to be evaluated) at the appointment stage.

More generally, the PLA has identified various approaches to pricing that have been adopted; for example, prices being fixed for an initial period of the framework,

[120] OGC (n 15) 4.

[121] Arrowsmith (n 1) 11-61–11-62.

[122] *Henry Brothers (Magherafelt) Ltd & Ors v Department of Education for Northern Ireland* [2008] NIQB 105, para 25.

[123] *Harmon v House of Commons* [1999] All ER (D) 1178, para 182.

or tendered prices being treated as maximum prices, but with the possibility of quoting lower prices in mini-competitions.[124] Arrowsmith has noted the Commission's Explanatory Memorandum to the original proposal for Directive 2004/18/EC which appeared to support scope for allowing some revision to prices in frameworks for 'markets which are constantly changing'.[125] It is not clear, however, how far this flexibility could be applied.[126]

If appointed suppliers were allowed to revise their price upwards at this second stage, this would risk breaching transparency and equal treatment principles from the perspective of suppliers not appointed to the framework because of the prices they tendered at the appointment stage. Price changes also need to be considered against the rule prohibiting 'substantial modifications' to frameworks under regulation 33(6), which, as discussed in chapter six, may apply the same principles as under the regulation 72 general rules on modifications of public contracts. Price changes could conceivably constitute substantial and thus non-permitted modifications on the basis that they introduce conditions which, had they been part of the initial procedure, would have achieved a different outcome (regulation 72(8)(b)) or a change in the economic balance of the contract in favour of the contractor (regulation 72(8)(c)).[127] Regulation 72(1)(a) provides for the possibility to lawfully modify a contract where provided for in a 'clear, precise and unequivocal review clause'; therefore, it is possible to provide for detailed objective pricing review mechanisms in clauses that may result in prices being revised upwards or downwards where certain conditions are met.[128] However, otherwise, it is difficult to see how a framework which generally permits suppliers to increase their prices at the mini-competition stage without reference to any detailed parameters could be compliant with regulation 72.

Following completion of the empirical research, an important High Court judgment was issued in *Consultant Connect*.[129] The court held that the pricing agreed with the winning tenderer bore very little resemblance to the pricing in the framework price matrix completed by the suppliers when tendering for places on the framework. The pricing bidders had to put forward for an IT pager device solution was for the cost to be measured by bands of numbers of device users. By contrast, the pricing agreed with the winner was for an 'enterprise licence' per service. This was held to fall 'on the wrong side of the dividing line between forbidden 'substantial modifications' to framework terms (regulation 33(6)) and permitted 'more precisely formulated terms' (regulation 33(11)

[124] PLA (n 27) 41.

[125] Proposal for a Directive of the European Parliament and of the Council on the coordination of procedures for the award of public supply contracts, public service contracts and public works contracts /* COM/2000/0275 final – COD 2000/0115 */ OJ 029 E, 30/01/2001 P. 0011–00111, 4.1 and 4.4.

[126] Arrowsmith (n 1) 11-63.

[127] See *James Waste Management LLP v Essex County Council* [2023] EWHC 1157, paras 160–189 for a recent case where the court applied the economic balance test in a holistic way and assessed whether any 'uncommercial sweeteners' were being given to the supplier.

[128] Standard boilerplate variation clauses are unlikely to satisfy the applicable conditions under reg 72(1)(a). See *Edenred v HM Treasury and others* 2015 UKSC 45 and *James Waste Management LLP v Essex County Council* [2023] EWHC 1157. Also, see *R (on the application of) Redwood Health Limited v NHS Purchasing and Supply Agency* [2009] EWHC 2511.

[129] *Consultant Connect Ltd v NHS Bath and North East Somerset, Swindon and Wiltshire Integrated Care Board & Ors* [2022] EWHC 2037 (TCC).

PCR 2015)'.[130] It was also held that the framework had not been operated 'transparently and even-handedly' as required under regulation 18.[131] This case confirms that the pricing used to award call-offs must at least relate back to the pricing or pricing mechanism established when the framework was awarded.

6.1.1. Establishing Pricing Terms in Practice under the PCR 2015

Holding a competition on price to award an ICT framework can be difficult when the precise requirements of each call-off are unknown, and the requirements are subject to dynamic pricing changes.

In interviews, virtually all legal advisers agreed that the law requires some competition on price to award the framework and that this represented good practice and provided a 'tested group of suppliers'.[132] However, many interviewees highlighted instances where well-known frameworks were established without any competition on price at the framework award stage.

Regarding approaches to establishing pricing at the framework award stage, commoditised and relatively price-stable ICT requirements might require suppliers to submit prices for specific items in the format of a price list which can be used for pricing purposes at the call-off stage when the contracting authority knows what specific items and quantities it requires. A CPA interviewee stated that in circumstances when a price is not readily available, a mini-competition is required or 'encouraged' but that 'customers do not always follow this and sometimes will just direct award'.[133] Another interviewee described the price evaluation exercise they conduct at the appointment stage whereby suppliers are asked to submit prices for a 'basket of items' with price changes at the call-off stage only being permitted to reflect any exchange rate fluctuations. They revealed that only a selection of items in the 'basket' are evaluated at the appointment stage, however.[134]

Problems can occur when using such models if bidders insert no or very low prices for some items. One interviewee relayed their experience of suppliers submitting excessively low prices to get on to frameworks. Complaints ensued from suppliers claiming that another had submitted an 'abnormally low tender' (under regulation 69) which should be investigated and rejected. The same interviewee appealed for more guidance on addressing abnormally low tenders for frameworks given their experience investigating tenders where suppliers refused to supply adequate evidence to explain their pricing.[135] As discussed in chapter ten, this is an aspect which should be subject to more systematic guidance.

Further, some experienced suppliers may be able to manipulate the 'basket of goods' approach in their favour. For example, where a bidder is aware that an item in the basket

[130] ibid para 217.
[131] ibid.
[132] LA3.
[133] CPB6.
[134] CPB8.
[135] CPB10.

is unlikely to be procured regularly, if at all, it may propose a very low price for that item to secure higher points in the tender evaluation and reserve its higher prices for commonly sought items. If the evaluation methodology has not been configured to incorporate the likely frequency of such purchases, a supplier may secure a place on the framework with the result that higher prices are paid for many items than would have been the case if a different supplier had been appointed or if the items had been secured outside the framework.

One interviewee considered that there was often little correlation between what is priced and what is subsequently purchased. They alluded to a CPA's attempt to impose profit margin limits on items, but which was ineffective as the scope was too broad and did not reflect how the industry worked. They stated that 'it is not appropriate to apply margin caps to highly specialised ICT items'. They also noted instances of fixed prices being applied to a basket of goods for two years but thought this was unrealistic due to the dynamic nature of the market.[136] Another interviewee had encountered a framework where suppliers' agreed prices were required to be uploaded to a framework portal, but which did not often happen; instead, a supplier's page on the portal stated, 'please contact us for a price'.[137] One interviewee explained that they avoided frameworks set up using the 'basket of goods' pricing approach because prices quickly became out-of-date; a regular benchmarking exercise indicated that best value was obtained by running a mini-competition instead.[138]

A framework for complex ICT solutions (eg, software development and hosting) presents an even greater pricing challenge, as pricing at the appointment stage may be based on hypothetical projects, the specifics of which will not be known until the call-off stage. Thus, whilst the appointment stage might, for example, require suppliers to submit hourly/daily rates or propose a price against a hypothetical project, the actual price for a particular project cannot be determined until the call-off stage when the full project scope is known. Poor practices were highlighted, including requiring rates to be submitted based on a standard industry rate, which would result in the same rate being tendered by each supplier.[139] The pricing for a particular project in such circumstances would usually be established through a mini-competition. Further, interviewees indicated the lack of correlation between 'indicative prices' offered at the appointment stage and prices offered at the call-off stage,[140] one commenting on the difficulty of applying the rules on abnormally low tenders to tenders based on hypothetical projects at the appointment stage because what was being priced was not a real project.[141]

Whilst a contracting authority might require the rates tendered at the appointment stage to be the maximum rates that can be used when pricing, many interviewees felt that some ICT suppliers employed experienced bidding teams to 'game' the

[136] EO5.
[137] CPB4.
[138] CA12.
[139] EO3.
[140] LA9.
[141] LA10.

process, putting SMEs without such resource at a disadvantage.[142] To counteract this, some CPAs may avoid using minimum scoring thresholds that SMEs are less likely to meet.

From a supplier perspective, the value of having a competition on price at the appointment stage was heavily questioned.[143] One interviewee had observed a supplier receiving full marks for its quality submission but coming nearly last in the price evaluation. They claimed that other suppliers must have submitted unrealistic, low prices against the hypothetical scenarios and expressed concern that 'customers never see or scrutinise the original pricing submissions to get on to the framework and so some suppliers do not see any material risk in moving away from the prices originally tendered'.[144]

Given the PCR 2015 requirements and experience highlighted in practice, the effectiveness of pricing competition in frameworks requires further investigation. As discussed in chapter ten, additional regulatory controls and/or guidance may be required.

6.2. Establishing Pricing Terms under the PA 2023

As indicated in chapter five, whereas the EU law definition of a framework agreement referred to the establishment of terms, in particular, regarding price, the new section 45(2) definition of a framework omits reference to price. Price is not even mentioned in section 45(4) in reference to 'core terms' in respect of awards without competition. It is only in section 45(5)(b) on information to be contained in a framework that there is reference to 'the price payable, or mechanism for determining the price payable under such contracts'. Further, whilst a framework is a public contract and, therefore, when following a competitive tendering procedure must be awarded to the MAT (section 19(1)), the provisions on award criteria do not specify that 'price' must always or generally be one of those criteria. Therefore, there is no apparent emphasis on requiring the procurement process used to set up the framework to include a competition to establish pricing and other terms.

It is conceivable that a contracting authority's duty to have regard to the importance of delivering value for money under section 12 would mean that, in practice, some competition on price and key commercial terms will usually be necessary to award the framework but it would have been preferable to include this as an explicit requirement. If a framework is intended to be a more focused tool for choosing a limited range of suppliers for repeat or aggregated purchases over the longer term, a substantive competition to appoint the suppliers and agree the terms of supply is surely a key element; otherwise, the discrete functional element that distinguishes frameworks from dynamic markets would be absent.

[142] LA15, LA11.
[143] EO2, EO3.
[144] EO2.

Instead, as indicated, section 45(5) only provides that a 'pricing mechanism' must be set out in the framework. Neither the legislation nor GCF guidance provides any steer on what this must involve and whether it is different or the same for each call-off procedure (competitive selection process and award without competition). From a value for money perspective, it is difficult to envisage how a direct call-off award without competition can be made unless the pricing mechanism in the framework is genuinely mechanistic (ie the application of rates and fixed prices agreed at the framework award stage to arrive at the price of a call-off) and does not require the submission of new pricing by suppliers at the call-off stage. It is submitted that the section 12 requirement to have regard to the importance of delivering value for money will not deter CPAs from setting up frameworks with incomplete pricing and permitting direct call-off awards without competition to be made. Therefore, it appears that the conditions are conducive to continuing use of extensive direct call-offs in multi-supplier frameworks.

7. Conclusions

Interviews have shown that full advantage has been taken of certain grey areas of the law when awarding frameworks eg the appointment of unlimited suppliers, use of supplementary selection and award criteria at the call-off stage, unclear choices between and provision of both direct and mini-competition call-off procedures, and questionable use of pricing mechanisms. As will be discussed in chapter eight, this has resulted in frameworks that may be difficult to manage and use with contracting authorities having to make risk-based assessments. For the most part, the PA 2023 requirements seem to either reflect the pre-existing position or constitute a further relaxation of it eg permitting the appointment of unlimited suppliers and enabling contracting authorities to introduce bespoke conditions of participation at the call-off stage. Moreover, price is no longer a central feature in the establishment of a framework. It can only be assumed that this has been done to enable flexibility as signalled generally in the Green Paper that precipitated the PA 2023. However, that the detailed PCR 2015 rules were not discussed in the Green Paper. Whilst some consultees requested the continued ability to make direct awards under frameworks,[145] the Cabinet Office's response did not indicate that it planned to relax the rules in the ways finally adopted. For balance, it should be acknowledged that the PA 2023 now expressly requires award criteria used at the call-off stage to relate to the award criteria against which tenders were assessed in awarding the framework. Whether this reform has any beneficial impact is likely to be determined by whether CPAs formulate award criteria in a relevant and bespoke way when awarding the framework or whether they resort to an approach that has been used in practice whereby the award criteria used at framework award are split into high-level 'quality' and 'price' elements only.

[145] Cabinet Office, 'Transforming Public Procurement: Government response to consultation', December 2021, CP 556, 48.

As repeatedly observed, it is striking that in respect of the set-up of frameworks, the PA 2023 correspond to the way in which many pan-public sector frameworks operated by large CPAs have been set up in recent years. As stricter legal provisions and firmer guidance have not been introduced to address poor procurement practices that have resulted, the inference is that the Government intends to continue to facilitate what has become a highly marketised framework model subject to few regulatory controls. If this is not the intention, it is likely to be the effect.

8

Using a Multi-supplier Framework

1. Introduction

Following consideration of the establishment of a multi-supplier framework in chapter seven, this chapter considers its use in practice. Venturing into the framework market can be daunting for contracting authorities looking to direct their procurement requirements through a framework, especially for those lacking expertise or capacity. As alluded to in chapter seven, uncertainties pervade the use and legality of many direct award and mini-competition procedures. Difficulties are regularly encountered when finalising the terms of call-offs and applying the legal rules on making modifications to call-offs. More recently, new forms of framework have been offered for use, but which create even greater legal uncertainty.

This chapter, focusing on contracting authority user experience, seeks to develop the findings in chapters six and seven by examining the following: general perspectives of using frameworks (Section 2); expertise, experience and capacity (Section 3); use of direct call-offs (Section 4); running mini-competitions (Section 5); finalising call-off terms (Section 6); evaluating price (Section 7); use of emerging framework models (Section 8); and contract modifications (Section 9), before offering concluding observations (Section 10).

2. General Perspectives on Using Frameworks under the PCR 2015

Chapter two highlighted the way in which the framework market has developed in the UK. Several interviewees from contracting authorities highlighted the difficulties of navigating the sometimes overlapping frameworks being introduced and reiterated at different times and the consequential strains on their organisation's capacity and expertise. It is somewhat paradoxical that the framework tool has been marketised to such an extent that there is more, rather than less, work for contracting authorities to do to identify a suitable framework.

As indicated in chapter five, a 'frameworks first' mentality persists. Several interviewees explained how their organisation adopted this approach, and one legal adviser confirmed, 'clients often say that they need to use frameworks to adhere to funding and internal policies and guidelines'.[1] It is apparent that some organisations go further

[1] LA5.

by highlighting the frameworks of a particular CPA that should be considered in the first instance, raising the obvious issue that, unless the contracting authority has been consulted and involved in setting up the frameworks, it is not clear how a recommendation to use a particular CPA can be made in general terms when other more suitable frameworks might exist.

However, many contracting authorities when 'framework shopping' struggle to identify frameworks that meet their specific requirements as 'they do not address individual needs'.[2] In the absence of the CPA conducting effective consultation with contracting authorities during the PME phase (as discussed in chapter five), the use of a framework to procure complex ICT requirements may carry unacceptable legal and commercial risks.

Whilst it appears that for some contracting authorities 'the decision whether to use a framework will largely be determined by the nature and complexity of the requirements ie whether seeking consultancy services, hardware or software and whether the requirement relates to a large project',[3] for many, speed and efficiency of contracting are equally, if not more, dominant factors. As one interviewee explained, 'some clients just don't want to have to run a full-blown competition'.[4] It appears that there is a risk that this can lead to a pre-determined result as contracting authorities may simply use a framework to justify an outcome they have already sought. For instance, legal advisers communicated concerns about the inappropriate use of frameworks by some of their clients with one commenting that much of their advice involves 'trying to justify the unjustifiable and legitimising client choice'.[5]

Legal advice is sometimes considered necessary, adding to the costs of using a framework. Advice is regularly sought on the grey areas of the law and the flexibilities allowed, including the permitted scope of a framework, the permitted user base and the consequences of exceeding a framework's estimated value, matters discussed in chapter six. Interviews indicated an apparent lack of awareness about recent case law on the important issue of exceeding the framework value, although this is generally considered to attract a low risk of challenge. One legal adviser stated, '[t]he total estimated value of a framework is often exceeded on the understanding that it is only an estimate and is permissible'.[6] This indicates the extent to which relaxed attitudes to compliance with fundamental requirements are emerging, calling into question whether regulation is effectively serving its function.

Another legal issue explained in chapter six and tackled in practice concerns the identification of the contracting authority user base eligible to use a particular framework. Several legal advisers had come across wide interpretations of framework documents by contracting authorities to justify using specific frameworks and it was acknowledged that many do not question whether the broadly scoped lists of eligible users are legally compliant. Interviewees pointed to a lack of enforcement by CPAs of the rules relating to the categories of eligible user contracting authorities. As one legal adviser highlighted,

[2] CA1.
[3] CA4.
[4] LA3.
[5] LA16.
[6] LA17.

not all frameworks require contracting authorities to sign 'access agreements' with the CPA, therefore a contracting authority may sometimes conclude a call-off directly with a supplier without any involvement of the relevant CPA. Consequently, the use of a framework can go 'under the radar' of the CPA.[7]

Further, in the case of CPA-led frameworks, with little to no involvement in their set-up, contracting authorities can be deterred from use due to lack of knowledge of how the framework operates and whether it can meet their requirements. Some interviewees pointed to the lack of control over the contracting process acting as a deterrent. This can relate to the fact that the selection and initial award stages have already been completed by the CPA and the framework may contain prescriptive procedures to follow and terms to apply when concluding call-offs, although, as indicated in chapter seven, the tendency appears to be towards increasingly less prescriptive call-off procedures for large multi-supplier frameworks. Moreover, as discussed in chapter six in respect of EU case law, as there has been no requirement for user contracting authorities to be parties to the actual framework itself and no requirement to involve them in framework design, it is perhaps unsurprising that a sense of lack of control and a disconnect may pervade between the framework provider and user. This disconnect also extends to relations with suppliers. As one interviewee highlighted, 'there is no guarantee that the framework suppliers will respond' when inviting them to participate in a mini-competition under a framework been set up for use by a wide range of contracting authorities and covering a broad scope of requirements.[8] This is a common problem for generic, pan-public sector frameworks and is, perhaps, unsurprising where relations are no longer closely bilateral between a contracting authority and select suppliers but, rather, impersonally intermediated by a CPA. Of course, this is not to say that close relationships do not exist under multi-supplier frameworks. Indeed, as discussed below, generic frameworks may also be used as a quick means of uniting contracting authorities with their preferred suppliers.

3. Expertise, Experience and Capacity

One of the largest variables in practice has been the levels of technical, commercial and legal expertise, capacity, and experience present within contracting authorities and their impact on framework use. Inevitably, how much expertise, experience and capacity is required to use a framework largely depends on the complexity of the requirement, contract terms and other framework documentation and the degree to which the framework addresses the associated technical, legal and commercial requirements.

As one interviewee put it, 'both rookies and experts are using frameworks with the experts getting what they want and the rookies being bamboozled by suppliers'.[9] According to another, 'when there are public sector funding cuts, there are usually consequential cuts to the procurement teams'. They referred to a lack of competence

[7] ibid.
[8] CA14.
[9] CA10.

and knowledge at the contract management level which appears to be 'exacerbated by a lack of good quality guidance on using frameworks either from central government or the CPAs'.[10] Whilst this book has focused largely on the contract award process, effective contract management will be critical to safeguarding against unlawful contract modifications and ensuring that what is delivered corresponds with what was called off under the framework.

Some frustration was expressed about CPAs putting the onus on contracting authorities to acquire the requisite skills and competencies to use frameworks. Some interviewees were aware of an earlier version of the Cabinet Office NPPS which mentions the need for them to ensure they have appropriate procurement skills and capability.[11] As one explained, however, 'at the moment, the procurement teams are stretched and already have lots of on-the-job training to do' which 'can lead to more use of frameworks as it is perceived that the legal risk is minimised when using a framework'.[12] Of course, it is at times of funding cuts and stretched resources that there will likely be the greatest emphasis on using frameworks to secure efficiencies. Contracting authority interviewees also indicated their expectation that CPAs should be more knowledgeable about the frameworks they set up and provide a quick route to contract for 'commoditised' and 'bottleneck' requirements, leaving contracting authorities to focus their resource on procurements of strategic value.[13]

Some contracting authorities benefit from experienced procurement professionals, ICT experts or in-house legal counsel with capacity to support the effective use of frameworks and the management of call-offs. However, interviewees representing well-resourced organisations indicated that frameworks allow them to 'play with the system', explaining how they would sometimes contact a supplier, ask them to source a product, negotiate a discount with them and then select a framework the supplier is on to contract the requirement incorporating the negotiated discount. They thought that this level of flexibility should be allowed when resourcing low-value items from frameworks. However, it is submitted that this is an example of a pre-procurement direct negotiation with a supplier and suggests an improper use of a framework. It would also appear to be an example of designing a procurement to artificially narrow competition (contrary to regulation 18(2)). This book has identified a number of instances where contracting authorities go outside the framework in order to achieve a desired outcome through the framework. It is conceivable that even less well-resourced contracting authorities may adopt similar approaches precisely because they lack dedicated resource, and direct call-offs may be a quick and easy route to contract.

For sector-specific frameworks designed for a small consortium of contracting authorities, it is common for collaborative working groups and management committees including representatives of participating contracting authorities to be set up. A good level of expertise tends to be present in the procurement teams of such contracting authorities, because they have invested time and resource in understanding frameworks

[10] CA14.
[11] Cabinet Office, 'Procurement Policy Note – National Procurement Policy Statement', Action Note PPN 05/21, June 2021, 2.
[12] CA14.
[13] CA15.

and share expertise. As one interviewee stated, 'they can detect suspect arrangements, loopholes etc and won't pay over the odds for their requirements'.[14]

By contrast, interviews confirmed some of the challenges for contracting authorities with limited resources and expertise. A few interviewees referred to the disproportionate amount of documentation that may deter framework use, especially where the contract subject-matter was low value and not complex. Examples were given of bundles of call-off documents including many schedules that failed to address the specific interests and objectives of different contracting authorities.[15] One interviewee stated that 'you need to have a decent knowledge of the market' to complete it and that 'many procurement officers would just sign the documentation without sufficient scrutiny'.[16]

More generally, irrespective of experience, interviewees viewed ICT procurement as particularly challenging because of 'the complexity of the requirements which does not sit well with the civil service mentality'. They had witnessed the successful use of frameworks divided into lots for the procurement of ICT infrastructure. However, 'the problems usually arise at the call-off stage when the service elements of the customer's requirement take it out of the commodity sphere' and the framework does not address the bespoke requirements of the contracting authority.[17] The inadequacy of frameworks to address specific requirements was a recurring theme that is clearly a significant problem for complex ICT requirements and calls into question whether frameworks are generally an appropriate procurement tool for many complex requirements.

Whilst one of the purported benefits of a framework is its speed and efficiency, the speed and efficiency objectives driving a contracting authority's use of a framework can lead to ineffective and unsatisfactory contracts being put in place. As one interviewee highlighted, the fluency of the call-off process can result in a lack of forethought being applied by inexperienced procurement officers who are tasked with running the call-off process and the finalisation of contract terms. An example was given of a procurement officer awarding a call-off to a supplier in very short order based on a high-level understanding of the requirement and a superficial, light-touch survey of the framework terms. When service delivery problems arose during the contract term, it was discovered that the call-off did not provide sufficient remedies and was unhelpfully vague in certain key areas. The contract had to be amended, leading to a significant increase in costs for the contracting authority. The same interviewee also gave examples of inexperienced procurement officers designing poor mini-competition processes. In one instance, a mini-competition was unintentionally determined based on price alone because the award criteria used to assess quality of solutions were poorly conceived and resulted in all bidders receiving identical scores. They also highlighted mini-competition documentation formulated in high-level and generic terms without any service-specific controls or any use of the facility to incorporate 'special terms' relevant to the contracting authority's requirements. They felt that 'there is a lot of education to be done here'.[18]

[14] CPB9.
[15] CA4.
[16] CA13.
[17] CA15.
[18] CA7.

Cost pressure is another important factor determining whether and when legal support is sought.[19] One legal adviser stated that they were rarely asked about the call-off process in advance 'because it is difficult for contracting authorities to justify the legal expense when frameworks are supposed to help reduce costs'. They were usually consulted later, 'when things get messy'.[20]

It is recalled from chapter four that, over the past two decades, there have been repeated calls for more detailed guidance on frameworks. The paucity of adequate central government guidance was also mentioned by many interviewees. Equally, concerns were expressed about what was perceived to be an excessive volume of general procurement guidance on other matters issued by central government in recent years. In the opinion of one interviewee, 'there is a ridiculous number of PPNs which are very confusing, sometimes inaccurate, and sometimes in conflict with each other'.[21] There were some concerns, therefore, that the introduction of more guidance on frameworks may not be beneficial unless it is focused, clear, concise, and non-contradictory.

Interviewees also mentioned the varying levels of knowledge, expertise, and experience present in suppliers. An interviewee stated that 'a significant problem is the lack of understanding by the suppliers' on how a framework operates due to a lack of experience and training and reliance upon sales representatives rather than their legal team.[22] Another interviewee stated that frameworks can provide barriers to entry for SMEs, which struggle with the complexities of public sector contracting. Whilst no statistics were shared, they observed that many SMEs have not joined ICT frameworks and queried whether it would be possible to establish some 'SME only' frameworks in the post-Brexit era to encourage and facilitate SME engagement.[23] As discussed in chapter ten, targeted training, guidance and support for SMEs would be beneficial and could increase the diversity of framework suppliers.

In contrast, many larger suppliers have extensive experience of contracting through frameworks and have built up valuable expertise. In the opinion of one legal adviser, 'customers need to upskill to match the skills of suppliers'. They have noticed that whilst contracting authorities might heavily scrutinise high-value call-offs, 'they fail to appreciate that value is not the sole determiner of risk' and sometimes do not properly scrutinise the commercial proposals of suppliers for lower value contracts. They had witnessed sophisticated commercial proposals for software development particularly in respect of the ownership of intellectual property rights.[24] Whilst the framework should settle the contract terms upfront as much as possible, an imbalance of expertise in the supplier's favour can sometimes lead to contracting authorities agreeing to less favourable conditions than those provided for in the framework at the call-off stage. This has risked the need to make substantial modifications potentially in breach of regulation 33(6).

[19] LA4.
[20] LA7.
[21] CA15.
[22] CA2.
[23] CA15.
[24] LA5.

3.1. Training and Support Available in Respect of Applying the PA 2023

In its response to its consultation on the *Transforming Public Procurement* Green Paper, the Cabinet Office revealed that questions had been raised 'about the capability of contracting authorities to select the best tool for their requirement between the proposed open frameworks, closed frameworks and dynamic markets, and requested guidance and training to be made available'.[25] It noted that 'often frameworks overlapped and suppliers felt the need to win a place on all relevant ones so as not to lose the opportunity to win business, leading to increased bidding costs for suppliers and potential duplication of available supply'.[26] The Cabinet Office proposed to issue guidance to provide suggestions on selecting the best tool for different requirements and advice on designing frameworks so that they contain all the relevant terms and, where appropriate, mechanisms for direct award.[27] It also proposed the introduction of a central register of commercial tools to provide a list of frameworks, which would bring greater transparency to the frameworks available to contracting authorities and reduce the current duplication of frameworks.[28]

As indicated in chapter four, the GCF has published a suite of guidance on the PA 2023 and has run a training programme. It is submitted, however, that whilst useful, it falls short of what was expected and does not provide sufficiently detailed advice on framework selection, design, and use and the key considerations that should be factored in. Instead of practical guidance that ensures a combination of good procurement practice and legal compliance, it tends to focus on explaining different purchasing tools and clarifying rules to aid interpretation. Many of the issues raised in this book are not considered or categorically addressed. Further, such high-level training is also no ready substitute for any shortfall in funding to recruit, train and retain procurement professionals.

The NAO has also recommended that the Government should expand its guidance on frameworks.[29] Further, the Public Accounts Committee has recommended that the Government produce a framework playbook.[30] In its response to the Public Accounts Committee, the Cabinet Office stated that it had done a lot of work to ensure that value is maximised when using frameworks. However, as the NAO subsequently observed, the Cabinet Office did not commit to developing a framework playbook or identify methods to ensure that framework hosts comply with good practice standards for frameworks.[31] The NAO reiterated its recommendation that the GCF publish

[25] Cabinet Office, 'Transforming Public Procurement: Government response to consultation', December 2021, CP 556, 48.

[26] ibid.

[27] ibid 49.

[28] ibid.

[29] NAO, *Lessons learned: Competition in public procurement*, Cabinet Office, Session 2022–23 19 July 2023, HC 1664, 13.

[30] House of Commons, Committee of Public Accounts, *Competition in public procurement*, Sixth Report of Session 2023–24, 13 December 2023, HC 385, 6.

[31] NAO, *Efficiency in government procurement of common goods and services*, CCS, Session 2024–25 HC 116, 40.

a playbook or good practice guidance for frameworks.[32] At the time of writing, no such playbook has been published.

4. Use of Direct Call-offs

4.1. Experiences of Using Direct Award Procedures without Competition under the PCR 2015

Chapter seven considered the legal and practical issues that arise in the set-up of direct call-off procedures. The PCR 2015 also contains very limited provision in respect of use of direct call-off procedures. This must be considered in light of the fact that there is necessarily more limited transparency because there is no competitive participation of multiple suppliers and, thus, such awards attract less scrutiny and oversight than the mini-competition call-off procedure. Regulation 50(4) provides that contracting authorities shall not be bound to send a notice of the results of the procedure for each contract based on a framework.

Overall, it seems that a risk-based approach to using direct award call-off procedures is taken. Most interviewees mentioned that direct call-off procedures are regularly misused with several interviewees observing that 'contracting authorities appear to be calling off as they like',[33] making direct awards 'for convenience only'.[34] One legal adviser described how 'purchasers seem to be relying more on their subjective discretion in choosing a supplier from frameworks rather than applying objective criteria' and '[c]lients often want to award to who they want and point to the guidance in the framework (as many of the framework user guides appear to permit this)'. This legal adviser encouraged clients 'to at least try to tie the award back to the scores in the original competition', highlighting that 'when using direct awards, you should be able to identify immediately who you should use'.[35] This does not always occur in practice, however. There is a perceived low legal risk of taking advantage of a loosely drafted framework guide to make direct awards without applying objective conditions set out in the framework as required by the PCR 2015. It is also perceived that it may constitute mitigation for contracting authorities to share the work around the framework suppliers to keep everyone satisfied.

Another interviewee perceived 'unlawful direct awards left, right and centre'. They acknowledged that the PCR 2015 introduced clarity on direct awards by explicitly requiring objective conditions to be used to select a supplier but observed frameworks allowing customers to make direct awards 'simply on the basis that they can determine which supplier can offer them the best solution for their requirement'.[36] It is apparent that the strict rules in the PCR 2015 applicable to making direct awards are not

[32] ibid 12.
[33] CPB4.
[34] CA3.
[35] LA15.
[36] CA14.

being complied with by all contracting authorities. Suppliers appear to take confidence from this with one interviewee drawing attention to suppliers' websites that advertise their products and services which can be bought directly through a framework. They viewed direct awards as 'being used as marketing tools' and questioned whether this is 'consistent with procurement ethics'.[37] It is important to acknowledge, however, that some interviewees were reluctant to use direct call-offs except for urgent requirements due to the lack of guidance on how to conduct these in a legally compliant manner.

There also appear to be instances in which contracting authorities have pre-determined their preferred supplier. Some contracting authorities take advantage of the direct award option if they know their precise requirements in advance of using the framework and the supplier they wish to deliver them. One interviewee described how their internal customer has usually 'done the deal with the supplier before they come to them looking for a route to contract'. One of their key suppliers was not reappointed to a particular framework and they 'had to hunt' for other frameworks that would allow them to use that supplier.[38] This is an archetypal example of 'framework shopping' representing poor procurement practice and, if widespread, calls into question the ongoing value of the framework tool and other regulated scoping mechanisms such as PME.

Nevertheless, frameworks that permit direct awards are appealing to contracting authorities because of the perceived speed and efficiency gains from not having to run any competition. Several legal advisers revealed that their clients frequently seek a framework allowing direct awards. Various interviewees highlighted that this could lead to direct award procedures being used inappropriately to procure solutions that, strictly speaking, should either be subject to mini-competition or a standalone competition outside the framework. An interviewee described a contracting authority using direct award procedures without spending sufficient time drawing up their specific requirements in advance. Rather than assessing their requirements against the service descriptions of the framework suppliers in a structured way, they stated that 'they jump straight to a supplier and engage in a series of clarifications to agree the scope and terms of a requirement'.[39]

Interviews also indicated that a direct call-off is not necessarily always an easy choice. One interviewee explained that they advise their customers to use this method only if, after considering the framework documentation and carrying out benchmarking, they can be assured it will enable a value for money solution but that disagreements on which supplier should be chosen through direct award still occur. As a result, they felt 'it is often fairer to run a mini-competition' rather than make a direct award.[40] It is submitted that if the application of a direct award procedure results in a debate over which supplier should be selected for a particular call-off, the framework does not contain sufficiently objective conditions to determine the call-off award in the first place.

Many legal advisers highlighted direct awards as one of the most legally problematic areas. As one explained, 'purchasers seem to be relying more and more on their

[37] CA10.
[38] CA12.
[39] CA8.
[40] CA12.

subjective discretion in choosing a supplier from frameworks rather than applying objective criteria'.[41] Their clients point to the vague buyer guides issued with frameworks as justification for using their subjective discretion to make direct awards. The consensus of legal advisers was that a contracting authority should be able to identify immediately which supplier should be chosen, applying the terms of the framework mechanistically. This would seem to be what is required by applying 'objective conditions' to select a supplier. Another legal adviser described the use of direct call-offs to procure requirements from suppliers that were not admitted to the framework, giving the example of an equipment and software framework (explained in chapter five) under which the reseller on the framework could not supply the required software itself, instead, offering to source it from a third party and charge 3 per cent on top of the subcontract price if it was procured through the framework.[42] This is corroborated by other studies, eg of procurement during the COVID-19 pandemic where suppliers appointed to frameworks that could not meet urgent requirements entered into arrangements with non-framework suppliers that could, raising a host of legal and practical problems.[43] Another interviewee described concluding a call-off with an incumbent supplier by way of direct award by roughly applying 'sole source principles' as justification. They used a direct award call-off mechanism from a framework on the understanding that this was permitted, notwithstanding that the objective conditions contained in the framework did not provide for this.[44] As indicated in chapter seven, this is not the only example of contracting authorities seeking to apply, by analogy, grounds for use of the negotiated procedure without prior publication of a contract notice (reg.32) to call-offs, the legality of which cannot be assumed.

Several suppliers mentioned the filtering tools incorporated in some of the largest pan-public sector ICT frameworks that allow direct call-offs and the resulting problems. One supplier had engaged with a customer contracting authority on a software requirement but lost the business to a competitor who directed the customer to a framework that allowed a direct award to be made to that competitor. The customer was unaware that the supplier was also on that framework, having not applied the filtering mechanisms properly.[45] As one interviewee stated, 'it is not in the customer's interest to input a vague requirement when using such tools'.[46]

4.2. Case Study of a Pan-public Sector, Direct Award-only Framework

There is a general perception that a few of the largest and most popular multi-supplier ICT frameworks have simply become 'transaction routes'[47] with call-off procedures leaving

[41] LA15.
[42] LA16.
[43] LRA Butler, *In Vitro Diagnostic Test Procurement During the COVID-19 Pandemic: Lessons Learnt and Recommendations* (BIVDA, 2022) 91.
[44] CA3.
[45] EO4.
[46] EO1.
[47] CPB1.

scope for significant abuse and circumvention of the legal rules. Most interviewees mentioned a specific framework that apparently 'has gargantuan levels of spend'[48] put through it. From the outset, it should be qualified that the framework is not named to preserve anonymity and this book does not purport to make any determination, inference or implication as to its legality but simply identifies the experiences of interviewees.

The framework is run by the largest CPA in the UK, is re-issued at regular intervals and only the direct award call-off procedure appears to be available. This framework is purportedly for the purchase of cloud-based solutions only and directs contracting authorities to an online digital marketplace where they can use an online search tool to filter and identify potential suppliers. This tool is used to create a longlist of suppliers' service offerings which is then refined to a shortlist that is evaluated and a supplier's service selected. With over 5,000 suppliers on the framework, contracting authorities must use keywords and filters to identify suitable suppliers and the service descriptions on offer; guidance is provided on how to do so. Irrespective of how many suppliers are identified from a search, it does not appear possible to hold a competition to award a call-off. Decisions must be based upon the service descriptions provided by suppliers although suppliers may be contacted to clarify their service description, terms and conditions, pricing or service definition documents. It is stated in the framework that no negotiation is allowed and that the award decision should be based on best fit using criteria relating to whole life cost, technical merit and functional fit, after-sales management and other non-functional characteristics.

However, interviewees identified uncertainty in applying the buyer guide that accompanies the framework. It provides that shortlisted suppliers can be evaluated using: (1) MEAT criteria or (2) direct award on lowest price only if they are comparable services. The guide also indicates that there are no specified evaluation weightings and that contracting authorities should determine their own evaluation criteria and weightings. It is suggested that, by referencing award criteria but also providing that these and corresponding weightings can be determined by each contracting authority, this call-off procedure appears to resemble an evaluation process that would be expected to be used for a mini-competition rather than for a direct award procedure without competition. It is not clear to what extent this call-off procedure complies with the requirement in regulation 33 to set out 'objective conditions' in the framework which are be used to determine which supplier should be awarded the call-off. By allowing flexibility in the criteria and weightings that can be applied, there may be a possible risk of user contracting authorities manipulating the criteria and weightings to award the contract to their preferred supplier.

Detailed views were expressed by interviewees on the use of this framework which justifies its treatment as a 'case study' for this book. Many interviewees stated that it provides a useful and swift route to contract particularly when the contracting authority knows which supplier it wants to use. As one interviewee remarked, a 'point and click' technique is used whereby 'purchasers generally know what they want and are fed a search term by the suppliers'.[49] Another interviewee found this framework 'very useful if an internal customer wants to use a particular supplier' and use 'particular phrases' in

[48] ibid.
[49] ibid.

the filtering tool to locate the supplier they needed to find.[50] Interviewees from suppliers supported this with one interviewee explaining how such frameworks are useful 'where a customer is seeking an extension to an existing call-off' or 'to deliver complementary services' and where it might not be economically feasible to switch from the incumbent supplier.[51] Another interviewee from a supplier noted that this framework can provide 'a low effort-high chance of winning' but said that 'for larger scale products such as digital transformations, it is only useful if the customer has a particular supplier in mind'.[52] However, this calls into question whether a direct award framework is being used in a way that is a less stringent alternative to using one of the grounds in regulation 32 PCR permitting use of the negotiated procedure without prior publication of a contract notice to make a direct award. Regulation 32 applies in very limited circumstances where there is only one or a limited number of suppliers that can perform a particular contract and provided certain conditions are satisfied. The sole fact that a particular supplier is an incumbent supplier is unlikely to be considered an 'objective condition' justifying a direct award under PCR rules on frameworks.

Many interviewees considered this framework to have been potentially misused. One referred to the 'magic word search' by contracting authorities which results in them asking suppliers 'clarification questions'. It was stated that this can morph into a 'pseudo-competition' by the contracting authority comparing supplier information.[53] Another interviewee explained that when using the filters and keyword search tools, it is not uncommon to get a list of over 100 suppliers that can meet a requirement. They described how suppliers upload their own 'service definition' document but, as there is no standardised format for this document, it is difficult to compare the respective offerings of each supplier.[54] Further, whilst another interviewee considered this framework to be useful for urgent, low-value ICT requirements, they considered that purchasers are not spending sufficient time drawing up a list of requirements and comparing them against the supplier service descriptions in a well-structured way. Instead, they identify a supplier and engage in a series of 'clarifications' to agree the scope and terms of a requirement.[55]

Interviewees highlighted how light the procurement procedure is for suppliers to get on to this framework. It was conveyed how contracting authorities may be using the framework under the misconception that the CPA running it has properly vetted all suppliers and so contracting authorities may not see the need for additional checks at the call-off stage. However, as one interviewee commented, 'in reality, very limited information is required from suppliers to get on to this framework' and that 'virtually the entire ICT marketplace is on there', adding, 'it constitutes a catalogue where you can select a software supplier completely freely, but it is badged as a framework not an electronic catalogue'.[56] As another interviewee observed, 'it often comes down to which suppliers have the best marketing teams'.[57]

[50] CA12.
[51] EO1.
[52] EO7.
[53] CPB4.
[54] CA5.
[55] CA8.
[56] CA14.
[57] LA18.

Relatedly, whilst this framework was cited by some as being SME friendly due to SMEs having been successful in securing work under it, this was not always the case. One interviewee referred to the 'propaganda' that surrounded its first iteration which included claims that the framework would be beneficial for SMEs; however, this interviewee perceived that 'SMEs get a very small proportion of the work on this framework'.[58] Other interviewees gave examples of the call-off contract values that have been put through this framework. These vary significantly depending on the subject-matter of the call-off. Two examples had contract values of £20 million and £100 million, respectively, demonstrating the enormous spend and indicating that large ICT suppliers have also been successful in securing work. This raises the question of whether frameworks are generally suitable tools for procuring solutions that range so significantly in value, also bearing in mind the legal obligations and practical exercise required in estimating the value of the framework.

Concerns were raised about a lack of monitoring and enforcement. One interviewee stated that no quality assurance was carried out by the CPA on the suppliers' products and services and there was no assessment of supplier sustainability. Instead, contracting authorities were told that 'caveat emptor' applied to this marketplace and that they must take responsibility for supplier due diligence. In this regard, they gave an example in which they had sought a product from a supplier on this framework but, after a series of clarifications with the supplier, it was revealed that they would be required to purchase it directly from a US parent company in US dollars, the UK entity simply acting as a 'shell company carrying out marketing activity'.[59]

A few interviewees had suggestions for how frameworks such as this could be set up to work better. Some considered that further shortlisting should be possible at the call-off stage followed by a genuine mini-competition. One interviewee appealed for a robust filtering system using a 'command set of data' followed by 'light-touch' clarification questions and physical demonstrations of solutions by suppliers.[60]

Some surprise was expressed that this framework had not yet been subject to a formal legal challenge. One interviewee stated that they had come across several instances of misuse involving, for example, the artificial narrowing of the supplier base that could meet a requirement, the use of the framework to procure ICT professional services not within scope of the framework and call-offs being entered into for well over the maximum call-off duration permitted under the framework.[61] Notwithstanding this and other concerns raised by interviewees, there was a general perception that each iteration and use of this framework attracts little practical risk of legal challenge. It has been endorsed and used widely across the public sector and there is little transparency in respect of how awards are made that may enable suppliers to make informed challenges. One interviewee stated that they allocated a low risk of challenge to using this framework provided that a reasonable justification for the approach taken could be documented and sufficient time allowed to conduct a fair evaluation of suppliers.[62]

[58] EO3.
[59] CA7.
[60] CA9.
[61] CA15.
[62] CA10.

A legal adviser stated that many direct awards are based on subjective assessments now but 'are so well established that it would take a brave claimant to challenge such practices'.[63]

4.3. Use of Direct Awards in Frameworks under the PA 2023

Similar to the position under the PCR 2015, it is recalled that under ss.45(3) and (4), it is permissible to set up a hybrid framework that allows awards pursuant to a competitive selection process or without competition. It is also permissible to set up a framework that only allows direct call-off awards without competition, thus the phenomenon of a 'direct award' framework will continue in the UK. As explained, the PA 2023 removes from the definition of a 'framework' the essential purpose of a framework focused on establishing the terms of call-offs and it is not strictly required to use pricing criteria to appoint suppliers to a framework. This risks the continued propagation of direct award frameworks with little to no substantive competition on, and settlement of, key terms at the framework award stage.

As explained in chapter seven, the PA 2023 relaxes the conditions that need to be satisfied for a contracting authority to make a direct award. It is recalled that section 45(4) provides that a multi-supplier framework may provide for the future award of a public contract without competition between suppliers if the framework sets out: (a) the core terms of the public contract; and (b) an objective mechanism for supplier selection. This introduces additional flexibility to the set-up and use of frameworks that allow direct call-off awards without competition. There is a risk, therefore, that the problems highlighted above on the use of direct award call-off procedures under frameworks will not be addressed and may even be compounded by the diluted provisions of the PA 2023. This risk needs to be assessed in light of other controls in the PA 2023, however, most importantly, the application of the section 12 procurement objectives and the transparency requirements with regard to the publication of notices. It remains to be seen to what extent these will provide effective constraint on the use of direct call-off procedures.

Regarding notices, pursuant to section 50(1), regulation 27(2)(h) PR 2024 provides that the contract award notice must contain certain information in relation to the framework including, for example, details of whether a competitive selection process or a direct award without further competition was used to award the public contract. Further, whereas regulation 50(4) PCR 2015 provided that contracting authorities were not required to publish notices of the results of call of procedures in contract award notices, under the PA 2023, where call-offs awarded pursuant to a call-off procedure under a framework constitute a public contract (ie are above threshold and not exempt), the same requirement will apply. This is the case whether the call-off was the result of a competitive selection process or direct award. Regulation 27(2)(h) PR 2024 provides that the contract award notice must contain certain information in relation to the framework, including for example, details of whether a competitive selection process or a direct award without further competition was used to award the public contract.

[63] LA9.

In addition, section 53(1) provides that a contracting authority must publish a contract details notice. In relation to the award of the framework regulation 33(2)(j) requires details of the selection process to be applied on the award of a contract in accordance with the framework. Regulation 34(2) provides that the contract details notice must contain certain information including details of whether the competitive selection process or award without competition was used and, if the latter, why the contracting authority considered that it applies by reference to section 45(4) ie to the framework setting out the core terms of the public contract and an objective mechanism for supplier selection.

Whilst the requirement to publish a contract award notice and contract details notice for the award of a public contract without competition under a framework increases the transparency of such direct call-offs, it is submitted that the level of transparency is somewhat limited and does not significantly increase transparency over the operation of the direct award procedures under the framework. For instance, there is no requirement to provide the framework suppliers with information about how the contracting authority has applied the framework call-off procedures before it signs the public contract with the selected supplier. Whilst an explanation of why the contracting authority considered that a direct award without competition could be made must be included in the contract details notice, this is post-contract award and it is not clear what level of detail is required to be included in the notice. A contracting authority will need to comply with the section 12 procurement objective to have regard to the importance of sharing information for the purpose of allowing suppliers and others to understand the authority's procurement policies and decisions but this does not clearly require full details of how the contracting authority has applied the framework call-off procedures to award the public contract. It is submitted that the GCF guidance should have clarified the level of information that needs to be included in the notice.

This increase in transparency is unlikely, by itself, to deter contracting authorities from setting up opaque direct award call-off procedures without competition nor from using them, particularly given the increased flexibility that has now been built into such call-off procedures compared with that available under the PCR 2015.

It is also significant that the requirement to publish a contract award notice does not apply to below-threshold contracts and a contract details notice need only be published for below-threshold contracts over a certain value (set out in section 87(4)); regulation 36 PR 2024 indicates that such a contract details notice need not include an explanation of why the contracting authority considered a direct award without competition under a framework could be made.

5. Running Mini-competitions

5.1. Running Mini-competitions and Use of Award Criteria in Practice under the PCR 2015

As indicated in chapter six, multi-supplier frameworks involving the appointment of unlimited or too many suppliers can have various consequences, including at the call-off stage. One of the largest barriers to using a mini-competition can be an excessive number of suppliers to manage and which negates the purpose and administrative efficiencies of using a framework, particularly if the framework simply replicates the size of the general market.[64]

As explained, there may be a lack of relevant expertise, experience and capacity to run an effective mini-competition. One interviewee had come across a contracting authority using a third party to run mini-competitions on their behalf instead and to administer the call-offs because of the lack of in-house expertise and capacity.[65] This explains the attractiveness of some frameworks operated by more professionalised and well-resourced CPAs who offer support in running mini-competitions but which is likely to attract additional cost.

The amount of flexibility permitted for contracting authorities to formulate award criteria and weightings appropriate for their call-off contract requirements is also an important factor influencing their decision of whether to use a framework. Whilst it appears that contracting authorities may appreciate a degree of flexibility, legal advisers explained that clients regularly ask them to advise on running a mini-competition, presumably requiring resource and expense.[66] One legal adviser had noticed less appetite for running mini-competitions in recent years on the basis that 'they are not considered as beneficial as they used to be' because of failures to limit the number of suppliers and difficulties in identifying which suppliers to invite.[67]

Chapter seven examined the legal rules on the formulation of award criteria to be used at the call-off stage and the attendant legal uncertainty. This has been borne out in practice with one interviewee explaining that 'it is not always clear whether you have to use such criteria, whether you can change them and whether you can change the weightings and if so by how much/how to go about doing this'. Whilst 'buyer guides' are issued by CPAs, there were pleas from this and other interviewees for more guidance and for clarification of the legal rules in this area. An interviewee stated that 'there used to be more uniformity years ago but as they have become more flexible they have diversified in their structure, content and rules', creating a burden.[68] They expressed a frequently held view that a CPA 'needs to educate buyers on how to use frameworks properly rather than focusing on how much revenue it can put through its frameworks'.[69]

However, some interviewees from contracting authorities were comfortable with the apparent flexibility allowed under many frameworks and the lack of detailed, prescriptive rules on the use of award criteria and weightings. However, it must be qualified that such contracting authorities usually have considerable expertise and experience in using frameworks and can gauge the practical risks of taking advantage of the perceived flexibilities. One interviewee described a framework that specifies generic award criteria, stating that whilst they were experienced and 'able to understand the grey areas between the black and white and how to use frameworks to the customer's advantage',

[64] LA1.
[65] LA7.
[66] LA6.
[67] LA7.
[68] CA12, CA4.
[69] CA10.

some contracting authorities lacked sufficient expertise and 'struggle to understand how to use the evaluation criteria to get the best outcome'.[70]

One legal adviser had come across instances of contracting authorities using 'materially different' mini-competition call-off procedures from those set out in the framework which were 'lacking in transparency'.[71] These could conceivably constitute unlawful 'substantial modifications' being made to the framework in breach of regulation 72.

From a supplier perspective, there were concerns about the ability of SMEs to compete successfully in mini-competitions. One interviewee stated, 'if they keep coming bottom in mini-competitions they will stop competing'.[72] Further, suppliers that had been successful in securing call-off contracts through direct awards clearly preferred these to mini-competitions. Nevertheless, there was acknowledgment from suppliers that contracting authorities need to run mini-competitions for some requirements. As one interviewee explained, mini-competitions are sometimes a 'necessary evil' for more complex requirements.[73] Participating in mini-competitions can be costly and time-consuming for suppliers, however, and suppliers appear to have become more selective about whether to participate in a mini-competition in recent years. One interviewee explained how they restrict their mini-competition bids to customers they already have a good relationship with and 'do not waste time on speculative bids'.[74] There are indications that further guidance may be needed to support both contracting authorities running mini-competitions and SMEs and other suppliers bidding through them.

The management of an existing incumbent supplier can also pose difficulties for contracting authorities looking to use a framework to procure a follow-on contract for an ICT solution. The incumbent might not be a supplier on the relevant framework meaning they would be unable to bid for the new contract. Even when the incumbent is on the framework, interviewees reported problems of using a mini-competition to award the call-off, particularly when the incumbent may have an advantage over other bidders. Incumbents may have access to more knowledge and information, may have embedded products that are difficult or costly to switch from, and will be familiar with the contracting authority's requirements. It is perhaps therefore unsurprising that contracting authorities may be led to frameworks on which an incumbent is an appointed supplier and where direct call-offs are permitted.

EU case law indicates that it is a well-established principle that a contracting authority needs to neutralise an incumbent advantage only to the extent that it is technically easy and economically acceptable, and where it does not infringe the rights of the incumbent.[75] However, incumbents might not be forthcoming with the information (eg, employee information, software ownership/licensing information and other technical information) required by the contracting authority to run a competition. As one interviewee stated, 'incumbents often can be very difficult to manage if they are unsuccessful

[70] ibid.
[71] LA17.
[72] CA10.
[73] EO2.
[74] EO7.
[75] Case T-345/03 *Evropaïki Dynamiki v Commission* [2008] ECR II-341. See also Case T-211-17 *Amplexor Luxembourg Sàrl v European Commission* ECLI:EU:T:2018:392 and Case T-10/17 *Proof IT SIA v European Institute for Gender Equality* ECLI:EU:T:2018:682.

on contract re-let and difficult tie-in issues have to be overcome'.[76] One interviewee described an incumbent sometimes submitting unsolicited proposals informally and attempting to influence the drafting of the specification to align with its solution.[77] The issue of managing incumbent suppliers is not exclusive to the use of frameworks but their closed nature and compressed tender timescales for a mini-competition can make it particularly challenging in the framework context.

5.2. Running Mini-competitions and Use of Award Criteria under the PA 2023

Concerning potential controls on the number of suppliers involved in a mini-competition, as explained in chapter six, it was implicit in the PCR 2015 provisions on frameworks that a limit should usually be placed on the number of suppliers appointed to the framework. However, as demonstrated in the case study above, frameworks have been set up and are being used which have not set any limit. By contrast, section 45 explicitly permits a framework to be set up with an unlimited number of suppliers. Again, it will be necessary to consider the section 12 procurement objectives as potential restraints on appointment with a view to their effects on the competitive selection call-off procedure. In particular, it may be conceived how having regard to the importance of value for money, sharing information and barriers to SME participation could lead to a contracting authority considering limiting the number of appointed suppliers to make the framework effective. However, as observed, it is not clear what, if any, practical impact these objectives may have.

Other tools exist that could be used to limit the pool of suppliers invited to participate in a competitive selection process. As with the PCR 2015 regime, section 18 provides that a contracting authority may divide a framework into lots with a limited number of suppliers on each lot. It is recalled from chapter seven that section 46(1) includes a new flexibility enabling contracting authorities to introduce supplementary conditions of participation when running a competitive selection process, and which could be used to reduce the pool of suppliers invited to tender for a call-off contract.

It is submitted, however, that it would have been preferable to expressly prohibit frameworks with unlimited numbers of suppliers, perhaps subject only to exceptionally justified instances where this may be necessary. This would have distinguished frameworks more clearly from other procurement tools such as dynamic markets and helped to drive better procurement practice by encouraging contracting authorities to focus on designing an effective procurement procedure to appoint the framework suppliers in the first instance.

Concerning the use of award criteria in a competitive selection process, the PA 2023 resolves some uncertainty in practice by clarifying in ss.46(8) and (9) that a competitive selection process may provide for the assessment of proposals 'but only by reference to one or more of the award criteria against which tenders were assessed in awarding

[76] CA6.
[77] CA7.

the framework' and that such criteria may be 'refined'. It is therefore not permissible to introduce wholly different award criteria at the call-off stage from those used to award the framework. The GCF guidance provides that 'additional sub-criteria may be included or the criteria explained further'.[78] Of course, the issue remains as to the permissible limits of refinement within a new regime ostensibly predicated on flexibility.[79]

The PA 2023 does not expressly address managing incumbents and the extent to which the playing field can be levelled for all framework suppliers participating in a mini-competition. Section 12 requires contracting authorities to 'treat suppliers the same unless a difference between the suppliers justifies different treatment' and '[i]f a contracting authority considers that different treatment is justified in a particular case, the authority must take all reasonable steps to ensure it does not put a supplier at an unfair advantage or disadvantage'. It is likely that similar considerations arising from the EU case law on addressing incumbent advantage will need to be considered under the new legal regime. Further, section 12 requires contracting authorities to have regard to barriers facing SMEs but this duty is not legally enforceable (section 100(5)).

Ultimately, other than introducing more flexibility in terms of the use of supplementary conditions of participation and clarifying the use of award criteria, the PA 2023 does not specify in detail how a competitive selection process should be conducted, nor does the GCF guidance elaborate on this matter. Contracting authorities using a CPA's framework are therefore likely to be faced with similar challenges as under the PCR 2015 when formulating a competitive selection process and still require training and support in this regard. This will particularly be the case if it is unclear how a CPA's framework procedures are to be operated or if the CPA leaves the majority of decisions on the process to the discretion of user contracting authorities.

6. Finalising Call-off Contract Terms

6.1. Finalising Call-off Contract Terms (for both Direct Awards and Mini-competitions) under the PCR 2015

As explained in chapter seven, it is integral to the PCR 2015 definition of a framework agreement that the procedure for awarding the framework should be used to establish the terms in as complete a form as possible, acknowledging that some terms may need to be finalised or refined at the call-off stage. As discussed, for most procurements, price should feature in the competition to award the framework and cannot be left solely to the call-off stage. This is especially important if the contracting authority wishes to limit the number of suppliers based on their tenders to proceed to the call-off stage. If there is no assessment of price at the framework award stage, the contracting authority would risk creating a closed list of appointed suppliers that have not been assessed by reference to a major award criterion, thereby restricting competition (contrary to regulation 18).

[78] GCF, 'Guidance: Frameworks', November 2024, 9.

[79] See generally, R Rees and LRA Butler, 'Using the right procurement procedures: selecting competitive award procedures under the Procurement Act 2023' (2024) 6 *PPLR* 345–400.

Under the PCR 2015, regulation 33(8)(a) indicates that the terms for call-offs awarded using a direct award call-off procedure without competition should be completely settled with framework suppliers at the time the framework is awarded. Call-offs can then be awarded based on these pre-agreed terms only. Regulation 33(11) indicates that for call-offs awarded pursuant to a mini-competition procedure, there is some scope for agreeing more precisely formulated and other terms.

6.1.1. *Finalising Call-off Contract Terms (for both Direct Awards and Mini-competitions) in Practice under the PCR 2015*

Despite the distinction made in the law between the degree to which call-off terms need to be settled when awarding direct call-offs as opposed to call-offs made by way of mini-competition, interviewees reported problems agreeing call-off terms with suppliers using both procedures and did not readily distinguish between them when describing the difficulties encountered. More generally, it is concerning that interviews suggested that, in practice, agreement of the call-off terms tends to occur at the end of the call-off procedure, which can delay contract conclusion and risks contracting authorities agreeing to substantial modifications to the framework terms.

From the outset, it is worth reiterating that interviewees stated that frameworks can be attractive because of the perceived ease of contracting in the knowledge that the contractual terms and conditions have already been either fully or at least substantially agreed.[80] As many interviewees from contracting authorities attested, a key driver affecting their decision to use a framework is whether the call-off contract terms are acceptable and appropriate. The applicable call-off terms are readily accessible online for many generic frameworks and this level of transparency was highlighted as being very helpful when surveying the framework market.[81]

However, many interviewees relayed practical difficulties when trying to agree the call-off terms with suppliers. Some frameworks were considered to have been set up without sufficient PME with the contracting authority and suppliers. There were also perceptions that the call-off terms on some frameworks had been designed for the specific requirements of a handful of contracting authorities, even though the framework was made available to a wider group of contracting authorities.

It was also felt that the call-off terms on some frameworks were not as favourable as they should be for contracting authorities because CPAs used the call-off terms to lure some major ICT suppliers to join. One interviewee commented that 'the terms and conditions are as a result often biased towards the big original equipment manufacturers'.[82] This attentiveness to supplier inputs above contracting authority users is another indicator of framework marketisation. In another interviewee's experience, certain large suppliers have secured 'preferential arrangements' by applying pressure to incorporate contractual options into call-offs 'which are not strictly allowed under the framework' and using this as a precedent for repeating such behaviour in future

[80] CA13.
[81] CA4.
[82] ibid.

call-offs.[83] Certain often-used call-off terms were highlighted as being problematic, including terms relating to liability, intellectual property, duration, making variations and, particularly for ICT contracts, data access, transfer and security. One interviewee had come across inappropriate standard data protection provisions and unacceptable data processing agreements proposed by suppliers. They experienced a conflict between the call-off terms set out in the framework and those proposed by the supplier at the point of call-off.[84]

There can also be a lack of clarity on the final agreed call-off terms. Some interviewees raised the difficult of agreeing on end user licence agreements with software suppliers in the supply chain not on the framework. Several interviewees were, however, accepting of the imposition of such end user licence agreements of large software suppliers at call-off stage, one considering that these simply highlighted how to use a licence and not viewing them as part of the call-off contract itself. They acknowledged that more transparency could be achieved by the end user licence agreements being provided upfront and as part of the agreed framework documentation, but considered that it was a case of '*caveat emptor*' and that software manufacturers were 'entitled to flow down these non-negotiable terms and conditions and it is simply up to the purchasing authority whether to accept them'.[85] This issue may not be exclusive to ICT requirements; it is possible to envisage third party contracts being relevant for other requirements where a contractor in the supply chain might require a direct contractual relationship with the end customer.

An 'order of precedence' approach adopted in many frameworks mitigates against suppliers presenting their own contract terms at the call-off stage.[86] This involves including a contract clause in the framework stating that the core terms of the framework will, in the event of conflict, take precedence over any other terms incorporated in the call-off documents. A call-off contract template will frequently be structured in a way that sets out the core framework terms in the main body, with separate schedules (some mandatory, some optional) in which contracting authorities and suppliers can insert the specific or 'special' terms applicable to the call-off. To clarify, the supplementation, and introduction, of new terms at call-off stage should only occur when using the mini-competition procedure due to the requirement for all the terms to be set out in the framework for direct call-off awards without competition. This difference requires clarification and guidance from the Government, however, due to the blurring of this distinction in practice. Another interviewee stated that 'some public buyers are not aware of the order of precedence and sometimes create a whole set of terms and conditions just using the call-off terms and the supplier's terms and are not aware that the framework conditions also apply'.[87]

Not all contracting authorities have the requisite expertise and experience to agree contract terms for ICT requirements, particularly when complex. Whilst schedules leave space to insert important requirements, as one interviewee witnessed, 'these schedules

[83] CA10.
[84] CA2.
[85] CA3.
[86] CA6, CA8.
[87] CA10.

include important aspects such as KPIs and score cards' and 'provide an opportunity for customers to insert much needed checks and controls to ensure satisfactory service delivery, but they are often left unpopulated – therefore a missed opportunity'. They thought that more guidance on using these schedules should be included in framework documentation.[88] Such omissions may only end up in further protracted negotiations with the supplier.[89]

There is a sense that the volume and complexity of the call-off documentation can be disproportionate to the subject-matter being procured and which can be a burden.[90] It seems that, as discussed in chapter ten, some upskilling and training is required for procurement teams using frameworks. This may be particularly challenging, however, given the CPA market and the significant variances between the different framework models used. If all frameworks followed a similar contractual structure and level of content, it would be easier for procurement teams to use and apply framework documentation in practice.

When the call-off terms are perceived to either party, it may be questioned whether it is possible to amend the relevant terms to make them more acceptable prior to concluding the call-off. Many contracting authorities will not use a framework that contains unacceptable terms. Difficulties can arise, however, when the chosen framework supplier proposes amendments to the core terms at the call-off stage. As one interviewee explained, contracting authorities faced with this possibility may consult their internal policies and seek legal advice, particularly when the proposed amendment would entail a significant change to the framework terms and, therefore, attract increased legal risk of non-compliance. Depending on which CPA 'owns' the framework, they might also consult the relevant framework lead for advice on whether the amendment can be made, and the degree of legal risk involved.[91] It appears that proposing amendments to call-off terms is a common occurrence when using ICT frameworks, which may highlight the difficulty or impracticability of agreeing call-off terms at the framework award stage for such requirements. For complex ICT requirements, there was a consensus amongst interviewees that not all terms can be agreed at the framework award stage, and much is left to the call-off stage to finalise, commonly referred to as 'backloading'. Some interviewees suggested that room for contract negotiation at the call-off stage should be expressly permitted by the rules and not just left to be dealt with by reference to the substantial modification rules in regulation 72. As explored in chapter five, the utility of frameworks for complex projects is doubtful; if significant changes to the call-off terms are needed at the call-off stage, this casts doubt on whether a framework was the most appropriate route to contract in the first place.

A few interviewees provided examples of opportunistic behaviour in which suppliers presented wholly different contract terms at the call-off stage and which was not limited to complex requirements. One interviewee procuring ICT consultancy services for a defined project described how a supplier proposed a new set of terms at the call-off stage involving a bundle of support services which would significantly increase the price.[92] Several

[88] CA4.
[89] CA13.
[90] CA9.
[91] CA8.
[92] CA7.

interviewees highlighted that the ICT sector is particularly prone to such behaviour. Another interviewee described how they escalate any such issues to the CPA but stressed how difficult it could be to finalise the contract when dealing with experienced suppliers.[93]

Interviewees from suppliers were in consensus that many contracting authority customers required assistance from suppliers in finalising call-off documentation.[94] Again, this depended on levels of expertise and capacity in contracting authorities, but it appears that ICT suppliers are commonly called upon by contracting authorities to pull together contract terms. This is hardly likely to discourage any opportunistic behaviour by suppliers keen to insert terms favourable to them at the final stage and is another indicator of framework marketisation. It would be helpful if all CPAs set out clearly in the framework documentation the rules applicable to finalising the contract terms.

The amount of competition between suppliers at the call-off stage may also influence their tactics when finalising the contract terms. As one legal adviser stated 'if there is no competition, they will ask a huge amount of clarifications' because 'otherwise, they will wait until they have won the call-off and then start negotiating'.[95] In one instance, a supplier took a transparent approach by issuing to the potential framework customers an 'information document about the different changes they would make for different call-off project scenarios'.[96] It is suggested that CPAs are best placed to control such supplier behaviours given their risk of late negotiations undermining equal treatment, and that more proactivity might help to drive better practice at this stage.

Some of the legal advisers indicated that it could be difficult to reconcile the negotiation of call-off terms with the strict legal rules. According to one interviewee, 'it is a very grey area in terms of how far you can go in amending the template terms' and that 'the easiest rule of thumb is that the more you are moving away from the standard framework terms the more risk you will attract'.[97] When contracting authorities are faced with the possibility of suppliers introducing their own contract terms or amendments to the framework's call-off contract terms, a risk-based approach is commonly adopted in consultation with legal advisers but it can be difficult to assess whether any such new terms or amendments to existing terms constitute unlawful substantial modifications to the framework under regulation 72. The rules on making modifications to frameworks are explored further below.

6.2. Finalising Call-off Contract Terms (for Awards without Competition and Using the Competitive Selection Process) under the PA 2023

It is implicit in the new provisions on frameworks under the PA 2023 that there is increased scope for agreeing call-off terms post-award of the framework. The increased flexibility may be an acknowledgement of the practices described above; namely, contracting

[93] CA14.
[94] EO2.
[95] LA5.
[96] LA4.
[97] LA7.

authorities having to spend time at the call-off stage negotiating and finalising the terms of call-offs with selected suppliers. The risk-based approach described above to agreeing call-off terms is therefore likely to persist.

Concerning call-off terms for awards without competition, as explained in chapter seven and above, the framework no longer needs to set out all the terms governing the provision of the works, services or supplies concerned, only the 'core terms' and there is a degree of uncertainty about what these comprise. It is also not clear what process is to be followed for agreeing the non-core terms given that no further competition is to be held between the framework suppliers. If the core terms do not constitute a complete set of terms that the parties would be able to contract under, a contracting authority that applies the 'objective mechanism' to select a supplier for a call-off may need to enter a period of negotiation with the selected supplier to agree the outstanding terms and finalise the call-off. A contracting authority can no longer point to a requirement that all the terms need to be set out in the framework to rebut the imposition of additional terms by a supplier at the call-off stage. This may give suppliers some bargaining power to impose additional terms with contracting authorities then needing to consider whether the introduction of such terms involves any substantial changes to the 'core terms' or otherwise constitutes a substantial change that would be unlawful under the new contract modification provisions in section 74 or breaches the PA 2023 in another respect eg the section 12 procurement objectives to 'treat suppliers the same unless a difference between the suppliers justifies different treatment'.

To take one example, a core term may be the 'pricing mechanism'. Given that there are no specific requirements in the legislation or guidance to explain what such a pricing mechanism should include, it is possible to envisage a pricing mechanism being set up in loose terms which evolves into a price negotiation exercise when the parties come to finalise the terms of a call-off. The list of example core terms in the GCF guidance and Explanatory Notes does not reference terms relating to intellectual property rights. It is therefore conceivable that suppliers in the ICT sector will continue to seek to introduce their own such terms.

Concerning call-off awards using the competitive selection process, there is now much more scope for agreeing terms at the call-off stage than under the PCR 2015. Regulation 33(11) required mini-competitions to be based on the same terms as applied for the award of the framework, where necessary, more precisely formulated terms and, where appropriate, other terms referred to in the procurement documents for the framework. The PA 2023 contains no such stipulation. Section 45(5) simply requires that the framework must include prescribed information but there is no reference to the establishment of call-off terms (except reference to a pricing mechanism) when using the competitive selection process. Similarly, there is no focus on the call-off terms when applying a competitive selection process for award of the call-off. Section 46 devotes most attention to conditions of participation and, only to a much lesser extent, assessment of proposals by reference to the award criteria at the framework award stage. There is no explicit provision in respect of agreeing call-off terms. Indeed, the focus on regulating conditions of participation at the call-off stage seems disproportionate when considered relative to the importance of negotiating and finalising call-off terms.

Ultimately, it looks somewhat anomalous that there is no meaningful provision in respect of call-off terms even acknowledging that certain issues will be a matter of contractual agreement. It is also surprising that no further guidance has been provided in respect of this decisive stage.

7. Evaluating Price

7.1. Evaluating Price in Mini-competitions in Practice under the PCR 2015

As submitted in chapter seven, a framework under which price is generally left to be determined at the mini-competition stage, without any reference to even a pricing mechanism established at the appointment stage, is unlikely to comply with the PCR 2015 and EU procurement principles. However, it is acknowledged that it can be challenging when setting up frameworks to establish pricing or pricing mechanisms to be applied to the award of call-offs. Many interviewees raised concerns about the pricing of call-offs, particularly for complex requirements.

Despite the legal requirements, there can be a lack of correspondence between the pricing exercise conducted at the framework award stage (if such exercise has even been carried out) and the pricing agreed for a particular call-off. The framework itself may omit entirely certain elements critical to pricing. One interviewee had experienced a supplier who had asked for payment in US dollars rather than pounds sterling, meaning that they had to account for the transaction and exchange rate fees, but the framework terms did not address this risk.[98] Even where the framework provides a pricing mechanism, it may be difficult to forecast prices based on hypotheticals as distinct from requirements as they arise at the call-off stage. One interviewee stated that 'day rates are often meaningless as the real price will come at the competition stage'.[99] Interviewees also gave examples of when the pricing quoted by a supplier in a mini-competition had only a weak link to the price list or schedule of rates agreed at the appointment stage, and instances in which there had been attempts by suppliers to replace the framework pricing methodology with their own at the call-off stage.[100]

Some interviewees noticed that the prices under frameworks can be higher than would be charged outside the framework, one interviewee describing how suppliers built an element of risk into their framework prices to address the perceived level of uncertainty about the volume and value of call-offs they might win under the framework.[101] Another interviewee had perceived 'suppliers taking advantage of complacent customers' and sought external consultancy support to verify the prices that suppliers were charging under frameworks, discovering that some were charging inflated profit percentages.[102]

Interviewees also raised concerns about value for money and pricing transparency when procuring through frameworks. A framework was described under which the

[98] CA4.
[99] ibid.
[100] CA14.
[101] CA10.
[102] CA12.

same pricing for commodity ICT items applied whatever the volume being procured, whereas a better deal based on volume purchased would have been achievable outside the framework.[103]

Notwithstanding, several interviewees highlighted that running mini-competitions was preferable to using direct award call-off procedures to obtain value for money in flushing out 'bad behaviours such as the loading of hours' due to the competitive tension present.[104] There was much less transparency in the use of direct award call-off procedures, with the result that some of these 'bad behaviours' went unchecked in respect of pricing.

Whilst the empirical research did not investigate the economic effects of frameworks in respect of pricing charged to public sector customers, as discussed in chapter ten, this is an area that certainly requires further investigation. It would be useful to compare pricing charged through frameworks with pricing charged for similar products and services outside frameworks.

7.2. Assessing 'Price' Using the Competitive Selection Process under the PA 2023

As explained above, there is much uncertainty on what is required at the framework award stage to establish the price payable or mechanism for determining the price payable under call-offs, for those awarded both with and without competition. Whilst the application of the section 12 procurement objectives, particularly having regard to the importance of delivering value for money, may help guide contracting authorities on the extent to which prices can and should be established at framework award, this places a discretionary burden on contracting authorities and may lead to poor procurement decisions driven more by objectives relating to simplifying the procedure to appoint the framework suppliers and leaving as much discretion as possible to user contracting authorities.

Nevertheless, it is assumed that there should be more scope for agreeing pricing at the call-off stage when using the competitive selection process than when making a call-off award without competition. That would be consistent with how the two call-off procedures have been distinguished in the PCR 2015. However, it is not clear how (or whether) the requirement in section 45(5)(b) to include in a framework 'the price payable, or mechanism for determining the price payable, under such contracts' differs between call-off awards made without competition and call-off awards made using the competitive selection process. This distinction is further elided when considering the requirement under section 46(8) and (9) that the award criteria used in a competitive selection process under a framework must be by reference to one or more of the award criteria against which tenders were assessed in awarding the framework although such criteria may be 'refined'. It is not clear what this means for pricing award criteria, particularly if it is sufficient to establish a 'pricing mechanism' in the framework rather

[103] LA10.
[104] ibid.

than the actual prices chargeable. When making a call-off award without competition, there is no explicit requirement that the price payable or pricing mechanism used relates back to any award criteria used to award the framework, although the 'charges and pricing mechanism' is given as an example in Explanatory Note to the PA 2023 of a 'core term' that must be set out in the framework.

The distinction between the establishment and use of prices and pricing mechanisms in respect of call-offs without competition and call-offs using the competitive selection process is a point that requires clarification and guidance.

8. A 'Framework Within a Framework'

8.1. A 'Framework Within a Framework' under the PCR 2015

Another aspect that has raised compliance concerns in practice is emerging concepts of a 'framework within a framework'. Several interviewees had come across this in the single-supplier framework context when a single supplier is awarded a framework and permitted under its terms to set up a framework type arrangement or supplier network at the sub-contract level. Interviewees mentioned the existence of certain 'neutral vendor' frameworks in operation. These can involve the award of a very broadly scoped framework to an intermediary company for use by the entire public sector. Contracting authorities liaise directly with the single supplier to identify a supplier at the sub-contract level that can meet their requirements. All interviewees who mentioned this phenomenon queried their compatibility with the PCR 2015.

The term 'framework within a framework' was also mentioned by interviewees in the multi-supplier framework context. First, the term was used to describe a supplier on a multi-supplier framework being awarded a call-off with a very wide, generic scope which was subsequently amended several times to incorporate additional supplies and services. An interviewee described how a supplier's sales team uses the framework documentation 'like order forms just to get the customer on contract and then the contract would gradually be inflated through change control'. One legal adviser had been asked to advise on a framework supplier being awarded a 'package of works' using a single call-off contract under a framework. They highlighted considerable uncertainty among contracting authorities about what is permissible to stay within the legal bounds of a framework.[105] Such arrangements are likely in the ICT sector given that technology evolves and changes become necessary.[106]

Second, the term was used to refer to a supplier on a multi-supplier framework being awarded a call-off under which it proposed to set up a network or 'sub-framework' of suppliers. A legal adviser referred to it as a 'neutral vendor agreement' similar to the arrangement that had developed in the single-supplier context.[107] For some suppliers, their entire business model is based on this sub-contracting model and acting as a 'thin

[105] LA17.
[106] CA10.
[107] LA4.

prime contractor' on frameworks. Again, a wide, generic scope of work is usually agreed when the call-off is issued but on the basis that the supplier will act as an intermediary by sourcing requirements on the contracting authority's behalf by sub-contracting to other suppliers not on the framework. A contracting authority indicated that the supplier's proposal to run a subordinate framework might only become apparent just before calling-off.[108] Another legal adviser said this 'amounts to buying from a supplier who does not have the capability', given their ultimate reliance on sub-contractors whose capability was not assessed at framework award.[109] Instances have even occurred where the entirety of requirements have been sub-contracted to a third party not on the framework. Reference was made to the *Lightways*[110] case and the risk of some call-offs involving delivery by suppliers not on the framework, thereby constituting unlawful direct awards.[111]

The above examples demonstrate how designing a framework in this way might circumvent the PCR 2015 (eg, regulation 18) in the absence of explicit rules on how a framework should be used. In both examples, awarding a call-off with an excessively broad scope and open-ended value to be performed in large part by non-parties to the framework could avoid the contracting authority needing to run a separate procurement or apply the framework procedures to award another call-off. It is possible to envisage any number of practical management issues that may arise eg in monitoring suppliers on the network, potential conflicts between the prime contractor bidding for other call-offs and its supply network which may affect disclosures on price, contract performance and other matters.

It is not clear what were the original drivers for setting up such arrangements eg whether led by contracting authorities seeking to outsource the procurement function and reduce the burden within their organisation, or market-led by suppliers, or both. At least 51 neutral vendor agreements have been identified on a basic search at the time of writing.[112] A much-publicised example of a 'neutral vendor framework' arrangement is the Ministry of Defence's £400 million 'Commercial X' involving the appointment of a single supplier to manage a host of suppliers.[113] This is identified as a 'Marketplace of pre-accredited Technology Providers which the MOD and pan-government participators can access' via the supplier in order to drive innovation.[114] The MOD has stated that the framework includes working with SMEs to remove barriers to entry. This book does not purport to assess the extent to which such specific examples may or may not comply with procurement legislation. Nevertheless, these are clearly described as market-led models that are considered to beneficial in various ways and which merit further research.

[108] CA13.
[109] LA6.
[110] *Lightways (Contractors) Limited v Inverclyde Council* [2015] CSOH 169.
[111] LA7.
[112] Information is available on a basic search of 'neutral vendor frameworks' at bidstats.uk/tenders/?ntype=tender.
[113] Information is available at www.gov.uk/guidance/ministry-of-defence-commercial-commercial-x.
[114] Information is available at www.constellia.com/solutions/public-sector-solutions/neutral-vendor-framework-for-innovation-nvfi/#:~:text=NVFi%20is%20an%20innovative%20commercial,goods%20and%20services%20across%20government.

8.2. A 'Framework Within a Framework' under the PA 2023

S.45(8)(b) introduces a new provision stating that section 45 on frameworks does not apply in relation to the award of a framework. The Explanatory Notes to the PA 2023 state that this means that this section 'does not regulate the award of a framework itself, but the award of contracts under a framework'. It is understood that this is intended to clarify that a framework cannot be used to award a framework under the PA 2023; however, ultimately, it does not categorically address the 'framework within a framework' concept because this provision is tied to the definition of a 'framework'. The two examples above do not relate to the use of a framework to award another framework, as defined. The first example concerns the award of a call-off with a very wide, generic scope which is subsequently amended several times to incorporate additional supplies and services. The increased flexibility permitted to agree the call-off terms combined with a similar set of provisions on contract modifications in section 74 means that the position under the PA 2023 is similar to that under the PR 2015, if not even more conducive to allowing such arrangements. The second 'neutral vendor' example described above whereby a framework supplier is awarded a call-off and sets up a 'sub-framework' is also not addressed by this provision. Again, the supplier network or 'sub-framework' is unlikely to meet the definition of a framework if, as would most often be the case, the establishing supplier is not a contracting authority under the PA 2023. This is because a framework is defined as 'a contract between a contracting authority and one or more suppliers'. As a result, there appear to be few regulatory controls in respect of such arrangements and which, as discussed in chapter ten, must be addressed.

9. Contract Modifications

9.1. Making Changes to Call-off Contracts under the PCR 2015

The risk of making an unlawful substantial change to a framework has been raised in various contexts in chapters six and seven, eg when exceeding the maximum framework value, use of call-off procedures and the finalisation of call-off terms. Modifications to call-off contracts subject to the PCR 2015 must be considered against the rule in regulation 33(6) that '[c]ontracts based on a framework agreement may under no circumstances entail substantial modifications to the terms laid down in that framework agreement'. Frameworks and call-off contracts are also subject to the dedicated rules on making modifications to concluded contracts during their term in regulation 72. In 2016, CCS published guidance which advised the following approach:

> Regulation 33(6) states that call-off contracts may not depart from the terms of the framework agreement in any substantial respect. This is because amendments to call-off contracts are subject to the terms of the framework agreement used to award them. Where an amendment to a call-off contract is proposed, the terms of the framework agreement should first be considered in the light of regulation 33. If however the framework agreement is silent,

and regulation 33 does not prevent the amendment, the rules in regulation 72 should be considered.[115]

There is no definition of 'substantial change' in regulation 33. In its absence, it is necessary to read across to regulation 72 which includes several safe harbours which permit modifications if the conditions are met. Regulation 72(1)(e) provides that a modification is permitted if it is not substantial, a substantial modification being defined in regulation 72(8) as occurring under the following circumstances:

(a) the modification renders the contract or the framework agreement materially different in character from the one initially concluded;
(b) the modification introduces conditions which, had they been part of the initial procurement procedure, would have:
 (i) allowed for the admission of other candidates than those initially selected,
 (ii) allowed for the acceptance of a tender other than that originally accepted, or
 (iii) attracted additional participants in the procurement procedure;
(c) the modification changes the economic balance of the contract or the framework agreement in favour of the contractor in a manner which was not provided for in the initial contract or framework agreement;
(d) the modification extends the scope of the contract or framework agreement considerably;
(e) a new contractor replaces the one to which the contracting authority had initially awarded the contract in cases other than those provided for in paragraph (1)(d).

It may be difficult to apply these grounds to a generic multi-supplier framework in practice. For instance, it may be difficult to assess whether a modification to a single call-off renders an entire multi-user, multi-supplier framework materially different in character, whether it shifts the economic balance in favour of a supplier or whether it changes the scope of the framework considerably. Further, given that a framework may be awarded flexibly to leave much for determination at the call-off stage, such that there may be a weak link between the two, it may be difficult to assess whether a proposed modification to a call-off entered into by just one of many user contracting authorities on a generic, widely used framework could have affected the outcome of the original procurement procedure used to set up the framework had it been included initially. This is quite apart from the general uncertainty of having to apply the modification grounds.[116]

9.1.1. Making Changes to Call-off Contracts in Practice under the PCR 2015

Several interviewees related call-off contract management issues they had experienced and the difficulties of applying regulation 33(6) to frameworks and call-offs.

[115] CCS, 'The Public Contracts Regulations 2015 & The Utilities Contracts Regulations 2016, Guidance on Amendments to Contracts During their Term', updated October 2016, 5.

[116] See generally, S Arrowsmith, *The Law of Public and Utilities Procurement: Regulation in the EU and UK*, 3rd edn, Vol I (Sweet & Maxwell, 2014) 6-267–6-306.

Uncertainty was expressed about the ability to make changes where the subject-matter is complex or bespoke, the market is constantly evolving or the call-off term is over several years, necessitating flexibility in contract terms.[117] Several interviewees offered examples of their approach to making such changes. Extensions to call-off terms were sometimes considered due to, for example, programme delays, security considerations or the need to maintain continuity of service. Changes to the scope of call-offs were also sometimes agreed to address programme changes by, for example, updating the product set or adding further ancillary workstreams. One interviewee cited the over-reliance on 'innovation' clauses in frameworks and how these are open to abuse with suppliers using them to add new technologies to a customer contract.[118]

More generally, there was a perception that poor contract management pervades call-offs in the ICT sector. Examples were given of excessive uses of change control mechanisms to correct misunderstandings of the requirement and solution, data not being recorded and project plans not being completed, leading to uncertainty and disputes. One interviewee highlighted that 'exit management' can be overlooked and left to be agreed when on contract, requiring using change control mechanisms to make the necessary changes, which attracted extra cost for the contracting authority.[119]

One legal adviser noted many breaches of regulation 33(6) when complex procurements were involved and that 'the rules on material change are being breached all the time but risk mitigation strategies are adopted to address the practical risks'.[120] This has led interviewees to query whether the framework model is an appropriate contracting tool for such complex, bespoke, dynamic and long-term ICT requirements, a recurring theme throughout this book.

Several interviewees suggested that the rules on making changes to call-offs should be made clearer and that frameworks might merit a separate set of rules altogether to guide contracting authorities on what changes can be made at the various stages of using a framework and managing call-offs. There was a perceived need for more flexibility in the ICT sector. Some suggested the possibility of setting out the mechanisms in advance for making future changes to call-off contracts and how useful it would be if the legal rules expressly endorsed this approach specifically for the framework model.[121] More than one legal adviser suggested that a specific safe harbour could be added to regulation 72 to clarify the circumstances in which changes can be made to a framework and call-offs that takes into account the unique aspects of the framework model.[122]

There is such uncertainty about the application of the legal rules when assessing the legality of changes in the framework context that the provision of additional guidance may be insufficient and reform of the legal rules may be required, as discussed in chapter ten.

[117] CA7.
[118] CA11.
[119] ibid.
[120] LA4.
[121] LA15.
[122] LA2, LA3.

9.2. Making Changes to Call-off Contracts under the PA 2023

The PA 2023 appears to adopt a similar approach to the PCR 2015 regarding the assessment of modifications to frameworks and call-offs made under them.

The *Transforming Public Procurement* Green Paper did not address whether the existing rules on making contract modifications to frameworks were suitable or needed reforming. It is therefore unsurprising that the PA 2023 adopts a similar approach to the PCR 2015. It is submitted that this is a missed opportunity, however, and that further reform in this area may be required, as discussed in chapter ten. Given that the PA 2023 creates even more scope for setting up generic, pan-public sector frameworks it may become increasingly difficult to apply the general rules on contract modifications to frameworks under the PA 2023.

Unlike the PCR 2015 which contained a specific reference to modifications in the provisions on frameworks (regulation 33(6)), there is no specific reference to modifications in the dedicated provisions on frameworks in the PA 2023, with the curious exception of section 49(9) which concerns substantial modification in the context of open frameworks. It is suggested that the absence of such an explicit reference could risk signalling a potential relaxation of the position on modifying frameworks. Instead, it appears that much is left to determination by application of section 74 which concerns the general provisions on contract modifications (broadly corresponding to regulation 72 albeit subject to important changes). This may, to some extent, address the 'read across' issue experienced under the PCR 2015 but the point remains that there is no specific emphasis on safeguarding against unlawful modifications of frameworks and call-offs in the framework provisions themselves.

Section 74 sets out the grounds on which a contracting authority may modify a 'public contract', the definition of which includes above-threshold, non-exempt frameworks and call-offs made under them. Similar to the set of safe harbours included in regulation 72, a list of 'permitted modifications' is referred to in section 74(1) and set out in Schedule 8. The list of 'permitted modifications' in Schedule 8 is similar to but expands slightly on the list of safe harbours in regulation 72. One notable addition is a ground that permits a modification due to the 'materialisation of a known risk' (Schedule 8, para 5). This applies when a contracting authority considers that a known risk has materialised otherwise than as a result of any act or omission of the contracting authority or the supplier and because of that fact, the contract cannot be performed to the satisfaction of the contracting authority. The contracting authority must consider that the modification goes no further than necessary to remedy that fact, and that awarding a further contract instead of modifying the contract would not be in the public interest in the circumstances. The modification must also not increase the estimated value of the contract by more than 50 per cent ignoring, for the purpose of estimating the contract value, the fact that the risk has materialised. This ground might seem like a useful one to address advances in technology and other changes required during the framework term. However, the 'known risk' that has materialised must be a risk that the contracting authority had identified in the tender or transparency notice for the award of the framework as a risk that could jeopardise the satisfactory performance of the contract, but because of its nature, could not be addressed in the contract as awarded. The possibility of relying on this ground must also be referenced in the notice. A strict set of conditions therefore applies to the application of this modification ground. To be able to rely upon it requires a degree of foresight by the contracting authority setting up the framework which may not be possible when it comes to rapid technology advances, many of which can be difficult to foresee.

A modification is also permitted if it is not a 'substantial modification' or is a 'below threshold modification', as defined. It should be noted that there has been significant change to the definition of a 'substantial' modification compared with the PCR 2015. As indicated, under regulation 72, it was provided that a modification would be a substantial one if the modification introduces conditions which, had they been part of the initial procurement procedure, would have allowed for the admission of other candidates than those initially selected, allowed for the acceptance of a tender other than that originally accepted, or attracted additional participants in the procurement procedure. This limb of the definition has not been included in the definition of a 'substantial modification' in section 74(3). Instead, a 'substantial modification' is a modification which would (a) increase or decrease the term of the contract by more than 10 per cent of the maximum term provided for on award, (b) materially change the scope of the contract, or (c) materially change the economic balance of the contract in favour of the supplier. Whilst it is not clear, this focus on materiality might be explained, at least in part, by the changed focus on the policy objectives of the PA 2023 compared with those of Directive 2014/24/EU. There is no longer a focus on free movement to create a single market and removing market access barriers to trade. Therefore, there may be less of an emphasis on conducting an analysis of the effects of procurement decisions on the wider supplier market and more of an emphasis on contracting authorities delivering value for money and achieving the other procurement objectives in section 12 (although the UK will continue to be subject to obligations of non-discrimination under international trade agreements). It is not yet clear to what extent this will provide even more flexibility to modify public contracts, including in the context of frameworks and to what extent section 12 objectives may act as any substantial restraint on modifications.

As part of the transparency agenda that has driven much of the PA 2023 reforms, section 75 provides that contracting authorities are now required to publish a contract change notice for most public contract modifications which will provide the market with certain information about the modification being made. It remains to be seen whether this will reduce the tendency to modify call-offs.

10. Conclusions

The empirical research has exposed, probably more than any other area of focus, the way in which the regulated framework model in the UK has become marketised and how a gulf between the application of the legal rules and practice has developed. It is evidenced by prominent references to 'framework shopping', 'opportunistic' and 'transaction routes'.

Contracting authorities and suppliers understand the need to acquire a sufficient level of technical, commercial and legal expertise and market knowledge to be able to transact effectively through frameworks in the ICT sector. The levels of expertise present vary substantially across different organisations, however. Many contracting authorities require more substantial support in this regard and such support could be provided by CPAs if they were required and configured to do so. Contracting authorities are attracted to frameworks so that they can take advantage of speed and efficiency gains, technical, commercial and market knowledge, and expertise developed by CPAs running the frameworks. The PA 2023 has made several reforms to frameworks which makes them even more flexible to use. Providing such flexibility means that contracting authorities may need to make decisions on various matters. Without clear guidance and support to drive the more effective use of frameworks, the poor and potentially legally non-compliant practices highlighted in this chapter are likely to continue.

Perhaps the most striking example of where the law is being flouted in this area relates to the use of direct call-offs without competition. Risk-based approaches are commonly adopted when making such call-offs where the call-off mechanism may not clearly comply with the PCR 2015 or is formulated in a way that may make it difficult to use whilst remaining legally compliant in practice. The case study explored provides an example of such a call-off procedure. It has been seen that these frameworks can be manipulated by contracting authorities and suppliers alike and can often be used in a market-led way by suppliers shepherding their customer contracting authorities to certain frameworks and supporting their use as suppliers attempt to secure a call-off. It is submitted that the problems highlighted are unlikely to be resolved by the PA 2023 due to the increased flexibilities introduced and the inadequate controls in the form of the section 12 procurement objectives and transparency requirements.

It has also been seen how the use of the mini-competition call-off procedure under the PCR 2015 has been subject to some legal uncertainty and some poor procurement practices. However, it can be difficult to use a mini-competition procedure effectively if an excessive number of suppliers are appointed to the framework. The PA 2023 expressly authorises such frameworks with an unlimited number of suppliers but includes some tools that might assist with reducing the numbers to invite to submit proposals as part of a competitive selection process (eg use of lots and introducing bespoke conditions of participation at the call-off stage). The PA 2023 provides little detail on how to run a competitive selection call-off process; therefore, contracting authorities will likely need training and support in this regard, again something that might potentially be best sourced from the CPA running the relevant framework.

The availability of pre-agreed terms and conditions is an attraction of using a framework for many contracting authorities. However, finalising the terms and conditions of a call-off can present problems when using both the direct award and mini-competition procedures, particularly regarding pricing. It seems that PME could be used by some CPAs to confirm proposed pricing methodologies and other call-off terms. Market dynamics are at play when it comes to the degree of contract negotiation and bargaining undertaken at the call-off stage and can lead to call-off terms being agreed in a way that is not provided for under the PCR 2015. The PA 2023 provides more flexibility for the agreement of terms at the call-off stage but there is a risk that this could lead to more protracted negotiations of contract terms at the call-off stage, particularly when using the competitive selection process. Whilst the PA 2023 framework provisions focus on conditions of participation and assessment of proposals at the call-off stage, it does not specifically address the finalisation of call-off terms.

Finally, difficulties are being encountered by contracting authorities when managing concluded contracts at the performance stage which may result in agreeing changes to the terms in breach of the prohibition in the PCR 2015 of making 'substantial modifications' to the terms of the framework. Further, the general rules on contract modifications can be difficult to apply to multi-supplier frameworks in practice. Similar issues are likely to arise under the PA 2023 and it is submitted that the Cabinet Office has missed an opportunity to create a more suitable set of legal rules to govern modifications to frameworks and call-offs.

Ultimately, an apposite note on which to end the substantive analysis of framework use in practice concerns the emergence of some questionable contractual constructs in the form of a framework within a framework. These appear to be motivated by new ways of outsourcing the procurement function to the private sector. The PA 2023 does not appear to address these directly but, as will be seen in chapter nine, they have come under the spotlight due to press coverage and legal challenges. These are one of the strongest recent indicators of framework marketisation and should be carefully monitored.

9

Review and Remedies

1. Introduction

The previous chapters demonstrated that setting up and using frameworks can give rise to breaches of procurement legislation, creating a risk of challenge.

The 2022 High Court *Consultant Connect*[1] judgment has put challenges to frameworks in the spotlight, the contracting authority being found to have run a disingenuous mini-competition by inviting just one supplier to tender, made substantial modifications to pricing provisions and failed to treat suppliers equally, transparently and proportionately. Unless an isolated incident (which is unlikely), the rules on frameworks have not deterred egregious practices. Notwithstanding, the risk of challenge is considered low and few challenges have reached UK courts.

This chapter briefly explores aspects of review and remedies as they relate to frameworks. As will be shown, multi-supplier frameworks have been designed to limit much of the risk of challenge even where there could be flagrant breaches. For example, large numbers of suppliers have been admitted or re-admitted where previously excluded, not necessarily because it makes good commercial sense or increases market access, but to limit the risk of challenge by suppliers. There is a certain irony that frameworks may be designed in breach of procurement rules to avoid challenge. This must also be considered in light of the lack of monitoring and enforcement of compliance, as discussed in chapter five.

The limited impact of the review and remedies system is another significant indicator of marketisation. The market's conspiracy of optimism is such that frameworks are perceived as too big to fail. As indicated in chapter one, it had been predicted that the introduction of a remedies regime would disincentivise framework use in order to 'dodge review'.[2] This has not been the case in the UK.

This chapter begins by introducing the emergent types of challenge (Section 2), followed by an overview of the PCR 2015 review and remedies rules (Section 3), perceptions of challenges in practice (Section 4) and bringing challenges under the PA 2023 (Section 5), before offering conclusions (Section 6). From the outset, it should be qualified that space does not permit a detailed analysis of review and remedies.

[1] *Consultant Connect Limited v (1) NHS Bath ICB (2) NHS Gloucestershire ICB and (3) NHS Bristol ICB (Interested Party: Monmedical Limited)* [2022] EWHC 2037 (TCC).

[2] CR Yukins, 'Are IDIQs Inefficient – Sharing Lessons with European Framework Contracting' (2008) 37 *PCLJ* 545, 568.

2. Bringing Challenges under the PCR 2015

Procurement challenges can only be brought in the High Court. Arrowsmith and Craven have found that very few are brought compared with EU Member States.[3] The two main deterrents are the cost of proceedings and fear of contracting authority retaliation, with others including conditions governing interim measures.[4] Guidance has been introduced to expedite proceedings.[5] However, it has been argued that lengthy and complex proceedings means that 'the system probably does not comply with the EU's requirement of effectiveness'.[6]

2.1. Challenges against CPAs under the PCR 2006 and 2015

There have been a few challenges to CPAs operating frameworks and carrying out other activities. For example,[7] in *Lion Apparel Systems Ltd v Firebuy Ltd*,[8] Firebuy, a CPA for UK fire authorities, procured uniforms and protective equipment; an unsuccessful tenderer sought but failed to secure an interim order preventing Firebuy from entering a contract on 13 different grounds. *Denfleet International Ltd v NHS PASA*[9] concerned a successful challenge against NHS PASA for acting outside the framework terms and *DeVilbiss v NHS PASA*[10] concerned an unsuccessful application for an injunction to suspend implementation of a contract purportedly awarded in contravention of the regulations.

Recent challenges by private sector organisations who operate frameworks are yet another indicator of marketisation. A recent example can be given, although the following makes no statement on the legality of any process undertaken.[11] In 2024, a provider of frameworks, DPS and other services commenced proceedings against an NHS Foundation Trust. The claim arose out of a contract notice published by the Trust for the award of an estimated £80 million 'National Professional Services Framework' open to use by other contracting authorities. The notice stated that the Trust was 'the public

[3] S Arrowsmith and R Craven, 'Public Procurement and Access to Justice: A Legal and Empirical Study of the UK System' (2016) 25 *PPLR* 227.

[4] S Arrowsmith, *The Law of Public and Utilities Procurement: Regulation in the EU and UK*, 3rd edn, Vol I (Sweet & Maxwell, 2018) 22–42, 22 129–22-145

[5] A Guidance Note on procurement proceedings has been published by the High Court Technology and Construction Court division which encourages less costly proceedings, particularly in relation to disclosure. See Courts and Tribunals Judiciary, 'The Technology and Construction Court Guide', October 2022, Appendix H, TCC Guidance Note on Procedures for Public Procurement Cases. Available at www.gov.uk/government/publications/technology-and-construction-court-guide.

[6] Arrowsmith (n 4) 22–67.

[7] See also *R. v Yorkshire Purchasing Organisation Ex p. British Educational Suppliers Ltd* [1998] ELR 195. *Medicure Ltd v The Minister for the Cabinet Office* [2015] EWHC 1854 (TCC); *Group M UK Ltd v Cabinet Office* [2014] EWHC 3659 (TCC); and *B2net Ltd v HM Treasury (Sued As Buying Solutions)* ([2010] EWHC 51 (QB)). These are referenced in J Chard, G Duhs and J Houlden, 'Body beautiful or vile bodies? Central purchasing in the UK' (2008) 2 *PPLR* NA26, 33.

[8] *Lion Apparel Systems Ltd v Firebuy Ltd* [2007] EWHC 2179 (Ch), [2007] EWHC 2179.

[9] *Denfleet International Ltd v NHS PASA* [2005] EWHC 55.

[10] *DeVilbiss Medequip v NHS PASA & Ors* [2005] EWHC 1757 (Ch) [2005] EWHC 1757.

[11] *Pagabo Limited v Alder Hey Children's NHS Foundation Trust*, Claim No HT-2024-000190.

sector legal entity responsible for hosting the tender process related to the framework award', but that a third-party supplier 'will manage the operational and practical aspects of selecting the suppliers and running the framework'. The claim alleged that without running a prior procurement process, the Trust directly appointed a particular private sector third party to provide services on its behalf and for the benefit of other users, 'being the management of selecting suppliers that will join the framework and the running of the framework'. The Particulars of Claim identified correspondence stating that 'to offer those frameworks within the marketplace, it requires a public sector Contracting Authority to host its tender processes' and the Trust would receive 'a proportion of the framework levy fees paid by suppliers'. The Particulars also highlighted a statement by the Trust that the third party approached and selected the Trust 'as their Host to run 'their frameworks' …', that it 'could select any willing public sector contracting authority it chooses' and that the Trust 'has no power over this choice'. The Trust denied that it had selected the third party on the basis that 'There are no services being provided to each other under this arrangement', stating that they were working together collaboratively and jointly and that the Trust took the contracting authority role, including issuing the contract notice and running the tender process. The third party was identified as leading on the management of the frameworks awarded resulting from that process. It was further stated that no public or non-public money was being spent by the Trust and that the third party would earn its income from its framework levy, of which the Trust would receive a small proportion. The challenger inferred that the third party would not receive payment from the Trust for its services under the contract, but would instead be permitted to generate revenues from other sources as a result of the appointment (eg from fees charged to suppliers and/or public authorities using the framework). As such, it alleged that the contract would be a concession and the appointment subject to the Concessions Contracts Regulations 2016 ('CCR 2016'). The claimant indicated that, in its experience, a service provider appointed to manage such a framework would expect to generate revenues that exceeded the financial threshold above which the CCR 2016 applies (pursuant to regulation 9(1)). Alternatively, it was argued that if the third party were to receive payment from the Trust for its services, the contract would be subject to the PCR 2015. The Trust denied that a concession contract had been created arguing that a concession would have to be a unique opportunity which only the Trust has to offer to the market but which was not the case because any public sector body can be a contracting authority host. Further, a concession contract requires a true transfer of risk, which was not the case.

From a marketisation perspective, the attempt to classify the arrangement as a concession is significant because, to a greater extent than other public contracts, it is a market-based transaction. This, of itself, implicitly suggests that a market exists for the provision of framework services. Regulation 3(4) CCR 2016 refers to 'the transfer of an operating risk in exploiting the works or services encompassing demand or supply risk or both' and 'the part of the risk transferred to the concessionaire must involve real exposure to the vagaries of the market, such that any potential estimated loss incurred by the concessionaire shall not be merely nominal or negligible'. Arguably, the contracting authority has commoditised the framework set-up and operation function into a profitable service.

Thus, it is a startling development that a private sector organisation is using the machinery of procurement law to challenge a framework hosting arrangement led by a competitor. It also indicates that various legal issues remain unresolved, not only the 'agency' or partnership relationship and basis for appointment but, even more fundamentally, the legal classification of the resulting contract.

It will be recalled that only a contracting authority could act as a CPA under the PCR 2015 and award a contract for the provision of centralised purchasing activities to a CPA without applying the PCR 2015 procedures (pursuant to regulation 37(8)). However, if a contracting authority has no meaningful role in frameworks set up in its name, it may be difficult to argue that the scenario can genuinely be described as conducting 'centralised purchasing activities' on 'a permanent basis' as required by the definition of a CPA (in regulations 2(1) and 37(1)). Otherwise, a competitive procurement process should be applied to appoint a provider to manage the framework. Were this the case, given the breadth of operations of certain private sector organisations, it is not clear how such a process would be scoped in a transparent way that does not represent an unlawful circumvention of the rules. The PA 2023 does not definitively address such matters.

2.2. Challenge to the Neutral Vendor Model under the PCR 2015

It will be recalled from chapter eight that the neutral vendor model has gained traction recently, a few examples of which can be found online.[12] One example is described in the following terms:

> A Neutral Vendor acts as a conduit between contracting authorities and pre-qualified suppliers across a wide range of services, goods & works. The Neutral Vendor offers a marketplace that suppliers can apply to join at a time, and wraparound service to support procurement activity. Awards can be direct or via further mini-competition with the process turnaround time for direct award being as short as one to five working days, and mini-competition within five to 10 working days.[13]

In a marketing 'flyer' for one example, reference is made to different level of fees charged depending on the 'service level' selected and call-off procedure used.[14]

Again, legal risk in respect of their use is increasing. Recently, a public law challenge was brought against a contracting authority's attempt to set up an apparent single-supplier neutral vendor framework.[15] The Good Law Project commenced judicial review against a consortium of local authorities for their decision to award a £70 billion 'Everything Net Zero' framework to a private company. It alleged that the proposed contract was 'a way of controlling how the entire public sector, from the NHS to local government offices, would award contracts even loosely connected to 'climate' issues, without having to comply with the usual public procurement rules' and 'seemed to have

[12] Examples include: nepro.org.uk/partnership; www.neutralvendorframework.com/; www.constellia.com/solutions/public-sector-solutions/neutral-vendor-framework-for-innovation-nvfi/.

[13] Information is available at www.neutralvendorframework.com/nv-explained/.

[14] An example can be found at www.neutralvendorframework.com/wp-content/uploads/sites/9/2022/03/MSP-Flyer-AEC-Framework.pdf.

[15] Information is available at goodlawproject.org/case/protect-net-zero-from-shoddy-procurement-practices/.

created a mechanism through which billions in public contracts could be awarded by the private company to other unspecified suppliers without open, transparent and fair competition'.[16] It also stated that the framework could be used by every public body and that the private company was the only supplier that submitted a tender for it. The Statement of Facts indicated that contracts would be awarded by a call-off to the private company which would then either perform the call-off itself or sub-contract with others using a 'pass-through' mechanism. Shortly after commencing proceedings, the consortium withdrew and paid some of the Good Law Project's costs. Again, as discussed, the PA 2023 does not decisively address such arrangements.

2.3. Examples of Challenges to Use of a Framework under the PCR 2015

There have been few challenges to call-offs but recent examples exist. The following two judgments occurred after conclusion of the empirical research.

The most prominent is *Consultant Connect*.[17] Consultant Connect brought a claim against three NHS bodies that jointly procured communications services to replace paging devices. Consultant Connect and two other suppliers (including Cinapsis, which was awarded the contract) were invited to participate in a product demonstration day but were not informed that this was being scored. On the previous day, the NHS bodies had held a private 'workshop' with Cinapsis. Unlike Consultant Connect, Cinapsis was one of 24 suppliers on a communications services framework. The NHS bodies also consulted three other suppliers on the framework but decided that only Cinapsis could meet their requirements. Following the demonstration day and these consultations, the NHS bodies held a mini-competition under the framework but only Cinapsis was invited to submit a tender, as the specification had been drafted such that only Cinapsis could meet it. The NHS bodies then negotiated with and awarded the contract to Cinapsis.

The court rejected their main defence that Consultant Connect did not have sufficient standing to challenge because it was not a member of the framework (on which see below). It went on to find that: (a) use of the framework to make a direct award was in breach of the equal treatment and transparency principles; (b) the mini-competition was not real and was in breach because only one supplier was invited to bid, the requirements were tailored to it, and the pricing agreed with it bore little resemblance to pricing in the framework; and (c) two staff members involved in the procurement had conflicts of interest that were not remedied, in breach of regulation 24.[18] For the first time in the UK, the court made an order shortening the contract, ordered payment of civil penalties, and found that the breaches were sufficiently serious to merit an award of damages on loss of chance principles.

This judgment is significant for many reasons. It is an indication of how market-engagement behaviours can impact negatively on frameworks and is a reminder of

[16] ibid.
[17] *Consultant Connect* (n 1).
[18] ibid paras 242, 212–216, 249 and 260–265.

the need for caution when choosing between pre-existing frameworks and other procurement options. It also sends a warning that established pricing structures and mini-competition procedures must not be abused.

Further, in *Optima v Department for Work and Pensions*,[19] under a CCS framework, Optima submitted a mini-tender for a call-off contract with the Department for Work and Pensions ('DWP'). The invitation to tender ('ITT') included a pricing schedule and explained that any bids for a service line exceeding the 'framework maximum prices' would be 'discounted'. DWP discovered that Optima had exceeded the prices in three out of 133 service lines having not spotted some changes in a revised pricing schedule issued by DWP and made some 'cut and paste errors'. Optima was excluded even though the errors had negligible impact on the overall pricing score; had Optima not been excluded, it would have been awarded the contract. The court considered this to be a notable element of the case. The Court of Appeal, overturning a decision of the High Court, concluded that the ITT did not contain a mandatory exclusion provision, and that no reasonably well-informed and normally diligent tenderer would have reached that view. A holistic interpretation of the ITT indicated that the obvious meaning of 'discounted' was 'reduced', not 'excluded' or 'disqualified' down to the framework maximum price.[20] The court also considered that DWP was obliged to seek clarification in the circumstances and that common sense was required when applying the procurement rules to ensure a healthy and fair competition and permit the proper evaluation of the tenders.[21] The court warned against adopting a strict and over-literal approach which may exclude the best tender for no objectively justifiable reason.[22]

This case again highlights the importance of clearly setting out requirements in call-off procedures and suppliers staying within the bounds of the pricing structures and established framework conditions. However, some of the Court of Appeal's reasoning is questionable. As indicated in chapter three, the reference to the purpose of the rules being 'the need for healthy and fair competition' is based on limited authority It is unclear what impact such unclear objectives may have on the application of the framework rules. The PA 2023 is no clearer in this regard in its inclusion of the section 12 objectives for covered procurement.

3. Overview of Rules on Bringing Challenges under the PCR 2015

The next few sections briefly set out the rules on bringing challenges for breaches of the PCR 2015 in respect of frameworks; public law challenges are not covered here.[23]

As discussed in chapter five, 'public contracts' and 'framework agreements' are defined separately in regulation 2(1). However, the rules on remedies in Chapter 6

[19] *Working on Wellbeing Ltd Trading as Optima Health v (1) Secretary of State for Work and Pensions (2) Department for Work and Pensions* [2025] EWCA Civ 127.

[20] ibid paras 43–50.

[21] ibid para 91.

[22] ibid.

[23] For a detailed analysis of all remedies rules, see Arrowsmith (n 4) ch 22.

PCR 2015 are stated to apply equally to frameworks and public contracts (including call-offs). Regulation 88(1) defines a 'contract' as covering frameworks as well as public contracts for the purposes of applying Chapter 6 (except in regulation 103 which deals with ineffectiveness of call-offs, considered below).

3.1. Standing in Relation to Frameworks under the PCR 2015

Under regulations 89 and 90 as originally drafted, contracting authorities owed a duty to suppliers (termed 'economic operators'[24]) from the UK and European Economic Area (and, where applicable, signatories to the WTO GPA or another international agreement) to comply with Part 2 PCR 2015 and any enforceable EU obligation in respect of a contract falling within the scope of Part 2.[25] Following Brexit, regulation 89 was amended so that the duty is only owed to a supplier from the UK or Gibraltar.[26] However, the duty is also owed to (a) a supplier from a GPA party where applicable[27] and (b) a supplier from a country party to a relevant international trade agreement where applicable.[28] Pursuant to regulation 91, a breach of this duty is 'actionable by any economic operator which, in consequence, suffers, or risks suffering, loss or damage'.

Case law has established that a supplier will not have standing to challenge if it was not in a position where it could suffer or risk suffering loss or damage. For example, in *Excel Europe*[29] it was held that no standing is present where a supplier has withdrawn from a competition and the challenge relates to breaches occurring after their withdrawal. Further, in *Lettings International*[30] it was held that there must be a 'significant chance' of being awarded the contract. In *Mears v Leeds City Council*,[31] it was held that this must be a 'real or significant as opposed to fanciful' chance of being put through to the next stage of the award procedure.

When awarding call-offs under a multi-supplier framework, it might be expected that only suppliers appointed to it would generally have standing to challenge. However, there have been two UK cases where it has been held that a supplier not a party to a framework had standing.

In *Lightways Contractors*,[32] Inverclyde Council awarded a call-off using a CCS framework to Amey Public Services LLP, which was not a framework appointed supplier. The relevant company in the Amey group on the framework was Amey OW Limited.

[24] Defined in reg 2(1) as 'any person or public entity or group of such persons and entities, including any temporary association of undertakings, which offers the execution of works or a work, the supply of products or the provision of services on the market'.

[25] The provisions on remedies in the PCR 2015 do not apply to other public procurement rules in the UK such as the Lord Young rules contained in Part 4 or to other legislative provisions on public procurement in the UK.

[26] Pursuant to The Public Procurement (Amendment etc.) (EU Exit) Regulations 2020, SI 2020/1319.

[27] Pursuant to reg 90A inserted by The Public Procurement (Agreement on Government Procurement) (Amendment) Regulations 2021, SI 2021/573.

[28] Pursuant to reg 90A inserted by The Public Procurement (International Trade Agreements) (Amendment) Regulations 2021, SI 2021/787. A relevant international trade agreement applies if the procurement is covered by an agreement listed in Schedule 4A of the PCR 2015.

[29] *Exel Europe v University Hospitals Coventry and Warwickshire NHS Trust* [2010] EWHC 3332.

[30] *Lettings International v London Borough of Newnham* [2008] LGR 908, para 141.

[31] *Mears v Leeds City Council* [2011] EWHC 1031 (TCC).

[32] *Lightways Contractors v Inverclyde Council* [2015] CSOH 169.

A competitor, Lightways, who was also not an appointed supplier challenged the call-off. The Scottish Court of Session held that Lightways had standing because of its status as a supplier affected by the decision to award a contract to its competitor without holding a new procurement process. The award to the non-framework supplier 'was not merely a clerical error; it was a fundamental error of substance'.[33]

As indicated, in *Consultant Connect* it was similarly held that a non-party to a framework had standing to challenge a call-off. The court acknowledged that they would not usually satisfy the causation of loss test in contrast to appointed suppliers who could show that the correct use of the framework would usually result in the award of a contract to a framework supplier. The court held, however, that the regulations did not rule out claims by a non-member if, on the facts, the contract award breached a relevant duty owed to them and they suffered or risked suffering loss in consequence. The alternative to an improper use of the framework was considered to be a procurement outside the framework, in which Consultant Connect could have bid.[34] This is an important reminder that challenges are possible by suppliers outside the framework, thereby reducing the perceived security of being able to freely award call-offs among appointees, especially where the framework is used as a convenient route to contract with a pre-determined supplier.

3.2. Time Limits

Pursuant to regulation 92(2), a supplier must commence proceedings within 30 days of the date when they first knew or ought to have known that grounds for proceedings had arisen.

However, the regulation 92 time limits for general claims brought under the PCR 2015 do not apply to claims seeking a remedy of ineffectiveness. Directive 2007/66/EC introduced this remedy whereby a review body can declare a contract to be set-aside or cancelled after it has been entered into where certain grounds are met, the consequences of which are determined by national law.[35] Importantly, one of the grounds relates to frameworks. Article 2(b), (c) and 2(d)(1)(c) provide for this possibility; for example, when a call-off exceeding the financial threshold has been awarded in breach of the rules concerning running a mini-competition (see regulation 99(6), as discussed below).

Instead, regulation 93 provides that the following rules apply. Firstly, where a contract award notice has been published, the time limit is within 30 days beginning the day after publication. This is relevant for the first ground of ineffectiveness where no call for competition has been published (see below). That notice must include justification of the decision to award without prior publication of a contract notice (regulation 93(4)). Second, where the contracting authority has informed the supplier of both the conclusion of the contract and a summary of the relevant reasons,[36] the

[33] ibid paras 6 and 8.
[34] *Consultant Connect* (n 1) paras 136–152.
[35] See Article 2d of Directive 2007/66/EC.
[36] The 'relevant reasons' means the reasons which the economic operator would have been entitled to receive in response to a request under reg 55(2).

time limit is 30 days beginning the day after the economic operator was informed. This circumstance is relevant where a procedure has been run pursuant to a call for competition.[37] Third, in all other cases, irrespective of whether the claimant knows or ought to know of the breach, the time limit is within six months beginning the day after the contract was entered into.[38] This acts as an absolute end-stop date.[39] Unlike with the rules for general claims, the court does not have the discretion to extend the time limits (regulation 92(4)).

3.3. Automatic Suspension and Other Pre-contract Remedies

Regulation 95 provides for an automatic suspension against concluding a framework or a call-off when a claim is issued. The suspension must remain in place until either: (a) the court brings it to an end by interim order (under regulation 96(1)(a)); or (b) the proceedings at first instance are determined, discontinued or otherwise disposed of and no order has been made continuing it (eg in connection with an appeal or the possibility of an appeal) (regulation 95(2)).

In addition, Article 2(1)(b) Directive 89/665/EEC requires that review bodies must be given powers to 'set aside or ensure the setting aside of decisions taken unlawfully'. Regulation 97(2) sets out the remedies that the court may grant where the contract has not yet been entered into. The court may, without prejudice to its other powers: (a) order the setting aside of the decision or action; (b) order the contracting authority to amend any document; or (c) award damages to an economic operator which has suffered loss or damage resulting from the breach.

3.4. Damages (Potentially Available Before and After a Contract has been Concluded)

3.4.1. Availability of Damages

The PCR 2015 provides that a court has the power to award damages both before (under regulation 97(2)(c)) and after (regulation 98(2)(c))[40] a contract has been concluded 'to an economic operator which has suffered loss or damage as a consequence of the breach'.

Until recently, it was settled case law that damages were, in principle, available for all breaches.[41] However, in *Nuclear Decommissioning Authority v Energy Solutions EU*

[37] In *Lancashire County Council v Brookhouse Group Limited* [2024] EWCA Civ 717 confirmed that where no competitive tendering exercise has been carried out, a six-month limitation period generally applies.

[38] As noted by Arrowsmith (n 4) 22–92, this six-month time limit cannot apply to proceedings to establish the unlawful nature of the award itself when a damages claim depends on establishing it, as this would also preclude the damages remedy. See Case C-166/14 *MedEval-Qualitäts, Leistungs und Struktur-Evaluierung im Gesundheitswesen GmbH* ECLI:EU:C:2015:779 confirming this position.

[39] In accordance with Article 2f(1)(b) Directive 2007/66/EC.

[40] This clarifies that this is irrespective of whether the court has also made a declaration of ineffectiveness or applies any penalty or fines or contract shortening.

[41] See eg *Harmon CFEM Facades (UK) Ltd v The Corporate Officer of the House of Commons* (1999) 67 ConL.R1 although cf *Nationwide Gritting Services v Scottish Minsters* (No2) [2014] CSOR 151.

Ltd,[42] the UK Supreme Court held that the availability of damages is limited by the so-called '*Francovich* conditions'[43] applicable to EU Member State failures to implement or comply with EU law; one such condition is that the breach must be sufficiently serious. The Supreme Court held that Directive 89/665/EEC permitted, and the PCR 2006 applicable at the time should be interpreted as meaning, that damages should be limited to cases of sufficiently serious breach, even though this was not explicitly stated in the regulations.

More recently, in *Braceurself*,[44] it was held that a single mistake made by the evaluators, was not, on balance, sufficiently serious to warrant damages even though it was held to be a 'manifest error' of assessment and had altered the outcome. The breach was considered inadvertent and minor in an otherwise well-planned procurement. The case went to the Court of Appeal[45] where it was confirmed that the 'sufficiently serious' test was concerned less with the consequences for the damaged party than the nature and quality of the breach itself.

3.4.2. *Quantifying Damages Claims*

When assessing damages, the UK courts have treated claims brought under procurement rules as claims for breach of statutory duty[46] and, therefore, damages put the claimant in the position it would have been had the contracting authority not committed the breach.[47] Thus, where the claimant would have been awarded the contract, the most obvious measure of damages would be its lost profits (although other losses may also be recoverable).[48]

The amount will depend on an assessment of the chances of winning. In *Harmon*,[49] it was held that damages could be recoverable based upon a 'loss of chance' principle and, as explained by Arrowsmith,[50] this probably requires the claimant to demonstrate a substantial chance that it would have been awarded the contract. If, for example, a claimant was considered to have a 50 per cent chance had the breach not occurred and stood to lose £1 million profit, it would be awarded £500,000.[51] According to *Harmon*, a claimant should be able to recover the entire value if it can show that it 'would have'

[42] *Nuclear Decommissioning Authority v Energy Solutions EU Ltd (now called ATK Energy EU Ltd)* [2017] UKSC 34.

[43] Set out in Joined Cases C-6/90 and C-9/90 *Francovich v Italian Republic* ECLI:EU:C:1991:428, [1995] ICR 722; [1991] ECR I-5357 and Joined Cases C-46/93 and C-48/93 *Brasserie du Pêcheur SA v Federal Republic of Germany, R v Secretary of State for Transport, Ex p Factortame* Ltd (No 4) ECLI:EU:C:1996:79, [1996] QB 404.

[44] *Braceurself Ltd v NHS England* [2022] EWHC 1532 (TCC); *Braceurself Ltd v NHS England* [2022] EWHC 2348 (TCC).

[45] *Braceurself Ltd v NHS England* [2022] EWCA Civ 837 and *Braceurself Ltd v NHS England No.2 Substantive Appeal* [2024] EWCA Civ 39.

[46] See eg *Energy Solutions v Nuclear Decommissioning* Authority [2015] EWCA Civ 1262, para 45.

[47] This principle was established in *Harmon* (n 41).

[48] See eg *Harmon CFEM Facades (UK) Ltd v The Corporate Officer of the House of Commons* (2000) 2 LGLR 372 where additional damages to cover bid costs and profits of other companies in the claimant's corporate group were held to be recoverable.

[49] ibid.

[50] Arrowsmith (n 4) 22-246–22-247.

[51] See eg *Lancashire County Council v Environmental Waste Controls Limited* [2010] EWCA Civ 1381.

been awarded the contract which could be shown if it had at least a 90 per cent chance of winning.[52]

A difficulty in the context of frameworks is how to determine damages where a claimant can successfully demonstrate that they would have been appointed to a framework had the contracting authority not breached the rules. This is because a multi-supplier framework may involve any number of call-offs to any number of suppliers with no guarantee of being awarded them.

In *European Dynamics SA v HM Treasury*,[53] the court had to consider whether to maintain an injunction regarding the establishment of a framework (divided into lots) for the delivery of software solutions. Lots were to be let to various suppliers whose services could be called upon by contracting authorities. In deciding to remove the injunction in relation to the three lots that the claimant had challenged (thereby allowing the framework for these lots to be concluded), the court held that damages would be an adequate remedy for the claimant, taking the view that '[t]he fact that damages may not be a perfect remedy is not material'[54] and acknowledging the possibility of assessing damages on a loss of chance basis, it being permissible for the court to do 'the best it can to assess damages when it is clear that there must have been some loss but it is difficult to assess'.[55] It suggested that a sensible way of calculating damages in that case could be: (a) assess on the basis of projections and previous framework type agreements entered into by the defendant and indeed on the actual operation of the proposed new frameworks what the likely value or range of values of the work will be over the period of the new agreements; (b) assess what the share of the claimant would be over the period of the agreements which could be done on a different number of bases (eg calculating the likely percentage share of work to be awarded based on its ranking in a particular lot if appointed to the framework); (c) assess what the profit and possibly overhead share was or would have been; or (d) discount the figure to allow for the receipt of the damages before some of the return would have been earned.[56]

In a similar vein, in *B2NET v HM Treasury*,[57] when considering an application for an injunction where the claimant had been refused admission to a tender stage for a framework, the court stated 'the evidence suggests that damages would be an adequate remedy, and more readily capable of calculation than many claims for damages for loss of business that come before the courts'. It was argued for the defendant that at the time when it comes to assessing damages 'the new framework will have been in operation for some time, and there will be data from which margins and other relevant figures can be found for the purposes of assessing damages'.[58] In holding that damages would be an adequate remedy for the claimant, the court agreed with the defendant that '[t]he longer any assessment of damages is deferred into the term of the new framework, the more evidence there will be'.[59]

[52] *Harmon* (n 49) paras 237–239.
[53] *European Dynamics SA v HM Treasury* [2009] EWHC 3419 (TCC).
[54] ibid para 22. The court referred to *Peaudouce SA v Kimberly Clark Ltd* [1996] FSR 680 in support.
[55] ibid.
[56] ibid.
[57] *B2NET v HM Treasury* [2010] EWHC 51.
[58] ibid paras 56 and 59.
[59] ibid para 59.

Another relevant case is *Exel Europe v University Hospitals Coventry and Warwickshire NHS Trust*,[60] which concerned a single-provider framework but involved several potential NHS clients. The court considered that damages would provide an adequate remedy for the claimant and found no difficulty in holding that 'if Exel's entitlement to damages includes the loss of the chance of tendering successfully, it will recover a reasonable amount for the profit lost on the custom that would have been generated'.[61]

Arrowsmith considers that these decisions on frameworks may be influenced by the domestic courts' inclination to limit remedies to avoid granting interim measures.[62] If the court considers that damages are an adequate remedy for the claimant, this may preclude the imposition of interim measures that could hold up a procurement.

Notwithstanding, it is possible to envisage difficulties when it comes to assessing the quantum of damages that should be awarded to a claimant who demonstrates that it has been wrongfully excluded from being admitted to a framework, particularly where a new framework with no previous iteration is being set up and there is little evidence on which to base estimations of future awards and values, or where the framework is a pan-public sector generic one with many suppliers admitted and very little transparency in terms of its likely use.

3.5. Remedy of Ineffectiveness

As indicated, Directive 2007/66/EC sets out three grounds which, if met, would permit the remedy of ineffectiveness, one of which specifically relates to the award of call-offs under a framework.

Regulation 98 provides that where a contracting authority has breached its duty to comply with the rules and the contract has already been entered into, a court must, if it is satisfied that any of the grounds for ineffectiveness applies, make a declaration of ineffectiveness in respect of the contract (unless regulation 100 requires the court not to do so). The three different grounds of ineffectiveness are set out below.

Ground 1: Direct awards without competition

Before the ineffectiveness remedy was introduced, a supplier might have not had a remedy at all where a contracting authority had awarded a framework illegally without advertising a contract and running any competition. This is because a supplier would have likely found it difficult to claim damages due to the need to show a loss of a chance and the absence of any bid costs.

Regulation 99(2)–(4) provide that the ineffectiveness remedy is available where a contract has been awarded without prior publication of a contract notice in any case where one was required by Part 2 (which contains the substantive provisions requiring such a notice to be published).

This ground will not apply where a contracting authority has, in good faith, considered that a call for competition was not required, published a voluntary transparency

[60] *Exel Europe v University Hospitals Coventry and Warwickshire NHS Trust* [2010] EWHC 3332.
[61] ibid para 49.
[62] Arrowsmith (n 4) 22-234–22-239 and 22-249.

notice to this effect with sufficient detail, and waited at least 10 days before entering into the contract (regulation 99(3)).

Ground 2: Substantive breach plus not following notification/standstill/automatic suspension rules

Article 2(d)(1)(b) Directive 89/665/EEC as given effect in regulation 99(5) provides that this ineffectiveness ground applies where: (a) a contract has been entered into in breach of any requirement imposed in relation to the notification and the standstill period, automatic contract suspension when a challenge has been made to contract award or interim orders made in respect of such automatic suspension;[63] (b) there has also been a breach of the substantive duties owed to economic operators (under regulations 89 and 90); (c) the breach referred to in (a) above has deprived them of the possibility of starting proceedings for the substantive breach or pursuing them to a proper conclusion before the contract was entered into; and (d) the substantive breach referred to in (b) above has affected their chance of obtaining the contract.

It is important to note that this ground will apply equally to standard public contracts, frameworks and call-offs (regulation 103(6)). With regard to call-offs, in respect of requirement (a) above, ineffectiveness will apply where a call-off is entered into in breach of the automatic suspension requirement/any order to maintain the suspension[64] and there has been a substantive breach relating specifically to the award of the call-off and the procedure relating to that award (regulation 103(6)(b)). Ineffectiveness applies in relation to a call-off entered into in breach of automatic suspension requirements because the UK Government has taken advantage of the derogation in Directive 89/665/EEC in declining to apply the notification and standstill requirements to call-offs (under regulation 86(5)(c)).

Ground 3: Breach of the rules in making call-offs

Under Article 2b(c) Directive 89/665/EEC, where a Member State opts to derogate from applying the usual notification and standstill obligations to making call-offs, a further ineffectiveness ground had to be made available by a Member State. As the UK took advantage of this derogation (under regulation 86(5)(c)), this ground applies in the UK and is set out in regulation 99(6). It applies to a call-off contract made under a framework or a DPS where: (a) the contract was awarded in breach of any requirement imposed by the rules on the award of contracts based on frameworks through reopening of competition or the rules on the award of contracts under DPS; and (b) the estimated value of the contract is equal to or greater than the applicable financial threshold (in regulation 5).

This third ground does not apply, however, if all the following apply: (a) the contracting authority considered the award to be in accordance with the provisions on the award of contracts based on frameworks through reopening of competition or the rules on the award of contracts under DPS, as applicable; (b) the contracting authority has voluntarily complied with the notification and standstill requirements (set out in regulation 86(1)–(4)); and (c) the contract has not been entered into before the end of the standstill period.

[63] That is, regs 87, 95 and 96(1)(b).
[64] Regulation 99(5)(a)(ii).

It should be noted that as well as this third ground not applying to a call-off with a value below the applicable financial threshold, it does not apply to a call-off with a value above it where it has been directly awarded in accordance with the framework without a mini-competition. As argued by Arrowsmith, there appears to be inadequate transparency controls over call-offs not made pursuant to mini-competitions as the standstill and ineffectiveness rules do not generally apply to them, even though such transparency controls are arguably more important for such direct call-off awards.[65]

It is important to note that in contrast with Ground 2, there are no additional conditions such as the requirement that the breach of the mini-competition rules must have affected the claimant's chances of winning the contract. Ineffectiveness will simply apply to all above-threshold call-offs where no notification/standstill has been observed and the contracting authority has breached the rules on running the mini-competition. In *Consultant Connect*,[66] the court decided that the conditions for this ineffectiveness ground were made out (due to a breach of the mini-competition rules in regulation 33(11)). As noted by Arrowsmith, there is a significant risk of ineffectiveness for call-offs on this ground as there is no scope for the court to preclude an ineffectiveness remedy based on the claimant's chance of success or the impact of the breach on the outcome, as with other remedies.[67] It is still possible, however, for a call-off to be maintained for overriding reasons of general interest, as discussed below.

3.6. Consequences of Ineffectiveness: Prospective Ineffectiveness

The consequences of a contract being declared ineffective are set out in regulation 101. Regulation 101(1) confirms that 'the contract is to be considered to be prospectively, but not retrospectively, ineffective as from the time when the declaration is made and, accordingly, those obligations under the contract which at that time have yet to be performed are not to be performed'.

3.7. Consequences of an Ineffective Framework and Call-off Contracts Made under it

As explained, the ineffectiveness remedy is available in respect of the overarching framework itself but strictly limited to grounds 1 and 2 described above (ground 3 being concerned with call-off).

In relation to call-offs generally, regulation 103(6) provides that a declaration of ineffectiveness can be sought both on the second and third grounds.

Directive 89/665/EEC does not expressly address the consequences for call-offs where the framework itself has been declared ineffective. If a call-off is entered into *after* a court has declared the framework to be ineffective, then if the call-off has a value

[65] Arrowsmith (n 4) 22-281.
[66] *Consultant Connect* (n 1).
[67] Arrowsmith (n 4) 22-279.

exceeding the applicable financial threshold and is not otherwise exempted under the PCR 2015, it would presumably constitute an unlawful direct contract award of a public contract. In the UK, there is a limited impact on call-offs entered into *before* a framework is declared ineffective due to the ineffectiveness remedy only applying prospectively in the UK. Regulation 103(2) provides that a call-off entered into before a declaration of ineffectiveness has been made in respect of the framework 'is not to be considered to be ineffective merely because a declaration of ineffectiveness has been made in respect of the framework agreement'. Pursuant to regulation 103(3)–(4), however, where a declaration of ineffectiveness has been made in respect of the framework, where an economic operator seeks a declaration of ineffectiveness in respect of a call-off, the court must make a separate declaration of ineffectiveness in respect of the call-off. As submitted by Arrowsmith, this seems to be aligned with the general principles of Directive 89/665/EEC as ineffectiveness should only be required to follow in the event of a challenge and should not apply automatically.[68] This would seem to strike a sensible balance between the interest of running a smooth procurement and the interests of suppliers in securing access to the market in accordance with the legal rules. However, in the context of multi-user frameworks, this means that there is a risk of a user contracting authority's call-off(s) being declared ineffective even though it has not committed any breach, the breach(es) having been committed by the lead contracting authority in awarding the framework.

Where a declaration of ineffectiveness is granted in respect of a call-off, it will apply prospectively as with the overarching framework. Regulation 103(4)(a) and (b) provide that the claimant must commence its challenge within the applicable time limit in respect of the call-off in question regardless of whether the challenge is brought at the same time as the challenge in respect of the framework or at another time.

Regulation 103(8) provides that where a call-off under a framework that has been declared ineffective is also declared ineffective, the consequences of ineffectiveness set out in regulation 101 apply but the requirement in regulation 102(1) to impose a civil financial penalty does not. This is presumably because any such financial penalty would have been addressed when the framework itself was declared ineffective.

3.8. Ineffectiveness – Overriding Interest Exception

Regulation 100(1) provides that the court must not make a declaration of ineffectiveness if a party raises an issue under regulation 100 during proceedings and 'the Court is satisfied that overriding reasons relating to a general interest require that the effects of the contract should be maintained'.

With regard to claims for ineffectiveness in respect of a call-off under a framework that has itself been declared ineffective, regulation 103(5) provides that this overriding interest exception can also apply to such call-offs 'insofar as the overriding reasons relate specifically to the circumstances of the specific contract'.

Regulation 103(9) and (10) provide that where the court refrains from making a declaration of ineffectiveness which would otherwise have been required, it must order

[68] ibid, 22-268–22-272.

that the duration of the call-off be shortened to the maximum extent possible having regard to the relevant overriding interests at issue.

3.9. Ineffectiveness – Alternative Penalties

Article 2e Directive 89/665/EEC provides for alternative penalties of fines and contract shortening in certain circumstances. These are intended to supplement other available remedies where challenges are made to concluded contracts.

These alternative penalties are set out in regulation 102 and their application is relatively extensive in the UK given its approach to limiting the availability of the ineffectiveness remedy to that strictly required by Directive 89/665/EEC. To briefly summarise: (a) as a result of the UK applying the ineffectiveness remedy prospectively not retrospectively, the court must impose a civil financial penalty in every case in which a declaration of ineffectiveness is made (regulation 102(1)); (b) where the court decides not to apply the ineffectiveness remedy overriding general interest reasons, it must order at least one, and may order both, of a financial penalty and contract shortening (regulation 102(2)(a) and 102(3)); and (c) where there is a breach of the automatic suspension or notification/standstill requirements but no declaration of ineffectiveness, the court must provide for one or both of a civil financial penalty and contract shortening.

Regulation 102(4) confirms that when considering what order to make, 'the overriding consideration' for the court 'is that the penalties must be effective, proportionate and dissuasive' and under regulation 102(5) the court must take account of all the relevant factors including the seriousness of the relevant breach, the behaviour of the contracting authority and the extent to which the contract remains in force. In *Consultant Connect*,[69] even though an ineffectiveness ground applied, the contract was not declared ineffective. Instead, the court held that for 'overriding reasons relating to a general interest', being the adverse effects on patient care, a contract shortening order should be made instead, reducing the term by 14 months. The court also imposed civil penalties and awarded damages.

4. Perceptions of Challenges in Practice under the PCR 2015

4.1. General Perceptions of Risk of Challenges to Frameworks

Notwithstanding the cases summarised above, there was a consensus amongst interviewees that challenges are not common although some had noticed increased activity. Challenges tend to be brought only where there is a clear breach. The costs and risks of bringing proceedings are significant. If the challenge is unsuccessful, suppliers might have to meet a significant proportion of the contracting authority's costs and compromise their reputation with a public sector customer. As one interviewee commented,

[69] *Consultant Connect* (n 1).

'most commercial organisations are not prepared to take these risks, preferring to focus on winning new contracts'.[70]

There was a general perception that the risk of challenge is more prevalent at the framework award stage than call-off. Some legal advisers had noticed a recent increase in challenges to framework awards, one revealing that they received seven letters of complaint about the framework appointment which led to three claim forms being issued and automatic suspensions imposed.[71] Another legal adviser stated that 'there is less goodwill amongst suppliers now with regard to avoiding challenges' and that 'suppliers are seeing others challenging and are seeing this as more standard business practice'.[72] It was noted that challenges still tend to be more commonplace in other jurisdictions, however.

As discussed in chapter seven, and corroborated by some interviewees, the growth of generic, pan-public sector frameworks with no cap on the number of suppliers has decreased the risk of challenge at the appointment stage. There was a perception that limiting the number of suppliers increases the risk of challenge from suppliers who did not get onto the framework. This is particularly the case where the framework is viewed as a key route to contracting with a particular customer and 'the requirement relates to a market where there are a small number of suppliers'.[73]

Given the above, the empirical research appeared to indicate that, even though challenges are not common, risk averse attitudes to challenges are informing choices about framework design in ways that compromise their effectiveness, a prime example being the admission of an unlimited number of suppliers to lower the risk of challenge.

4.2. Challenges and Complaints when Awarding Frameworks

It is common for contracting authorities setting up frameworks to receive informal complaints from unsuccessful bidders. This is because the closed nature of a framework means that they will be locked out of the framework for its duration. Many interviewees commented that only a small proportion of these ever progress to a formal legal challenge, being 'dealt with relatively swiftly'[74] or which 'fizzle out relatively quickly'.[75] However, a few instances were reported of frameworks being delayed by months due to informal complaints.

A frequent complaint relates to perceived errors in the evaluation of tenders or insufficient, misleading or ambiguous information being provided to justify the scores given. One interviewee had experienced a formal challenge from a large ICT contractor where the evaluation process had not been documented properly leading to a lack of justifiable evidence upon which to rely, thereby giving the challenger a reasonable ground of challenge. Ultimately, the contracting authority appointed the supplier to the framework simply to diffuse the challenge and avoid delay and excessive legal costs.[76]

[70] LA16.
[71] LA13.
[72] LA18.
[73] CPB4.
[74] ibid.
[75] CPB2.
[76] CA5.

One interviewee mentioned that complaints are sometimes made when a challenger perceives that another bidder has reverse engineered the framework award process and submitted an 'abnormally low bid' that should have been investigated and rejected (pursuant to regulation 69),[77] an aspect raised in chapter seven as needing further guidance and also requiring more sophisticated technical expertise within contracting authorities when formulating pricing evaluation methodologies used in frameworks to mitigate this risk.

A few interviewees had experienced complaints about the evaluation and award of lots under frameworks, particularly when a bidder had been awarded multiple lots. An example was given of a bidder being awarded six out of eight lots, where insufficient due diligence had been carried out on the bidder's capacity to deliver on all six.[78] Sometimes, the methodology applied to determine the apportionment of lot awards is unclear, particularly when a bidder has won more than one. As discussed in chapter six, whilst it is possible to award contracts combining several or all lots, under regulation 46(6), the objective criteria used to determine how the award of combinations of lots is to be made should, in accordance with the principle of transparency, be set out in the procurement documents.

As indicated, the risk of challenge to a framework award may be significantly limited by admitting multiple suppliers. Several interviewees gave examples of suppliers making sometimes baseless complaints but which were appointed to the framework to avoid mounting costs and stretched capacity.[79] Another interviewee identified a supplier tactic of complaining during any standstill period which would lead to suspension of the period until the complaint was resolved.[80] Suppliers also relayed their experiences of successfully reversing award decisions.[81] There was a sense among smaller suppliers that larger ICT organisations can exert their commercial weight to tip the balance in their favour and win places on frameworks in such circumstances.

4.3. Transparency, Complaints and Challenges when Awarding Call-offs

As discussed in chapters seven and eight, as there were few transparency requirements applicable to call-offs under the PCR 2015, breaches have not always been easily detectable at the call-off stage. For direct awards without competition, there is no requirement to inform other suppliers on a framework of a proposed direct award. Nor is there any requirement to publish a contract award notice for call offs made with or without competition. Regarding call-off awards made with competition, under regulation 86(5)(c), contracting authorities have been exempt from the requirement to notify bidders of their award decision and run a standstill period before entering into the call-off.

Some interviewees expressed concerns about the absence of these requirements. Regulation 99(7) provides that contracting authorities may mitigate the risk of an

[77] CPB10.
[78] LA13.
[79] CPB3.
[80] CPB9.
[81] EO3.

'ineffectiveness' claim regarding a call-off awarded using a mini-competition by voluntarily applying the notification and standstill rules. CCS guidance recommends that this is done[82] and it would seem a sensible course of action unless, for reasons of urgency, the consequential delay in award is not justifiable or if the contracting authority is confident that it has applied the mini-competition rules correctly. However, removing this risk of ineffectiveness does not seem to be a predominant factor when deciding whether to apply the notification and standstill procedures to the award of a particular call-off. Rather, it is seen more as a useful means of identifying early complaints and preventing challenges generally.

CPAs tend to leave the decision to run a standstill period at the call-off stage to contracting authorities, although some recommend that one is run as a matter of good practice. For some contracting authorities, this decision is based on the value, subject-matter and complexity of the call-off requirement. In the experience of one interviewee, 'the vast majority of customers do run standstill periods if they have the time to do so'.[83] Another interviewee described their policy of running standstill periods for all call-offs, providing detailed bidder debriefs and disclosing more rather than less detail to help suppliers improve future tenders, stating that being open and transparent in this way helped to prevent further questioning.[84]

For other interviewees, however, not running a standstill at the call-off stage was preferable in the ICT domain. As one interviewee stated, 'no one wants to paint a target on themselves',[85] allowing the possibility that running a standstill period and providing bidders with feedback might attract a higher risk of challenge than running no standstill at all. The risk of providing tender feedback through a standstill stage that is flawed in some way (eg by being overly subjective) was raised by several interviewees and could act as a deterrent to issuing standstill letters at the call-off stage.[86]

When awarding a framework, regulation 50(1) provides that contracting authorities are required to publish a contract award notice on the UK's Find a Tender service no later than 30 days after the award of a contract or conclusion of the framework. Regulation 50(4) provides that no such requirement applies to the award of call-offs. However, PPN 01/23 provides that for call-offs made via direct award and mini-competition, contracting authorities are required to publish an 'awarded opportunity notice' within a specified timescale on the UK's Contract Finder service (including specified information) where the value of the call-off exceeds a certain value.[87] Many interviewees revealed that such notices were not always published in practice, particularly for direct call-offs.[88]

Several interviewees raised the lack of transparency and disclosure obligations in respect of call-offs as reasons why challenges to call-offs awards are few and far between.

[82] CCS, 'The Public Contracts Regulations 2015 & For Utilities, The Utilities Contracts Regulations 2016, Guidance on the standstill period', updated October 2016, 8.

[83] CPB5.

[84] CA12.

[85] CPB1.

[86] CA3.

[87] PPN 01/23, Cabinet Office, 'Guidance on the Transparency Requirements for Publishing on Contracts Finder', 18 January 2023, 4.

[88] EO4.

One legal adviser queried whether 'more oversight is potentially needed'[89] and suggested that the new Procurement Review Unit ('PRU') introduced by the PA 2023 might be able to provide such. It would seem, however, that more substantive changes may be required to increase the transparency of call-offs and enable breaches to be addressed before concluding contracts, particularly in respect of direct awards.

Concerning complaints in respect of call-offs, there was a general perception that challenges and complaints against call-offs are not as common as those brought against awards of public contracts outside of frameworks. The risk of challenge is perceived to be very low for frameworks used by many contracting authorities with numerous call-offs to be awarded. One interviewee observed an 'acceptance by suppliers that you win some and lose some' and that 'they are content so long as they get some regular business through the framework'.[90] Most complaints and challenges relate to the appointment stage as suppliers see some frameworks as being key to their marketing and business winning strategy. It was observed by interviewees anecdotally that complaints and challenges to call-off awards are less common and relate predominantly to mini-competitions, not direct awards.[91] There may be any number of other reasons that could explain the low levels, just some of which are identified here.

First, some CPAs offer support to contracting authorities to diffuse complaints and challenges. As one interviewee explained, it is in their commercial interests to 'help the customers nip the complaint in the bud before it becomes a serious issue'.[92] However, some take a more 'hands-off' approach. As discussed in chapters five and eight, it has been questioned whether CPAs could offer more support throughout the call-off award process.

Second, as explained, it may be difficult to detect non-compliance in order to bring a challenge, particularly in the context of direct awards as transparency controls are lacking.

Third, a common perception conveyed was that, as framework suppliers benefit from being admitted to a framework for the duration, they are reluctant to bite the hand that feeds.[93] A legal adviser stated that 'frameworks accentuate the problem of suppliers being unwilling to challenge their customer for breach of the procurement rules' on the basis that 'there is a limited pool of suppliers and so more opportunities to get business and they want to be reappointed to the framework'. They continued that 'suppliers will therefore send softer letters of complaint whilst highlighting that they do not intend to raise any legal challenge'.[94]

Fourth, it may be difficult to identify who to bring a challenge against, on what basis, and whether they have standing to challenge. Hurdles to bringing a challenge include not knowing which organisation to challenge (ie the CPA or user contracting authority); identifying a strong ground on which to base a challenge; ensuring the time limit for bringing a challenge has not expired; and ensuring that sufficient legal standing is

[89] LA3.
[90] CA2.
[91] CA7.
[92] CPB6.
[93] LA14.
[94] LA11.

present to bring a challenge. One interviewee stated that there was a lower risk of a challenge for call-offs because non-framework suppliers would not usually have sufficient legal standing to bring a legal claim; the contracting authority only needed to be concerned about the pool of framework suppliers. It should be noted, however, that, as indicated above, there have been at least two cases in which non-framework suppliers had standing to challenge call-offs.

Fifth, from a commercial perspective, there can be a lack of incentive to bring a challenge due to the non-obligatory nature of most frameworks in the UK. Framework suppliers are generally not exposed to contract delivery risk and according to one interviewee, 'are not really losing out'. They stated that 'it is different if a framework requires you to be oven-ready to deliver from the point of admission'.[95]

Whilst formal legal challenges to call-offs might be few, interviewees nevertheless gave some examples. One legal adviser described a challenge brought on the ground that a proposed call-off would result in the originally estimated total framework value being increased from £5 million to £15 million.[96] This would appear to represent a good ground of challenge based on making a substantial modification to the framework.

Some legal advisers highlighted that whilst they generally advise that the practical risk of a challenge against the award of a call-off is low, sometimes they must advise that there is a high risk that *if* a challenge were to be brought, the challenge would likely be successful. One legal adviser commented that 'it often helps to reduce the practical risk if the cake is divided up and shared fairly amongst suppliers'.[97]

Therefore, factors against bringing a challenge appear to outweigh those that might prompt a challenge. This is problematic if market-related considerations are put above the effective functioning of the regulated procurement system.

4.4. Views on Liabilities and Remedies

Interviewees expressed a range of views in respect of the issue of liability and remedies under the PCR 2015.

Interviewees raised concerns about the apportionment of liabilities between CPAs and user contracting authorities under regulation 37. It was perceived that CPAs have a 'get out of jail free card' under regulation 37 as contracting authorities bear the legal responsibility for conducting a reopening of competition under a framework that has been concluded by a central purchasing body.[98] As discussed in chapter five, greater clarity is needed on this issue. Relatedly, questions were also raised about when time for commencing legal proceedings starts to run and when the time limit expires in the framework context given that frameworks may be set up by one contracting authority eg a CPA but user contracting authorities do not call-off contracts under it until some time later. There was uncertainty particularly where flaws in the framework have been present since the framework was set up (eg provision for unlawful call-off mechanisms).

[95] LA4.
[96] LA18.
[97] LA6.
[98] LA11.

As one legal adviser queried, 'if no challenges have been brought against the framework set-up after six months, are future challenges in respect of the framework set-up time barred?'.[99]

There was also some apparent uncertainty around available remedies. A few legal advisers highlighted the anomalous third ineffectiveness ground which applies to a call-off awarded in breach of any requirement imposed by the rules on award pursuant to a mini-competition but not direct call-offs. One legal adviser considered this to be illogical as it imposes a higher standard of legal compliance for call-offs than for standard public contracts with even 'an innocent, minor mistake being caught'.[100] This third ground appears to catch any breach of the rules on running mini-competitions which contrasts with the second ineffectiveness ground in regulation 99(5) which has conditions attached. However, this has arguably been addressed in the PA 2023, as explained below.

More generally, questions were raised about the effectiveness of the institutional machinery for addressing complaints, given that, as discussed in chapter five, issues have also been raised about the ability of CPAs to provide effective monitoring and oversight of frameworks. For instance, the Cabinet Office's Mystery Shopper scheme (renamed the Public Procurement Review Service ('PPRS') in 2011) was mentioned by some interviewees.[101] This service provides an alternative route for suppliers to anonymously raise concerns about procurement practice (even when attempts at resolving issues with a contracting authority or a first-tier supplier have failed) and provides feedback to enquirers on their concerns. It can also carry out spot checks on procurement processes and publishes the results of cases. It can make recommendations to contracting authorities to help drive better practice but cannot award any specific remedies to suppliers or mandate actions to be taken by a contracting authority. The consensus amongst interviewees was that this service has not been very useful, criticisms including the absence of any remedies, the lack of urgency of review which is not helpful for 'live' procurements and the lack of 'teeth' in that the service can only make non-binding recommendations. There was support amongst interviewees for an entity with more robust legal powers to enforce compliance and sanction non-compliance in a timely and efficient way, such as a tribunal. It is uncertain what role any new units such as the PRU (discussed in section 5) will have under the PA 2023.

5. Bringing Challenges under the PA 2023

5.1. Transparency

It is recalled that there were few transparency requirements applied in respect of call-offs, in particular, direct call-offs under the PCR 2015 which has affected the ability to detect

[99] ibid.
[100] ibid.
[101] Information is available at www.gov.uk/government/publications/public-procurement-review-service-scope-and-remit.

breaches and, thus, mount a challenge. As explained in chapter eight, under the PA 2023, the contracting authority must usually publish a contract award notice containing details of whether a competitive selection process or a direct award without further competition was used (s.50(1)). A contracting authority must also publish a contract details notice after the contract has been awarded including details of whether the contract was awarded using a competitive selection process or directly without competition (s.53(1)). However, as indicated, this transparency remains limited given that it is provided post-award. This may limit opportunity to challenge the award before the contract has been entered into and avoid the need to make an application for the contract to be set aside.

5.2. Apportioning Liability

As discussed in chapter five, difficulties can arise in ascertaining where legal responsibility lies if both a CPA and user contracting authority are implicated in a breach of the PCR 2015 in applying a framework as this is not definitively addressed in the provisions on apportioning liability (regulation 37). The short time limit for commencing proceedings has reduced the practical risk of a challenge against the CPA leaving a contracting authority using a framework exposed.

The PA 2023 does not include specific rules on the allocation of responsibilities. Rather, it simply refers to a contracting authority carrying out a procurement or covered procurement: (a) on its own behalf, including where it acts jointly with or through another person other than a CPA, and (b) if the contracting authority is a CPA: (i) for or on behalf of another contracting authority, or (ii) for the purpose of the supply of goods, services or works to another contracting authority. This does not explicitly address the delegation of authority and liability in a way covered by the PCR 2015. By contrast, the GCF guidance appears to do so but through an explanation of what constitutes 'in the business of' when considering whether a contracting authority is acting as a CPA. It is recalled from chapter four that the definition of a CPA in section1(4) is 'a contracting authority that is in the business of carrying out procurement for or on behalf of, or for the purpose of the supply of goods, services or works to, other contracting authorities'. The GCF guidance states that, 'in the business of' ensures that only contracting authorities that specialise in this activity rather than on an ad hoc basis can be CPAs.[102] This is stated to be important because contracting authorities can only lawfully delegate responsibility (and liability) for procurement to a CPA. It continues that if two contracting authorities conduct a joint procurement, they are both responsible (and liable) for any contracts they award, whereas if a contracting authority procures via a CPA, it delegates liability for the award of contracts by the CPA, eg establishment of frameworks, but not for awards it makes itself under such an arrangement, eg call-off contracts.[103] The Explanatory Notes include similar statements.[104] Thus, it appears from the guidance that 'in the business of' is intended to confirm delegation of responsibility and liability as was the case under the PCR 2015 with 'in the business of' importing much of the

[102] GCF, 'Guidance: Covered Procurement Objectives', December 2024, 3.
[103] ibid.
[104] Explanatory Notes to the Procurement Act 2023, ch 54, 9.

same meaning. Legal uncertainty persists, therefore, as the guidance does not address the issue of when there might be a joint breach of the PA 2023 with regard to the use of a framework; for example, where an unlawful call-off procedure designed by a CPA is used by a contracting authority.

It is also observed that the distinction between when a contracting authority will be considered 'in the business of' carrying out procurements for the benefit of other contracting authorities, thereby potentially constituting a CPA, and when it will be acting jointly with other contracting authorities is not clear in the PA 2023. Take, for example, a small group of local authorities that habitually set up frameworks through which to procure various requirements but that do not set up a special purpose vehicle for this purpose. Should the lead contracting authority here be considered as 'in the business of' carrying out procurements for the benefit of other contracting authorities or is it acting on an ad hoc basis? To what extent, if at all, could it be relevant whether the repeat set-up of frameworks was for very similar or even overlapping requirements as distinct from a range of very different requirements? The 'more ad hoc basis' reference is characteristic of much of the vague GCF guidance and it is not clear whether this constitutes the introduction of an additional test which may be difficult to apply. The distinction is important because of the apportionment of liabilities in the legislation.

The PA 2023 has also seemingly introduced a more restrictive regime for joint procurements. Under the PCR 2015, regulation 38 on occasional joint procurement provided that where the conduct of a procurement procedure is not in its entirety carried out in the name, and on behalf of, the contracting authorities concerned, each contracting authority shall be jointly responsible only for those parts carried out jointly but shall have sole responsibility for fulfilling its obligations in respect of the parts it conducts in its own name and on its own behalf. There appears to be no such provision on sole responsibility in the PA 2023. The GCF guidance appears to confirm this, stating that:

> Where contracting authorities are not centralised procurement authorities and are acting on a more ad hoc basis to carry out procurements on behalf of other contracting authorities, including setting up frameworks that other contracting authorities can use, then contracting authorities cannot delegate any part of their obligation to comply with the Act and remain fully liable for any unlawful award made by them as a consequence of the arrangement. In terms of frameworks established by a contracting authority for use by itself and other contracting authorities, this means that the contracting authority procuring under the framework must be satisfied that the framework itself complies with the Act as it will be liable both for compliance with the Act when establishing the framework and when carrying out a procurement and awarding a call-off contract under the framework.[105]

In light of the ambiguous divide between CPA and joint procurement arrangements, it is not necessarily clear why a lead contracting authority acting in such a 'joint' capacity with other contracting authorities should be liable for all call-offs entered into pursuant to a framework set up in this way whereas a CPA bears no such responsibility.

The GCF guidance does include a checklist for contracting authorities when considering whether to use a third party's framework. It highlights that if a contracting authority wishes to award a call-off under a framework established by another contracting authority, it must ensure that the framework is suitable for the contract it intends to

[105] GCF, 'Guidance: Frameworks', November 2024, 3–4.

award. It sets out some important checks that a contracting authority should make, in particular that:

(a) the framework has been established by a contracting authority;
(b) as relevant, a tender or transparency notice has been published;
(c) the tender or transparency notice (where relevant) and framework:
    (i) clearly identify the contracting authority as one of those permitted to use the framework;
    (ii) include goods, services or works of a type to be awarded under the call-off contract;
    (iii) set out the other matters required by section 45(5) and regulation 20 or 26 PR 24 (as relevant), such as the price payable, or mechanism for determining the price payable under the call-off contract and any selection process to be applied;
(d) the total value of call-off contracts awarded under the framework to date does not exceed the estimated value of the framework as set out in the tender notice and framework.[106]

The GCF guidance also provides that contracting authorities should understand the liability position for the framework, in particular, where a framework has been established by another contracting authority acting as a CPA and where a contracting authority is liable as principal for a third party framework set up on a more ad hoc basis.[107] As explained above, this may not be straightforward to determine for some cases in practice. It also reminds contracting authorities that when awarding a call-off, the contracting authority must comply with the selection process set out in the framework, noting, in particular, when it is permissible to award a contract without following a competitive selection process.[108]

For multi-user frameworks established by CPAs, therefore, contracting authorities will continue to have responsibility to check that the framework has been established in a way that has been well-informed by the potential user base and the relevant supplier market and has been sufficiently scoped to meet their needs. Contracting authorities using a third-party framework will essentially bear the risk of challenge when making decisions on using the framework. The increase in transparency generated by the PA 2023 will put such decision-making in the spotlight and, so, contracting authorities will need to ensure that, in addition to carrying out any necessary checks of suppliers relating to exclusions and debarment, the framework has been set up lawfully and that they can use it for their specific requirements in a way that achieves value for money and, for public contracts, has regard to the importance of the section 12 objectives.

5.3. Review Forum

It is recalled that concerns were raised about the effectiveness of the review system given exclusivity of the High Court as a review forum. In the *Transforming Public Procurement*

[106] ibid 10.
[107] ibid.
[108] ibid.

Green Paper, the Cabinet Office originally proposed reforms to certain court processes, including speeding up the resolution of challenges.[109] It also indicated that it would investigate the introduction of a tribunal system to determine low-value claims and issues in ongoing procurements.[110] The Cabinet Office did not proceed with the tribunal system option but suggested it would keep it under review and focus instead on exploring options for faster and more accessible routes for challenge. It did not set out any concrete proposals other than mentioning that it would look at reform to court processes such as decisions on written pleadings, early and enhanced disclosure and a dedicated procurement judge.[111] These reforms have not been incorporated in the PA 2023; it is assumed that any such reforms will be addressed in further updates to the Civil Procedure Rules and/or Technology and Construction Court Guidance.

5.4. Remedies

The provisions in the PA 2023 that relate specifically to bringing challenges are similar to those in the PCR 2015 except that they are intended to encourage challenges to be brought more promptly and before the public contract is concluded. This is reflected, for example, in the fact that section 101(1) provides that a suspension on the award only applies if proceedings are commenced during any applicable standstill period (usually eight working days which, again, is optional for call-offs under frameworks) and the contracting authority is notified of such proceedings. It is not clear that this will have any significant impact on whether challenges are brought in respect of frameworks. A challenger would still need to follow the court procedure rules and fund the associated costs as well as establish a breach of the duty to comply with the PA 2023 that has caused or risks causing loss or damage (section 100(3)).

Regarding standing, the position under the PA 2023 is similar to that under the PCR 2015. Section 100(3) provides that proceedings may be brought by a supplier that: (a) is a UK or treaty state supplier, and (b) has suffered, or is at risk of suffering, loss or damage in consequence of a breach of the duty. It is likely, therefore, that similar considerations with regard to challenges brought by non-parties to the framework will still apply.

The time limits for bringing a challenge under the PA 2023 are also similar to those under the PCR 2015. The main differences relate to the standstill period which is now eight working days in all cases and the automatic suspension only applies if proceedings are commenced within the standstill period, as indicated.

Regarding the availability of damages, the PA 2023 does not expressly refer to any test of 'sufficiently serious breach' building on existing UK case law. Section 104(2)(b) simply states that the court 'may, in any case, make an order for the award of damages'. The GCF guidance also provides that an award of damages is 'effectively a form of compensation to the claimant for the loss or damage it has suffered as a consequence of

[109] Cabinet Office, *Transforming Public Procurement*, December 2020, CP 353, 60–61.
[110] ibid 63.
[111] Cabinet Office, 'Transforming Public Procurement: Government response to consultation', December 2021, CP 556, 57.

the breach by the contracting authority of its statutory duty'.[112] It goes on to state that '[i]n all cases, whether this is a pre-contractual remedy or a post-contractual remedy, it is for the court to decide whether the breach caused the damage or loss suffered by the claimant and therefore whether an award of damages is appropriate in the circumstances'.[113] However, it is noted that in *Braceurself*, Coulson LJ in the Court of Appeal made the following statement:

> In a public procurement claim, where an unsuccessful bidder claims damages against the contracting authority, the claimant must prove [...] that the breach is 'sufficiently serious' to warrant an award of damages (sometimes called Francovich damages). Although this is a concept originating in European Law, it remains unamended by the new Procurement Act 2023. It is not a test that fits very easily either into the English common law generally, or the world of public procurement challenges in particular.[114]

At the time of writing, therefore, it is not entirely clear whether the same 'sufficiently serious' test will apply under the PA 2023.

Concerning the ineffectiveness remedy, this is now termed 'set aside'. The set aside conditions are different to the ineffectiveness provisions in the PCR 2015 but as the GCF guidance states, 'they reflect the same intent: that a supplier should have the option of bringing a claim to set aside the contract where it has been denied the opportunity to bring a claim before the contract has been entered into or the modification made'.[115] The grounds of set aside reflect the augmented transparency brought about by the increased information that must be provided in notices before a public contract is entered into and focus on circumstances when a supplier has been denied the opportunity to seek a pre-contractual remedy.

It should be observed that the specific ineffectiveness ground related to breach of the mini-competition provisions has not been carried forward into the PA 2023. It will be recalled that there was no ineffectiveness ground related specifically to breach of the direct award provisions.

Under section 105, there are six conditions for set aside which are broader and less specific to particular breaches compared with the three PCR 2015 ineffectiveness grounds. These can apply both to frameworks and call-offs. Importantly for call-offs, one of the set aside conditions in section 105(1)(d) is in the case of a contract that does not require a mandatory standstill period (which would include a call-off under a framework), where the breach became apparent only on publication of a contract award notice. This would cover the award of call-off contracts using the competitive selection process where no standstill has been run as well as where a call-off has been awarded directly. This relates to the fact that the use of both call-off procedures now requires a contract award notice to be published prior to entering into the call-off. Further, the sixth set aside condition in section 105(1)(f) relates to where 'the breach became apparent only after the contract was entered into or modified'. This appears to be somewhat of a catch-all condition which could potentially have a very broad application to any

[112] ibid 8.
[113] ibid.
[114] *Braceurself* (n 46) para 1.
[115] GCF, 'Guidance: Remedies', November 2024, 3.

circumstance where a breach has not been published sufficiently such that it should have been 'apparent' to a potential challenger prior to the contract being entered into.

Aside from the court system of remedies, it will be recalled that some interviewees mentioned the PPRS. Under the PA 2023, the PPRS will continue to operate, but as part of the new PRU, established to operate the procurement oversight regime, as well as a new exclusion and debarment regime.[116] The PRU monitors compliance across contracting authorities and focuses on investigations into contracting authorities that demonstrate patterns of repeated non-compliance (referred to as 'institutional non-compliance'). A pattern of non-compliance could also be across a number of different contracting authorities (referred to as 'systemic non-compliance'). The GCF guidance indicates that an investigation into an individual procurement will only be in response to a supplier's complaint, in line with PPRS.[117] A recommendation can be issued to a contracting authority under section 109 following an investigation and the PRU will manage the publication of any investigation reports, including any recommendations issued, and progress reports submitted by contracting authorities (or notice of a contracting authority's failure to submit a progress report). These will be published on a dedicated gov.uk page, which will also serve as the mechanism for suppliers and other stakeholders to raise a concern regarding a contracting authority's compliance. Therefore, the PRU is given only slightly more powers than the PPRS. It is conceivable, however, that if it is sufficiently resourced and operates efficiently, it could have a more positive and widespread impact on compliance moving forward.

6. Conclusions

There have been relatively few challenges to frameworks in the UK, although the legal risk profile is potentially changing given recent high-profile cases. Many contributing factors have been identified. There is the difficulty of determining who is legally responsible for a breach. The High Court is the only review forum, other informal resolution processes lacking effective enforcement powers (eg the PPRS). Further, frameworks may be designed to limit the risk of challenge eg admitting many suppliers or re-admitting excluded suppliers, which may, itself be unlawful. In addition, there is a general lack of transparency on call-offs in the absence of mandatory standstill and notice requirements necessary to inform a challenge. Suppliers may not want to bite the hand that feeds, given that a framework provides a basis for future and repeat business. Otherwise, the review and remedies rules do not appear to place significant constraints on the ability to secure review and remedies. Suppliers which are not parties to frameworks have been able to challenge call-offs under them and have been able to make claims of contract ineffectiveness and damages as well as secure other remedies.

Thus, perhaps symptomatic of the absence of regulatory pressure brought to bear on framework set-up and use, the review and remedies regime has not been a significant deterrent to framework marketisation.

[116] Information is available at www.gov.uk/guidance/procurement-review-unit.

[117] GCF, 'Guidance: Procurement Oversight', November 2024, 3.

The PA 2023 provisions on notices should increase transparency of call-offs but it is unclear whether this will significantly improve the ability to detect breaches. Relatedly, the grounds for set aside conditions appear to be broader than the ineffectiveness grounds, including in respect of direct call-offs although detection of breach remains an issue. Otherwise, there is continuing uncertainty as to determining who is liable and the approach to remedies appears to be similar to that under the PCR 2015. A new PRU may provide greater oversight than the PPRS although whether it will be effective remains to be seen. Therefore, there are few indications that the new review and remedies regime will address many of the issues raised.

PART IV

Reform

10

Regulatory Reform of Frameworks in the UK

1. Introduction

Parts II and III revealed extensive framework marketisation as well as general legal uncertainty which has compromised the efficacy of frameworks in practice.

This chapter focuses primarily on the need for further reform of regulation. Of course, regulation alone will not address the many issues. There is also a need for institutional and industry reform to change an entrenched culture that seems to consider a 'commercial' approach to procuring through frameworks as involving the identification of quick, convenient routes to contract, and even the ability to generate revenue. The fundamental purpose of frameworks must be renewed to put the focus back on use only where appropriate and securing value for money in public service delivery. Notwithstanding, there are reasons to revisit regulation specifically.

First, returning to the intuitions of chapter one, regulation appears to exert increasingly less pressure in constraining or guiding framework use. A broad legal definition has been exploited, particularly in the case of generic multi-supplier frameworks. The definitional purpose of holding a rigorous competition to appoint select suppliers and establish an agreement ie a 'framework' of core terms governing future 'call-offs' has been eroded. Instead, only a notional competition may be held to appoint many suppliers with loose arrangements for determining call-offs. In certain instances, frameworks have been set up without complying with basic rules eg by entities which do not even constitute 'contracting authorities'. Further, whilst the growth of centralised purchasing, including fee-charging, has incentivised framework use, there are many other forms of marketisation. There has been a normalisation of the perception (developed beneath the regulatory radar) that frameworks are easy and low risk, and which is more prevalent than any particular concern to realise the benefits of aggregated procurement. Therefore, there is a need to recalibrate regulation to ensure that it acts as both an effective enabler and constraint.

Second, as discussed in chapter four, there have been several missed opportunities to address regulation and decisive action is now required. Brexit was a once-in-a-generation opportunity to 'transform' procurement. However, as will be discussed, the Cabinet Office consultation expressed fundamental uncertainty on how to regulate purchasing tools, and consulted on neither the framework definition, procedures and rules, nor on practice when setting up and operating them. Instead, largely uninformed by empirical evidence, it simply proposed to retain the closed framework with limited changes and introduce an open framework option. As discussed throughout Part III, the PA 2023 appears to provide continuity or even extend flexibility rather than introduce regulatory rigour to ensure more responsible framework use. The new rules do little to address much of the pre-existing legal uncertainty and introduce new uncertainty. More flexibility might have been tenable had this been accompanied by detailed guidance addressing compliance and commercial practice issues (although, arguably, additional hard rules would have been necessary in any event), but this has not been the case. This is difficult to square with the new Labour Government's rhetoric indicating a tougher stance on frameworks. Moreover, successive governments have appeared ambivalent on the extent to which they intend to further regulate.

Third, lack of effective regulation is not a problem specific to the UK. Albano and Nicholas's review of international experience has indicated that whilst framework design and implementation can be improved without regulation, 'the regulatory system needs to provide rules and guidance to supplement primary law and regulations in more detail than many systems currently do'.[1]

This chapter identifies certain areas for regulatory reform. It is not intended to be comprehensive and the (de)merits of various options would need to be carefully considered. The objective is to simply concentrate policy-makers' minds on regulation rather than continuing to leave matters largely to the vagaries of the market. The chapter begins by reinforcing the need identified in chapter two to examine more systematically the characteristics and economics of the UK framework market in order to better inform policy interventions (Section 2). It will then consider potential further substantive reform of procurement rules (Section 3) as well as the role of other areas of regulation eg competition law (Section 4). It also briefly indicates the need for longer-term institutional reform (Section 5) and calls on industry to act (Section 6). The chapter then offers concluding observations (Section 7).

2. UK Framework Market

As indicated in chapter four, previous consultations on reform have not been informed by any systematic understanding of the characteristics, in particular, economics of the UK framework market. This can lead to assumptions about how frameworks are operating, the development of rules without any clear understanding of whether they are targeting the right issues or using the most appropriate regulation (eg hard or soft law) and their potential impact, or even a reluctance to make policy interventions claiming a lack of evidence of the problem. There have been studies of the economics of frameworks[2] but none have focused specifically on the UK; an exception appears to be limited albeit useful research on construction frameworks.[3]

[1] GL Albano and C Nicholas, *The Law and Economics of Frameworks: Designing Flexible Solutions for Public Procurement* (Cambridge University Press, 2016) 323.

[2] See generally, Albano and Nicholas, ibid, and citations therein.

[3] TYM Lam and K Gale, 'Highways maintenance: impact of framework agreements upon project financial importance' (2014) 32(5) *Construction Management and Economics* 460–72; TYM Lam and K Gale, 'Framework procurement for highways maintenance in the UK: can it offer value for money for public-sector clients?' (2014) 11(5) *Structure and Infrastructure Engineering* 695–706; TYM Lam and K Gale, 'A performance-driving model for public-sector construction framework procurement in England' (2023) 13(6)

This lack of evidence matters when it comes to reform. For instance, the Cabinet Office Green Paper precipitating the PA 2023 claimed that frameworks have the intention of 'speeding up and simplifying the process of awarding contracts for particular needs as well as aggregating demand to drive competition between suppliers and leverage better prices and quality'.[4] Whilst this may be the intention, it is by no means clear that frameworks do always speed up procurement relative to a full procurement process or have enabled simplified processes. A major reason why contracting authorities use CPA-led frameworks is precisely because the award of a framework is a complex process (whatever simplification is achieved by a call-off stage instead of a full procurement). Indeed, as the Green Paper itself acknowledged, frameworks may be set up by CPAs that can have a very wide scope which can still result in a complex process rather than a simple call-off, as intended, although stating that lots can mitigate this[5] (it did not address the complexity that can be introduced by lotting structures, however). The Green Paper did not actually identify those aspects of framework practice that create complexity and undermine speed and simplicity and how they should be reformed. Similarly, it did not address the potential over-simplification of frameworks that lack proper process eg limited supplier due diligence checks on appointment, excessive discretion given to contracting authorities as to the use of call-off procedures and contract terms etc.

It is also not necessarily clear that frameworks do suit particular needs. If they did, significant amendments to call-off terms should not be necessary and new product lines would not need to be added during their term to meet requirements. Further, Part III demonstrated that frameworks may not always be suitable for pricing complex requirements, which led to consideration of whether frameworks should be used for complex requirements at all or adaptations made to address complexity.

Similarly, it is not clear that the aggregation of demand necessarily drives competition and leverages better prices and quality. It is recalled from chapter five that it has been queried whether the ability of some CPAs to secure lower prices for some aggregated demand may, paradoxically, result in higher prices being paid on other frameworks and through other procurement routes, a so-called 'waterbed effect'.[6] This raises the question of whether further regulatory controls are necessary to address how purchasing techniques facilitate aggregated demand.

Thus, there needs to be less reliance on general understandings or anecdotal evidence of some of the claimed advantages and disadvantages of frameworks and more focus on evidence-led findings in order to develop more responsive regulation.

As indicated in chapter two, integral to this approach is a need to better understand the dimensions of the UK framework market, and which comprises various aspects.

2.1. Demand and Supply

As a starting point, it is obviously important to better understand the nature of demand. Whilst CCS has developed categories that can help forecast demand and category

Built Environment Project and Asset Management 781–98; and S Tennant and S Fernie, 'The commercial currency of construction framework agreements' (2012) 40(2) *Building Research & Information* 209–20.

[4] Cabinet Office, *Transforming Public Procurement*, December 2020, CP 353, 43.

[5] ibid 44.

[6] Section 3.2.1.

management techniques exist, it is not clear what are the patterns of demand for certain types of goods, services or works to be procured through frameworks as distinct from other forms of procurement. This is relevant to regulation because, as Part III revealed, the type of purchase may influence the regulatory design. For instance, under the PCR 2015, DPS were identified as a distinct tool to procure commoditised requirements; DPS do not permit direct awards but it might be thought such would be useful to quickly procure basic requirements. Yet, frameworks continue to remain the most popular route for procuring commoditised items. Further, as indicated, frameworks may be used to procure complex requirements in circumstances in which they may not be suitable. It can only be known which are the most suitable types of purchasing tool to use once it is known what is the nature of the goods, services and works being procured through different purchasing tools.

Another aspect is the demand for aggregation of purchases. The operating assumption of large CPAs (eg, CCS) is that the more that goods and services are aggregated, the better value for money; this has been posited as a justification for seeking to capture more of the aggregated spend market for certain categories. Therefore, it is necessary to better understand the drivers of demand aggregation, where aggregation is considered useful and not, how demand is aggregated, and its effects. This is important because frameworks may aggregate requirements in ways that fail to meet demand eg the offer of generic products on a framework that do not meet a contracting authority's specific needs, resulting in them procuring a sub-optimal solution or suppliers adding product lines outside the initial scope of the framework. This is quite apart from the extent to which aggregation does actually achieve better value for money; the waterbed effect issue was identified above, for example. More generally, there seems to be little focus on differentiating frameworks for aggregated requirements and for bespoke requirements. To date, only a basic distinction has been drawn in regulatory terms between single-supplier frameworks and multi-supplier frameworks ie based on the number of suppliers, not the nature of the demand being met.

Of course, aggregation has all sorts of other implications. It may impact supply side behaviour if it forces industry consolidation or rationalisation to meet larger demand and which may impact on SMEs used to bidding for smaller requirements. It could also lead to concentration of buying power and buyer-supplier collusion. Aggregation is also relevant to the wider policy question of the extent to which procurement should be further centralised. This too has a regulatory dimension, namely, the extent to which certain CPAs and purchasing techniques should be mandated.

There also needs to be a greater understanding of the supplier base. As indicated in chapter two, 'strategic suppliers' appear to play a significant role, raising the issue of who has access to frameworks in what share.[7] Further, chapter five indicated that the way that supply markets are structured may even impact the framework model, eg where original suppliers not admitted to frameworks can dictate the prices offered by resellers on frameworks, rendering mini-competitions redundant.[8] It is also not clear to what extent there are risks for supply side collusion. There is also limited information on the

[7] Section 3.2.
[8] Section 3.4.1.

types of services offered by the private sector to assist in management of frameworks. It is suspected that many types of consultancy and other services are not subject to full competitive procurement procedures.

2.2. Sectors

Whilst this book has focused on the ICT sector, there appears to be little other sector-specific research (except some in construction). The characteristics and economics of each sector may have a bearing on how frameworks operate and should be regulated. There may well be commonalities or differences that necessitate the same or different approaches to regulation. For instance, as discussed below, the assumption has been that flexibilities should apply to frameworks in the utilities and defence sector which appear to have been largely accepted unquestioningly. A prime example is permitting double the maximum duration of a framework. Further, as discussed in Part III, there have been calls for sector-specific adaptations of framework rules which raises the question of how to accommodate such differences within a uniform regulatory regime without undermining it.

2.3. Centralised Purchasing

This book has only focused on the role of CPAs in the context of analysing the impact of framework regulation in practice. It has not examined the actual procurement functions and business operations of CPAs more generally. For instance, it has not investigated any similarities and differences between central government and regional CPAs, how they engage private sector operators in the provision of procurement support services, their market engagement activities, their interactions with contracting authorities and suppliers in designing frameworks, their internal corporate governance structure, their monitoring and enforcement of frameworks, the setting of fees etc. This could inform approaches to regulating issues such as whether duties should be imposed on CPAs to consult framework parties, to monitor framework compliance with internal processes and procurement law, and the setting and use of fees.

Further, it is recalled that an emerging issue concerns the role of CPAs as competitive service providers on a market. This includes the extent to which CPAs are in (in)direct competition with public and/or private sector entities, what arrangements exist between 'friendly competitors' and the effects. Again, this is relevant from the perspective of regulation, in particular, competition law.

2.4. Framework Models

Whilst this book has not focused on single-supplier frameworks, Part III raised various issues. Single-supplier frameworks are different in certain important respects from multi-supplier frameworks, not least given that they are characteristically more like standard binary contracts and involve longer-term strategic partnerships. Their differences in practice relative to multi-supplier frameworks merit further investigation because it is by no means clear that they should be regulated in the same way and current regulation does not clearly differentiate between these two models. Further, as discussed in chapter eight, evidently, new types of framework model are emerging; for example, the neutral vendor and managed service provider models which raise a host of legal and practical issues.[9]

2.5. Competition

A critical issue requiring further investigation is the extent to which frameworks impact on competition. This includes not only the extent to which they provide for competition but also the ways in which their use may have anti-competitive effects.

As indicated in chapter two, both the NAO and PAC have observed the lack of any clear understanding and management of levels of competition.[10] The NAO has recommended that competition within frameworks could be enhanced by obtaining better data to improve design of call-off procedures and upskilling smaller contracting authorities to use mini-competitions more effectively.[11] The NAO goes even further and appears to have suggested the need for 'greater rivalry between framework providers'.[12]

However, more fundamentally, it is questionable to what extent there is a problem of lack of competition and whether the introduction of more is a solution to many of the issues arising. For instance, to what extent is competition really closed off if a multi-supplier framework can be established admitting hundreds of suppliers or if a supplier not admitted to one framework is admitted to a parallel framework on similar terms? If no rigorous competition is held at framework award stage only to be supplemented by a mini-competition, is this better in competition terms than where a rigorous competition is held and only supplemented by direct call-offs? To what extent is a framework competitive if many suppliers are appointed but very few are awarded call-offs? Alternatively put, part of the problem may be that frameworks do not provide *meaningful* competitions (howsoever determined) and the focus should be on addressing the myriad issues necessary for frameworks to operate more effectively.

Determining the extent to which frameworks enable or prevent competition is important because it can affect how rules are formulated. Again, to give a familiar example, what is the effect of setting a certain framework duration on competition? Should the law impose a maximum and what is appropriate based on an understanding of the impacts? As discussed in chapter three, EU law has set a four-year maximum for public sector contracts, although it is not clear that this was informed by any particular understanding of the effects on competition. Yet, it is recalled that it has been suggested under EU law that contracting authorities must consider the effects of setting framework durations on competition and may even be precluded from setting a particular duration

[9] Section 8.

[10] Section 3.4.

[11] NAO, *Efficiency in government procurement of common goods and services*, CCS, Session 2024–25 HC 116, 39.

[12] ibid 42.

below the maximum.[13] In the Green Paper consultation, the UK appeared to become fixated on this issue but seemed confused. To explain, the Green Paper proposed, on the basis of an apparent concern about 'locking out' suppliers, that closed frameworks would be permitted for up to four years, meaning the market would be closed but 'offering a period of stability and reducing bureaucracy that may be appropriate in some situations'.[14] This decision to not differ from EU law may be contrasted with the seven-year duration the UK proposed when seeking reform of the Directives (modelled on the defence rules). The Green Paper proposal appeared to suggest that the four-year rule would apply to *all* contracts despite defence and utility contracts previously permitting effectively double the maximum duration (seven or eight years). Therefore, it would appear that the policy justification was simply to ensure uniformity across all contracts; there was no indication that this decision was based on an assessment that allowing longer durations for certain types of contract could have adverse effects on competition.

The Green Paper proposal clearly proved to be problematic, evidencing considerable confusion. First, in the consultation response, it was acknowledged that the main concern raised by the utility sector was the reduction in maximum duration for utilities 'as the utility sector relies on long term relationships that would be undermined by shorter framework terms'.[15] No specific indication was given of the prevalence of such relationships for which types of utilities contracts and the ways in which a shorter duration would undermine them. In response, the Government simply u-turned, stating that in response to the concerns raised about 'the potential loss of flexibility from the existing regime', it proposed to allow a longer term for utilities (but was silent on defence contracts).[16]

Second, it seemed to be concerned to ensure a short four-year term to avoid closing off the market to competition but was silent on the fact that under the PA 2023, it would actually permit an extension beyond the maximum without significant constraints. This even applied to defence and security and utilities contracts already subject to an eight-year maximum.

Third, it seems that it was considered that closing off the market could be traded off against the apparent benefit of 'achieving value for money, particularly where the contracting authority needs a longer-term relationship, for example in construction and infrastructure' through allowing open frameworks. Yet the proposal was not to enable extension of the maximum duration solely for construction contracts but, indeed, any; moreover, open frameworks create a set of other issues which does not address the problems of closed frameworks, including the issue of maximum duration and its extension.

Fourth, it should not be overlooked that the Government actually increased the maximum duration for defence contracts from seven years under the Defence and Security Public Contracts Regulations 2011to eight years under the PA 2023 and provided no reasons. Presumably, doubling the maximum duration would necessitate compelling policy justifications given the apparent concern about shutting out competition.

[13] Section 4.2.

[14] *Transforming Public Procurement* (n 4) 46.

[15] Cabinet Office, 'Transforming Public Procurement: Government response to consultation', December 2021, CP 556, 48.

[16] ibid 48.

Again, in case the above seems abstract, in the PA 2023 guidance on defence and security contracts (but not in the frameworks guidance), it is stated that:

> Contracting authorities should consider the terms of frameworks on a case by cases basis bearing in mind that utilising the maximum permitted duration in developing or volatile markets might effectively stifle competition and innovation leading to poor value for money.[17]

This guidance is interesting given that, as indicated, there seemed to be no strong objection to allowing eight-year defence and security frameworks originally, in particular, based on concerns about 'stifling competition' or innovation. This also renders it unclear to what extent section 12 may require the impacts on competition to be considered having regard to ensuring value for money when setting framework duration.

Thus, it is important to understand the effects that frameworks have on competition and how this should inform rule-setting.

Relatedly, it is recalled from chapter three that the EU introduced rules designed to prevent the improper use of frameworks, in particular, because of their potential anti-competitive effects and it has even been argued that the application of framework rules should be constrained by a legal principle of 'competition'. The UK has not introduced such rules under the PA 2023. Were it to consider such, it is difficult to see how such rules could be properly formulated and applied without any clear understanding of the effects of frameworks (and the application of framework rules) on competition.

2.6. Other Economic Analyses

The authors defer on those aspects that should be studied further by economists but it would be useful to know from economic analyses which areas necessitate particular policy interventions. For instance, the latest National Procurement Policy Statement states that 'there are currently too many similar agreements across the public sector, leading to unnecessary transactional costs'.[18] However, it is not clear what is the evidence of the transaction and other costs involved in frameworks. Similarly, little is known about the outcomes of frameworks; research on construction frameworks has observed that 'despite widespread adoption of construction frameworks, there is scarce empirical evidence about their performance outcomes and implementation procedures'.[19] Another major aspect concerns pricing. The example of waterbed effects has already been mentioned. It is also recalled from chapter eight that there appears to be uncertainty on prices charged to public sector customers versus the private sector and the possibility that contracting authorities may get better prices by not using frameworks (even using consultants to verify whether this is the case).[20] In addition, it is recalled from chapter two that major CPAs like CCS have not been able to develop effective ways of measuring the 'commercial benefits' of frameworks. Economic analysis of the framework market will be particularly important if it is envisaged that competition law should play an increased role.

[17] Cabinet Office, 'Guidance – Defence and Security Contracts', updated 16 May 2025, para 37.
[18] Cabinet Office, *National Procurement Policy Statement*, 13 February 2025.
[19] Lam and Gale, 'A performance-driving model' (n 3) 782.
[20] Section 7.1.

2.7. Intra-UK Procurement

It would also be useful to gain a better understanding of how frameworks operate within each nation and cross-border. There is often much discussion of central government CCS frameworks but regional and sector-specific frameworks increasingly play a prominent role. It is not clear what is their impact on regional and national trade. This could be relevant to any consideration of whether to mandate the use of certain CPAs that are not central government led. Further, as indicated in chapter four, each nation may set their own policies on frameworks (eg, on speculative frameworks), which raises the issue of how policy and practice may differ across the nations.[21] In addition, it is not clear how frameworks operate 'cross-border'. For instance, the PA 2023 has recently been amended to enable otherwise excluded devolved Scottish authorities to access UK Government (ie CCS) frameworks (section 115A). Indeed, Wales indicated that one reason for opting in to the PA 2023 was the amount that Welsh contracting authorities spend on call-offs from CCS frameworks (£295m in 2022/3)[22] and the Cabinet Office has identified the need to preserve such 'commercial arrangements'.[23] This evidences the extent to which the marketised framework model may even override fundamental national political imperatives.

3. Reform Through Regulation

The authors acknowledge the UK's ambition to introduce more flexibility in procurement, including frameworks. In principle, it is difficult to object to flexibility provided there are sufficient residual legal constraints on the exercise of any additional discretion and substantial guidance to aid decision-making. However, the PA 2023 has not provided such and, whatever flexibility is introduced, there is still a need for certain additional hard-law rules on some issues. Going forward, regulatory reform should not only focus on addressing existing legal uncertainty or extant concerns about aggregation of purchases or concentration of buying power but also market-related behaviours. Part III included a brief analysis of PA 2023 provisions pertaining to issues raised by interviewees. Building on that analysis, this Section offers just some suggestions for further reform.

Before doing so, it will be suggested that the UK Government needs to identify a clearer policy vision regarding the aims and objectives of frameworks within the UK procurement system; this is essential for developing a principled regulatory policy. In addition, whilst beyond the scope of this book, reform should be informed by comparatives experiences of EU Member States, certain of which have regulated in this area,[24] as well as other countries with extensive experience (eg, the US).[25]

[21] Section 3.1.

[22] Explanatory Memorandum to The Procurement (Wales) Regulations 2024, 11 June 2024, 12.

[23] GCF, 'Guidance: Devolved Contracting Authorities', October 2024, 6.

[24] A useful starting point is the national central purchasing chapters featured in M Comba, 'CPBs in the European legal space: an unresolved misconception' in C Risvig Hamer and M Comba (eds), *Centralising Public Procurement: The Approach of EU Member States* (Edward Elgar, 2021).

[25] A useful overview is provided in Albano and Nicholas, (n 1) ch 6.

3.1. Objectives

It is difficult to discern what is the UK Government's policy on the purpose of frameworks and the circumstances of their use. Of course, their functions can be identified in general terms eg speed and simplicity, demand aggregations, economies of scale etc. However, there is little clarity as regards their specific aims and objectives, ie what are the precise circumstances in which they are intended to operate to achieve what ends. If this is not clear, it is not possible to develop targeted regulation, an issue which may be compounded if the objectives of the procurement system overall are also unclear.

For example, the Green Paper appeared to express uncertainty and contradiction on the role of frameworks, seemingly reflecting a more general uncertainty on the role of purchasing techniques within the UK system.

On one hand, it stated that frameworks are 'ideal for situations such as catalogues and markets requiring high volume commodity items and call-offs, stable long-term relationships, especially where direct award call-off is allowed and a high degree of stability and certainty exists in a market'.[26] This seemed to suggest that frameworks should mainly be used for transactional purchasing in stable markets. Yet, as indicated in chapter three, one reason for introducing EU rules on frameworks was to address the need for purchasing arrangements in volatile markets ie where it was not possible to establish prices from the outset. As indicated, it is therefore no longer clear what differentiates a framework from a DPS, for example. Further, the Green Paper did not address whether frameworks are beneficial for purchasing more complex requirements where there is less market certainty (although this is alluded to, as discussed below). It is also questionable whether frameworks are intended to foster long-term stable relationships (and whether up to four years can really be considered such). On one reading of the Green Paper, it could even be suggested that it endorses repeat direct call-offs to the same supplier, raising the question of whether this is considered preferable over mini-competitions. Thus, the above seems to refer to a combination of single-supplier and multi-supplier framework models without distinguishing each, the former tending more towards 'relational' strategic partnering arrangements, the latter more transactional. Whilst single-supplier frameworks are more suited to this partnership model and where direct call-offs may be standard, it is questionable whether the same is the case for multi-supplier frameworks (especially if the framework award stage did not involve a robust competition) but the Green Paper did not address this distinction.

On the other hand, the Green Paper suggested that 'innovation' had been 'stifled by the limited flexibility offered in PCR-style frameworks' and necessitated reform to 'make it easier to achieve value for money, particularly where the contracting authority needs a longer-term relationship, for example in construction and infrastructure'.[27] Yet, as indicated, it was stated that frameworks are supposed to be ideal for procuring high-volume commodities ie items that, in fact, will involve the least innovation. It is not at all clear that frameworks have ever been specifically intended to enable innovation in process or outcome. The references to construction and infrastructure are also curious given that, presumably, construction

[26] *Transforming Public Procurement* (n 4) 45.
[27] ibid.

projects will typically be complex involving a mix of goods, services or works, not just the purchase of high-volume commodities. It is by no means clear that frameworks would generally be used in the construction sector to procure innovation.

The result is confusion as to what frameworks are for and when they should be used. This should be considered in light of the fact that the Green Paper referred to 'using the best commercial purchasing tools'. It is not clear how it is decided what is the 'best' purchasing tool and how frameworks should be viewed in 'commercial' terms. This is to say nothing of the confusion as to the proposals made for a 'DPS +' model which was abandoned and replaced with a 'dynamic market', the discrete functions of each tool and the exercise of choice between them.

More broadly, the UK Government has not provided a particularly clear set of objectives for the procurement system overall. As indicated in Part III, it has legislated to include statutory objectives in section 12 PA 2023 to which contracting authorities must have regard. These include, for example, value for money and maximising public benefit. There is no equivalent of a claimed objective of 'competition', for example, as discussed in chapter three. As repeatedly observed, it is not clear how the rules on frameworks must be interpreted in light of these objectives. Also, certain objectives are not even enforceable in civil proceedings (eg to have regard to barriers facing SMEs: section 100(5)). As Albano and Nicholas have previously observed:

> A statement of objectives may give some general guidance as part of a package of tools to support the use of framework agreements – emphasising the importance of administrative efficiency, for example – but it does not give rights to or place obligations on procuring entities or suppliers, which are the backbone of a public procurement system.[28]

It is beyond the scope of this book to address what and how objectives (and principles) should be framed for the procurement system, including through regulation, and their application to frameworks. However, at the very least, there could be clearer guidance and illustrations of how the rules on frameworks may be applied in light of the section 12 objectives. Further, in the absence of an express competition objective, it may also be considered whether an anti-circumvention rule of some kind should be introduced into the PA 2023 to prevent improper design and use of frameworks similar to that previously found under EU law but accompanied with clearer guidance and/or other controls to avoid some of the legal uncertainty that has arisen. Of course, the need for such rules might be obviated by other rules on frameworks that impose clearer obligations on contracting authorities (including CPAs) when setting up and operating frameworks and by greater enforcement under competition law.

3.2. Definition of a Framework

It is recalled from chapter five that section 45(2) now defines as a 'framework' as:

> a contract between a contracting authority and one or more suppliers that provides for the future award of contracts by a contracting authority to the supplier or suppliers.

[28] Albano and Nicholas, (n 1) 311.

Chapter five identified various issues with this definition.[29] As indicated, the very purpose of a framework, namely, an 'agreement' to establish at the first stage terms (particularly, price and quantity) governing contracts to be awarded has been removed. Instead, its purpose is replaced by a tautology of sorts: a framework is a contract for the future award of contracts. Conceptually, it is thus not necessarily clear whether there is now less emphasis on using competition to formalise the framework. Further, the fact that a framework is both a 'public contract' (section 3(3)) and a 'contract' creates potential uncertainty in various respects. One is whether agreements imposing binding obligations to purchase and supply should be treated as a standard public contract not subject to the framework provisions at all. Another is the fact that it appears that a framework (as a public contract) can be directly awarded, raising the issue of whether this is sound in principle. Yet another is the possible conflation of frameworks and dynamic markets and the effects. Thus, a framework may be awarded following a competitive tendering procedure, participation in which may be limited to members of a dynamic market. A supplier may be charged fees when awarded a contract based on dynamic market membership (eg, when being admitted to a framework) and when awarded a contract under the framework.

Relatedly, whereas proportionality-related requirements have been incorporated in some PA 2023 provisions, the ability to set up a framework with an unlimited number of suppliers has not been made subject to any proportionality considerations where such reference would be useful. It is also not clear to what extent the section 12 objectives may bear on determinations about the number of suppliers admitted.

When combined with certain other messaging which describes frameworks as 'commercial vehicles' (which is difficult to reconcile with the notion that contracting authorities should not be operating on a commercial basis) and the relaxed legal controls over using frameworks (particularly in respect of the design and use of call-off procedures), the new definition is unlikely to change perceptions or dissuade behaviours identified in this book.

It is submitted that a form of the old definition should be reinstated alongside clear guidance which reinforces the purpose of a framework in order to better condition contracting authorities on appropriate use. After all, a framework is not intended to be merely a supplier list given that dynamic markets are intended to fulfil that function. Additional guidance should also help refine the scope of a framework, eg in terms of the number to appoint, estimation of contract value etc.

The fact that reference to price has been removed from the definition raises the need for a more detailed focus on addressing competition on price both in the definition and at the appointment stage. If a pricing competition is held at the appointment stage, the pricing established needs to feed into, or at least have a strong link, to the prices agreed for call-offs or else the initial pricing competition loses its purpose. For example, chapter seven revealed that problems can occur when using a 'price list' or 'basket of items' model for suppliers to complete when applying to join a framework if the suppliers insert no prices or very low prices to get on to frameworks.[30] Questions can then arise

[29] Section 2.2.
[30] Section 6.1.1.

as to whether suppliers have submitted an 'abnormally low tender'. The effectiveness of pricing competition requires further investigation and additional controls and/or guidance may be necessary to drive better pricing practices, a key aspect of ensuring value for money.

3.3. Oversight of the Decision whether to Set Up and Use a Framework

The PCR 2015 did not expressly regulate the decision whether to set up a framework or use an established framework as against other options, including choices between overlapping frameworks or other purchasing tools. Similarly, the PA 2023 does not include any explicit duty to carefully consider between procurement options, including frameworks.

It could be argued that the section 12 objectives may need to be considered when making such choices because they apply to 'covered procurement' (section 1) which includes any step taken for the purpose of award or a part of the procurement. Further, the PA 2023 contains general provisions that regulate certain choices made in designing a framework eg that when setting conditions of participation for an award (including a framework) (section 22(1) and (5)) or competitive selection process for call-off (section 46(5)), these must be proportionate, having regard to the nature, complexity and the cost of the contract. However, these do not go as far as explicitly addressing various framework-related choices. As indicated in the Green Paper consultation response, contracting authorities considered that the choice between purchasing tools was complex and necessitated guidance.[31]

Albano and Nicholas have observed that, in theory, it would be possible to introduce a formal legal requirement to consider and justify the use of frameworks and impose conditions on use; however, they also point out that whilst it forces consideration of the effectiveness of the choice, it may become a tick-box exercise, adding to the administrative burden, and it may be difficult to enforce. They also identify the possible alternative of defining or describing the permitted circumstances for use of frameworks. In any event, they suggest that rules or guidance that set out the planning process and record keeping of such could be suitable measures in practice.[32]

Going forward, possible considerations might include: an explicit requirement for the selection of any procurement route to be considered in light of the section 12 objectives; a requirement for an explanation of the choice of a particular framework model in a tender notice (beyond simply identifying whether a closed or open framework has been chosen); or a duty to identify whether there are other similar frameworks on the register and to provide an objective justification in the tender notice for the choice. As indicated, at the very least, the responsible exercise of choice between using a framework over other procurement options is an area that would benefit from further guidance.

To put the above in wider context, there is increased focus at the EU and domestic level on the regulatory implications of choice between procurement options. For

[31] 'Transforming Public Procurement: Government response to consultation' (n 15) 48.
[32] Albano and Nicholas, (n 1) 311–14.

example, the EU *Irgita*[33] case involved a choice between an in-house transaction and conventional procurement. Article 12 Directive 2014/24/EU sets the conditions for determining whether an award is excluded on the basis that it is in-house. However, Lithuania introduced additional conditions to the effect that an in-house transaction may only be concluded when a procurement procedure cannot ensure continuity, quality or availability of services. The CJEU held that Member States could impose such further criteria provided these are compatible with EU law. Relatedly, as discussed below, it is possible to suggest that EU law style in-house transaction tests could be applied by analogy to decide whether a CPA should be subject to certain procurement rules. This focus on choice would also be consistent with the latest Ministerial statements which seem committed to placing more controls on making value for money assessments when deciding between procurement options (eg, whether to in-house or outsource).[34]

More generally, Albano and Nicholas point to the proliferation of overlapping frameworks without binding commitments in the UK as leading to 'under-use' of certain frameworks given that contracting authorities may shop around and suppliers may not recoup their costs in being admitted to so many but not receiving work under them, creating 'less-than-optimal administrative efficiency'. On this basis, they state that, from a policy perspective, there is a need to encourage the appropriate level of framework use and that periodic review of the extent and scope of use should be undertaken.[35] This is something which could potentially be achieved through guidance and policy requirements relating to the incorporation of periodic reviews in the governance and internal procedures of contracting authorities.

Of course, the above is predicated on contracting authorities having free choice between procurement options. As discussed below, it should be considered whether it would be useful to reduce the choice available and introduce a requirement mandating use of certain frameworks or CPAs, given the multitude of CPAs active in the market and overlapping frameworks likely to be accessible.

3.4. Preliminary Market Engagement

It is recalled from chapter six that the PA 2023 includes provisions on PME, even particularising the purposes for which it is permitted, as well as obligations to publish a PME notice and a pipeline notice in certain instances.[36]

However, whilst this may increase transparency of PME, it does not address some of the opportunistic behaviours encountered in the framework context, such as use of PME to identify and maximise the potential profitability of the framework, to engage in selective bargaining within certain suppliers and, in the extreme case, the facilitation of collusive behaviour. For instance, there is a provision designed to prevent PME conferring an unfair advantage and to ensure that competition is not distorted (section 16(3)) but this appears to focus, in particular, on the effects of PME on the instant procurement

[33] Case C-285/18 *Irgita* ECLI:EU:C:2019:829.
[34] Statement made on 13 February 2025, by Georgia Gould, Parliamentary Secretary for the Cabinet Office.
[35] Albano and Nicholas, (n 1) 320.
[36] Section 2.2.

process, rather than any wider impact. It is also not clear that the need to have regard to the section 12 objectives when carrying out PME will have significant impact on CPA behaviours when setting up frameworks.

The provisions on PME could be expanded to prohibit its use for certain purposes or ensure its use only for prescribed purposes. In addition, there could be separate prescription of requirements for CPAs regarding, for example, the permitted scope for collaborating with other CPAs, investigating the degree of market overlap that would result from the proposed framework, engaging effectively with the proposed contracting authority user base and the scope for using lotting in a framework and facilitating SME access. More explicit guidance could also be published warning against the marketisation related risks identified above and to steer CPAs away from adopting anti-competitive behaviours.

3.5. Choice of Procedure to Award a Framework

The PA 2023 no longer prescribes forms of open, restricted or negotiated procedure but, rather, a single-stage tendering procedure or competitive flexible procedure (s.20). It follows that there is more flexibility to design a procedure for award and which may, therefore, result in variation in design among different contracting authorities. Further, it is possible to directly award a framework. Therefore, there is increased flexibility regarding framework awards, although it is not apparent that such increased flexibility is desirable for frameworks. The PA 2023 and guidance provide no guidance on how to use these procedures to award frameworks. In addition, the requirements for tender notices and associated tender documents provide increased transparency but many are vaguely worded. Combined, such requirements are likely to be further conducive to the award of broadly scoped frameworks.

If the definition of a framework was reformulated to provide more clarity about its purpose, with a focus on competitive award, consideration could be given to whether a bespoke competitive procedure should be developed or at least detailed guidance provided on the use of competitive procedures to facilitate more effective awards. This focus could result in call-off stages that would involve a more straightforward ordering procedure (whether by direct award or a light touch further competition on certain terms). Suppliers would likely welcome a uniform and streamlined procedure used for the set-up of frameworks rather than having to deal with multiple different versions of the competitive flexible procedure given the number they are often expected to apply for.

3.6. Identifying User Base, Estimating Maximum Framework Value and Setting Framework Duration

As discussed in chapter six, the PA 2023 provides that a contracting authority must set out 'the contracting authorities entitled to award public contracts in accordance with the framework' (section 45(5)(f)).[37] The PR 24 provides that the tender notice

[37] Section 4.2.

requires listing the names of those authorities or by describing categories of authorities (regulation 20(2)(e)). The same information is required in a transparency notice for a direct award of a framework (regulation 26(2)(w)(iii)).

As under the PCR 2015, it is not clear what level of precision is required when referring to eligible user contracting authorities, to what extent, if at all, a contracting authority must consult users or obtain their consent or obtain details of their estimated usage of the framework. The law and guidance need to be much clearer on these aspects. Further, if it is intended to prohibit non-contracting authorities from using a framework, this also needs to be made more explicit.

Similarly, as discussed in chapter six, the PA 2023 and guidance has not introduced any tighter controls on the estimation of value exercise.[38] Whilst it may not be desirable to introduce a strict requirement to specify a maximum framework value and a strict rule outlawing any call-offs in excess, consideration could be given to specifying the steps a CPA or other contracting authority must take to derive an informed estimated value so that it is a meaningful indication of likely throughput.

Further, as indicated above, given the uncertainty regarding the basis for setting the maximum framework duration, further guidance should be provided on the factors that should inform this determination, in particular, where extending beyond the maximum. The same should be the case in respect of the duration of frameworks under an open framework.

3.7. Single-supplier Frameworks

This book has not covered single-supplier frameworks in detail. Notwithstanding, as indicated in chapter five,[39] it should be explored whether these should be treated as standard public contracts (with clarifications on binding obligations and pecuniary interest) or whether specific framework rules should be created.

3.8. Eligibility to be a CPA and Private Sector Frameworks

It is recalled from chapter four that under the PA 2023, a CPA means 'a contracting authority that is in the business of carrying out procurement for or on behalf of, or for the purpose of the supply of goods, services or works to, other contracting authorities'.[40] The GCF guidance states that, 'in the business of' ensures that only contracting authorities that specialise in this activity rather than on an ad hoc basis can be CPAs;[41] this is important because contracting authorities can only lawfully delegate responsibility (and liability) for procurement to a CPA. However, it is recalled that the reference to 'in the business of' and factors such as whether a contracting operates on a 'commercial basis' and 'operates on a market that is subject to fair and effective competition' provides little

[38] Section 5.2.
[39] Section 2.2.1.
[40] Section 5.1.
[41] GCF, 'Guidance: Frameworks', November 2024, 3.

clarity as regards the characterisation of CPA activities and which may be relevant to determining the application of competition law. Further, the PA 2023 does not conclusively resolve the issue of private sector entities purporting to act as CPAs and setting up and managing frameworks for use by contracting authorities. There are also no further specific provisions regarding procurement activities undertaken specifically by CPAs and CPA governance in relation to the set-up and operation of purchasing tools.

It is submitted that reissuing guidance on speculative or flag of convenience frameworks of the kind outlined in chapter four will not be sufficient as this has evidently been ineffective. In policy terms, a clearer differentiation must be made between categorically prohibiting private sector organisations from setting up and operating frameworks and legitimate provision of their services in support of CPA established frameworks. As regards the latter, it must be made clear that attempts by CPAs to award contracts for such services cannot become means by which a private sector organisation effectively provides the framework. Otherwise, in such instances, the contracting authority would not be 'in the business of' ie specialising in this activity. As there is no discrete provision on CPAs and no clear rules on the apportionment of responsibility and liability, it is strongly arguable that it is necessary to clearly delimit in legislation what sorts of arrangements are permitted.

One option would be to follow the approach adopted in some EU Member States whereby contracting authorities are mandated to use frameworks of specific CPAs. This would place the responsibility on the Government to determine the lawfulness of the CPA and the frameworks that it directs contracting authorities to use. This could specify which CPAs are to be used based on, for example, the type of contracting authority and sector coverage (eg central government, local government, health, education, defence), location (with regional CPA hubs mandated for contracting authorities based in particular regions), value of procurement (with some CPAs specialised in standard, off-the-shelf procurements and others specialising in more complex projects). Of course, there are advantages and disadvantages of such models and, as indicated, any decision would need to be informed by a much better understanding of the impact of CPAs on the framework market.

Alternatively, a change in behaviour may be achieved by amending the legal definition of a CPA and introducing additional conditions to constitute a CPA. For instance, it might be possible to apply, by analogy, established rules on 'in-house' arrangements to ensure public sector control over CPAs and limit private sector influence. In essence, such rules provide that an arrangement between public sector entities will be exempt from complying with all rules if one entity exercises control over the other similar to that which it exercises over its own departments and the other performs most of its essential activities for it ie a parent-child or 'vertical' arrangement. The PA 2023 could require that the relationship between a user contracting authority and a CPA needs to satisfy some or all of the 'control' conditions in Schedule 2 of the PA 2023 and that details of this relationship are included in the new register of commercial purchasing tools.[42] Thus, it might be required that user contracting authorities together be parent

[42] A similar suggestion was made in the Consultation Response to the Cabinet Office's consultation on the Green Paper from Trowers & Hamlins LLP (19 March 2021) (retained on file).

undertakings of the CPA, that no other person exert a decisive influence on its activities or hold shares in it and that more than 80 per cent of its activities are carried out for or on behalf of the user contracting authorities. Another possibility might be to consider application of the rules on 'horizontal arrangements' in which a contracting authority awards a contract to another provided the parties are cooperating to achieve common objectives solely in the public interest, albeit permitting a limited number of activities to be carried out for non-public purposes. However, such in-house rules are complex and would require careful consideration in their design.

A wider policy issue is not just whether to limit private participation in contracting authorities but whether the Government wishes to prevent or limit contracting authorities, in particular, CPAs, from also providing their services to the private sector. This would inevitably affect the approach then taken to various other reform options.

In any event, to address the immediate risks, if it is intended to prohibit private sector entities from purporting to act as an 'agent' of a contracting authority in circumstances where the contracting authority is not genuinely 'in the business of' being a CPA at all, some clearer guidance could be published to explain this prohibition. This should clarify that whilst a private sector entity might legitimately be awarded contracts to provide services in managing a framework, only a contracting authority can be a CPA and party to a framework and needs to take an active role in its set-up and management.

In addition, as indicated in chapter eight, the PA 2023 does not categorically address various emerging framework within a framework models eg the neutral vendor framework.[43] The apparent prohibition on being able to award a framework under the provisions on frameworks (section 45(8)(b)) should be clarified to address such models.

3.9. Liability and Responsibilities of Contracting Authorities, in Particular, CPAs

As discussed in chapter nine,[44] the PA 2023 does not include clear rules on the allocation of liabilities. Instead, the GCF guidance explains that if two contracting authorities conduct a joint procurement, they are both responsible (and liable) for any contracts they award, whereas if a contracting authority procures via a CPA, it delegates liability for the award of contracts by the CPA, eg establishment of a framework, but not for awards it makes itself under it, eg call-offs.[45] The guidance does not address the issue of joint breach eg where an unlawful call-off procedure designed by a CPA is used by a contracting authority nor the fact that the user authority will bear the practical risk of challenge given that the time limit for bringing a challenge against the CPA will have likely passed.

Similarly, the PA 2023 and guidance do not clearly differentiate the responsibilities of CPAs. Some provide support services to contracting authorities using their frameworks, including guidance on use of their frameworks, and even run mini-competitions for

[43] Section 8.2.
[44] Section 5.2.
[45] GCF, Guidance: Covered Procurement, March 2024, 3.

users. This raises the question of whether a CPA bears or should bear more regulatory compliance risk if providing such support at the call-off stage.

It is possible to conceive of more targeted regulation on CPA responsibilities and liability.

Regarding responsibilities, it is recalled from chapter four that 2008 OGC guidance stated that, whilst a contracting authority should not have to 'supervise the processes' of the CPA, it should include inclusive protective provision committing the CPA to comply with the regulations, such that if a contracting authority is in breach and incurs costs or damages, the CPA will compensate it. The guidance indicated that any such arrangement was a matter for the parties. This raises the question of whether such important legal matters should be a matter of exclusively contractual agreement rather than statutory regulation. It is possible to conceive of basic rules on how contracting authorities instruct CPAs, duties in respect of framework design, and duties to consult users as regards certain measures taken by a CPA. After all, as suggested above, it is possible to think of other duties to consult users eg on the estimation of framework use. Obviously, this is a delicate balance because the purpose of using a CPA is for them to have the flexibility to set up the framework but there are also clear risks where a CPA is subject to no instruction or account at all to contracting authorities, especially when issues arise at the call-off stage.

Further, the 2008 OGC guidance appeared to only conceive of provision to hold a CPA to account for the purposes of indemnifying a contracting authority following an action against it for breach. It is possible to envisage imposing obligations on CPAs that could mitigate the risk of breaches occurring by requiring more proactive framework management. This could include obligations to ensure periodic monitoring of use of call-off procedures.

Similarly, as the evidence suggested that CPAs may also have limited oversight because of a lack of information provided by user authorities and suppliers, reporting obligations could be imposed on the parties. CPAs could be given audit rights to step in and examine framework use. This might better ensure that contracting authorities comply with framework terms.

In addition, further corporate governance controls could be considered eg requiring minimum levels of procurement support and guidance for contracting authorities, monitoring of application of exclusion grounds and other due diligence requirements that apply to suppliers and the potential removal and replacement of suppliers (eg based on repeated checks of legal and financial capacity) and the vetting of call-off procedures proposed to be used by contracting authorities.

As regards liability, ultimately, consideration could be given to whether, in circumstances where a contracting authority's use of a CPA's framework involves a breach of the PA 2023 that originates in whole or in part from a CPA's breach in setting up the framework, the CPA should bear a joint risk of liability with the user authority. This could act as a deterrent to CPAs setting up incoherent frameworks which fail to set sufficiently objective call-off mechanisms or which incorporate other flexibilities that, if used by a contracting authority, would involve a breach. Of course, it is possible to foresee difficulties with operating this in practice ie in determining when the breach relates to any act or omission by the CPA and the extent of the CPA's responsibility for the breach.

If it is considered too difficult to regulate based on apportioning liabilities in this way, another option previously recommended by the NAO is for the Cabinet Office to introduce a formal system of accreditation of framework providers before they are made available for use.[46] This process could be used to verify the lawfulness of the framework including its call-off procedures. This obviously would not prevent a framework still being used unlawfully in individual cases, especially where circumstances may not have been foreseen at the outset (eg certain modifications become necessary) but it would mitigate the risk.

Related to the above, currently, there is no formal policy to address how CPAs go about establishing governance structures and processes for the use of frameworks. There is a need for CPAs to revisit their internal governance processes given that contracting authorities may be inclined to treat these as authoritative and a way of mitigating legal risk for their call-offs, which is not satisfactory. This will involve some changes to the corporate governance structure of how CPAs operate.

3.10. Fees

It is recalled from chapter five,[47] that the PA 2023 provides for the charging of fees at a fixed percentage of the estimated value of any contract awarded (section 45(7)). However, neither the PA 2023 nor GCF guidance adopted the Green Paper proposal that fees should be 'proportionate and used solely in the public interest',[48] suggesting the need for fees to be reinvested back into public services. The effect, then, has been to explicitly authorise use of fees and it appears that it will be left to market factors to determine their application. The requirement to include information on fees chargeable in the tender notice may increase transparency of fees but does not address underlying fee charging behaviours or lack of visibility regarding how they are applied.

The NAO has previously recommended the need for a reduction of fees.[49] It may be preferable to place explicit controls on the level that can be charged, eg based on strict cost recovery principles only. If the framework market continues to expand through private sector entities setting up and managing frameworks, further controls may be necessary, eg by requiring a percentage to be shared with the user authority and restricting the remainder to the necessary costs associated with framework management on behalf of users. Further, the basis for calculating fees as a fixed percentage of the estimated value of any contract awarded is not clear as there is often a discrepancy between the estimated value and actual value recovered by suppliers. Fees have traditionally been based on invoiced values and an amendment to this effect would therefore seem appropriate. It is also possible to conceive of further institutional oversight eg for HM Treasury to conduct periodic reviews of fee arrangements.

[46] NAO, (n 11) 40.
[47] Section 4.2.
[48] 'Transforming Public Procurement: Government response to consultation' (n 15) 53.
[49] NAO, (n 11).

3.11. Call-off Procedures

It is recalled from chapter seven,[50] that under the PA 2023, there is a lack of clarity and guidance on the formulation of call-off procedures, making the choice between them and, most importantly, legal compliance and best practice regarding their use, particularly direct awards. The only residual control is the need to have regard to the section 12 objectives when designing call-off procedures.

It would be helpful for further guidance to advise on factors to consider, relating, for example, to the number of user authorities and whether each might need to apply additional conditions of participation (meaning that a further competition procedure would need to be run), the nature of the market concerned, the number of suppliers to be appointed, and the extent to which it is commercially feasible to establish pricing and other terms at the framework award stage.

Guidance could also usefully explain more clearly what terms constitute the 'core terms' to be set out in the framework for a call-off without competition. The GCF guidance gives some examples of such terms but creates uncertainty about what collection of terms suffices to constitute sufficiently key 'core terms' that would justify an award without competition.

For both types of call-off procedure, the PA 2023 indicates that it is sufficient for a 'pricing mechanism' to be set out in the framework. Guidance could explain what degree of flexibility is allowed to devise a pricing mechanism that can be applied to determine the pricing of a call-off, particularly in respect of call-offs without competition where the supplier is not asked to submit a proposal (in contrast to where the competitive selection call-off process is used).

Also, the PA 2023 clarifies the need for there to be a linkage between the award criteria used to award the framework and those used to award a call-off pursuant to the competitive selection process. However, no such explicit linkage applies between the award criteria used to award the framework and the objective mechanism used to select a supplier without competition. It is submitted that this difference should be reconsidered. This is because, unlike the PCR 2015, a framework under the PA 2023 does not need to set out all the terms of the call-off contract for an award without competition to be made, just the 'core terms' and, as stated above, it is only necessary to include a 'pricing mechanism' in the framework rather than actual prices. Therefore, there is a need to ensure sufficient correspondence between stages.

As indicated, the PA 2023 states that a framework may provide for a call-off without competition if the framework sets out the core terms and 'an objective mechanism for supplier selection' (section 45(4)(b)). The GCF guidance provides the examples of a 'taxi-rank' system where call-offs are awarded on a rotational basis, or a 'highest ranking' system with a limitation on the number or value of call-offs awarded to any one supplier.[51] However, it is submitted that citation of just two examples is not particularly helpful, and nor is it necessarily clear that these would comply with the section 12 objectives.

[50] Sections 5.2 and 5.4.
[51] GCF (n 41) 9.

It is difficult to see how awards by rotation will generally demonstrate value for money for a particular contracting authority's call-off requirements. Guidance should be published on how to configure a mechanism that supports contracting authorities in identifying the most advantageous tender for their specific call-off requirement.

Alternatively, given that there is no specific regulation of the design of call-off procedures, a requirement could be introduced to consult user authorities on their design. Compliance with this requirement or not could be a material factor in considering who should be liable when there is a breach in applying a call-off procedure.

It will also be recalled from chapter eight[52] that the PA 2023 introduces more ex-post transparency of call-offs made without competition through requirements to include details of which call-off procedure a contracting authority has used in the contract award notice and contract details notice and an explanation of why it considered that an award without competition could be made in accordance with section 45(4) in the contract details notice. Whilst welcome, the information is published after a contracting authority has already applied the call-off procedures. Consideration should be given to whether ex-ante transparency should be provided through a requirement to notify all framework suppliers in advance of the intention to award without competition including a justification. The practicality of this would clearly need to be considered (eg possibly made subject to an exception in cases of urgency).

3.12. Bespoke Modification Rules

It was explained in chapter eight[53] that the general rules on making modifications can be difficult to apply, particularly when a generic, multi-supplier framework is concerned. Those rules were based on a codification of CJEU jurisprudence regarding amendments to binary public contracts, not frameworks. It is not clear to what extent consideration was given to whether these rules were easily transferable to the framework context. Such rules do not include any controls or safeguards that account for the fact that a user authority may not have been involved in establishing the framework and, thus, may not have had the opportunity to incorporate provisions to address any known risks or other changes that might be required during the contract term. Similarly, the PA 2023 modification rules also do not distinguish between frameworks and other public contracts

Thus, bespoke modification rules for frameworks would be useful. After all, the PA 2023 already provides flexibility to modify special regime contracts (eg, section 74(2) regarding light touch contracts). This could include, for example, a definition of 'substantial modification' tailored to the risks and concerns that arise in frameworks such as changes to or misapplication of call-off procedures, changes made to the core terms established at framework award and specific rules relating to any changes made to the price or pricing mechanism. It is also possible to conceive of how the flexibility in rules may need to differ as between single- and general multi-supplier frameworks, given the

[52] Section 4.3.
[53] Section 9.2.

need for individual user authorities to tailor call-offs to their requirements in the case of the latter (although this would need to be accompanied by appropriate safeguards).

3.13. A More Practical Open Framework Tool

It is recalled from chapter four[54] that in its submission for reform of the Directives, the UK proposed an optional 'open' framework on the basis that closed frameworks limit competition. It did not acknowledge any potential disadvantages of open frameworks. The Green Paper similarly proposed an open framework for all types of contract for up to eight years with an initial three-year closed period but, again, explained neither the policy rationale nor the relative advantages or disadvantages. It was simply stated that it would 'make it easier to achieve value for money, particularly where the contracting authority needs a longer-term relationship, for example in construction and infrastructure'.[55]

It is recalled that section 49(2) PA 2023 provides for an open framework model in which an initial framework is established and then reopened at least once within three years of award, followed by the award of at least one more within five years. In principle, it is understandable why the notion of a framework in which suppliers can be added or removed during its term may be attractive. The UNCITRAL Model Law provides a formulation of an 'open framework agreement' under which suppliers may be admitted at any time[56] and the DPS in Directive 2014/24/EU is predicated on a similar model. Such formulations would seem to be genuinely open arrangements. However, the PA 2023 open framework is largely predicated on a closed framework model albeit with successive reopening points; it does not therefore appear to be more beneficial in many respects than setting up a series of short-term back-to-back closed frameworks.

Several observations may be made. First, the policy justifications for the three- and five-year durations up to an eight-year maximum are unclear. The maximum three-year term for the first framework is actually shorter than the maximum four-year term for a closed framework. Further, the framework may well be open to new entrants and evolve over time but the basic model will still be in place for eight years. It also cannot be extended unlike closed frameworks (section 47(2)).

Second, as indicated in chapter five, each framework must be on substantially the same terms (section 49(9)). Such a restriction would not apply were each framework to be awarded as a discrete closed framework in succession

Third, the Green Paper acknowledged but did not fully elaborate on the implications for administration, management and risk exposure. If each framework constitutes a public contract, a tender notice will need to be published to advertise a framework each time it is reopened, requiring the assessment of any new suppliers, as well as tenders, including those from existing suppliers where a limit is placed on the number of framework suppliers. The Cabinet Office acknowledged the administrative burden depending

[54] Section 2.3.2.
[55] *Transforming Public Procurement* (n 4) 45.
[56] UNCITRAL Model Law on Public Procurement, Articles 60 and 61.

on how many times the framework is reopened.[57] If a contracting authority decided to open up the framework frequently (eg, every six months or every year), this burden would be very high and it is difficult to envisage many circumstances in which this would be desirable or practicable. It would also expose a contracting authority to the risk of challenge each time.

Fourth, questionable claims were made in the Green Paper about the benefits of open frameworks. It was stated that these would encourage competition, allow new market entrants to join, and prevent suppliers from being 'locked out' for the duration, and be of 'particular benefit' to small businesses in facilitating access because of more opportunities to participate.[58] However, it is not necessarily clear how open frameworks will encourage more competition than successive iterations of closed frameworks or significantly benefit 'new market entrants', in particular, SMEs, as distinct from established suppliers. For example, an open framework does not address the problem of incumbent advantage. This could potentially be more problematic under an open framework if an incumbent supplier is allowed to sit on it for the whole duration, enabling it to develop knowledge and experience of supplying over a long period which puts it at an advantage over new entrants joining part way through. Further, whilst reopening the framework reduces the extent of lock out, it does not eliminate it, especially if the framework is only reopened infrequently.

Finally, key practical aspects were not explained in consultations. For instance, how much scope is there for each framework to deviate from the earlier iteration? How can a contracting authority apply the same requirements and award criteria to different tenders submitted at different points in time ie would all suppliers (both those already on the framework and new applicants) need or want to submit a tender at each framework opening? Would some controls on the number of times a framework could be reopened be desirable? Should open frameworks be restricted to procurement of certain types of requirements subject to static market conditions, such that tenders submitted at different points in time can be fairly evaluated against each other?

Thus, there appears to have been little consideration of how an open framework is preferential to a back-to-back series of closed frameworks.[59] The PA 2023 open framework appears conceptually confused in borrowing features from both a closed framework and a DPS. What results is a tool that can be set up with an unlimited number of suppliers but with award procedures more appropriate for a closed framework involving a limited number of suppliers.

An alternative option might have been to limit the number of suppliers at the outset and allow for the removal and addition of suppliers during a framework's term based on the occurrence of certain trigger events eg the replacement of a supplier subject to an exclusion ground or who no longer meets applicable conditions of participation, the need for an additional supplier due to the voluntary departure of an existing supplier, or the unforeseeable need for further supply capacity on the framework. A reserve list of

[57] *Transforming Public Procurement* (n 4) 46.

[58] ibid.

[59] In this regard, see S Arrowsmith, 'Transforming public procurement law after Brexit: early reflections on the Government's Green Paper' (SSRN, 30 December 2020) 7, available at papers.ssrn.com/sol3/papers.cfm?abstract_id=3749359.

suppliers could be established for this purpose when awarding a framework or a simplified competitive tendering procedure required to be followed to add a new supplier.

3.14. Guidance and Training

Chapter four indicated that over the last two decades, consultations consistently revealed the need for better guidance. Of course, various trade-offs may need to be made in deciding whether to regulate a matter through hard-law rules or soft-law guidance, and, if soft law, whether its focus should be on prescribing policy, addressing legal interpretation and compliance, best procurement practice, or a combination. The tendency has been to focus largely on ensuring compliance. Ultimately, successive Governments may have been content to largely leave it to contracting authorities and suppliers to develop framework models and practices. However, this is no longer sustainable. In its response to the Green Paper consultation, the Cabinet Office acknowledged that there was a general call for guidance and that this would be provided but, as indicated, the GCF guidance and the learning module are largely explanatory guides to the PA 2023 provisions and provide limited useful examples of how these might apply in practice.

As indicated throughout Part III, there is a need for more targeted guidance focusing on substantive issues. Aspects have already been identified in this chapter, just some of which are identified here. Concerning the preparatory phase, there is a need for clear guidance on the choice between procurement options and on PME. Regarding framework design, there is a need for guidance on: setting conditions of participation; refining award criteria and weightings at the call-off stage; how to select between call-off procedures and run them; the potential for supplementing and introducing other commercial terms at call-off stage (particularly now that the PA 2023 allows direct call-offs without competition to be made where only the 'core terms' are set out in the framework); guidance on setting pricing mechanisms; and relatedly, guidance on conducting investigations of abnormally low tenders submitted at the framework award stage. There is also a need for guidance on effective monitoring of frameworks.

Consideration could also be given to increasing the standardisation of framework model templates for contractual terms. If all frameworks followed a similar contractual structure and content, it would be easier for procurement teams to use and apply framework documentation. It is recognised that individual CPAs tend to use standard templates for their various frameworks but contracting authorities are likely to find it more helpful and frameworks more accessible if an industry standard was created and implemented across different CPAs to the extent possible. It is acknowledged, however, that the commercial imperatives driving some CPA frameworks may militate against this possibility.

Concerning the form which guidance should take, there is a need for more best practice focused guidance that assists the exercise of 'commercial' decision-making, that is, to guide discretionary decision-making in ways that ensure value for money. This could take the form of a 'playbook' as recommended by the NAO.[60] This would still need

[60] NAO, (n 11) 12.

to engage with the technical legal issues but also address the marketised behaviours that have emerged. Additional guidance could also be published by the GCF. Other bodies concerned with specific types of contracting authority, eg the Local Government Association and the Regulator of Social Housing could develop bespoke guidance for their respective sectors. The Competition and Markets Authority could also consider publishing guidance on the competition law risks.

In addition, Part III indicated that there are varying levels of knowledge, expertise and experience in respect of frameworks. The useful PA 2023 training and guidance focuses on acclimatising stakeholders to the legal regime rather than systematically addressing its implementation and wider behaviours that are not addressed by it. More focused training is therefore required. On the supply-side, a lack of experience and training can be a barrier to contracting with the public sector, in particular for SMEs; therefore, more targeted supplier training would be beneficial and could help increase the diversity of framework suppliers.

4. Other Regulation

Regulatory reform should not focus exclusively on procurement regulation but rather holistically alongside other areas of regulation.

As indicated, one aspect that is not definitively addressed by procurement regulation concerns the impact of frameworks on competition. Various competition-related issues have been raised. These include: risks of collusion between framework suppliers, framework suppliers and non-party suppliers and contracting authorities and suppliers; MoUs between government departments and suppliers setting prices or other terms; whether CPAs are acting as providers of services on the market such as to constitute undertakings subject to competition law; and private sector organisations benefitting from prices negotiated in procurement processes for public sector customers.

Neither the PCR 2015 nor PA 2023 provide definitive regulatory responses to these issues, although EU Directives did, at the very least, include provision or references to address behaviours that may prevent, restrict or distort competition. The section 12 objectives may impose some general constraints given the need to act and be seen to act with integrity in procurement, for example. However, there is no categorical provision addressing anti-competitive practices. As discussed, it should be considered whether rules and guidance should be introduced to address potential anti-competitive effects.

Competition law could also potentially play a more prominent role. Regarding the appropriate response at the EU level, it has been observed that it is not easy to imagine a solution but one possibility might be to acknowledge the public nature of CPAs and to admit them as an exception to competition rules, which means that CPAs must be considered as equivalent to in-house entities and their relationships with other contracting authorities constituting a form of institutional collaboration in their capacity as non-competitive institutions.[61] This would entail treating CPAs as exercising public

[61] AG Campos Sánchez Bordana made comparisons with *Irgita* in Case C-3/19 *ASMEL v ANAC* ECLI:EU:C:2020:423 at paras 60–68.

powers and prohibiting them from providing procurement services on the market and any involvement in the market for procurement services; although it has been considered that this might still not strike an adequate balance that respects freedom to provide services and the grant of exclusive rights.[62] It is not clear that this would be sufficient in the UK, however, given the sheer number of CPAs in operation, their wide ranging customer base and the involvement of private sector entities in running the business of CPAs; more targeted regulation may be necessary.

Regarding possible competition law enforcement, most recently, the Competition & Markets Authority has expressed increasing willingness to investigate procurement contracts (eg bid rigging in school improvement contracts) and suggested that it should play a more substantial role in procurement in the Green Paper consultations.[63] A good starting point would be to undertake a study investigating whether there is a CPA 'market' which includes public and private sector entities competing against each other to provide centralised purchasing services for the public and other sectors. Any such 'framework market' would need to be defined for the purposes of such investigation, before any practices are investigated.

It is also open to consider whether there could be more specific regulation of CPA activities. Questions arise about the degree to which CPAs should be free to establish and manage frameworks for the entire public sector, what scope of purchasing and support services CPAs should provide, and what responsibilities CPAs should have with regard to managing frameworks and enforcing legal compliance, as discussed.

5. Political and Institutional Reform

As indicated in chapter two, the NAO has recently scrutinised CCS's institutional role in the context of framework provision.[64] Chapter five also indicated that a disincentive towards further centralised purchasing has arisen, in part, precisely because of the sheer market and institutional dominance of certain CPAs (including CCS) and which may lead to conflict.[65]

It should therefore be considered whether there could be a further separation of functions and allocation of responsibilities between government departments. Whilst it is not suggested that there is an overt conflict of interest between the Cabinet Office in its role of formulating procurement policy and its Trading Fund and Executive Agency, CCS, as the largest CPA, the empirical research alluded to an apparent conflict here. There is an apparent risk of the Cabinet Office setting policy on frameworks drawing on its experience through CCS, which may not necessarily be representative across the wider public sector. It also appears somewhat incongruous that CCS is looking to drive further centralisation whilst the Cabinet Office seems to leave the choice of whether to

[62] M Comba, 'CPBs in the European legal space: an unresolved misconception' in C Risvig Hamer and M Comba (eds), *Centralising Public Procurement: The Approach of EU Member States* (Edward Elgar, 2021) 35.

[63] Competition & Markets Authority, *Transforming Public Procurement Response from the Competition and Markets Authority*, 10 March 2021.

[64] Section 4.

[65] Section 3.1.2.

use centralised procurement to the individual discretion of each contracting authority. This may reflect a certain wider ambivalence about Government policy on centralised procurement, and which requires clarification. The NAO has recommended that CCS needs to focus less on growing its market share and commercial benefits and more on its purpose to maximise the wider benefits of central purchasing for the public sector, acting as the 'system leader for the procurement of common goods and services'.[66] However, as indicated, there is a need to examine more fundamentally the current institutional configuration of centralising purchasing in the UK given the systemic issues that appear to have arisen and which have not been addressed by the PA 2023. It is not necessarily clear that CCS should be assigned system leader.

It is beyond the scope of this chapter to explore this issue in depth but it is also possible to consider how external controls may be introduced. As indicated in chapter two, HM Treasury historically had a greater role in procurement before many roles and responsibilities were assigned to the Cabinet Office. Given the significant sums of public money involved in frameworks, HM Treasury could be given additional oversight powers in respect of large-scale central government frameworks, as it has already intervened on fee charging. This could even contribute to a wider debate on whether there is a need to establish an independent regulator and policy-maker for procurement.[67]

6. Industry Reform

Finally, it is submitted that given the prominent role of the private sector not only in providing goods and services but also framework management, it is incumbent on it to consider how it can more responsibly engage the public sector in this space.

To be clear, this book is not intended to be excessively critical of suppliers who exploit market opportunities where there are grey areas of law or policy. They have a different *raison d'être* to public sector organisations in that they are necessarily profit-orientated, even if they share the goal of providing effective public services. They fill a void in providing professional support services that contracting authorities may not have the resources or expertise to provide, and parties are willing to pay higher fees for better customer service (which raises the question of whether fees should be legitimated but more effective controls placed on them).

Nevertheless, it is important to distinguish between standard commercial behaviours and blatant opportunism that undermines the regulatory model. A prime example is pro-actively seeking out willing contracting authorities to act as hosts for their own frameworks, charging excessive fees, or requiring non-disclosure arrangements which undermine transparency.

Ultimately, to date, there does not appear to have been any significant private sector-led initiative to discourage exploitative practices. As indicated in chapter four, this must be contrasted with industry association and other initiatives to promote accredited 'gold

[66] NAO, (n 11) 13.

[67] LRA Butler, 'Responsible public procurement: towards a public service contract regulator?' (2019) 5 *PPLR* NA 198.

standard' framework contracting. None of the existing initiatives include an emphasis on an ethics of responsibility when providing services in respect of the management of, or supplying under, frameworks.

It is possible to identify any number of industry-side initiatives that could be developed. This could include a supplier focused playbook and codes of practice eg one for framework providers and one for framework suppliers. Such initiatives could be led by central government, or public sector-led organisations or associations. To incentivise the practical uptake of such initiatives, compliance with industry codes could result in accreditation as an ethical or responsible provider which could be registered and potentially authenticated by a public sector entity (eg, the PRU).[68] After all, there are no indications that the Cabinet Office will be undertaking any advance or ongoing checks on compliance of frameworks with the PA 2023 according to information populated on the central register. Accreditation does not eliminate the risk of unlawful practices but does mitigate it. At the time of writing, a number of experts in the field (including the authors) are in the formative stages of developing an ethical frameworks initiative.[69]

7. Conclusions

This book has highlighted the extent of framework marketisation in the UK. It has provided a detailed examination of the impact of regulation on this trend and on the efficacy of frameworks in practice. As indicated, the UK has already introduced reform under the PA 2023. Whilst it is still too early to determine its impact, preliminary analysis indicates that it is unlikely to 'transform' the use of frameworks in line with stated ambitions. It appears that the regulatory conditions are conducive to yet further marketisation and legal uncertainty.

This chapter has made a compelling case for considering further reform through regulation which goes beyond further tweaks or inclusions in the PA 2023. Fundamentally, the Government needs to ask searching policy questions about the role that frameworks (and centralised purchasing) should play in the procurement system; clear objectives can then be reflected in regulation. Decisions about the appropriate policy interventions need to be informed by economic analyses and an appreciation of the impact and potential use of other areas of regulation. Further, consideration should be given to political and institutional reform given the formative role that central government has played in setting the rules of the framework game whilst also being its largest player. The private sector should also ensure more responsible ethical framework use. There is a need for a shift in the procurement culture as much as a shift in regulation. Importantly, this book should draw on comparative experience in considering all of the options going forward. Given the focus on regulatory reform, this chapter has identified various potential reforms of the PA 2023 as well as areas in which further guidance could be introduced.

More generally, it is observed that as procurement practice continues to evolve, the trend appears to be towards the greater use of agile, more responsive or 'dynamic'

[68] The authors are grateful to Dr Rebecca Rees for raising this possibility.

[69] Led by Alan Heron of Places for People and Dr Rebecca Rees of Trowers & Hamlins.

purchasing techniques than a standard competitive procedure. The PA 2023 has introduced open frameworks and dynamic markets in this regard. In order to avoid a repeat of the last two decades, it is important to learn from the experience of frameworks in developing such techniques.

As indicated in chapter one, 'public procurement' has firmly entered the public consciousness. Questions have already been asked about frameworks and will continue to be asked. This book has shown that real reform of regulation and practice is now long overdue.

APPENDIX

Interview References

Reference	Role
CA1	ICT Procurement Lead
CA2	Deputy Head of Procurement
CA3	ICT Category Manager
CA4	ICT Procurement Consultant
CA5	Commercial Procurement Manager
CA6	Director of ICT Procurement
CA7	Senior Commercial Manager
CA8	ICT Category Manager
CA9	ICT Category Manager
CA10	ICT Category Manager
CA11	Procurement Consultant
CA12	Head of Procurement
CA13	Solicitor and Head of Public Procurement
CA14	Strategic Procurement Officer
CA15	Head of Procurement Policy
CA16	Deputy Director – Procurement
CA17	Head of Procurement
CA18	Solicitor – Procurement
CPB1	ICT Category Lead
CPB2	Commercial Policy Lead
CPB3	ICT Category Lead
CPB4	ICT Category Lead
CPB5	ICT Category Lead
CPB6	ICT Category Lead
CPB7	Procurement Manager

(continued)

(Continued)

Reference	Role
CPB8	ICT Category Lead
CPB9	Head of Category Management
CPB10	ICT Commercial Lead
CPB11	Frameworks Lead
CPB12	Managing Director
EO1	Head of Framework Management
EO2	Public Sector Framework Bids Manager
EO3	Managing Director
EO4	Head of Commercial
EO5	Public Sector Frameworks Manager
EO6	Account Manager
EO7	Public Sector Portfolio Lead
LA1	Specialist Procurement Counsel
LA2	Legal Director
LA3	Partner
LA4	Partner
LA5	Senior Associate
LA6	Partner
LA7	Legal Director
LA8	Partner
LA9	Senior Associate
LA10	Partner
LA11	Barrister
LA12	Principal Associate
LA13	Partner
LA14	Legal Director
LA15	Specialist Procurement Counsel
LA16	Partner
LA17	Partner
LA18	Partner
LA19	Partner
LA20	Senior Solicitor

INDEX

www.ingramcontent.com/pod-product-compliance
Ingram Content Group UK Ltd.
Pitfield, Milton Keynes, MK11 3LW, UK
UKHW020232290926
15470UKWH00002B/492

9 781509 985623